3RD EDITION

METAL MATTERS

ENGLISCH FÜR METALLBERUFE

von
Georg Aigner
Isobel Williams

sowie
Manfred Thönicke und Jörg Trabert

unter Mitarbeit der Verlagsredaktion

Cornelsen

Verfasser/in:	Georg Aigner, Landshut
	Isobel Williams, Berlin
Verfasser KMK-Seiten:	Manfred Thönicke und Jörg Trabert, Hamburg
Berater/innen:	Antje Baehr, Essen; Annette Fauth, Freiburg; Jan Richter, Freiberg
Projektleitung:	Simone Conrad
Außenredaktion:	James Abram
Redaktionelle Mitarbeit:	Christine House, Oliver Busch (Wörterverzeichnisse)
Bildredaktion:	Thomas Adam, Gertha Maly, Christina Scheuerer
Layoutkonzept:	finedesign, Berlin
Gesamtgestaltung und technische Umsetzung:	vitaledesign, Berlin
Umschlaggestaltung:	vitaledesign, Berlin
Coverfoto:	Fotolia/Kalinovsky Dmitry
Illustrationen:	Oxford Designers & Illustrators

Erhältlich sind auch:
Handreichungen für den Unterricht mit MP3-CD und Online-Zusatzmaterialien
ISBN 978-3-06-451512-3

Soweit in diesem Lehrwerk Personen fotografisch abgebildet sind und ihnen von der Redaktion fiktive Namen, Berufe, Dialoge und Ähnliches zugeordnet oder diese Personen in bestimmte Kontexte gesetzt werden, dienen diese Zuordnungen und Darstellungen ausschließlich der Veranschaulichung und dem besseren Verständnis des Inhalts.

www.cornelsen.de

Die Webseiten Dritter, deren Internetadressen in diesem Lehrwerk angegeben sind, wurden teilweise von Cornelsen mit fiktiven Inhalten zur Veranschaulichung und/oder Illustration von Aufgabenstellungen und Inhalten erstellt. Alle anderen Webseiten wurden vor Drucklegung sorgfältig geprüft. Der Verlag übernimmt keine Gewähr für die Aktualität und den Inhalt dieser Seiten oder solcher, die mit ihnen verlinkt sind.

1. Auflage, 4. Druck 2021

Alle Drucke dieser Auflage sind inhaltlich unverändert und können im Unterricht nebeneinander verwendet werden.

© 2017 Cornelsen Verlag GmbH, Berlin

Das Werk und seine Teile sind urheberrechtlich geschützt. Jede Nutzung in anderen als den gesetzlich zugelassenen Fällen bedarf der vorherigen schriftlichen Einwilligung des Verlages.
Hinweis zu §§ 60 a, 60 b UrhG: Weder das Werk noch seine Teile dürfen ohne eine solche Einwilligung an Schulen oder in Unterrichts- und Lehrmedien (§ 60 b Abs. 3 UrhG) vervielfältigt, insbesondere kopiert oder eingescannt, verbreitet oder in ein Netzwerk eingestellt oder sonst öffentlich zugänglich gemacht oder wiedergegeben werden. Dies gilt auch für Intranets von Schulen.

Druck und Bindung: Livonia Print, Riga

ISBN 978-3-06-451510-9
ISBN 978-3-06-451511-6 (E-Book)

PEFC zertifiziert
Dieses Produkt stammt aus nachhaltig bewirtschafteten Wäldern und kontrollierten Quellen.
www.pefc.de

Vorwort

Metal Matters 3rd edition ist die vollständige Neubearbeitung des bewährten Englisch-Lehrwerks für Auszubildende in Metallberufen, die am Berufsschulunterricht oder an betrieblichen Fortbildungen teilnehmen.

Das Lehrwerk setzt Englischkenntnisse voraus, die dem Niveau A2 des Europäischen Referenzrahmens (*Common European Framework of Reference*) entsprechen. Es deckt die Themen der aktuellen Lehrpläne der Bundesländer für Englisch in der Berufsschule konsequent ab.

Metal Matters 3rd edition besteht aus zwölf Units, die flexibel einsetzbar sind. Jede Unit umfasst vier abgeschlossene Lernsituationen, die jeweils in einer Doppelstunde bearbeitet werden können. Eine Unit ist wie folgt aufgebaut:

Foundation: Diese Doppelseite bietet Ihnen mit technischem Grundwissen und elementarem Themenvokabular einen Einstieg in das Thema der Unit.

Part A/B: Diese stark technisch ausgerichteten Module können je nach Umfang der Inputmaterialien jeweils zwei oder drei Seiten umfassen. Hier werden fachspezifische Schwerpunkte der Unit mithilfe authentischer und aktueller Materialien behandelt.

Communication: Berufliche Kommunikation steht im Fokus des abschließenden *Communication*-Teils. Ein „Das kann ich"-Kästchen – eine Checkliste zur Selbstevaluation – rundet die Unit ab und ermöglicht es den Lernenden, über ihren persönlichen Lernerfolg zu reflektieren.

Alle Lernsituationen sind so konzipiert, dass sie ausgelassen oder zu einem anderen Zeitpunkt behandelt werden können. Somit berücksichtigt die Modulstruktur einer jeden Unit die organisatorische Vielfalt des Englischunterrichts und schafft größtmögliche Flexibilität im Unterricht.

Besonderer Wert wird in diesem Lehrwerk auf **Handlungsorientierung** und direkten Berufsbezug gelegt: Jedes Modul beginnt mit einer branchenspezifischen *Situation* und führt über handlungs- und kompetenzorientierte Lernschritte zu einem Handlungsprodukt. Dieses Lernziel ist jeweils zu Beginn des Moduls mit einem Pfeil gekennzeichnet und ermöglicht so eine schnelle Orientierung.

Unterschiedliche Aktions- und Sozialformen ermöglichen zudem den Einsatz von kooperativen Lernformen und fördern **eigenverantwortliches Lernen**.

Um der Heterogenität der Auszubildenden gerecht zu werden, finden sich zahlreiche Aufgaben zur **Binnendifferenzierung** in den Units. Diese sind mit einem Strich unter der Aufgabenziffer gekennzeichnet und verweisen auf editierbare Kopiervorlagen in den Handreichungen, die alternative Bearbeitungsmöglichkeiten für die jeweilige Aufgabe zur Verfügung stellen.

Zur Vorbereitung auf die **KMK-Prüfung** für Niveau A2 und B1 werden anhand von sechs Unterrichtseinheiten und einer kompletten Musterprüfung prüfungsrelevante Materialien und Aufgaben angeboten und so eine systematische Prüfungsvorbereitung ermöglicht.

Grundlegende grammatikalische Strukturen werden durchweg im **situativen Kontext** vermittelt, ergänzt durch eine systematische Grammatikübersicht im Anhang. Zur Erweiterung des berufsrelevanten Wortschatzes wird schwieriges **Fachvokabular**, das zum Verständnis der Materialien notwendig ist, in jedem Modul in einer *Toolbox* gesondert hervorgehoben. Eine umfangreiche *Unit word list* mit allen neuen Wörtern in chronologischer Reihenfolge wie auch eine *A-Z word list* mit allen neuen Wörtern in alphabetischer Reihenfolge befinden sich im Anhang, ebenso wie berufsbezogene *Useful phrases*, die eine effektive berufliche Kommunikation erleichtern.

Sämtliche Audiomaterialien finden Sie in den Handreichungen für den Unterricht. Typische Sprachhandlungssituationen im Berufsalltag werden multimedial mit visueller Unterstützung trainiert: Diese visualisierten Hörtexte sind mit ▶ gekennzeichnet und schulen effektiv das Hör- und Sehverstehen. Ein Webcode, mit dem Sie die visualisierten Hörtexte aufrufen können, befindet sich ebenfalls in den Handreichungen.

Der Verlag, die Autoren sowie die Berater wünschen Ihnen viel Erfolg und Freude mit *Metal Matters 3rd edition*.

Table of contents

Unit	Content	Situation	Language	
1 My company				6
FOUNDATION	A company profile	Writing a profile of your company	Asking for information Giving directions Saying where something is Talking about jobs Offering help/refreshments	
PART A	The layout of a company	Describing your workplace		
PART B	The structure of a company	Describing the structure of your training company		
COMMUNICATION	Introductions and small talk	Looking after a visitor to your company		
2 My workplace				14
FOUNDATION	Health and safety in the workplace	Making a safety poster for your workshop	Giving orders and instructions Describing what people are doing in photos Talking about your work Talking about what you do regularly Giving telephone numbers	
PART A	My job	Writing a short profile of yourself		
PART B	The dual system of vocational training	Giving a short presentation about vocational training		
COMMUNICATION	Telephoning	Leaving a voicemail message		
KMK Exam practice 1				22
3 Tools of the trade				24
FOUNDATION	Favourite tools	Making a list of tools in English	Asking and answering questions Saying where things are Talking about what you usually do Using polite language in emails Salutation and complimentary close in emails	
PART A	Hand tools	Writing a tool trolley checklist		
PART B	Machine tools	Explaining how a machine works to a new colleague		
COMMUNICATION	Emails	Writing an email to a customer		
4 Materials of the trade				34
FOUNDATION	The right materials for the job	Giving a presentation about the materials your company uses	Describing properties of materials Comparing things 2D and 3D shapes Structuring a presentation	
PART A	The Stirling engine	Answering a request for help on a user forum		
PART B	A specific workpiece	Describing and drawing workpieces		
COMMUNICATION	A short presentation	Giving a presentation about your work		
KMK Exam practice 2				44
5 Manuals and safety instructions				46
FOUNDATION	Numbers and measurements	Phoning a supplier to clarify details	Giving dimensions Asking for and correcting information Talking about safety rules Discussing how to solve problems Describing graphs	
PART A	Safety precautions	Creating a safety poster for a new machine		
PART B	Machine maintenance	Using a checklist to solve a problem		
COMMUNICATION	Graphs and charts	Preparing notes on graphs for a presentation		
6 Advising customers				56
FOUNDATION	Conversations at a trade fair	Advising a customer about equipment	Advising a customer Talking to a salesperson Asking for information Telling the time in English-speaking countries Giving dates, days and times	
PART A	A CNC turning machine for serial production	Writing a report on a new machine		
PART B	Installation of the machine	Explaining the advantages of a control unit		
COMMUNICATION	Arrangements for meetings	Writing emails to make arrangements		
KMK Exam practice 3				66

Unit		Content	Situation	Language	
7	**Communicating with colleagues**				68
	FOUNDATION	Internal communication	Doing a survey about means of communication	Talking about quantities Using first names Giving an oral report Describing an incident	
	PART A	Relocation of production	Writing a memo		
	PART B	Problems abroad	Giving a short report to your supervisor		
	COMMUNICATION	Reports	Writing a report on an incident		
8	**Presenting a technical project abroad**				78
	FOUNDATION	International standards	Making a list of international standards your company uses	Defining things more closely Talking about possibilities Describing processes Giving a presentation	
	PART A	An automated washing system	Writing a description of the system		
	PART B	The presentation of the washing system	Creating slides for a presentation		
	COMMUNICATION	Business trips	Doing research on other cultures		
	KMK Exam practice 4				88
9	**Enquiries and offers**				90
	FOUNDATION	A video conferencing system	Writing a report on a suitable system	Comparing items Structuring a report Structuring an enquiry Salutation and complimentary close	
	PART A	An enquiry for linear drives	Writing an enquiry to a manufacturer		
	PART B	A desktop CNC milling machine	Researching and presenting a suitable machine		
	COMMUNICATION	The layout of business letters	Writing business letters		
10	**Ordering technical products**				100
	FOUNDATION	Aluminium containers	Confirming an order by email	Describing objects Describing technical specifications of a car Writing an enquiry Writing an offer	
	PART A	A vintage car data sheet	Ordering spare parts by email		
	PART B	An order for spare parts	Ordering spare parts by letter		
	COMMUNICATION	Enquiries, offers and orders	Writing enquiries, offers and orders		
	KMK Exam practice 5				110
11	**Problems and complaints**				112
	FOUNDATION	Recycling	Replying to a comment on a web forum	Discussing problems with a sales representative Talking about consequences Troubleshooting problems Making a telephone complaint Dealing with telephone complaints	
	PART A	A delivery of a new robot	Writing an email of complaint		
	PART B	Problems with a 3D printer	Replying to an email of complaint		
	COMMUNICATION	A telephone complaint	Dealing with a telephone complaint		
12	**A job application**				122
	FOUNDATION	Where do I go from here?	Writing about your apprenticeship	Talking about skills Thinking about possibilities Expressing your wishes Asking for clarification	
	PART A	Job adverts and applications	Writing a job application		
	PART B	Job interviews	Practising interviews		
	COMMUNICATION	A CV and a covering letter	Studying CVs and covering letters		
	KMK Exam practice 6				132

Partner files	134	Transcripts	162	Talking about numbers	220
KMK Mock exam	143	Unit word list	174	Conversion tables	221
Useful phrases	148	A–Z word list	201	Abbreviations	222
Grammar	157	Basic technical vocabulary	219	Irregular verbs	223

1 My company

FOUNDATION: A company profile

Situation: You are an apprentice with a German company that also has lots of trainees from abroad.
→ **You write a short profile of your company in English for the apprentice file.**

1 Reading a company website

Before you write the profile, you read another company's English profile online.

AT Adler Technology Group – a global player

A The Adler Technology Group is a German producer of cables and connectors. Its head office is in Duisburg in North Rhine-Westphalia. The company was founded in July 1948 by Hans-Joachim Adler and his wife, Luise. Today, Adler Technology Group is still a family business. It is run by Wolfgang and Suzanne Adler and their two children, René Adler and Mareike Adler-Schmidt.

B The structure of the company looks like this:
Wolfgang Adler – Chairman of the Board, General Partner
Mareike Adler-Schmidt – General Partner, Senior Vice President Finance and Purchasing
René Adler – General Partner, Senior Vice President New Technologies
Suzanne Adler – Partner, Senior Vice President Sales and Marketing

C Although it is a family business, Adler is also a global player. There are 11 factories, located in Germany, the Netherlands, France, Great Britain, Romania, the USA and China. Forty-seven sales companies look after Adler's customers worldwide. The company employs around 6,000 people, including over 500 engineers and research scientists.

D Adler Technology Group develops, manufactures and sells electrical and electronic cables and connectors. Our products are used in mechanical engineering, factory automation, power generation and distribution as well as industrial electronics and telecommunication.

E Vocational training and apprenticeships for young people play a central role in the company.

A Match the headlines 1–6 to the paragraphs A–E. There is one headline more than you need.

1 Company structure
2 Interesting information for trainees
3 About Adler
4 Adler's customers
5 Introduction to Duisburg
6 Adler worldwide

 TOOLBOX

apprentice – *Lehrling, Auszubildende/r*
apprenticeship – *Lehre, Ausbildung*
customer – *Kunde/Kundin*
electrical/electronic – *elektrisch/elektronisch*
engineer – *Ingenieur/in*
vocational training – *Berufsausbildung*

My company Unit 1

B Say if the following statements are true or false according to the text. Correct the false statements.

1 Adler Technology Group is a multinational company.
False: Adler Technology Group is a family business and is well known abroad, but it is not a multinational.
2 Adler's head office is in Germany.
3 The company was founded in 1948.
4 No one from the original family works for the company any longer.
5 All production is done in Germany.
6 Adler has an international sales team.
7 The company sells to customers in many different sectors.
8 There are no training possibilities at Adler.

2 Introducing a company

A group of young people are introducing themselves and the companies they work for.

2))) Copy the grid below into your exercise book. Then listen and complete the grid.

Name of company	Sector	Head office	Size
BCC Electronics			medium-sized
International Solutions			start-up
Nilsson Construction	building		
Han Gao			
Jahn Services			
Aikon			

3 Making notes about your company

A Make notes that you can use to give a short description of your company. Cover the points below:

— name of the company
— sector
— location
— number of employees
— what the company does
— target group/customers
— some competitors

> **Asking for information**
>
> **Who** do you work for?
> **What** is the name of your company?
> **Where** is the company located?
> **How many** employees does your company have?

› Grammar: Questions and short answers, page 157

B Talk with a partner. Your partner will ask you questions about your company. Use the notes above. You have three minutes to answer. › Useful phrases: Describing your company, page 148

4 Writing the company profile

Now it is time to write the company profile for the apprentice file.

On your own, or with your partner, write a short profile of your company. Structure your information under the headings you used for exercise 3A above. Present your company to the class and be prepared to answer questions from the audience. › Useful phrases: Describing your company, page 148

 TOOLBOX

automotive sector – *Automobilbranche, -industrie*
electronic equipment – *elektronische Geräte/Ausrüstung*

medium-sized company – *mittelständischer Betrieb*
multinational company – *multinationaler Konzern*

PART A: The layout of a company

Situation: You work at Mech-On, an international mechanical engineering firm based in Nuremberg. Today, you are going to start work at the UK subsidiary of the company in Newcastle.
→ **You describe your workplace at your training company in Germany.**

1 Describing places in a company

You are waiting at reception for your supervisor, Martin Foster. You refresh your knowledge of English words for departments and places in a company while you wait.

Match the photos (A–J) with words from the list. There are two more words than you need.

CNC milling · construction · dispatch · drilling · finance · grinding · locker rooms · marketing · measuring room · stores · turning · waterjet cutting

 TOOLBOX

CNC milling – *CNC-Fräsen*
construction – *Konstruktion*
drilling – *Bohren*
grinding – *Schleifen*

supervisor – *Ausbildungsleiter/in, Vorgesetzte/r*
turning – *Drehen*
waterjet cutting – *Wasserstrahlschneiden*

8

My company   Unit 1

2 Going on a tour of the factory floor

Martin Foster meets you and the other new apprentices at reception. He takes you on a tour of the factory.

A Before you listen to the tour, study the floor plan and make sure you know all the words.

B 3))) ▶ Now listen and match the names of the missing departments to the numbers on the drawing. The words from exercise 1 will help you.

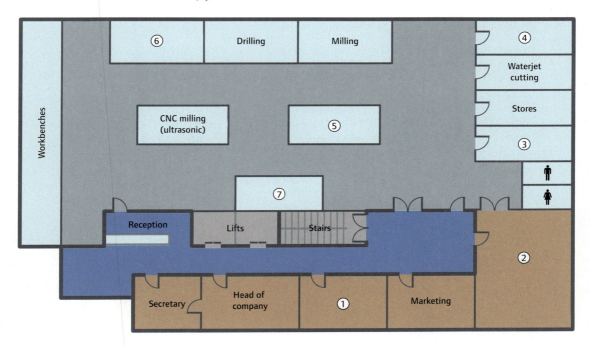

3 Giving directions and describing locations

Martin Foster wants to make sure that you know exactly where everything is on the factory floor.

👥 Work with a partner. Use the floor plan from exercise 2 and take turns to describe how to get to the different locations.

A *How do I get to the stores from reception?*
B *Go along the corridor, past the offices, then turn left into the production area. The stores are on your right, just past the toilets and the locker rooms.*

> ➔ **Giving directions; saying where something is**
>
> **Turn right/left** into the factory and **go straight ahead** till you get to the workbench. The milling machine is **over there**, **next to** the grinding machine, **opposite** the stores. The Human Resources department is **on** the first floor.

› Grammar: Imperatives, page 157

4 Describing your workplace

Martin Foster asks you to describe your workplace at your training company in Germany.

👥 Work in groups with students from the same company. Decide together what places you are going to have on your floorplan then draw a rough sketch.

Agree on a starting point, e.g. the entrance to the factory floor, then take turns to describe the way to different locations.

> *The locker rooms are next to the toilets. Go along this corridor, then turn right at the stores.*

9

PART B: The structure of a company

Situation: It is your first day at the subsidiary of Mech-On in Newcastle. Your supervisor, Martin Foster, describes the structure of the UK branch.
→ You describe the structure of your training company in Germany.

1 Understanding an organization chart

First of all, Martin Foster shows you an organization chart of the UK branch of Mech-On.

A Work with a partner. Study the chart and make sure you understand all the words in the list below.

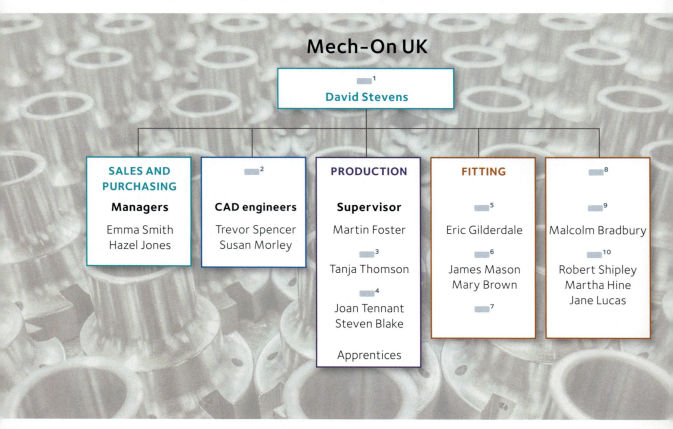

B Now listen and complete the chart with words from the list.

Apprentices · Construction · Fitters and turners · Foreman · Head of division · Line manager · Quality control · Quality control manager · Skilled workers · Test technicians

 TOOLBOX

CAD engineer – *Technische/r Zeichner/in*
fitter – *Monteur/in*
fitting – *Montage*
foreman/-woman – *Vorarbeiter/in; Meister/in*

head of division – *Bereichsleiter/in*
quality control – *Qualitätskontrolle*
skilled worker – *Facharbeiter/in*
turner – *Dreher/in*

My company   Unit 1

2   Reading emails to Mech-On

Martin Foster would like to test your understanding of the organization of the Newcastle branch. He gives you excerpts from five emails to Mech-On.

👥 Work with a partner. Decide together which department they should go to.

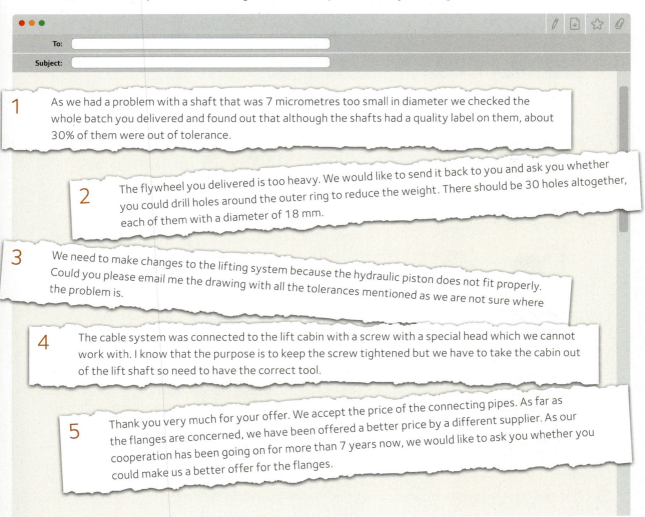

1   As we had a problem with a shaft that was 7 micrometres too small in diameter we checked the whole batch you delivered and found out that although the shafts had a quality label on them, about 30% of them were out of tolerance.

2   The flywheel you delivered is too heavy. We would like to send it back to you and ask you whether you could drill holes around the outer ring to reduce the weight. There should be 30 holes altogether, each of them with a diameter of 18 mm.

3   We need to make changes to the lifting system because the hydraulic piston does not fit properly. Could you please email me the drawing with all the tolerances mentioned as we are not sure where the problem is.

4   The cable system was connected to the lift cabin with a screw with a special head which we cannot work with. I know that the purpose is to keep the screw tightened but we have to take the cabin out of the lift shaft so need to have the correct tool.

5   Thank you very much for your offer. We accept the price of the connecting pipes. As far as the flanges are concerned, we have been offered a better price by a different supplier. As our cooperation has been going on for more than 7 years now, we would like to ask you whether you could make us a better offer for the flanges.

3   Describing the Mech-On head office

Now Martin Foster wants to know about the structure of the Nuremberg head office.

👥 Work with a partner. Partner A: Look at File 1 on page 134. Partner B: Look at File 9 on page 138.

4   Describing the structure of your training company

A   👥 Work in groups with students from your own company. Decide together what you are going to include on your organization chart before you draw it. Make sure you include the names of the main departments and the names and positions of people in important positions.

B   Explain the company to someone from another group.   › *Grammar: Simple present, page 157*

COMMUNICATION: Introductions and small talk

> **Situation:** You work at Mech-On, a Nuremberg-based mechanical engineering company.
> → You look after a visitor from England until your supervisor, Ms Müller, is ready to meet him.

1 Introducing yourself and others to colleagues

The Human Resources department at Mech-On stores information about its employees on computerized personnel files.

A 5))) Listen to the people introducing themselves. Copy and complete the entries in your notebook.

Name: Martyna Nowak
Age: ▭¹
Place of birth: Poland
Job description: ▭²

Name: Halil Özdemir
Age: ▭³
Place of birth: ▭⁴
Job description: Training supervisor

Name: Deema Mansour
Age: ▭⁵
Place of birth: Syria
Job description: ▭⁶

Name: Robert Klein
Age: 21
Place of birth: ▭⁷
Job description: ▭⁸

Name: Canan Tolon
Age: ▭⁹
Place of birth: Turkey
Job description: ▭¹⁰

Name: Alexei Melnyk
Age: 39
Place of birth: ▭¹¹
Job description: ▭¹²

B You have three minutes to introduce yourself to the other people in the class.

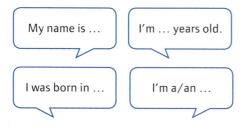

> → **Talking about jobs**
> What **do you do**? – I'm **a** trainee. / I'm **an** energy engineer.
> What **is** your job? – I'm **a** mechanic. / I'm **an** electrical engineer. (NOT: ~~My job is ...~~)

C Introduce one of the people you met to the rest of the class.

My company Unit 1

2 Making formal introductions

A   Work with a partner. Introduce yourself in a formal way to your partner (a visitor).

B   Now formally introduce your partner to another pair.

3 Making small talk

A   In groups, choose suitable topics for small talk in business. Say which topics you should avoid.

holidays   your city/town   religion   the journey to the meeting place

illnesses   sport   politics   the weather   pay   where someone works

B   Match the questions (1–6) to the possible responses (a–f).

1 Is this your first time in Berlin?
2 How is your hotel?
3 It's lovely weather, isn't it?
4 How was your journey?
5 Where are you based?

a Yes. It's fantastic. We've been very lucky this year.
b Very nice. I travelled by train this time.
c Yes. I've heard that it's a very interesting city.
d Fine. I have a good view from the window in my room.
e In Scotland. In Edinburgh, in fact.

4 Meeting and greeting the visitor

Now it is time to meet the visitor. You know that the person Ms Müller is expecting is called Mr Brown.

A   Work in groups of three. Complete the dialogue. Then close your books and practise the dialogue.

You	*Excuse¹ me. Are you²* Mr Brown?
Visitor	Yes, I am.
You	I'm (own name). ___³ do you do? ___⁴ to Mech-On.
Visitor	Thank you. It's ___ ___ ___ ___⁵.
You	I'm afraid Ms Müller has been held up, but she'll be here in a few minutes. ___ ___ ___⁶ your coat?
Visitor	Yes, thank you. Here you are.
You	___⁷ you like something to drink?
Visitor	Yes, please. I'd like a cup of coffee with milk and sugar.
You	Here you are. Is this your ___ ___⁸ in Germany?
Visitor	No. I've been here before, but only on holiday.
You	Oh. Here's Ms Müller now. Mr Brown, ___ ___⁹ Ms Müller.
Ms Müller	___¹⁰ morning, Mr Brown. Sorry to keep you waiting.
Visitor	No problem. Your assistant has been looking after me very well.

> **Offering help/refreshments**
>
> Can I take your coat?
> Would you like something to drink?
> Would you like some tea or coffee?

› *Useful phrases: Showing visitors around the company, page 148*

B   Write your own dialogue and practise it in your group.

DAS KANN ICH (Unit 1)
- Ein kurzes Firmenprofil meines Ausbildungsbetriebs auf Englisch erstellen. (Foundation)
- Meinen Arbeitsplatz im Ausbildungsbetrieb auf Englisch beschreiben. (Part A)
- Die Struktur meines Ausbildungsbetriebs auf Englisch beschreiben. (Part B)
- Eine/n englischsprachige/n Besucher/in empfangen und jemandem vorstellen. (Communication)

2 My workplace

FOUNDATION: Health and safety in the workplace

Situation: An accident happened in your company recently, so all apprentices are sent on a safety training course.
→ You make a safety poster for your workshop.

1 Talking about hazards at work

The trainer gives a short talk about dangers at work before she asks you to discuss your own ideas.

> Welding, panel beating, paint spraying – these are just three of the jobs you might be doing in the workshop. We all enjoy being there, but there could be some dangers attached to the work. Not using eye protection when welding could result in "arc eye" or you could have problems with your breathing. Not wearing ear protection when panel beating could result in permanent or temporary deafness. Safety in the workshop is very important. …

A 6))) ▶ Listen and answer as many of these questions as you can.

1. What protective clothing does the trainer mention?
2. What examples of messiness on the floor are given?
3. What is the safety rule for emergency switches?
4. How should you fill a shelf?
5. How can you make sure you have enough ventilation in the workshop?
6. What problems related to guards and screens does the trainer mention?
7. What advice does the trainer give about tools?
8. What tools does she give as examples?

B When you have finished, work in groups and compare your answers.

 TOOLBOX

emergency cut out switch – *Not-Aus-Schalter*
guard – *Schutzvorrichtung*
hard hat – *Schutzhelm*
paint spraying – *Spritzlackieren*
panel beating – *Spenglerarbeiten*

protective clothing – *Schutzkleidung*
screen – *Schutzschirm*
ventilation – *Belüftung*
ventilator – *Abzug, Ventilator*
welding – *Schweißen*

My workplace   Unit 2

2 Reading safety guidelines

Complete the safety guidelines with imperative forms of the verbs in the list.

~~keep~~ · make sure · not distract · ~~not smoke~~ · not wear · not work on · open · shut down

1 *Keep* your workplace clean. *Do not smoke* in the workshop.
2 ___ jewellery around machines.
3 ___ another employee while he/she is working.
4 ___ electrical appliances while they are plugged in.
5 ___ machinery before cleaning or maintenance.
6 ___ the windows so there is enough air in the workshop.
7 ___ you know the safety rules.

> **Giving orders and instructions**
>
> **Do not block** emergency exits.
> **Keep** emergency stop buttons free.
> **Switch off** machinery before you remove the safety cover.

› *Grammar: Imperatives, page 157*

3 Describing accidents and emergencies

👥 Work in groups. Describe an accident or emergency you know of that happened due to dangers in the workshop. Report to the class.   › *Grammar: Simple past, page 158; Past progressive, page 158*

I was standing on a ladder. A colleague bumped into the ladder and I fell off.

4 Recognizing safety signs

Match the signs (A–J) to the meanings (1–10). What do the different colours of the signs mean?

1 danger: high voltage
2 fire extinguisher
3 emergency exit
4 wear gloves
5 acid
6 highly flammable
7 no entry
8 no naked lights
9 first aid
10 wear safety goggles

5 Making a safety poster

Now it is time to make a poster for your workshop showing how to stay safe at work.

A 👥 Work in groups. Think of a headline for your poster and draw safety signs. Make a short list of safety rules in English (use imperatives).

B When you have finished your poster, pin it on the wall and do a gallery walk. Rank the posters using the categories below. Give points from 1–5 for each category.

headline · design · correct signs · instructions/imperatives · overall effect

 TOOLBOX

acid – *Säure*
emergency exit – *Notausgang*
fire extinguisher – *Feuerlöscher*
first aid – *Erste Hilfe*

flammable – *brennbar*
high voltage – *Hochspannung*
naked lights – *offene Flammen*
safety goggles – *Schutzbrille*

PART A: My job

Situation: You are doing part of your apprenticeship in the British subsidiary of your company.
→ You write a short profile of yourself for the company's intranet.

1 Talking about engineering jobs in the UK

Your supervisor explains that you will be working with colleagues from different sections of the company. He gives you a list of their job titles.

> **Describing what people are doing in photos**
>
> He**'s doing** maintenance on a heating system.
> They**'re looking** at a technical drawing.
>
> › *Grammar: Present progressive, page 157*

A 👥 Work with a partner. Match the job titles (a–e) to the people you can see in the pictures (1–6). Explain your answer. There is one more photo than you need.

a Mechanical Design Engineer
b Maintenance Technician
c CNC Specialist
d Mechanical Fitter
e Project Manager

B Read these statements from the colleagues above. Say who is talking.

1 I work mainly on the computer. I draw things like parts for the machinery we produce or different templates.
2 Precision is the most important thing when you produce parts for machinery on a CNC machine, so everything I do has to be very accurate. It's a challenge to be accurate to 1000th of a millimetre.
3 Once the different parts are manufactured, I assemble them into a mechanical system.
4 My job is to make sure that heating and water supply systems are in good condition and work properly.
5 My responsibilities include pre-planning and other technical activities related to the work that has to be done. I also make sure that our tasks are completed according to plans.

🧰 TOOLBOX

maintenance – *Wartungsarbeiten*
mechanic / mechanical technician – *Mechaniker/in*

template – *Vorlage, Schablone*

Unit 2 My workplace

2 Describing your German job in English

When you write your job profile, you will have to be able to explain your duties and responsibilities.

A 👥 Work with a partner. Read excerpts from the profiles of five other apprentices (1–5). Decide together which of the jobs in the list the writers have been trained to do.

Anlagenmechaniker/in · Industriemechaniker/in · Kraftfahrzeugmechatroniker/in · Werkzeugmechaniker/in · Zerspanungsmechaniker/in

1. When we talk about tools, we often think about pliers, screwdrivers, hammers, and so on. What we do is produce special tools for mass production in industry, different moulds or templates. We also mount these complex tools, test their functions and commission them.
2. I work with specialists for automotive technology. We do repair work and maintenance on passenger cars, lorries and other vehicles. We install special accessories according to the customers' wishes.
3. In my job, I store gases, liquids or compressed air in safe vessels or pipes. The company builds, mounts and repairs pipeline systems at refineries, power plants or refrigeration systems.
4. Everything turns, either the workpiece or the tool, such as a turning tool or a milling cutter. I produce precise workpieces for machines, appliances and production systems. I use technical data like cutting speeds and feed rates to help me plan the production process and to program the machinery.
5. We make sure that industrial production works properly and smoothly. We assemble machines or whole production plants and commission them. We also do the maintenance work to reduce wear and tear and to prevent breakdowns.

B 👥 Work in groups. Talk about your job and responsibilities. Use your dictionary and make notes. Keep your notes for exercise 3.

> **➔ Talking about your work**
>
> **It is** my job **to repair** …
> My responsibilities **include servicing** and **repairing** …
> I'**d like to get** more experience.
> I **enjoy working** in a team.

> 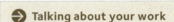 *Grammar: Verb +* to*-infinitive or* -ing *form, page 159*

3 Writing your profile for the company intranet

> **❗ What's my job in English?**
>
> The following is a selection of jobs in small and medium-sized metal engineering companies:
> *Elektriker/in*   electrician / electrical engineer
> *Feinwerkmechaniker/in*   precision mechanic
> *Maschinenbauer/in*   machine builder
> *Schneidwerkzeugmechaniker/in*   cutting tool mechanic
> *Werkzeugmacher/in*   tool maker
> *Mechatroniker/in*   mechatronic systems engineer
>
> Many jobs cannot be translated directly into English, so you may have to describe what you do, e.g.:
> *I am an industrial mechanic. I produce workpieces out of steel and plastics and assemble them. I also …*

Your training supervisor asks you to prepare your profile for the company intranet.

Write some sentences about yourself and your job using the following ideas.

- your name and where you are from
- who you work for
- your job
- your responsibilities
- what you enjoy doing at work

> *Useful phrases: Describing your job, page 148*

PART B: The dual system of vocational training

Situation: You are working at the British subsidiary of your company.
→ **You give a short presentation about vocational training in Germany to your British colleagues.**

1 Reading about the dual system

Your supervisor suggests you use information from the following text for your presentation.

Learning by doing in Germany

Most students in Germany complete their high school education between the ages of 15 and 18. After that, some of them enter a dual training scheme at a vocational college.

5 The dual system combines hands-on learning with classroom learning. This means that the apprentice gets job experience at work and a deep knowledge of their trade at school.

One company that offers apprenticeships is
10 Mech-On, a medium-sized company in the metal trade based in Nuremberg. Mech-On offers apprenticeships in mechanics, electronics and mechatronics.

Gaining a vocational college qualification in
15 trades like these gives young workers good chances in their future lives. The qualification standards are the same throughout the whole of Germany, which means that the degree is recognized by every company.

20 Taking on an apprentice costs a lot of money but, at the end of the day, the company often benefits. By training their own expert staff, businesses of every kind create the next generation of workers. Apprentices who are offered a permanent position at the end of 25 their apprenticeship are already familiar with the structure of the company and the way things work. Another advantage of keeping on apprentices is that a company reduces recruitment costs. 30

Learning by doing is an important part of the German education system. Whether someone is a mechanic or a workshop manager, he or she has probably gone through the dual education system at some time in their life. 35 Even though the German degree is not recognized in some countries, the fact that someone has trained in Germany is often enough to get them a good position abroad.

A Say if the following statements are true or false. Correct the false statements.

1 Vocational college training is only for students who have been to university.
2 Apprentices must have job experience before they can get a place at a college.
3 Mech-On trains people for different types of jobs in the metal industry.
4 A vocational school qualification is accepted by every German firm.
5 Training young people doesn't cost a company anything.
6 There are no advantages for a company that trains young people.
7 A lot of qualified workers have attended vocational college.
8 German dual system qualifications are recognized all over the world.

My workplace Unit 2

B Find the words in the text that match the following definitions.

1. a school that teaches the skills that are necessary for particular jobs
2. learning by doing
3. an exam that you have passed
4. particular areas of business
5. advantages
6. a long-time job
7. finding new people to join a company
8. completed

C Work with a partner. Note down information in the text that you can use in your presentation.

> German students complete high school between 15 and 18.
> dual system = hands-on learning + classroom learning

2 Making a mind map

You continue with your preparation, brainstorming and making a mind map.

A Work with a partner. Describe your working/training situation in Germany using the points below. You can add more points if you like. Make notes.

- what you are training for
- what you like / don't like about your training: breaks, canteen, noise in workshop, …
- how many weeks you spend in the company
- weekly/daily working hours, overtime work, pay, holidays
- working alone/supervised
- how many days/weeks you spend at vocational college
- what you learn at college

> **Talking about what you do regularly**
>
> We **usually** work for … hours a week.
> We **sometimes/never** have to work overtime.
> We **always** have a break for 15 minutes at 9 o'clock.

German vocational schools

The following are the official terms for German vocational schools:

Berufsschule	vocational college
Berufsfachschule	technical college of vocational education
Technikerschule / Meisterschule	technical college of further education
Fachoberschule / Berufsoberschule / technisches Gymnasium	technical college of higher education

B Use your notes to make a mind map. The ideas on the right should start you off. Add more branches if you need to.

3 Giving a presentation

It is time to write up and give your presentation.

A Continue to work with your partner. Use the notes you made for exercise 1C and the mind map you produced for exercise 2 to write up your presentation.

B When you are ready, take turns to give your presentation to the class.

› Useful phrases: Giving a presentation, page 149

COMMUNICATION: Telephoning

Situation: You are working in the UK subsidiary of HUM Maschinenbau GmbH.
→ You call a client and leave a voicemail message. Later, you take a message.

1 Making a telephone call

Your supervisor has left you a note asking you to call a customer, Mr Dalton.

First, check the phrases for making a call. Put them in the order you will use them when you call.

- a   Could you ask … (*name*) to call me back?
- b   Good morning/afternoon.
- c   I'd like to speak to/leave a message for … (*name*).
- d   I'm calling on behalf of … (*name*).
- e   It's about the …
- f   My number is …
- g   Thank you. Goodbye.
- h   The details are as follows: …
- i   This is … (*name*) from HUM Machines Ltd.

> - Phone Esher Engineering to confirm the service checks on their lathes.
> - Say that you're calling on my behalf.
> - Ask to speak to Roger Dalton. He's the factory manager.
> - Tell him that two maintenance technicians will be at the factory at 8.30 on Tuesday, 7 June.
> - All checks should be completed by 12.30 at the latest.
> - If you only get voicemail, ask for Mr Dalton to call you back to confirm the date and time.
> - Give him your mobile number. Thanks.

2 Leaving a voicemail message

When you call Esher Engineering, you only get voicemail, so you have to leave a message for Mr Dalton.

Work with a partner. Use the phrases in exercise 1 and the note above to complete the voicemail message. Each gap represents one word.

"Good morning. This is ▬ ▬¹ from HUM Machines Ltd. I'm calling ▬ ▬ ▬² my supervisor, John Hall. I'd like to ▬ ▬ ▬ ▬³ Mr Dalton, the ▬ ▬⁴. It's ▬ ▬⁵ service checks on your lathes. The ▬ ▬ ▬ ▬⁶: We'll be sending ▬ ▬ ▬⁷ to your factory at 8.30 on Tuesday, 7 June. All checks should be completed by 12.30 ▬ ▬ ▬⁸. ▬ ▬ ▬⁹ Mr Dalton ▬ ▬ ▬ ▬¹⁰ to confirm the details? My ▬ ▬¹¹ 0177 58412503. ▬ ▬¹². Goodbye."

3 Preparing to take a call in English

Match the English sentences (1–10) to the German equivalents (a–j) on page 21.

1   I'm sorry, I didn't understand. Could you repeat that, please?
2   I'm afraid the line is engaged.
3   I'm sorry, … (*name*) is unavailable at the moment.
4   Please hold the line.
5   Who's calling, please?
6   Would you like to speak to someone else?
7   Would you like to leave a message?
8   I'm trying to connect you.
9   I'll put you through.
10 Could you spell your name, please?

TOOLBOX

to be unavailable – *nicht zu sprechen sein*
to connect sb – *jdn verbinden*

engaged – *besetzt*
extension – *Durchwahl*

My workplace   Unit 2

a   Bleiben Sie bitte dran.
b   Der Anschluss ist besetzt.
c   Ich stelle Sie durch.
d   Ich habe nicht verstanden. Bitte wiederholen Sie.
e   Buchstabieren Sie bitte Ihren Namen.
f   Möchten Sie mit jemand anderem sprechen?
g   Ich versuche, Sie zu verbinden.
h   Möchten Sie eine Nachricht hinterlassen?
i   Die Person, mit der Sie sprechen möchten, ist im Moment nicht da.
j   Wie ist Ihr Name, bitte?

4 Taking a message

Your colleague, Julie Matthews, takes a call from a supplier.

7 Before you listen to the call, complete the dialogue using phrases from exercise 3. Then listen and check.

Julie	HUM Machines Ltd. Julie Matthews speaking.
Liam	Can I speak to Martin Brown in the workshop, please?
Julie	*Who's calling please* ¹?
Liam	This is Liam Donnelly.
Julie	I'm sorry, ▬▬ ▬▬ ▬▬ ▬▬ ▬▬, ▬▬ ²?
Liam	It's L I A M D O double-N E double-L Y. I'm calling from Machine Tools in Manchester. It's about the drills Mr Brown ordered.
Julie	Thank you, Mr Donnelly. I'll try Mr Brown for you. Please ▬▬ ▬▬ ▬▬ ³.
Liam	Thank you.
…	
Julie	Mr Donnelly. I'm sorry, Mr Brown is ▬▬ ⁴ at the moment. Would you like to ▬▬ ▬▬ ▬▬ ▬▬ ⁵?
Liam	Yes. All right. Anyone in the workshop will do.
Julie	Thank you. I'll ▬▬ ▬▬ ▬▬ ⁶.
…	
Julie	I'm sorry, Mr Donnelly. I'm afraid the line ▬▬ ▬▬ ⁷. Would you like to ▬▬ ▬▬ ▬▬ ⁸ for Mr Brown?
Liam	Yes, please. Would you tell Mr Brown that the drills he ordered aren't available and ask him to call me to discuss an alternative. My telephone number is 161 839 5005 and the extension is 822.
Julie	▬▬ ▬▬ ⁹. I didn't ▬▬ ¹⁰. Could you ▬▬ ▬▬ ▬▬ ¹¹, please?
Liam	Sure. It's 161 839 5005, extension 822.
Julie	Thank you, Mr Donnelly. I'll make sure that Mr Brown gets the message.

> **Giving telephone numbers**
> Say each digit separately, except for double digits, e.g. 01233455 = "oh (AE: zero) one two double-three four double-five".

5 Role-play: A telephone call

👥 Work with a partner. **Partner A** and **Partner B:** Look at File 3 on page 135.

› *Useful phrases, Telephoning, page 149; Taking telephone calls, page 150*

DAS KANN ICH (Unit 2)
– Ein Plakat mit Sicherheitsvorschriften für die Werkstatt gestalten. (Foundation)
– Mich und meine Arbeit in einem Tätigkeitsprofil auf Englisch beschreiben. (Part A)
– Eine kurze Präsentation über die duale Ausbildung auf Englisch halten. (Part B)
– Eine Nachricht auf einer Mailbox hinterlassen; eine Nachricht weiterleiten. (Communication)

 TOOLBOX

mobile phone (AE: cell phone) – *Handy*
to put sb through – *jdn durchstellen*

voicemail – *Mailbox*

KMK Exam practice 1

1 Hörverstehen: B1

Sie haben sich erfolgreich um einen Praktikumsplatz in einem metallverarbeitenden Betrieb in Gloucester beworben. Heute ist Ihr erster Tag in der Firma, und Sie werden offiziell gemeinsam mit anderen Praktikanten/Praktikantinnen aus anderen Ländern begrüßt.

8))) Um sich möglichst schnell zu orientieren und den Betrieb kennenzulernen, machen Sie sich während der Begrüßungsansprache einige Notizen zu Namen, Produkten usw. Sie haben die Rede mit Ihrem Smartphone aufgezeichnet und hören sie sich später noch zwei Mal an. Dabei füllen Sie den folgenden Stichwortzettel in deutscher Sprache aus.

Wichtige Personen und deren Aufgabenbereiche			
Mr Brady		Mr Bird	
Ms Lawrence		Walter Bright	
Fred McKenzie		Barbara Collins	
Produkte			
Erwartungen an jeden Mitarbeiter zur Qualitätsverbesserung			
Einsatzbereiche			
1. Woche			
2. Woche			
3. Woche			
Besonderes Ereignis / Wichtiger Termin			

2 Produktion: B1

Sie arbeiten in der Hamburger Filiale einer Londoner Firma namens Xellent UK plc. Dieses Unternehmen ist in Fachkreisen als Spezialist für digitale Fernsehtechnik und High-End-Produkte im Bereich DVD/Blu-Ray-Rekorder und -Dekoder geschätzt. Für ihr neues Image soll eine neue Webseite kreiert werden. Eine Unterseite trägt den Titel „About Us". Sie soll in knapper und übersichtlicher Form die Firmengeschichte wiedergeben.

Da man weiß, dass Ihre Englischkenntnisse sehr gut sind, gibt man Ihnen den Auftrag, den Text anhand der Angaben auf Seite 23 zu verfassen.

1961	"Radio Shack" founded in Oxford / radios and antennas
1965	Also portable transistor radios, own factory in Wales (until 1973)
1970	Number of staff employed 250
1977	Affiliate in the Netherlands. Name changed (reason: companies of the same name in other countries)
1985	German affiliate
1990	Production: UK: TV sets; NL: pocket-size radios; Germany: video cassette recorders
1991	NL: satellite dishes only (pocket-size radios abandoned)
1994	Crisis (wrong advertising strategies)
1995	Successful TV spots
1997	Introduction of new product lines: MP3-players, DVD players / Number of staff: 1400
2000	2nd crisis (increase in competition)
2002	New Marketing Manager (Mr Rudolph): Elimination of unsuccessful products
Since 2010	Further improvements and completely new product range

3 Interaktion: A2

When you started your apprenticeship, you were told that wearing the right clothes was very important for the safety of metal workers.

Study the drawing below and discuss with your partner(s) which of the rules apply for the following jobs:

- Cutting Machine Operator
- Foundry Mechanic
- Technical Product Designer

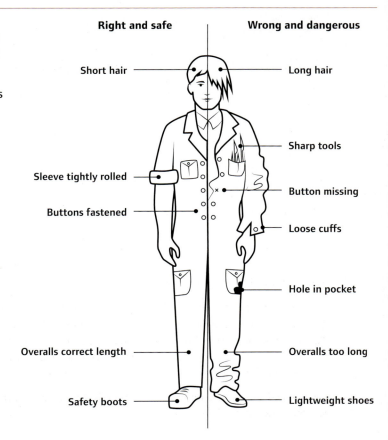

3 Tools of the trade

FOUNDATION: Favourite tools

Situation: You work at an international technology company in Germany which employs technicians from all over the world.
→ You make a list of expressions for tools in English.

1 Using the right tools

Three employees talk about some of the tools they like to use and what they use them for.

Marcus Beyer
Machine builder

Imre Akdeniz
Mechatronics technician

Pavel Denisovic
Precision mechanic

A 9))) Read what the employees say and decide who is talking. Then listen and check.

a I enjoy working with my vernier callipers. They're used for measuring thicknesses, inside diameters, outside diameters and depth. It's the best measuring tool ever. It's much more accurate than a normal ruler. That can only measure down to 1 millimetre, or maybe 0.5 millimetres if you have a good one. Good vernier callipers can measure within 0.1 millimetres. The second tool I like is my inspection mirror. I use it when I'm working on machines to check for screws and things that might have become loose during vibration testing.

b I spend a lot of time on the factory floor, checking and repairing machinery and devices. If something's not working properly, I have to diagnose the problem – find out what's wrong – then I have to fix it. In this case, I use a multimeter that measures voltage, current and resistance or one that can measure the capacitance, inductance and current gain of transistors. That one's a very advanced, high-tech tool. At the other end of the scale, I often have to use a soldering iron which is a very simple tool. My father taught me how to use a soldering iron when I was a kid.

c I like working with the centre punch I made myself. Basically, you use a centre punch to mark the centre of a hole when drilling holes. A drill can wander if it doesn't start in a hole, so you use the punch to form a dent to guide the tip of the drill. You place the tip on the point where you want the hole, then hit it hard with a hammer. An automatic centre punch operates without the need for a hammer, but I really prefer the one I made. It's just a metal rod with a shaped tip on the end that has been hardened.

Tools of the trade   Unit 3

B Look at the close-up photos of tools from the text. With a partner, try to guess which tools they are.

2 Naming tools in English

You are working in the tool store. As your supervisor can't speak English and some of the technicians don't speak German, he asks you to make a list of the tools for him in English.

A Work with a partner. Make two columns in your exercise book. Copy the English words for tools you have learned on these pages in the second column. Find the German expression in the wordlist and write it in the first column.

Handwerkzeuge	Hand tools
Messschieber	vernier callipers
	inspection mirror

B Add the German expressions for other tools you know. Check your dictionary for the English words. Keep adding to this list.

› Part A, exercise 2, page 26

3 Game: What's in my toolbox?

Twenty questions is a game to test your knowledge of the English names for tools.

A Choose two tools that you like working with or tools that you and your colleagues use every day. (Use your dictionary if you don't know the English word.) Do not show your list to anyone.

B Now work in groups of four. Take turns to ask and answer yes/no questions to find out what tools your partners are thinking of. Who has most points when the game is over?

> *Twenty questions: Rules*
> 1. *You are only allowed to ask yes/no questions.*
> 2. *You are only allowed to ask 20 questions. Someone should keep a note of how many questions have been asked.*
> 3. *The person who names the tool first gets one point.*
> 4. *If all 20 questions have been asked and no one has guessed the name of the tool, then the person thinking of the tool gets the point.*

> **→ Asking and answering questions**
> **Do you use** this tool in the workshop?
> – Yes, **I do**. / No, **I don't**.
> **Did you make** this tool yourself?
> – Yes, **I did**. / No, **I didn't**.
> **Can you carry** it in your pocket?
> – Yes, **you can**. / No, **you can't**.
> **Is it** small? – Yes, **it is**. / No, **it isn't**.

I'm thinking of a small tool that I use a lot.

Is it a centre punch?

Yes, that's right. / No, it isn't.

› *Grammar: Questions and short answers, page 157*

25

PART A: Hand tools

Situation: You are doing work experience as a fitter for RoboCron Ltd in York. It's your first day and you are working with hand tools in the workshop.
→ You make a tool trolley checklist for your supervisor.

1 Identifying workshop sounds

🔊 10 As you enter the workshop, you hear a lot of different noises.

👥 Work with a partner. Listen to the sounds of six hand tools and match them with the pictures below (A–F).

> I think that's a(n) …

> Sorry, I don't agree. It's a(n) …

| A | B | C | D | E | F |
| electric drill | handfile | hammer | hacksaw | jigsaw | ratchet |

2 Naming workbench tools

Your supervisor shows you the workbench where you will be working.

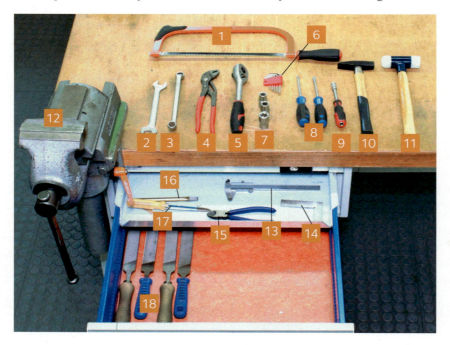

 TOOLBOX

electric drill – *elektrische Handbohrmaschine*
hacksaw – *Bügelsäge*
handfile – *Handfeile*

hand tool – *Handwerkzeug*
jigsaw – *Stichsäge*
ratchet – *Ratschenschlüssel*

Tools of the trade Unit 3

A Match the tools (1–18) in the photo on page 26 to the words in the list.

Allen head wrench set · angle · chisel · double ended ring spanner · double open ended spanner · engineer's hammer · flat files · hacksaw · nut driver · ratchet · screwdrivers · side cutting pliers · socket wrench · soft faced hammer · three corner scraper · vernier callipers · vice · waterpump pliers

> **Saying where things are**
>
> The … is **beside** / **next to** the …
> The … is **on** the workbench.
> The … are **in** a drawer.
> There is a … **on top of** the workbench.
> There is a … **on the left** / **on the right**.

B Now say where the tools are in the photo.

3 Choosing the right tools for the job

Your supervisor would like to find out how much you know about working with hand tools.

A Work with a partner. Write sentences saying which tools you need for the jobs below.

To repair a pump first of all you need spanners or socket wrenches. Then you need …

1 repair a pump
2 mount an assembly line
3 service a car
4 measure and mark out workpieces
5 produce a die plate

B With your partner, write about two other jobs you do regularly. Make sentences like the ones above, saying which tools you use.

> **Talking about what you usually do**
>
> I **always/usually/often** use spanners to repair a pump.
> I **sometimes / hardly ever / never** use a …

4 Fixing screws, nuts, bolts and washers

Your supervisor tests your knowledge of fasteners and the tools you need to fix them.

A Work with a partner. Match the screws and screwdrivers (1–6) with the correct names.

Cross slot / Phillips · Hexagon · Pozidriv · Security T · Slotted · Torx

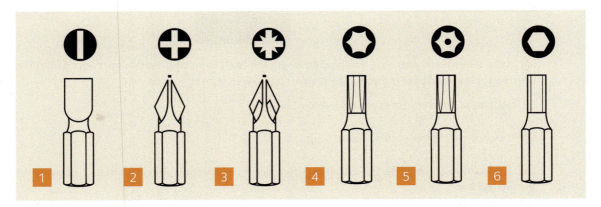

🧰 **TOOLBOX**

Allen key/wrench – *Innensechskantschlüssel*
double ended ring spanner – *Doppelringschlüssel*
double open ended spanner – *Doppelmaulschlüssel*
screwdriver – *Schraubendreher*
socket wrench – *Aufsteckschraubenschlüssel*
workpiece – *Werkstück*

B 👥 Work with a partner. Match the nuts, bolts, screws and washers (1–12) with the correct names.

cap nut · hex nut ·
nylon insert lock nut ·
square nut

hex bolt · machine bolt · sheet metal screw · thread cutting machine screw

external tooth lock washer · flat washer · internal tooth lock washer · split lock washer

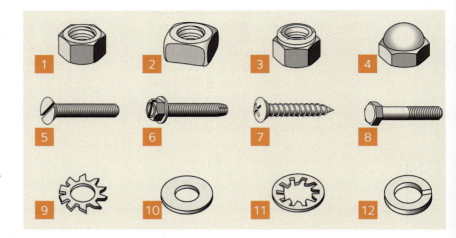

C 👥 Work in groups. Make a list of other fasteners you use in your job. Say which tools you use to fix them.

5 Writing a checklist for the tool trolley

Your supervisor asks you to write a checklist for the tool trolley, saying where the tools are and why.

A 👥 Make a list of the tools that you use every day and a list of other tools that you need but don't often use. Discuss where to put the tools in the tool trolley. Remember that heavy tools should go at the bottom.

The … should go in the top drawer because …

Do you think so? I think that the … should go in the bottom drawer because …

B 👥 Make a numbered checklist list showing where the tools should go. Add a short note giving the reason why the tools are in these drawers. Two drawers have been started for you.

1 Top drawer (tools we use every day): screwdrivers, …
  …
5 Bottom drawer (heavy tools): power tools, …

C 👥 Compare your checklists in groups. Do you agree on which tools should go in each drawer? What are the differences?

🧰 **TOOLBOX**

bolt – *Schraube (zur Befestigung von Muttern)*
drawer – *Schublade, Schubfach*
nut – *Mutter*
screw – *Schraube (zur Befestigung von Teilen mit Innengewinde)*
tool trolley – *Werkzeugwagen*
washer – *Unterlegscheibe*

Tools of the trade Unit 3

PART B: Machine tools

Situation: You are doing work experience as a fitter at RoboCron Ltd in York. This week you are working in a different workshop.
→ You explain how one of the machines works to a new colleague.

1 Identifying machine tools

A Match the machine tools (1–7) with the names from the list.

bandsaw · drilling machine · grinding machine · milling machine · off-hand grinder · power hacksaw · turning machine

B 11)) Listen to the sounds of five machine tools. Which ones can you see in the photos?

2 Describing three different machine tools

Your supervisor shows you three of the machine tools that are used at RoboCron. He gives you three different tasks to test your knowledge of the machines.

A Work with a partner. Complete the text with words from the list.

column · chuck · dial · head · motor · swivelled · vice

A **drilling machine** is composed of a base that supports a ___¹, which in turn supports a table. Workpieces can be supported on the table with a ___² or hold down clamps, or the table can be ___³ out of the way to allow tall workpieces to be supported directly on the base. The column also supports a ___⁴ containing a ___⁵ which turns the spindle at a speed controlled by a variable speed control ___⁶. The spindle holds a drill ___⁷ to hold the cutting tools.

TOOLBOX

bandsaw – *Bandsäge*
chuck – *Spannfutter, Bohrfutter*
clamp – *Klemme*
column – *Säule*
drilling machine – *Bohrmaschine*
grinding machine – *Schleifmaschine*

milling machine – *Fräsmaschine*
off-hand grinder – *Handschleifmaschine*
spindle – *Spindel*
to swivel – *schwenken*
turning machine – *Drehmaschine*
vice – *(Maschinen-)Schraubstock*

B Read the description of the milling machine. Then complete the vocabulary card with English words and expressions from the text.

The **milling machine** is a frequently-used workshop machine tool. Milling machines are usually used to machine flat surfaces, but can also produce irregular surfaces. They can also be used to drill, bore and produce slots. The most common type is a vertical spindle machine with a swivelling head. A milling machine removes metal by rotating a multi-toothed cutter that is fed into the moving workpiece. Most milling machines are equipped with a power feed for one or more axes. The power feed can produce a better surface finish because it is smoother than a manual feed.

Milling machine	
a	ebene Flächen bearbeiten
b	unebene Flächen herstellen
c	Schwenkkopf
d	mehrzahniges Fräswerkzeug
e	automatischer Vorschub
f	manueller Vorschub

C Read the description of the turning machine. Then use your dictionary to write your own vocabulary card. Keep your card safely. You will need it for exercise 4.

Turning machine

The **turning machine** is another very common machine tool in the workshop. A turning machine rotates a workpiece against a tool whose position it controls. It is used to manufacture parts and features that have a circular cross section. The spindle, which is driven by an electric motor through a system of gear trains, is the part of the turning machine that rotates. The tailstock can be used to support the end of the workpiece with a centre, or to hold tools for drilling, threading, or cutting tapers.

 TOOLBOX

axis, axes – *Achse*
to bore – *innendrehen*
centre – *Reitstockspitze*
cross section – *Querschnitt*
to drill – *bohren*
gear train – *Getriebe*

slot – *Schlitz*
swivelling head – *Schwenkkopf*
tailstock – *Reitstock*
taper – *Kegel*
to thread – *Gewinde schneiden*
vertical spindle machine – *Maschine mit senkrechter Spindel*

Tools of the trade   Unit 3

3 Understanding how a turning machine works

Your supervisor shows you the turning machine and gives you a list of parts.

A Work with a partner. Match the following parts to the turning machine on page 30. Add new words to the vocabulary card you made for exercise 2C.

- a apron
- b bed slideways
- c chuck
- d compound slide
- e control unit
- f headstock
- g protective hood
- h rack
- i tailstock
- j tool holder

B What does each part of the turning machine do? Match these descriptions to the parts of the turning machine in exercise 3A.

1. This part makes sure that the workpiece which has to be machined is held right in the centre.
2. This serves as housing for the driving pulleys, back gears, headstock spindle, live centre and the feed reverse gear.
3. This is located between the headstock and tailstock and supports, guides and feeds the tool against the workpiece during operation.
4. This protects the lathe operator from flying chips or coolant during operation.
5. This slides along the bed to accommodate different lengths of workpiece between the centres.
6. This is fastened to the compound slide and it houses the gears, clutches and levers required to move the cross slide.
7. The working parts of the lathe, such as the headstock and tailstock are mounted on this heavy, rugged casting. It provides a base for the carriage assembly which carries the tool.
8. Here you can type in all the data necessary for manufacturing a workpiece. The emergency-stop switch is also here.
9. This is located below the headstock and contains a number of different sized gears to change speed and direction of rotation.
10. This is mounted on the compound rest and it rigidly clamps the cutting tool at the correct height.

4 Explaining how the turning machine works

Your supervisor asks you to explain how the turning machine works to a new colleague.

A Work with a partner. Use your vocabulary card from exercise 2C and phrases from exercise 3 to make notes. Make sure you cover all the parts of the turning machine mentioned in exercise 3.

You can start like this:
A turning machine is a machine tool which holds the workpiece rigidly between two rigid and strong supports called centres or in a chuck which revolves. The cutting tool is held and supported in a tool holder which is fed against the revolving workpiece. The cutting tool is normally fed either parallel or at right angles to the axis of the workpiece.

B Work in groups. Use your notes to explain the different parts of the turning machine.

TOOLBOX

apron – *Schlosskasten*
bed slideways – *Maschinenbett*
compound slide – *Kreuzschlitten*
control unit – *Steuergerät*

headstock – *Spindelkasten*
protective hood – *Schutzhaube*
rack – *Zahnstange*
tool holder – *Werkzeughalter*

COMMUNICATION: Emails

Situation: You work at Technical Tools, a supplier to the technical trades, where your supervisor asks you to take care of a customer enquiry.
→ You write an email to a customer.

1 Giving email addresses over the phone

You check the English for some of the symbols that appear in email addresses.

A Match the symbols (1–6) to the words (a–f).

1	+	4	-	a	at	e	plus
2	_	5	.	b	dot	e	number
3	@	6	3	c	hyphen	f	underscore

B 12))) Listen to your supervisor and a customer on the phone. Which email addresses are correct?

1
a tm.martin@technical-tools.de
b tmmartin@technical_tools.de
c tm.martin@technical_tools.de

2
a maryannbrown@5+5_services.net
b mary-anne-brown@5+5services.net
c maryann-brown@5+5services.net

C Work with a partner. You are going to dictate email addresses to each other.

Partner A: Look at File 2 on page 134.
Partner B: Look at File 10 on page 138.

> Can you spell that, please?

> Could you repeat that, please?

2 Writing a subject line

The first indication of what is in an email is the subject line. This must state clearly what the email is about.

A Work with a partner. Study the subject lines (1–6) below and find an email which …

1 is a request for information.
2 gives information about a meeting.
3 asks for assistance.
4 contains new information.
5 announces a change of plan.
6 is a covering letter for a brochure

a Subject: Need your help with English
b Subject: New venue for event on Saturday
c Subject: Flyer (attached)
d Subject: Meeting 25.03. Starting time?
e Subject: Update on project
f Subject: Agenda

B With your partner, write suitable subject lines for the following emails (1–6).

1 Sorry, I would like to change the date of the meeting to Friday 12 July.
2 Could you send me information about the presentation, please?
3 I am on holiday from 21.03 till 04.04 inclusive and will answer emails when I return.
4 I am writing to confirm your application for a stand at the Technical Trades Fair. The stand number is C208.
5 As promised, here is the link to the website for email tips.
6 This is just to let you know that I am interviewing a new technician at 12.30.

TOOLBOX

hyphen – *Bindestrich, Minus*   underscore – *Unterstrich*

Tools of the trade Unit 3

3 Writing a reply to an email enquiry

Your supervisor gives you the enquiry below and asks you to reply by email.

> Dear Sir/Madam
>
> We have studied your catalogue on the Internet and are interested in your Phillips screwdrivers (catalogue number SP 492876) and your slotted screwdrivers (catalogue number SS 8592201).
> We would like to order 100 of each type of screwdriver.
> We would also like to order 1,000 boxes of Phillips screws and 1,000 boxes of slotted screws.
> Please let us know if you have these items in stock.
>
> Yours faithfully
> Robert Johnson
>
> Robert Johnson Building Ltd

Use a suitable greeting and subject line and reply to Mr Johnson. Include the following points:

- Thank him for his enquiry.
- Say that the screwdrivers and the screws are in stock.
- Say you will dispatch them next week.
- Say that you look forward to doing business with him in the future.
- Use the correct complimentary close.

› Useful phrases: Writing emails, page 150

Using polite language in emails

Could and *would like* are more polite than phrases with *can*, *need* or *want*.
~~Can~~ you let me know by Monday? → **Could** you let …
I ~~need~~ the information today. → I **would like** the …
We ~~want~~ to have a meeting. → We **would like** to …

› Grammar: Modals and their substitutes, page 161

Salutation and complimentary close in emails

If you do not know the name of the person you are writing to, begin your email with *Dear Sir or Madam*.
If you do not know your business partner well, use a formal salutation and complimentary close.

	Salutation	Complimentary close	
Formal (to unknown person)	Dear Sir or Madam	Yours faithfully	
Formal (to person whose name you know)	Dear Ms/Mr Smith	Regards Best regards	Best wishes Yours sincerely
Less formal	Dear Paul / Hi Paula Good morning, Paul	Regards Best regards	Best wishes All the best

DAS KANN ICH (Unit 3)

- Eine Liste der englischen Bezeichnungen für Werkzeuge zusammenstellen. (Foundation)
- Eine englische Checkliste für den Werkzeugwagen schreiben. (Part A)
- Die Bestandteile einer Drehmaschine auf Englisch benennen und beschreiben. (Part B)
- Die E-Mail eines britischen Kunden auf Englisch beantworten. (Communication)

TOOLBOX

Best regards / Regards – *Schöne Grüße*
complimentary close – *Grußformel (am Briefende)*
salutation – *Anrede*

subject line – *Betreff*
Yours faithfully – *Mit freundlichen Grüßen*
Yours sincerely – *Mit freundlichen Grüßen*

4 Materials of the trade

FOUNDATION: The right materials for the job

Situation: Your company is taking part in an international trade fair.
→ You give a short presentation at the fair about the materials your company uses.

1 Classifying materials

Your supervisor suggests that you start your presentation with an overview of materials the company uses.

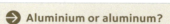
Aluminium or aluminum?
BE: alu**min**ium: the stress is on the third syllable
AE: **alu**minum: the stress is on the second syllable

A Copy and complete the grid with materials from the list.

carbon fibre · cast iron · glass ·
glass fibre · lead · magnesium · stone ·
titanium · wood · zinc

Metals		
ferrous metals	non-ferrous metals	
e.g. *steel* ▭¹	heavy metals e.g. *copper* ▭² ▭³	light metals e.g. *aluminium* ▭⁴ ▭⁵
Non-metals		
natural materials	artificial materials	compounds
e.g. ▭⁶ ▭⁷	e.g. ▭⁸ plastics	e.g. ▭⁹ ▭¹⁰

B Make a mind map showing the materials your company works with.

🧰 TOOLBOX

aluminium/aluminum – *Aluminium*
cast iron – *Gusseisen*
copper – *Kupfer*
lead – *Blei*

steel – *Stahl*
titanium – *Titan*
zinc – *Zink*

Materials of the trade   Unit 4

2 The mechanical properties of materials

You decide to check what you know about the properties of metals.

A Combine the words and phrases to make sentences describing the mechanical properties of materials.

1 Elastic		a	absorb energy when it is deformed elastically.
2 Flexible		b	bend or deform in response to an applied force.
3 Hard		c	deform under compressive stress without developing defects.
4 Hard-wearing	can	d	reduce weight while preserving strength.
5 Light-weight	material will	e	withstand shock and plastically deform without fracturing or rupturing.
6 Malleable	is able to	f	withstand surface indentation and scratching.
7 Resilient		g	last a long time and remain in good condition.
8 Tough		h	resist a distorting influence or stress and return to its original size and shape when the stress is removed.

B With a partner, choose two materials. Decide together what type of material they are and describe their properties. Make notes.

C When you are ready, find another pair and take turns to describe the materials you have chosen. Ask them to guess the materials.

> **Describing properties**
>
> Carbon fibre is a **good** material for crash helmets.
> Plastic is a **useful** material for household goods.
> Steel is **hard**.
> The metal feels **rough**.

It's a silvery-grey metal. It's light-weight and flexible.

I think it's aluminium.

› *Grammar: Adjectives and adverbs, page 160*

3 Presenting the materials

It is time to prepare, structure and give your presentation.

A Work with a partner. Decide together what materials you are going to talk about. Use your mind map from exercise 1B and add the qualities of the materials to it.

B Use your mind map to make a vocabulary handout that you can give your audience.

C Now make notes about what you are going to say in your presentation. The structure below will help you.

Introduction:	The main part of the presentation:	Conclusion:
– Greet the audience. – Give a very short introduction about yourself. Say where you work and what you do. – Say what you are going to talk about and distribute your handout.	– Classify the types of materials you work with. – Describe the qualities of the materials and how these qualities are necessary for the jobs you do. – Refer to your handout when necessary.	– Summarize what you have said in the main part of the presentation. – Ask and answer questions from the audience. – Thank everyone for coming and say goodbye.

D When you are ready, give your presentation.

› *Useful phrases: Giving a presentation, page 149*

35

PART A: The Stirling engine

Situation: You are working at the subsidiary of an American engineering company that also produces Stirling engines.
→ You answer a request for help on the user forum on the company's website.

1 The parts of a Stirling engine

Your supervisor tests your knowledge of the Stirling engine.

A Match the expressions in the list with the numbers (1–5) in the photo.

base · cooler ·
flywheel · motion link · stand

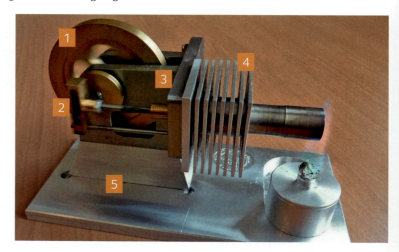

B Use the table below. Say which materials are used for the parts of the Stirling engine and explain why.

Physical properties of materials				
	density in g/cm³	elasticity in kN/mm²	thermal expansion in 10^{-6} K^{-1}	thermal conductivity in W/(m·K)
steel	7.85	206	11.5	50
aluminium	2.7	70	23.1	236
cast iron	7.3	128	10.0	54
brass	8.4	108	18.5	113

> **Comparing things**
>
> The cooler is made of … because it is **denser / less dense than** …
> The … is made of … because it expands **more / less slowly** under temperature **than** …

› *Grammar: Comparatives and superlatives, page 160*

 TOOLBOX

---

base – *Grundkörper*
brass – *Messing*
cooler – *Kühlkörper*
density – *Dichte*
elasticity – *Elastizität*

flywheel – *Schwungrad*
motion link – *Kulisse, Kulissenführung*
stand – *Ständer*
thermal conductivity – *Wärmeleitfähigkeit*
thermal expansion – *Wärmeausdehnung*

Materials of the trade **Unit 4**

2 Reading about engine maintenance

You decide to find out more about Stirling engines and their maintenance, so you read the following extract from your company's user manual.

Displacement axle and crankshaft oils

Ready-assembled models are already lubricated and must not be lubricated further. For self-assembled models, lubricate as follows:
- Only use AeroShell Fluid 12: do not use any other oil. The manufacturer's warranty will be void if other oils or lubricants are used.
- The Stirling engine will not start if there is excess oil on the displacement axle or excess ceramic paste on the working piston. In this case, the engine must be partially disassembled and cleaned thoroughly. Oil may only be applied after the first trial run on the displacement axle (1 oil droplet, diameter 1mm). DO NOT regrease!
- The bearings must NEVER be lubricated.
- In crankshaft models, it is recommended that the 4mm axle in the centre (between the aluminium flanges, where two rods on the axle are located) be lubricated with 1 drop of oil (1mm diameter) after prolonged use.

Piston cleaning

The model may no longer run properly if the pistons are not cleaned or too much oil is used.
- Clean the working pistons regularly and do not relubricate the model unless the engine is completely disassembled and rebuilt.
- Over time, black abrasion dust builds up in the friction bearing (piston/cylinder) which settles in the cylinder and may cause the the model to run poorly or even come to a standstill. Clean the inside of the piston and the cylinder on the sliding surfaces regularly. Remove the piston and clean the piston and working cylinder with a dry cloth. Clean the brass cylinder inside down to the bottom. Reassemble dry WITHOUT lubricant.

As a rule, Stirling engines are to be kept oil-free with working pistons.

Surface oxidation and ageing

Brass is subject to natural oxidation processes and it is intended that the Stirling engine model will tarnish and get a patina over time. Fingerprints may be seen but will also darken.
- Avoid contact with sweaty palms, water and moisture.
- The brass may be polished with standard brass polishes!
- Allow the model to age normally: after a few years it will have the desired brass patina.

Source: www.en.boehm-stirling.com

 TOOLBOX

abrasion – *Abrieb*
axle – *Achse*
bearing – *Lager*
crankshaft – *Kurbelwelle*
displacement – *Verdrängung*

flange – *Flansch*
lubricant – *Schmiermittel*
piston – *Kolben*
trial – *Versuch*
warranty – *Garantie*

A Find the English meanings for these German expressions in the text on page 37. They are in the same order.

1 geschmiert
2 unwirksam
3 Arbeitskolben
4 zerlegt
5 Probelauf
6 länger andauernd
7 Abriebsstaub
8 Stillstand
9 wieder zusammenbauen
10 anlaufen

B Another colleague who read the text has misunderstood several facts. Say which of his statements are true or false. Correct the false statements.

1 Never oil a new engine.
2 Lubricants made by other companies can be used as well.
3 The working piston must be oiled well.
4 After the first run, you may oil only once.
5 Lubricate the bearings well.
6 If you use enough oil, you won't have to clean the piston.
7 If there is too much abrasion in the friction bearing, the engine stops.
8 Clean the piston and the cylinder from time to time.
9 Brass rusts.
10 As brass gets older, it starts to look nicer.

C Sie haben einen Stirlingmotor in Ihrer Werkstatt. Lesen Sie den Text und fassen Sie die wichtigsten Punkte zur Pflege und Wartung auf Deutsch für Ihre Kollegen und Kolleginnen zusammen.

3 Replying to a request for help

As you are interested in the Stirling engine, your supervisor asks you to reply to a customer who has a problem with his new model.

Read the forum request and answer it using information from the text.

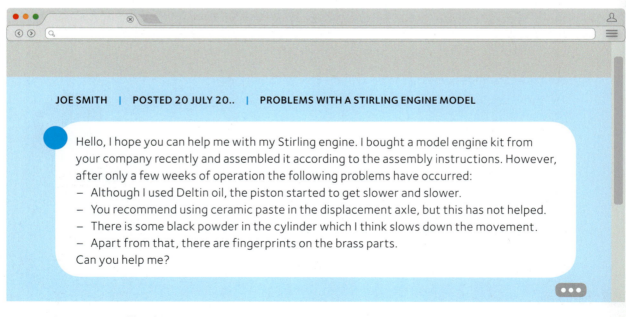

JOE SMITH | POSTED 20 JULY 20.. | PROBLEMS WITH A STIRLING ENGINE MODEL

Hello, I hope you can help me with my Stirling engine. I bought a model engine kit from your company recently and assembled it according to the assembly instructions. However, after only a few weeks of operation the following problems have occurred:
– Although I used Deltin oil, the piston started to get slower and slower.
– You recommend using ceramic paste in the displacement axle, but this has not helped.
– There is some black powder in the cylinder which I think slows down the movement.
– Apart from that, there are fingerprints on the brass parts.
Can you help me?

You can start like this:

Hi Joe,
Thanks for your request for help. We're sorry to hear that your Stirling engine model is not working properly. First of all, we think you ...

Materials of the trade Unit 4

PART B: A specific workpiece

Situation: You work for a metal engineering company that produces specific workpieces for customers.
→ **You describe workpieces and draw a workpiece according to a customer's specifications.**

1 Adding dimensions to a drawing

Your supervisor calls an English customer because some dimensions on a sketch of a workpiece are missing.

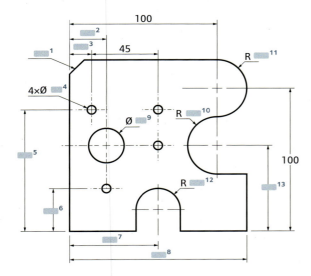

A 13))) Listen to their conversation and note down the missing dimensions.

B Where can you see the following information on the drawing? What do these lines mean?

continuous line · thin chain-dotted line · dimension line

C 13))) Close your books. Listen again and draw the full workpiece on a separate piece of paper.

2 Describing shapes

Your supervisor asks you to write a list of English expressions for describing workpieces. You label some sketches so that she can keep them by his phone.

A Copy and complete the drawings with the following information.

chamfer · circumference ·
concave · convex ·
diameter · groove · radius

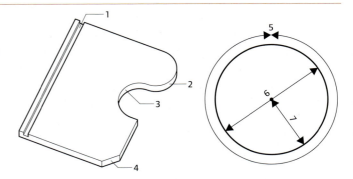

 TOOLBOX

chain-dotted line – *strichpunktierte Linie*
chamfer – *Fase*
continuous line – *durchgezogene Linie*

edge – *Kante*
groove – *Nut*

39

B Complete this word families table with the missing adjectives. Use your dictionary if necessary.

2D shapes			3D shapes		
shape	noun	adjective	shape	noun	adjective
	square	*square*		cube	*cubical*
	rectangle			rectangular solid	
	triangle			cylinder	
	circle			sphere	
	semi-circle			hemisphere	*hemispherical*
				cone	

› *Grammar: Adjectives and adverbs, page 160*

C Match the drawings (1–10) to the words in the list.

bar · block · casting · film · plate · rod (circular bar) · sheet · strip · tube · wire

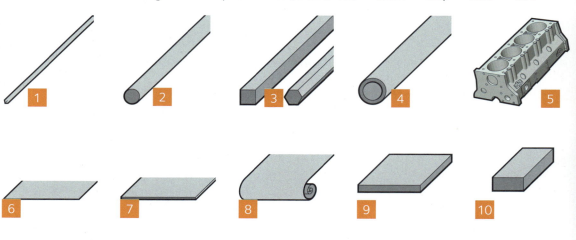

3 Practising describing workpieces

Part of your in-company training programme is a monthly test. You prepare for this month's test by checking descriptions of workpieces.

40

Materials of the trade Unit 4

A   Match the workpieces (1–5) to the descriptions (a–e).

a   This workpiece is a rectangular solid with a radius on the left, a cylinder on the right and a thread through it. It is machined from a casting.
b   This workpiece has a thread with a nut on the left and a sphere on the right. It is made from a rolled rod.
c   This workpiece is cylindrical and is made from rolled steel.
d   This workpiece is conical and is made from sheet metal.
e   This workpiece is an L-shaped rectangle and is made from sheet metal.

B   Work with a partner. Say what you think the workpieces are.

4 Describing workpieces to your partner

It is time to draw a workpiece according to a customer's specifications.

A   Work with a partner. Look at the drawing of an apron together, then complete the description with the missing dimensions. Which part (1–5) of the turning machine does the drawing match?

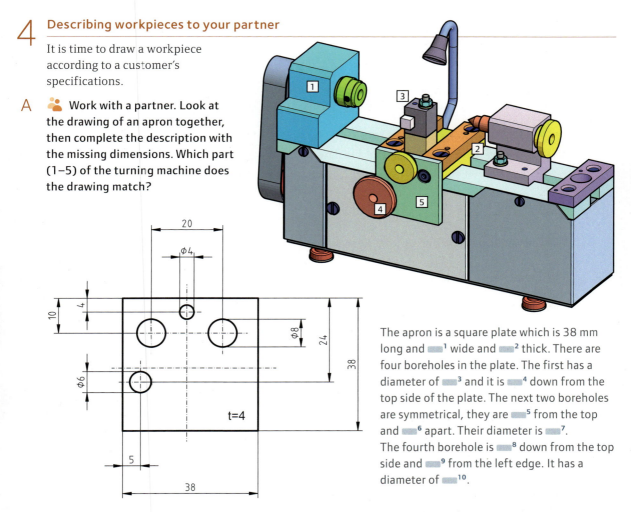

The apron is a square plate which is 38 mm long and ▬¹ wide and ▬² thick. There are four boreholes in the plate. The first has a diameter of ▬³ and it is ▬⁴ down from the top side of the plate. The next two boreholes are symmetrical, they are ▬⁵ from the top and ▬⁶ apart. Their diameter is ▬⁷. The fourth borehole is ▬⁸ down from the top side and ▬⁹ from the left edge. It has a diameter of ▬¹⁰.

B   Work with a partner. Partner A: Look at File 6 on page 136. Partner B: Look at File 14 on page 140.

Sit back to back and take turns to describe workpieces from the turning machine.

› Useful phrases: Describing size and dimensions, page 151

 TOOLBOX

thread – Gewinde

COMMUNICATION: A short presentation

> **Situation:** Some trainees from the UK are soon going to start work at your company.
> → You give a short presentation to the new trainees about your work.

1 Thinking about the contents of a presentation

Your supervisor gives you a list of points you should include in your talk.

what the company does · your department · what you do

A 👥 Work with a partner. Read the list and decide together what you would like to add to your supervisor's list above. Make notes.

B 👥 Compare your notes with another pair and decide on the final points you will cover. Make a mind map.

C 👥 Agree on the order you will present the contents. Make a numbered list. Write the name and date of your talk at the top of the list.

Presentation to new trainees: 08.07.20..
1 Introduction (self/the company)
2 ▬
3 ▬

2 Writing the presentation

A Use your mind map and the list from exercise 1 to write your text. Follow this structure.

Introduction	– Say in a few words what you are going to talk about.
Main part	– Use one paragraph for each topic. – Use signposts to move from one subject to the next.
Conclusion	– Summarize the main ideas. – Invite questions from the audience.

B Check the text together for clarity and correctness as follows.

- Is the information in the text correct? If not, correct it.
- Is the spelling and grammar correct? Use your dictionary and the list of phrases on page 43.

3 Making a prompt card

A presentation comes across best when the presenter looks at the audience and speaks naturally. As it is difficult to do either of these things when you read from a text, you should make yourself a prompt card.

A Follow the steps below.

- Highlight important words and phrases in your text.
- Copy the words and phrases onto an index card.
- Include signposts to structure the ideas.

> - manufacturing company
> - workshop
> - apprentice ...

B Practise your presentation in your group, using only your prompt card.

Materials of the trade **Unit 4**

> **Structuring a presentation**
>
> Introduction
> My name is … and this is my colleague, …
> We are … apprentices at … (*name of company*) in Germany.
> This morning/afternoon I'm / we're going to give a short talk/presentation on …
> I/We will be happy to answer any questions at the end of the talk.
>
> Main part
> I've/We've divided the talk/presentation into … parts.
> First/Firstly … / Second/Secondly, … / After that … / Finally …
>
> Signposts
> To begin with … / Next …
> Now … / I would also like to mention …
>
> Conclusion
> To conclude, … / To sum up, …
> I'd/We'd be happy to take questions now. / Does anyone have any questions?
> Thank you for listening.

4 Giving your presentation

It is time to give your presentation and to give each other feedback.

A Decide who is going to speak first in your group. When it is your turn, stand up, look directly at the audience and smile. Then speak freely and clearly using your prompt card. Ask for questions at the end.

B Give each other feedback using this feedback sheet. Give points from 1 to 3.
(1 point = needs improvement,
2 points = good,
3 points = very good)

› *Useful phrases: Giving a presentation, page 149*

Presentations feedback		Points
Content	you covered all the necessary points	
	you used examples to support your points	
Structure	your talk was easy to follow	
	you used useful phrases to structure your talk	
	you summarized the main ideas in your conclusion.	
Presentation	you smiled and looked friendly	
	you spoke clearly and freely	
	you looked at the audience when you spoke	
Dealing with questions	you dealt with questions in a friendly manner	
	you answered all the questions clearly	
Overall score for the presentation		/30

> **DAS KANN ICH (Unit 4)**
> – Eine kurze Präsentation über die Materialien halten, die meine Firma verwendet. (Foundation)
> – Auf ein Problem, das in einem Webforum gepostet wurde, eingehen. (Part A)
> – Ein Werkstück auf Englisch beschreiben sowie nach einer englischen Beschreibung skizzieren. (Part B)
> – Eine kurze Präsentation über meine Arbeit für neue Auszubildende halten. (Communication)

KMK Exam practice 2

1 Mediation: B1

Ihr Ausbildungsbetrieb erwartet in vier Wochen Besuch von drei Praktikanten/Praktikantinnen aus verschieden Ländern. Alle drei sprechen Englisch. Sie werden von Ihrem Ausbildungsleiter gebeten, die Praktikanten per E-Mail auf Englisch zu kontaktieren, um ihnen als erste Information die Sicherheitsbestimmungen beim Bedienen von elektrischen Werkzeugen zukommen zu lassen. Von Ihrem Ausbildungsleiter erhalten Sie die untenstehenden Sicherheitsbestimmungen auf Deutsch als Vorlage.

Übertragen Sie die untenstehenden Sicherheitsbestimmungen in Form einer Checkliste ins Englische. Es wird keine Übersetzung erwartet.

> **Sicherheit beim Bedienen von elektrischen Werkzeugen**
> - Um Verletzungen vorzubeugen, ist es wichtig, dass Sie mit schnelldrehenden elektrischen Maschinen wie z. B. Bohrern, Fräsen oder Schleifmaschinen stets konzentriert arbeiten. Das gilt nicht nur für Sie, sondern auch für andere Personen.
> - Vergewissern Sie sich, wo der Not-Aus-Schalter ist, um die Maschine im Notfall zu stoppen. Sie müssen wissen, wo das Notfalltelefon ist.
> - Geeignete Schutzkleidung und -schuhe sind unbedingt erforderlich. Denken Sie auch an passenden Augenschutz. Für manche Arbeiten ist das Tragen von Handschuhen Vorschrift. Generell ist es notwendig, bei längeren Haaren ein Haarnetz zu tragen.
> - Befestigen Sie die Werkstücke und kontrollieren Sie Werkzeughalterungen gut.
> - Lassen Sie eingeschaltete Geräte nie unbeaufsichtigt!
> - Sollten Sie Reinigungsarbeiten an einem elektrischen Werkzeug vornehmen wollen, so trennen Sie es vorher vom Stromnetz.
> - Säubern Sie Ihren Arbeitsplatz.

2 Produktion: A2, B1

Schreiben Sie nun die E-Mail an die Praktikanten/Praktikantinnen, in der Sie über sich berichten, in welchen beiden Abteilungen Ihres Betriebes Sie am liebsten waren und warum (oder welche beiden Tätigkeiten Sie am liebsten ausführten).

Erwähnen Sie den Grund Ihrer Mitteilung und weisen Sie auf die Wichtigkeit der Sicherheitsbestimmungen im Anhang hin. Gern stehen Sie für gemeinsame Unternehmungen nach Dienstschluss mit Rat und Tat zur Verfügung. Schließen Sie die E-Mail mit dem Satz, dass Sie sich auf den Besuch freuen.

3 Leseverstehen: B1

Sie sollen im Rahmen einer Architekturtagung eine Präsentation über Metallarten, die bei der Herstellung von Geländern vorrangig benutzt werden, halten. Bei Ihrer Internetrecherche stoßen Sie auf den untenstehenden Text.

Werten Sie den Text auf Seite 45 auf Deutsch aus, indem Sie sich Notizen für die vorgegebenen Aspekte machen.

Iron railings – all time favourites

Hundreds of years ago, it took a lot of hard work and skill to manufacture metal railings. This made metal railings a very expensive item which only the rich or members of the elite classes could afford. With the introduction of new technology, for example welding, working with metal has become much easier and metal is now the most popular material for railings with people from all classes.

Fashion always changes with the times, but metal railings still remain popular. Although kings and the aristocratic class preferred other valuable metals, such as gold and silver, in many household articles, iron was often used in the construction of railings. Metal does not decompose and is extremely durable. This one characteristic of iron has helped it survive the changing fashion.

In the 17th century, only wrought iron or cast iron railings were available; however there are now three types of iron railings available today: wrought iron, cast iron, and steel.

Wrought iron railings: Railings made of wrought iron are very expensive, as a lot of hard work and skill is required to fabricate them. Pre-heating iron and hammering the red hot iron into the desired shape is a laborious process. The hard work involved makes the supply of wrought iron railings limited and expensive.

Cast iron railings: Cast iron railings are manufactured by casting molten iron into sand moulds of the desired shape and design. Although the railings are made from iron, they can be very fragile and once broken they are hard to repair; in this case, they may simply need to be replaced.

Mild steel railings: Mild steel became popular straight away after it was introduced in the 18th century. Working with mild steel was comparatively easy as heating was not necessarily required. Two pieces could be joined by riveting rather than welding them. Because of its low maintenance cost, its strength and elegance, steel has become the most popular material for manufacturing railings and other articles.

Ihre Notizen für Ihre Präsentation:

Gründe, warum früher Geländer selten aus Metall hergestellt wurden:		
▬	▬	▬
Kundenkreis daher:	▬	
Kundenkreis heutzutage:	▬	
Im Text aufgeführte Geländerarten und deren Vor- und Nachteile:		
Geländerarten	Vorteile	Nachteile
▬ ▬ ▬ ▬ ▬	▬ ▬ ▬ ▬ ▬	▬ ▬ ▬ ▬ ▬

45

5 Manuals and safety instructions

FOUNDATION: Numbers and measurements

Situation: You work at Metall Wagner GmbH, a manufacturer of trolleys, ladders and scaffolds.
→ You phone a British client and clarify the details of a product he is interested in.

1 Talking about numbers

Before the phone call, you check your knowledge of the English terms for mathematical operations.

A 14))) Listen to the recording, then match the symbols to the English mathematical terms.

1 is approximately equal to
2 degree
3 divided by
4 is equal to / equals
5 is greater than
6 is less than
7 minus
8 multiplied by / times
9 per cent
10 squared
11 plus or minus
12 is not equal to

a	≠	b	−	c	>	d	=
e	×	f	≈	g	<	h	°
i	%	j	x^2	k	±	l	÷

› Talking about numbers, page 220

B Work with a partner. Partner A: Look here. Partner B: Look at File 4 on page 135.

Read out these mathematical statements. Partner B will write them down. When you have finished, check that Partner B has written them correctly.

1 A > B
2 3 x 6 = 18
3 x ≠ y
4 0.65 ÷ 5 = 0.13
5 3% of 1,387,669 = 41,630.07
6 10 ± 0.3

2 Describing dimensions

You now check the words for describing dimensions.

A Copy and complete the drawings with the words from the list.

depth/deep · diagonal · height/high · ~~length~~/long · thickness/thick · width/wide

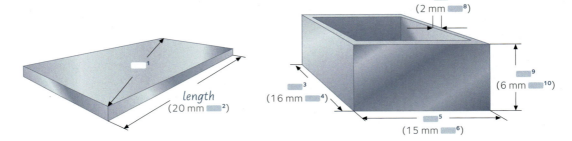

length
(20 mm ▭²)
(16 mm ▭⁴)
(15 mm ▭⁶)
(2 mm ▭⁸)
(6 mm ▭¹⁰)

46

Manuals and safety instructions Unit 5

B Describe these boxes to your partner.

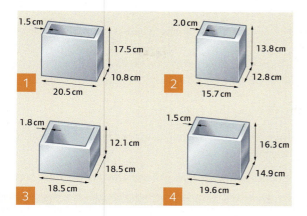

> **Giving dimensions**
>
> The box is 15 mm **w**ide / has a **w**idth of 15 mm.
> The metal plate is 2 mm **th**ick. / The **th**ickness of the metal plate is 2 mm.
>
> Dimensions or measurements of rectangular solid shapes are given in reverse alphabetical order – **w**idth (side to side), **h**eight (top to bottom), **d**epth (front to back):
> The box is 20.5 cm **by** 10.8 cm **by** 17.5 cm.

› Useful phrases: Describing size and dimensions, page 151

3 Role-play: Giving specifications on the phone

Your supervisor at Metall Wagner GmbH has emailed a drawing of a platform trolley to a client in Britain. Unfortunately, some of the information is incorrect. You phone the client to clarify the details.

Work with a partner. Partner A: Look here.
Partner B: Look at File 11 on page 139.

You work for Metall Wagner GmbH. Phone Partner B (the client) and give him/her the correct information about the platform trolley he/she is interested in.

> **Clarifying details**
>
> **Asking for information**
> What does it say about … ?
>
> **Correcting information**
> I'm afraid the dimensions of the … are wrong/incorrect. They should be …
>
> The trolley is made of …
> The castors are made of …

PLATFORM TROLLEY / aluminium
1000 x 655 x 620 mm

Other information: Four castors on the bottom made of rubber.
They measure approximately 160 mm in diameter and 40 mm in width.
Both back wheels are fitted with wheel brakes.

When you have finished your call, compare the information. Are Partner B's dimensions now correct?

TOOLBOX

brake – *Bremse*
castor – *Laufrolle*
depth – *Tiefe*

height – *Höhe*
length – *Länge*
rubber – *Gummi*

thickness – *Dicke, Stärke*
width – *Breite*

PART A: Safety precautions

Situation: You are working in the British subsidiary of your company where a technician is installing a new turning machine.
→ You create a poster for your colleagues explaining the safety hazards of the new machine.

1 Understanding safety instructions

The technician leaves you a list of rules that turners must follow when using the machine. She also gives you some warning decals that you can stick on the machine.

A Read the safety instructions and say if the statements below are true or false. Correct the false statements.

Safety instructions:
read before operating this machine

- Always wear safety goggles when working with this machine.
- Do not operate with the door open.
- The machine is automatically controlled and may start at any time.
- Improperly clamped parts may be ejected and cause fatal injuries.
- Chucks must be greased weekly and regularly serviced.
- Chuck jaws must not protrude beyond the diameter of the chuck.
- Hydraulic pressure must be set correctly to securely hold the workpiece without distortion.
- Do not press POWER UP / RESTART on the control panel until after the installation is complete.
- Never service the machine with the power connected.
- Windows must be replaced immediately if damaged or severely scratched.
- Do not operate without proper training.

1. Operators must wear eye protection.
2. The machine can be operated with the door open.
3. The machine only starts when the turner presses the ON button.
4. Loose workpieces are a serious health risk.
5. Hydraulic pressure is set automatically.
6. The machine must be unplugged before maintenance work begins.
7. You must complete installation of the workpiece before you start operating the machine.
8. The machine is easy to use and anyone can operate it.

TOOLBOX

decal – *Aufkleber*
distortion – *Verzug*
to eject – *auswerfen*

hydraulic pressure – *Hydraulikdruck*
to protrude – *vorstehen*
safety precautions – *Sicherheitsvorkehrungen, -maßnahmen*

Manuals and safety instructions   Unit 5

B   Study the warnings (1–7) and match them to the warning decals (a–g).

1   Automatic machine may start at any time
2   Electrocution hazard
3   Lock the main switch
4   Moving parts can crush
5   Moving parts can entangle, trap and cut
6   Risk of eye or ear injury
7   Risk of fire and explosion

a

b

c

d

e

f

g

2   Listening to operating instructions

You and your colleagues are listening to the technician who is setting up the new turning machine.

A   Match the German words (a–j) to the correct English expressions (1–10).

1   to connect
2   control cabinet
3   to disassemble
4   drive
5   line voltage
6   lubrication
7   no-load running
8   sound level
9   switching device
10 warranty regulations

a   Antrieb
b   demontieren
c   Garantiebedingungen
d   Lärmpegel
e   Leerlaufbetrieb
f   Netzspannung
g   Schaltgerät
h   Schmierung
i   Steuerungskasten
j   verbinden, anschließen

B   15))) ▶   Listen to the conversation and answer the following questions.

1   Which three sections of the operating manual does the fitter mention?
2   Where is the main switch?
3   What is the line voltage of the turning machine?
4   What does the fitter have to do with the motors and switching devices?
5   Who is allowed to modify or disassemble the machine?
6   Under what conditions is the sound level measured?
7   What is the maximum sound level?
8   When can the machine start normal production?

   TOOLBOX

3-phase current – *Drehstrom*
electrocution – *(Tötung durch) Stromschlag*
to entangle – *sich verfangen*
hazard – *Gefährdung*

to modify – *verändern*
operating manual – *Betriebsanleitung*
seal – *Siegel*
to trap – *einklemmen*

49

3 Role-play: Working safely with a turning machine

The technician explains how to work safely with the machine.

 Work with a partner. **Partner A:** Ask the technician questions about the safety precautions you have to follow when working with the machine. **Partner B:** You are the technician. Answer Partner A's question.

Follow the German instructions below and role-play the dialogue.

You

Fragen Sie, welche Sicherheitsmaßnahmen während der Arbeit mit der Drehmaschine beachtet werden müssen.

Fragen Sie, was beim Werkstückwechsel beachtet werden muss.

Fragen Sie, wie die Werkzeuge ausgetauscht werden müssen.

Fragen Sie, ob die Maschine gesichert werden muss, damit sie nicht von alleine anläuft.

Fragen Sie, ob das auch für Wartungsarbeiten gilt.

Bedanken Sie sich für die Tipps.

Technician

Antworten Sie, dass die Tür immer geschlossen bleiben muss, während die Maschine läuft.

Antworten Sie, dass nur der Dreher selbst die Tür öffnen, das Werkzeug wechseln und die Tür wieder schließen darf, bevor das Programm wieder anläuft.

Antworten Sie, dass der Maschinenraum vollständig leer sein muss, bevor die Maschine wieder automatisch anläuft.

Antworten Sie: Ja, dazu muss der Not-Aus-Taster gedrückt bleiben.

Antworten Sie: Nein, dazu muss unbedingt der Netzstecker gezogen werden.

Beenden Sie das Gespräch.

› *Useful phrases: Talking about health and safety, page 151*

4 Making a safety poster

Your supervisor wants to make sure that everyone knows how to work safely with the turning machine. He asks you to prepare a poster for the workshop.

A Work in groups of four. Make a poster showing safety rules for working with a turning machine. Use visuals and colours to attract people's attention. Keep information/rules as short as possible. Use the imperative form of the verb for the rules.

→ **Talking about safety rules**

Always read the safety instructions.
Never work without your safety goggles.

› *Grammar: Imperatives, page 157*

B When you have finished your poster, pin it on the wall and do a gallery walk. Rank the posters, using the categories below. Give points from 1–5 for each category.

Headline · Design · Visuals · Instructions / Imperatives ·
Does the poster do its job?

Manuals and safety instructions Unit 5

PART B: Machine maintenance

Situation: You work in the British subsidiary of your company. A new turning machine has been set up and aligned in the workshop.
→ You solve teething problems with the machine using a troubleshooting checklist.

1 Understanding maintenance instructions

Before you start work with the new machine, your supervisor wants to make sure that you understand the regular maintenance routines.

A Match the German words (a–j) to the correct English expressions (1–10).

1	central lubrication	a	Abscheuerung
2	chafing	b	Feuchtigkeit
3	clamping force	c	Keilriemen
4	connection terminal	d	Kühlflüssigkeit
5	coolant	e	Leck
6	hose	f	Rohr
7	humidity	g	Schlauch
8	leakage	h	Spannkraft
9	pipe	i	Verbindungsklemmen
10	V-belt	j	Zentralschmierung

B 👥 Work with a partner. Look at the photos and decide which regular maintenance routines they show. Compare your answers with another pair.

C Now match the photos (1–8) with the regular routines and maintenance instructions from the user manual on page 52.

1 **Daily**
1.1 Remove chips from working space.
1.2 Check coolant level and top up if necessary.
1.3 Check central lubrication oil level and top up if necessary.
1.4 Visual inspection of machine for any damage, deformation, leakage, loose or missing bolts.
1.5 Check all wiring, cables and pipes or hose lines for proper position.

2 **Weekly**
2.1 In case of cast iron machining, dismount and clean the wipers.
2.2 Check the filter inserts and clean or replace them if necessary.
2.3 Check clamping force of the power chuck.

3 **Monthly**
3.1 Check V-belt tension (main drive, cross drive).
3.2 Check guideway and tailstock wipers and replace if necessary.
3.3 Check window shield for cracks and other major damage.
3.4 Check the air conditioning system and fans (if any) for proper function.

4 **Every six months**
4.1 Clean the coolant tank.
4.2 Check all sealing points.
4.3 Check all control devices for proper function.
4.4 Renew filters and similar elements where dirt may gather (lube system, etc.).
4.5 Check hose lines and piping for tight mounting and possible chafing.

5 **Once a year**
5.1 Headstock gear: change oil and filters.
5.2 Check the internal plug connectors for corrosion (humidity?).
5.3 Check connection terminals inside switch cabinet (tight fit?).
5.4 Inspect each bearing and readjust clearance where required.
5.5 Check function of power supply chain; check power feed lines for damage.

2 Understanding a checklist

The troubleshooting checklist for diagnosing problems with the machine has become smeared with oil. Your supervisor asks you to complete the sections that cannot be read clearly.

Work with a partner. Read the causes of five problems that may occur with the machine, then discuss how to solve them. Complete the checklist with words from the list.

chuck · cross slide taper · cutting pressure · headstock (x2) · main bearing · quill · steady rest(s) (x2) · tailstock · taper · tightly

	Problem	Causes	Remedy
A	The workpieces clamped overhung are not turned cylindrically.	The main spindle centre line is not parallel to the bedways.	→ Re-align the ▬▬[1].
B	The workpieces are not turned cylindrically when using the tailstock.	The lathe centre of the tailstock is displaced in relation to the turning axis.	→ Re-align the top of the ▬▬[2].
C	The workpieces are not turned properly.	The workpieces are not clamped tightly enough.	→ Clamp workpieces more ▬▬[3].
		Unsteady workpiece	→ Clamp workpieces without constraint, reducing the ▬▬[4] or cutting section by a large amount. Use ▬▬[5] if appropriate.
		Quill force too high or too low	→ Change ▬▬[6] pressure.
		Too much clearance in the main bearing	→ Readjust ▬▬[7].

D	The workpieces are not faced exactly.	There is no right angle between turning axis and cross slide guideways.	→ Re-align the ___8.
		The cross slide has too much leeway.	→ Readjust ___9 gib.
E	The turned faces of the workpieces are imperfect.	The slides have too much play in their guideways.	→ Readjust ___10 gibs.
		An overhung workpiece projects too much.	→ Reduce the projection of the workpiece and check clamping force of ___11.
		A workpiece clamped between centres is unsupported for an excessive length.	→ Use one or more ___12.
		Wrong tool or incorrect clamping	→ Clamp tools with as little projection as possible. Make sure you are using a suitable tool.

3 Troubleshooting with the checklist

In the first few days of operation there are a few teething problems with the machine. You solve them together using the troubleshooting checklist.

Work with a partner. Role-play a trouble shooting dialogue using the information from the checklist. Troubleshoot remedies for these problems:

- workpiece not turned cylindrically
- turned faces of workpiece are imperfect

> **→ Discussing how to solve problems**
>
> We **should** check if the main spindle is parallel to the bedways.
> Is the main spindle parallel to the bedways?
> If it isn't, / If that's the case, we **need to** realign the headstock.
> That's not the problem. It **must** be something else.

› Grammar: Modals and their substitutes, page 161

This workpiece is not turned cylindrically. There must be a problem.

OK, we should check first that the … . If it isn't, we need to …

The workpiece is … . That's not the problem. It must be something else.

Then we should check if … . In that case, we need to …

Change roles if you want and prepare to perform your dialogue for the class.

 TOOLBOX

to align – *ausrichten*
bearing – *Lager*
cause – *Ursache*
chips – *Späne*
clearance/play – *Spiel*
constraint – *Auflage*

damage – *Schaden*
fan – *Ventilator*
gib – *Bolzen*
leeway – *Abdrift*
quill – *Pinole*
remedy – *Abhilfe*

to top up – *auffüllen*
unsteady – *wackelig*
visual inspection – *Sichtprüfung*
wiper – *Abstreifer*

COMMUNICATION: Graphs and charts

Situation: Your union representative is speaking at an international conference next week.
→ You prepare notes on some graphic information that he can use in his talk.

1 Describing graphs

You refresh your knowledge of the English expressions for describing graphs.

A Match the names in the list to the graphs (a–c). There is one name more than you need.

bar chart · line graph · pie chart · table

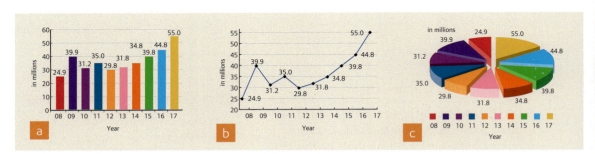

B Match the words/phrases (1–15) to the graphs (a–h). For some graphs, several expressions can be used.

1. to remain constant / stay the same
2. to go up / down
3. to increase / the increase
4. to hit a maximum / minimum
5. to flatten out / to level off
6. to decrease / the decrease
7. to drop / the drop
8. to rise / the rise
9. to fluctuate / the fluctuation
10. to fall / the fall
11. to climb / the climb
12. to peak / the peak

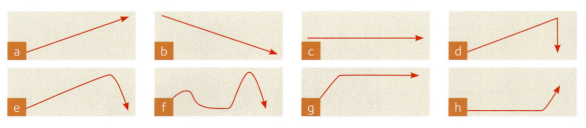

C 👥 Work with a partner. **Partner A:** Look here. **Partner B:** Look at File 5 on page 136.

Describe this line graph to Partner B. Partner B will draw it. Check Partner B's graph when you have finished.   › *Useful phrases: Describing graphs, page 151*

Manuals and safety instructions Unit 5

2 Talking about figures

At the conference, your union representative uses a table to describe sales of technical products worldwide in the last financial year.

A 16))) Listen and decide which of the tables is being presented.

A

Quarterly sales (millions of euros)				
Area	Q. I	Q. II	Q. III	Q. IV
UK	10.3	11.4	8.2	10.5
Germany	8.9	9.3	8.6	7.1
E. Europe	0.2	0.8	1.7	3.6

B

Quarterly sales (€m)			
Q. I	Q. II	Q. III	Q. IV
10.3	11.4	8.2	10.3
8.0	8.3	8.1	6.2
0.3	0.9	3.8	4.5

C

Quarterly sales (€m)			
Q. I	Q. II	Q. III	Q. IV
10.3	11.4	8.2	10.7
8.2	7.4	8.0	9.5
0.5	1.6	2.3	2.3

B Work with a partner. Choose one of the tables and describe the sales figures for Germany or Eastern Europe. Your partner should say which table you are describing.

3 Describing a table

Your union representative would like to compare and contrast average working hours in Germany with conditions in other countries. You have found the following table.

	Working hours per week	Working day*	Lunch break
Germany	41.1	07.30/08.30–16.00/17.30	30–45 mins 12.00–13.30
France	37.9	08.00–18.00	60 mins 12.00–14.00
GB	41.4	08.00/09.00–17.00/18.00	60 mins 12.00–14.00
Scandinavia	39.1	08.00–16.00	30 mins 11.30–12.00
USA	40+	08.00–17.00+	30 mins 12.00–13.00

* The working day: Blue collar workers in some countries begin work one hour earlier than white collar workers.

 Work with a partner. Study the table and write notes, using the following headings:

Introduction
The table shows information about …

A Working hours per week
The shortest working hours per week are to be found in …

B Working day
In Germany, most people begin work between 7.30 and 8.30 and finish …

C Lunch breaks
People in France and Great Britain have the longest …

DAS KANN ICH (Unit 5)
– Maße und andere Produktdetails am Telefon auf Englisch erklären. (Foundation)
– Ein Sicherheitsplakat für eine Drehmaschine auf Englisch entwerfen. (Part A)
– Eine englische Fehlerbehebungscheckliste verwenden, um Probleme zu lösen. (Part B)
– Notizen anhand einer Grafik auf Englisch erstellen. (Communication)

6 Advising customers

FOUNDATION: Conversations at a trade fair

Situation: You work for World Medical, a company that manufactures medical equipment, and you are at the company's stand at a trade fair.
→ You advise a customer about some portable X-ray equipment.

1 Showing a customer a product

A customer who is in charge of a team of swimming pool attendants enquires about pulse and blood pressure monitors. Your supervisor shows her a suitable product.

A 17))) ▶ Listen to the conversation and say if the following statements are true or false. Correct the false statements.

1. The supervisor shows the customer a pulse and blood pressure monitor.
2. These monitors can only be used indoors.
3. The screen can be adjusted if the weather is sunny.
4. The pulse and blood pressure monitors are easy to operate.
5. The model shown is 100% accurate.
6. The customer thinks the monitor is too heavy.
7. It is not expensive.
8. The customer places an order immediately.

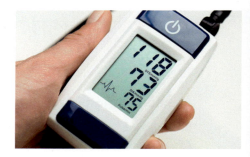

B 17))) ▶ Listen again and complete the specifications with the missing information.

WM 206 Pulse and Blood Pressure Monitor

Specifications
– Accuracy: ▭¹ bpm (beats per minute)
– Size: 11.6 × 6.5 × ▭² cm
– Touch screen: 6.1 × ▭³ cm
– Cover: slip-on, ▭⁴, 12 × ▭⁵ × 3 cm
– Weight: ▭⁶ g (without batteries)
– Power: ▭⁷ V (rechargeable batteries supplied)

Price: € ▭⁸
Delivery details: Within ▭⁹ days after payment
Packaging details: small ▭¹⁰ case

 TOOLBOX

adjustable – *verstellbar*   rechargeable battery – *Akku*   waterproof – *wasserdicht*

Advising customers   Unit 6

2 Role-play: Advising a customer

Another customer visits the stand and enquires about portable X-ray equipment.

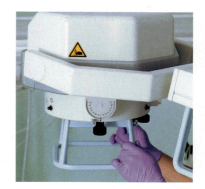

Work with a partner. Partner A: Look here. **Partner B:** Look at File 13 on page 140.

You are working at the World Medical stand at the trade fair. A doctor would like to know about some equipment.

Before you start, read the description of the product and prepare to answer the doctor's questions.

Top-X Portable X-ray Equipment

General information
- Small size and light weight
- Can be used anywhere
- Works without a darkroom
- Low radiation dose
- Can be connected to a computer

Price: €960.00

Specifications
- X-ray tube voltage/current:	80 kV/0.5 mA
- Power supply:	90–240 V, 50 or 60 Hz
- Power consumption:	70 VA
- Net weight:	8 kg
- Gross weight:	13 kg
- Size of handheld case:	66 x 53 x 22 cm

Delivery details: Within 3 days after payment
Packaging details: Aluminum case and carton

Start like this: *Good morning/afternoon. How can I help you?*

Change roles if you want. Prepare to perform your roleplay for the class.

➔ **Advising a customer**

Greeting
Good morning/afternoon. How can I help you?

Showing the product
This is our latest model.
How about this one?
This one has some nice features.
There's a five-year guarantee.

Making suggestions
I wouldn't recommend that one.
You could try this one instead.
It might be better to take this model.
I would take that one if I were you.

➔ **Talking to a salesperson**

Asking for advice
I'm looking for a(n) …
I need a(n) … for my …

Asking about the product
How much does it weigh?
How many batteries will I need?

Accepting/rejecting suggestions
Yes, I think that's the right one for me.
Good. I'll take it/them.
Sorry, I don't think that's what I had in mind.
I'm afraid that's not really what I'm looking for.

3 Talking about customer service

While you are on the stand at the trade fair, you realize how important contact with customers is for your company.

Work in small groups. Discuss the things that you think are most important for customer service. Make a list and present it to the class.

Do …
- smile and be friendly.
- …

Don't …
- sell the customer something he/she doesn't want.

57

PART A: A CNC turning machine for serial production

Situation: You work at the British subsidiary of Mech-On. The company needs a new CNC turning machine to increase the serial production of workpieces.
→ You write a report on a new machine for your supervisor.

1 Talking about requirements

The factory manager, David Stevens, asks your supervisor, Martin Foster, to find out about a new CNC turning machine.

18)) Listen to their conversation and answer these questions.

1. Why does Mech-On need a new CNC turning machine?
2. How many extra shafts will Mech-On have to produce every day?
3. What are the dimensions of the shafts that Brooks requires?
4. What length and diameter of shafts should the new turning machine be able to produce?
5. Which control units do most of the machines in the factory have at the moment?
6. What extra option does Martin Foster suggest that Mech-On should order for the turning machine?

2 Role-play: Making a phone call

Martin Foster asks you to call the manufacturer and enquire about the most suitable CNC turning machine for the factory.

A Work with a partner. Before you start, complete these notes, using information from exercise 1.

> **→ Asking for information**
>
> How many pieces do you **need** to produce?
> **Would** you like any extras?
> **Could** you send me an offer?
>
> › Grammar: Modals and their substitutes, page 161

Mech-On UK info@mechon.co.uk.

Requirements: new ▭¹ for bulk production; up to ▭² workpieces per year

Max. diameter of workpieces: currently ▭³ mm; maximum of ▭⁴ mm

Max. length of workpieces: currently ▭⁵ mm; maximum of ▭⁶ mm

Control unit: ▭⁷

Extra options: ▭⁸

 TOOLBOX

chip conveyor – *Späneförderer*
chip tank – *Spänetank*
feature – *Merkmal, Funktion*

serial production – *Serienfertigung*
shaft – *Welle*

Advising customers Unit 6

B

Work with a partner. Now role-play the telephone conversation using your notes and the instructions below.

Partner A: Apprentice at Mech-On	Partner B: Representative of DMG MORI
• Introduce yourself and explain why Mech-On needs a new CNC turning machine. • Answer Partner B's questions. • Ask for information on the machine and an offer. • Give your email address. • Thank the representative for his/her help.	• Ask Partner A questions about what they require. • Recommend the NEF 400. • Promise to send information and an offer by email. • Ask for an email address. • End the conversation politely.

› Useful phrases: Advising customers, page 151; Asking for advice, page 152

Partner B starts:
Hello, DMG MORI. This is … (name) speaking. How can I help you?

Change roles if you want. Prepare to perform your role-play for the rest of the class.

3 Reading about the new machine

The email with the information about the NEF 400 has arrived. There are some problems with the English version of the text.

Read the text and replace the German words in brackets with English expressions from the list.

components · customized · performance · precision · productivity · serial production · series · single workpiece · turning · user

NEF 400
The 5th generation NEF | The best technology in its class worldwide – at an unbeatable price

The benchmark for ▬¹ *(Produktivität)* and flexibility. The NEF 400 machines offer an outstanding level of ▬² *(Leistung)*, which has never before been achieved in this price-performance category worldwide. The latest NEF generation uses high-tech ▬³ *(Bauelemente)* to make efficient and precise ▬⁴ *(Drehen)* capabilities available even to the entry-level ▬⁵ *(Anwender)* – at the highest possible level of quality. NEF operators benefit from high flexibility for ▬⁶ *(Einzelteil)* manufacturing and achieve maximum ▬⁷ *(Genauigkeit)* and dynamics in ▬⁸ *(Serienfertigung)*. Numerous options allow ▬⁹ *(kundengerecht angefertigt)* configurations of the machine to reach maximum productivity in manufacturing – from individual workpieces to small series. The NEF ▬¹⁰ *(Baureihe)* ensures success and opens up new opportunities in the marketplace.

Source: DMG MORI

 TOOLBOX

to achieve – *erreichen*
benchmark – *Maßstab*
capabilities – *Möglichkeiten, (Leistungs-)Vermögen*

efficient – *leistungsfähig*
to ensure – *garantieren, sicherstellen*

4 Analysing an offer

You have received an offer for the NEF 400 with several extra options.

NEF 400 V1	– 5th generation, ISM 2-axis universal turning machine, turning length 650 mm – Main spindle as integrated spindle motor – drive power 8/11,5 kW 100/40% ED, 4500 min-¹ – 12 stations disc turret Sauter reception VDI 30, DIN 69880-30 for fixed tools – automatic tailstock – chip tank with coolant equipment – CELOS® with Siemens 840D sl or Heidenhain without CELOS®	€90,000.00*
NEF 400 V3	– 5th generation, ISM 2-axis universal turning machine with second spindle (C-axis), turning length 650 mm – main spindle as integrated spindle motor – drive power 8/11,5 kW (100/40 % ED), 4500 min-¹ – 12 stations disc turret Sauter reception VDI 30, DIN 69880-30 for fixed tools with tool drive for 6 stations connection/drive acc. DIN 5480 – C-axis and spindle brake (hydr.) – automatic tailstock – chip tank with coolant equipment – CELOS® with Siemens 840D sl or Heidenhain without CELOS®	€100,000.00
	Chip conveyor, discharge height 1250 mm (49.2 in), right side discharge	€5,000.00
	1 set of additional documentation	€500.00
	Commissioning incl. instruction	€1,500.00
	DMG MORI Tool Cart: the right tool at a single grasp	€700.00
	Training package: Programming, setting up and operating, without C-/Y-axis for 2 participants	€3,000.00
	Packing cost for road transport, means of transport and transport locks	€800.00
	Freight costs: **in Europe** +5% **outside Europe** per package on request	

Source: DMG MORI *All prices are examples only.

A Work with a partner. Find the three differences between the NEF 400 V1 and the NEF 400 V3.

B Decide together which of the machines, and which of the additional extra options, you would recommend your company to buy. Say why. Make notes.

5 Writing a report

Martin Foster wants to order the NEF 400 V3. He asks you to write a report about it for David Stevens.

Use your notes from exercise 4B and the phrases below to write a report.

› *Unit 7, Communication, page 76*

To: David Stevens	Subject: Recommendation for new CNC turning machine
I have studied the offer from … and compared … . I would recommend …	
Reason: Although the … is sufficient for our current needs, the … is a better investment in the future of … . The … has three advantages: … . These additions mean that we can …	
Extra options: I would recommend the … because …	

Advising customers Unit 6

PART B: Installation of the machine

Situation: You work at the British subsidiary of Mech-On. The company has ordered a NEF 400 V3 and it will soon be delivered.
→ You explain the advantages of the control unit to a new colleague.

1 Estimating the space requirements

Your supervisor asks you to help to find a suitable space for the new machine on the factory floor.

A Read the definitions of parts of the machine (1–8) and match them to the parts listed below the plan.

1 a device to transport small cut pieces of metal
2 the control centre for electric currents and functions
3 the connection for compressed oil
4 the device which pumps liquids to reduce temperature on cutting tools
5 machine for bulk production of round parts
6 the connection for compressed air
7 the electrical connection on the back of the machine
8 the area where you work in front of the machine

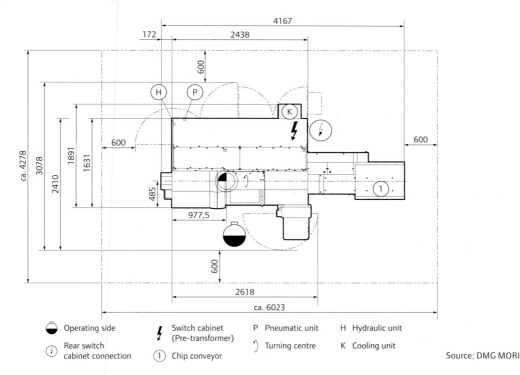

● Operating side   ⚡ Switch cabinet   P Pneumatic unit   H Hydraulic unit
ⓘ Rear switch   (Pre-transformer)   ⌒ Turning centre   K Cooling unit
   cabinet connection ① Chip conveyor

Source: DMG MORI

B 👥 Study the plans with your partner and answer these questions.

1 What's the length and width of the machine, including the chip conveyor and tank?
2 How much space does the machine require, including the necessary working space around it?
3 What's the approximate distance between the electric and the pneumatic connection?
4 What's the approximate distance between the pneumatic and the hydraulic unit?
5 What's the length of the chip conveyor?

61

2 Completing the electrical installation

Your supervisor asks you to email the electrician the electrical specifications of the NEF 400 V3.

Copy the table and complete it with information from the box.

10 mm² · 21 kVA · 31 A · 35 A · 400 V · 50 Hz · L1, L2, L3 · PE

Operating Voltage (U)	1
Phases	2
Protective earth	3
Main fuse (slow blow)	4
Nominal current (I)	5
Frequency (f)	6
Nominal apparent power (S)	7
Conductor cross section (A)	8

3 Reading about a control unit

Before you explain the Siemens controller to a new colleague, you read this brochure.

NEF 400
Up to 50% increased productivity thanks to exclusive technology cycle for SIEMENS with ShopTurn 3G.

Easy Tool Monitoring
- Driven tool load monitoring during the machining process in order to avoid damage to the machine, workpiece and equipment.

Alternating speeds – for vibration-critical set-ups
- Automatic and repeated modification of the spindle speed in order to avoid tool vibration during the machining process.

Multi-thread cycle
- This cycle provides an interface for entering the angle, number of threads and contour of the thread.

Technology cycle highlights
- Exclusive technology know-how.
- Simply enter the parameters into a graphical dialogue.
- Exclusive context menus with parameters.
- Easy to learn thanks to pre-defined input screens – no programming knowledge required.
- Program generation by the machine operator – no complicated DIN programming.
- Cycle to produce a thread with free contours, e.g. for large power transmission threads or special threads.

Source: DMG MORI

 TOOLBOX

alternating – *wechselnd*
angle – *Winkel*
apparent power – *Scheinleistung*
conductor cross section – *Leiterquerschnitt*
fuse – *Sicherung*
increased – *gesteigert*
modification – *Änderung*

multi-thread cycle – *Multigewindezyklus*
nominal current – *Nennstrom*
operating voltage – *Betriebsspannung*
protective earth – *Schutzleiter*
set-up – *Aufspannung*
slow blow – *träge*
tool load – *Antriebslast der Werkzeuge*

Advising customers **Unit 6**

A Read the text and find out what the following expressions are in English.

1. gesteigerte Produktivität
2. Antriebslastüberwachung
3. schwingungskritische Aufspannung
4. Spindeldrehzahl
5. Multigewinde
6. vordefinierte Eingabemaske
7. Maschinenbediener
8. großes Bewegungsgewinde

B Read the text again and answer these questions.

1. What does Easy Tool Monitoring do to protect the machine and workpieces from damage?
2. How does the control unit avoid tool vibration during the machining process in vibration critical set-ups?
3. What information can you enter on the multi-thread cycle interface?
4. How are the parameters of the workpiece entered into the control unit?
5. What programming knowledge does the machine operator need to operate the machine?

4 Role-play: Explaining the control unit

Now it is time to explain the Siemens control unit to your colleague.

 Work with a partner. Role-play the following dialogue in English using the prompts below.

Partner A

Erklären Sie, dass die neue Drehmaschine mit einem Siemens Steuergerät mit ShopTurn 3G ausgestattet ist.

Antworten Sie, dass ShopTurn fertige Technologiezyklen enthält und man dadurch bis zu 50 % Produktivitätsvorteil hat.

Antworten Sie: Es überwacht die Antriebslast der Werkzeuge zur Vermeidung von Schäden an Werkstücken und an der Maschine.

Antworten Sie, dass man diese für schwingungskritische Aufspannungen verwendet, wenn zum Beispiel Exzenter gedreht werden.

Antworten Sie, dass dies ganz einfach sei, da die Parameter in einem graphisch geführten Dialog eingegeben werden.

Antworten Sie: Nein, es gibt hierfür vorgefertigte Eingabemasken, und Programmierkenntnisse sind nicht erforderlich.

Verneinen Sie und sagen Sie, dass in ShopTurn auch der Maschinenbediener programmieren könne.

Partner B

Fragen Sie, warum sich die Abteilung für Siemens und ShopTurn entschieden hat.

Fragen Sie, welche Aufgabe das Easy Tool Monitoring hat.

Fragen Sie, für welchen Zweck man die alternierende Drehzahl verwendet.

Fragen Sie, wie die Parametereingabe erfolgt.

Fragen Sie, ob das schwierig zu erlernen sei und ob Programmierkenntnisse erforderlich seien.

Fragen Sie, ob in DIN programmiert wird, denn das sei für den Maschinenbediener recht kompliziert.

63

COMMUNICATION: Arrangements for meetings

Situation: You work at Juncker Anlagenbau GmbH in Dusseldorf. The company is taking part in the Ecological Trade Fair next week.
→ You write three emails to make arrangements for meetings with customers.

1 Setting up a meeting with a client

Paul Smith, the Chief Engineer at Juncker, asks you to arrange a meeting with a customer. He gives you the following instructions.

> Pls. get in touch with Mary Doyle at Waste Water Solutions, Dublin; set up a mtg. to present our filter presses. Ms Doyle wants to discuss some details before ordering.
> Suggest we meet at ETF in Glasgow: 26 April, morning any time until 12.30 p.m.; or 27 April, betw. 12.30 and 6.30 p.m. Need about 3 hrs. Ask which day is suitable (pls. book room for mtg.).
> Thanks. Paul

→ **Telling the time in English-speaking countries**

When telling the time in English, use the short forms, a.m. and p.m.
a.m. *(ante meridiem)* = between midnight and midday
p.m. *(post meridiem)* = after 12.00 noon
In English-speaking countries the twenty-four hour clock is generally only used for timetables.

Work with a partner. Complete the email to Ms Doyle using words and phrases from the notes above.

From: trainee@juncker_anlagenbau.de
To: m.doyle@wastewatersolutions.ie
Subject: Meeting with Paul Smith to discuss filter presses

Dear Ms Doyle

Paul Smith, Chief Engineer at Juncker Anlagenbau, has asked me ___¹ with you in order to ___² a meeting. Mr Smith would like to ___³ our filter presses and ___⁴ with you before you place your order.

Mr Smith will be at the Ecological Trade Fair in Glasgow next week so he ___⁵ either of the following dates: 26 April at any time in the ___⁶ until 12.30 p.m. or 27 April between 12.30 and 6.30 p.m.

He thinks that the meeting will take about ___⁷.

Please let me know if either of these dates ___⁸.

I hope to hear from you by tomorrow as I need time to ___⁹ a room for the meeting.

Yours ___¹⁰

 TOOLBOX

filter press – *Filterpresse*   waste water – *Abwasser*

Advising customers Unit 6

2 Replying to the invitation to the meeting

Complete Mary Doyle's reply using words and phrases from the list.

An appointment · Best wishes · booked · invite · look forward · reserve · Thank you · We are in

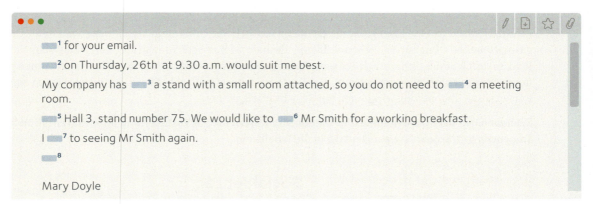

_____¹ for your email.

_____² on Thursday, 26th at 9.30 a.m. would suit me best.

My company has _____³ a stand with a small room attached, so you do not need to _____⁴ a meeting room.

_____⁵ Hall 3, stand number 75. We would like to _____⁶ Mr Smith for a working breakfast.

I _____⁷ to seeing Mr Smith again.

_____⁸

Mary Doyle

3 Changing arrangements

Because Paul has to set up a small presentation for Ms Doyle on Thursday morning, he postpones a breakfast meeting with his business partner, Ian Duncan.

Write Mr Smith's email to Ian Duncan to postpone the breakfast meeting. Explain the situation and use details from the itinerary below to suggest a new date and time for a meeting, e.g. for lunch or dinner.

→ **Giving dates, days and times**

at 6 p.m., **at** lunchtime
at night, **at** the weekend
on Monday, **on** 21 June
in the morning, **in** January, **in** 2017

ITINERARY	– Wed 25th – Sat 28th		
Wed 25	Flight LH 134 07.20 → Glasgow (arr. 08.40)		Dinner: Hans Treder 19.00 (Wallace Restaurant)
Thur 26	~~Breakfast: Ian Duncan 7.30 – 9.00~~ Mary Doyle (presentation) 9.30 – 12.30	Meeting: SysMet 14.00 – 16.00	
Fri 27	Stand: 10.00 – 12.00	Meeting: KL Pipes 14.00 – 18.00	
Sat 28	Golf: Harry Jones 11.00		Flight LH 918 19.15 → Dusseldorf (arr. 21.25)

› *Useful phrases: Making arrangements, page 152*

DAS KANN ICH (Unit 6)

- Eine/n Kunden/Kundin beim Kauf eines technischen Geräts beraten. (Foundation)
- Einen Bericht über eine CNC-Drehmaschine auf Englisch schreiben. (Part A)
- Ein Steuerungssystem für eine CNC-Drehmaschine auf Englisch erklären. (Part B)
- Ein Treffen mit englischsprachigen Kunden/Kundinnen per E-Mail organisieren. (Communication)

KMK Exam practice 3

1 Leseverstehen: B1

Ihr Arbeitsplatz ist eine Eisengießerei, die hauptsächlich Maschinenteile und Pumpen herstellt. Die gasbetriebenen Öfen dürfen nicht abkühlen – deshalb wird in Schichten gearbeitet. Abgesehen von den Risiken durch Staub, Schmutz, Hitze und Vibrationen wird die Gesundheit der Mitarbeiter/innen gerade durch die Schichtarbeit stark belastet. Die Geschäftsleitung ist darüber besorgt und hat Sie um eine kurze Präsentation über die Auswirkungen der Schichtarbeit gebeten.

Sie haben den nachstehenden Text gefunden und werten ihn zur Vorbereitung Ihrer Präsentation aus. Tragen Sie Ihre Ergebnisse auf Deutsch in die Tabelle ein.

Social Jet Lag
Irregular sleep patterns are dangerous for our health

People who sleep during the day and stay awake at night put their health at risk. They may suffer from a phenomenon that we refer to as jet lag, a term originally used in connection with travelling through different time zones.

This does not only refer to partygoers, but also to workers whose sleeping times follow their working hours. To some extent it applies to anyone who does not set the alarm at the weekend and gets up later, but it is especially true for shift workers. They also sleep in shifts, which results in a "social jet lag". Moreover, they sleep longer on their days off, and shorter before and after shifts. This removes them from their body's natural rhythms.

Changing sleep schedules is like flying from Frankfurt to Shanghai and back within a few days. But there is a big difference between travel jet lag and social jet lag: light. Arriving in Shanghai often means beginning a day by daylight. With social jet lag, your body cannot adapt to the day-night rhythm – and the disorder is permanent. You keep living in a wrong time zone.

This has various negative effects. This risk of becoming overweight or obese rises dramatically. How does this happen? If you sleep against the biorhythm you simply do not get enough sleep. If you feel tired you are less likely to go in for sports or to prepare healthy meals. Studies have shown that people with irregular sleep patterns burn fewer calories when they are at rest.

Weight gain is not the only problem. It is more difficult to maintain friendships with people who live on different schedules. If you postpone your bedtime to go out with friends you make your problems worse.

You are more likely to depend on addictive substances like nicotine or alcohol; your coffee consumption will increase. Your upset body clock may even take revenge by making you depressive.

Aspekt	Ihre Ergebnisse
Erklärung des Begriffs "sozialer Jetlag"	
Vergleich der Begriffe: a) „Jetlag" im herkömmlichen Sinn b) „Sozialer Jetlag"	Übereinstimmung: Unterschiede:
Gesundheitsrisiken:	Gründe für Gewichtszunahme: Weitere:

2 Leseverstehen: A2

Sie sind bei einer großen Baumarktkette in der Nähe des Frankfurter Flughafens beschäftigt. Sehr oft haben Sie mit Englisch sprechenden Kunden/Kundinnen zu tun, die nach den Unterschieden zwischen den einzelnen Batteriearten fragen.

Ihre Aufgabe ist es, sich gründlich mit dem folgenden Text zu befassen, um besser mit den ausländischen Kunden/Kundinnen umgehen zu können. Wie beantworten Sie folgende Frage, die Ihnen auf Englisch gestellt werden können? Füllen Sie den Fragebogen auf Englisch aus. Tragen Sie Stichwörter ein.

BATTERIES

Everyone knows what a battery is: It's one of those little tubes that you put in your walkman or your torch so that you can have music or light wherever you go. It's portable electricity.

In fact, batteries come in many shapes and sizes, not simply tubes, and we should really call them cells, because a battery is a number of cells linked together. They range from the button-size cells which keep your watch going for more than one year to the heavy batteries which can power submarines.

There are two different types of cells: one is called a primary cell, and the other one is known as a secondary cell. Both kinds change chemical energy to electricity. Primary cells are thrown away when the chemicals they contain are used up. Secondary cells can be recharged and used again and again.

The most common and cheapest kind of primary cells is the zinc-carbon cell. It consists of a zinc can which contains two chemicals. The zinc is the negative electrode. One of the chemicals, manganese dioxide, forms a positive electrode. Millions of cells like this are used every year in radios, torches, and tape recorders.

More and more people want a cell which can be used again and again. The NiCad cell fits in this description. It's a secondary cell with a nickel positive electrode and a cadmium negative electrode. Ni for nickel, Cad for cadmium – NiCad. NiCad cells are more expensive, but they can be recharged hundreds of times. They are used in many cordless appliances such as portable phones.

Source: Oxford English for Electronics

Customers' questions	Your findings
Which are the two most important features of a battery?	▬ ▬
How does a battery work?	▬
What are batteries used for?	▬ ▬
What is the main difference between a primary and a secondary cell?	primary cell: ▬ secondary cell: ▬

7 Communicating with colleagues

FOUNDATION: Internal communication

Situation: Your firm is carrying out measures to improve internal communication.
→ You do a survey to find out which means of communication colleagues use and what improvements they would like.

1 Talking about communication at work

A   What method(s) of communication do you use most at work? Make a list.

B   👥 Work with a partner. Talk together about the advantages/disadvantages of the means of communication on your lists.

C   👥 Work with another pair. Rank the types of communication according to how useful they are when you are at work.

2 Getting the message across

Three trainees are discussing their company's decision to improve internal communication. (The discussion is in three sections.)

David
Construction mechanic

Marta
CAD engineer

Janek
Energy engineer

 TOOLBOX

to access information – *auf Informationen zugreifen*
face-to-face meeting – *persönliches Treffen/Gespräch*
to share information – *Informationen teilen*
to synchronize files – *Dateien abgleichen/synchronisieren*

Communicating with colleagues **Unit 7**

A **19 ▶ Listen and say who expresses the following opinions.**

1 A face-to-face meeting is good when you want to make a quick decision.
2 When you want a quick decision in writing, it's better to send a text message.
3 It doesn't take long to write an email.
4 You need to be at work to access the intranet.
5 You can access cloud storage from anywhere.
6 Slides should only be used for graphic images and shouldn't have a lot of text.

B **19 ▶ Listen again and complete the notes on the advantages and disadvantages of the different types of communication systems below.**

1 If the other person isn't around, you can't have a ▬ .
2 Good options for making a ▬ are using the telephone for a phone call or a message.
3 One of the things people really dislike about emails is that ▬ .
4 The advantage of using the cloud is that the company can ▬ with clients.
5 An intranet is ▬ so it's easy to find the information you're looking for.
6 When they're full of writing, slides are ▬ .

3 Carrying out a survey

You do a survey among your colleagues to find out their ideas about internal communication.

A In class, brainstorm ideas for questions for your survey.

- Do you use … at work?
- How often do you use … at work?
- In your opinion, what are the advantages/disadvantages of … ?
- What type of communication would you like to use at work?

> **Talking about quantities**
>
> **How many** text messages do you get at work every day?
> – I get **a lot**. **A lot of them** are instructions from my supervisor.
> **How much time** do you spend answering emails?
> – Too **much** time.
>
> › *Grammar: Much, many, a lot (of), page 161*

B Make two charts to record the results of your survey.

1 Communication we use at work			
type of communication	How many people use this?	advantages	disadvantages
email	|||| ||	you can send attachments	too many emails every day

2 Communication we would like to use at work	
type of communication	advantages

C Use the results of your survey to make suggestions on how to improve internal communication in your firm.

PART A: Relocation of production

Situation: You work for Schmidt Ltd in Cork, Ireland, a subsidiary of Schmidt AG in Dortmund. The company is relocating the production of thermal fuses from its factory in Cork to Bangkok in Thailand.
→ You write a short memo about the preparations for the installation of machinery in the new factory.

1 Reading about thermal cutoff fuses

You will be travelling to Thailand with the project manager, Kate O'Brien, to supervise setting up the machinery in Bangkok. Before you leave, you read the company's website to check your knowledge of the company's product.

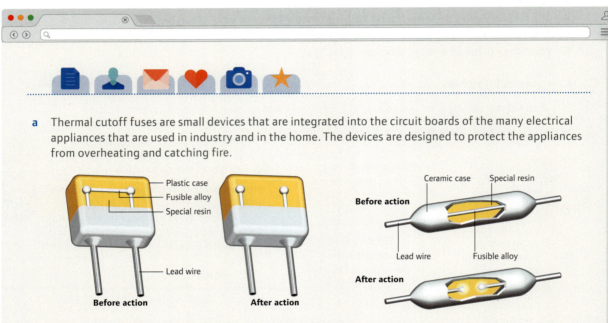

a   Thermal cutoff fuses are small devices that are integrated into the circuit boards of the many electrical appliances that are used in industry and in the home. The devices are designed to protect the appliances from overheating and catching fire.

b   Each device contains a thermal pellet made of an organic material or fusible alloy. In order to guarantee hermetic sealing, each device is resin-sealed. When the ambient temperature of the appliance containing the device reaches a specific temperature, the thermal pellet in the device will melt. As soon as this happens, the electrical current to the appliance is immediately interrupted to protect the appliance. It should be noted that once thermal reaction has happened, the thermal cutoff device must be replaced. Schmidt AG produces a broad range of thermal cutoff fuses to suit the operating temperatures and rated currents of each type of electrical appliance.

c   Our thermal cutoff fuses conform to environmental standards and regulations. Due to their small size, they are extremely sensitive to abnormal temperatures. The fuses cover a wide range of operating temperatures (73°C – 240°C) and some versions are able to operate under large currents (0.5A – 15A range). The high-quality resin-seal guarantees the high reliability and accuracy of the thermal cutoff fuses.

d   Our thermal cutoff technology is used in many domestic appliances and commercial applications. These include: domestic irons, hair dryers, refrigerators, electric kettles, coffee makers; air conditioners, ventilation fans, electric fans, gas boilers; transformers, adaptors; chargers, battery packs; photocopiers, laser beam printers.

Communicating with colleagues **Unit 7**

A Skim the information and match the headings (1–5) to the paragraphs (a–d). There is one more heading than you need.
1 Advantages of Schmidt's thermal fuses
2 Applications
3 How they work
4 Installation instructions
5 Thermal cutoff fuses

B With a partner, take turns to find the answers to the following questions.
1 Where are thermal cutoffs used?
2 How is the cutoff fuse made waterproof and airtight?
3 How is the circuit interrupted?
4 Why must the thermal cutoff device be replaced after it has done its job?
5 What is the maximum current for the cutoff?
6 What is the maximum temperature for the cutoff?
7 Name at least three household devices that use Schmidt's thermal cutoff fuses.
8 Name at least three industrial or commercial uses for thermal cutoff fuses.

2 Communicating with a colleague abroad

A few days before your flight, Kate has a video conference with Surat Meesang, the factory manager in Bangkok. They discuss the installation of the resin-sealing unit, which is vital for the production of the thermal fuses.

A Work with a partner. Before you listen to the conversation, decide together which of the words below you might hear.

1 crate
2 forklift truck
3 nuts and bolts
4 screwdrivers
5 drill and drill bits
6 glue
7 data cables
8 power cables
9 cable trunks
10 flooring
11 pneumatic hose
12 temperature detection

B 20))) Now listen and check your answers.

C 20))) Listen to the conversation again and answer these questions.
1 When will the resin-sealing unit arrive at the factory?
2 Why should it be left in its crate until you and Kate arrive?
3 How heavy is the machine?
4 What is the DFG 435 and why can it not be used for the installation?
5 What does Kate suggest instead?
6 How is the machine going to be fixed to the floor?
7 What equipment will the electricians use to fix the machine?
8 What is going to be laid under the flooring?

! Using first names

If a person is in a higher position than you, you should always use their surname until they specifically ask you to use their first name. If you and a colleague are at the same level, you may suggest using first names if you wish.
Please call me Kate.
Thank you. My first name is Surat.

TOOLBOX

appliance – *Gerät*
cable trunk – *Kabelkanal*
circuit board – *Leiterplatte*, *Platine*
cutoff – *Abschaltung*
domestic – *Haushalts-*
electric circuit – *Stromkreis*
flooring – *Fußboden*
forklift truck – *Gabelstapler*
fusible alloy – *Schmelzlegierung*
hermetic sealing – *hermetische Abdichtung*
resin-seal – *Gießharzverguss*
thermal fuse – *Thermosicherung*

3 Role-play: Discussing what is going to happen

Before your write the memo for the files, you check some of the details with Kate O'Brien.

 Work with a partner. **Partner A:** You are the apprentice at Schmidt Ltd in Cork. **Partner B:** You are Kate O'Brien. Discuss in English who is going to do what in the process of setting up the resin-sealer.

You

Fragen Sie, wann die Versiegelungsanlage bei der Fabrik ankommen wird.

Kate O'Brien

Antworten Sie: am 29. November.

Fragen Sie, wer die Kiste nun auspacken wird.

Antworten Sie, dass die Kiste bis zur Ankunft in Thailand nicht ausgepackt werden soll.

Fragen Sie, ob der richtige Gabelstapler bereitsteht.

Antworten Sie, dass Herr Meesang einen TFG 540 von einer Fabrik in der Nähe besorgen wird.

Fragen Sie nach den Bolzen und der Bohrmaschine.

Antworten Sie, dass die Bohrmaschine und die 18 mm-Bolzen schon am Arbeitsplatz sind.

Fragen Sie nach dem Kleber, mit dem die Bolzen in den Boden geklebt werden.

Antworten Sie, dass es den Kleber im Materiallager der Fabrik gibt.

Fragen Sie, ob Sie einen Kabelkanal für das Anschlusskabel und die Datenleitung legen müssen.

Antworten Sie, dass das Kabel unter dem Boden verlegt werden kann.

Fragen Sie, wann sie die Anlage in Betrieb nehmen möchte.

Antworten Sie: am 3. Dezember.

› *Grammar: Future with* will *and going to, page 158*

4 Writing a memo for the files

Now you write a short memo on the most important details of the video call for the project files.

Look back at your answers to exercises 2B and 3 and use them to write the memo.

Schmidt Ltd, Cork, Ireland

Project no. 1603: Relocation of production of thermal cutoff fuses to Bangkok

Report update: 21/11 – Installation of resin-sealing unit

Project manager, Kate O'Brien, planning installation with Surat Meesang, factory manager, Bangkok

The following points were covered:

1. The resin-sealer has arrived at …
2. It will be delivered to the … on …

…

Communicating with colleagues Unit 7

PART B: Problems abroad

Situation: You work for Schmidt Ltd in Cork, Ireland. You and your supervisor, Kate O'Brien travel to Thailand to supervise setting up a new factory for thermal cutoff fuses. There are some problems to solve before the factory can start production.
→ **You give a short report to your supervisor about the installation when you return to Cork.**

1 Reading a report for the supervisor

The day after you arrive, Kate sends a report on the current status of the project to her supervisor, Frank Cox, in Cork.

A Skim her email below and find the words that match the pictures on page 74.

From: kate.obrien@schmidt.ie
To: frank.cox@schmidt.ie
Subject: Current status of work in Thailand

Dear Frank

We arrived safely in Thailand yesterday with no delays and we are now in the factory. I'm afraid we are having a few problems and have not been able to start on the installation.

As agreed with Mr Meesang, the resin-sealer was still in its crate when we arrived. However, when we unpacked it, the control unit and the recycler for the excess resin were not there. Mr Meesang phoned the customs inspector in Bangkok port and his contact there is checking to see if there is another crate with the missing parts somewhere in the port.

The second problem is that the forklift truck that Mr Meesang promised us was not available. Instead, he has offered us a gantry crane. I'm not very happy about this for safety reasons and have asked the factory safety officer to make sure that no one stands underneath the hanging load.

The next thing is that the air conditioning system in the factory is broken, so the glue for the bolts to fix the machine on the floor might not dry for days. The chief electrician says he will need one day to repair the system.

The electricians have laid all the cables, but the fuse box in the power distribution is not suitable. This means that we're going to need a new distribution board for our NH-fusage and residual current circuit breakers. It will take too long to get a replacement from Europe, but the chief electrician says that he can get a Chinese one locally which will work just as well.

As you suggested, I gave Mr Meesang an earlier finishing date (3rd December). It's good that we planned in an extra week here.

Best wishes
Kate

B Now read the email carefully and say if the following statements are true or false. Correct the statements that are false.

1 Kate is happy to report that everything is going well with the installation.
2 The resin-sealing unit had been unpacked before Kate got to the factory.
3 All parts of the machine have been delivered.
4 Mr Meesang has been in touch with Bangkok port customs about the missing parts.
5 There is no forklift truck on site that can lift the machine.
6 The safety officer will make sure that everyone takes care while the gantry crane is in use.
7 The chief electrician overhauled the air conditioning system before Kate arrived at the factory.
8 The power and data cables have not been laid.
9 The electrician is going to order a new distribution board from Europe.
10 Kate is worried that the work won't be done by 3rd December.

2 Mediation: An email to a colleague at Schmidt AG in Germany

You and a friend at the German headquarters always keep in touch about work.

A Make a list of the problems Kate O'Brien mentions in her email and how they will be solved.

Probleme	Lösungen
Kiste mit Steuerungssystem …	…
…	

B Write a short email to your friend in German describing the problems with the installation of the resin-sealing machine in Thailand.

 TOOLBOX

air conditioning (system) – *Klimaanlage*
distribution board – *Stromverteilung*
gantry crane – *Portalkran*

NH-fusage – *NH-Sicherungen*
residual current circuit breaker (RCCB) – *FI-Schutzschalter, Fehlerstrom-Schutzschalter*

Communicating with colleagues Unit 7

3 Installing pneumatic hoses

Kate asks you to check that the pneumatic hose is installed correctly.

👥 **Work with a partner. Look at the drawings and say which of the pneumatic hoses are correctly or incorrectly installed. Use the words in the list to help you.**

large radius · loose hose · minimum radius · round fitting/connection piece · sharp bend · straight fitting/connection piece · straight piping · tight bending · tight hose

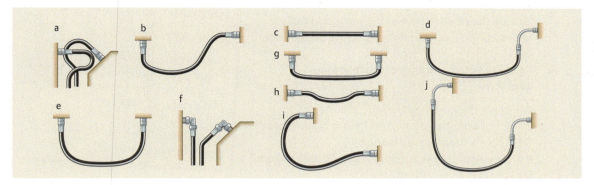

4 Checking your to-do list

The problems have been solved, but you cross-check your to-do list again before production begins.

👥 **Work with a partner. Take it in turns to read the points on the to-do list and say whether they have been done. Use the prompts to help you.**

Installation of resin-sealer: to-do list	
· control unit and excess resin recycler at customs	→ deliver to factory ✔
· no proper forklift truck available	→ lift machine into place using gantry crane ✔
· air conditioning system in factory broken	→ electrician to repair system ✔
· glue for bolts not dry (too warm)	✔
· bolt machine to floor	✔
· install data and power cables and pneumatic hose	✔
· European power distribution board not available	→ replace with Chinese distribution board ✔

You can start like this:
A: *The control unit and the excess resin recycler were held up at customs.*
B: *OK, they have now been delivered to the factory.*

› *Grammar: Present perfect, page 158; Passive forms, page 159*

5 Giving a short report to your supervisor

You fly back to Cork while Kate stays in Thailand to supervise the first week of production. Your supervisor, Frank Cox, asks you to tell him what happened during the installation.

👥 **Work with a partner. Use the to-do list in exercise 4 and take turns to describe the problems and explain how they were fixed.**

You can start like this:
When we arrived at the factory, ... First, we unpacked the resin sealer. Then we ...

> **Giving an oral report**
> There **was** no suitable forklift truck so we **used** a gantry crane instead.
> Some parts of the machine **were held up** at customs.

› *Grammar: Simple past, page 158; Passive forms, page 159*

75

COMMUNICATION: Reports

> **Situation:** You work in the maintenance department of a British factory.
> → You prepare a report for your supervisor on a health and safety incident.

1 Reading a notice

You are the first to arrive at the workshop this morning. You find the following notice on the door.

IMPORTANT NOTICE: NO ENTRY!
Maintenance Workshop 2.01

Fire damage: workshop closed.
Please go to the Quality Control Workshop (1.01) in the building opposite and report to Irene McCartney, QC Manager

Andy Murray, Workshop Manager
9 p.m. Tuesday, 13/07/20..

A Read the notice and answer the following questions.

1. Why is the workshop closed?
2. Which workshop do workers have to go to instead?
3. Where is the other workshop?
4. Who should workers report to when they get there?
5. Who wrote the notice?
6. When was the notice written?

B Write a short text message to your colleagues telling them not to come to the workshop. Explain the situation in a few words and tell them where to go instead.

2 Reading statements about the fire

Andy Murray gives you these statements to read so that you can write a short report about the fire.

A Who said what? Match the statements (1–4) to the names of the people who made them (a–d).

a Tommy Atkins, Construction Mechanic
b Andy Murray, Workshop Manager
c Jackie Stewart, Security/First-aider
d Angela Thomson, Welder

1 It was just before 8 o'clock. I was working in the office when I heard shouting in the workshop next door. I ran in there and saw Tommy Atkins trying to put out a fire on the floor. Angela Thomson was using the fire extinguisher but the fire was spreading. I set off the alarm and went with Tommy and Angela to the assembly point outside the building.

2 I was welding. Suddenly, there was a crash and Tommy shouted. I smelled acetone so I turned off my welding equipment. It was too late. There was a flash and then the floor started to burn. Tommy started stomping on the flames but that didn't work. I got the fire extinguisher off the wall but the flames were everywhere. Acetone keeps on lighting even after you stomp on it. Andy got Tommy and me out of the workshop and took us to the assembly point. We were taken to hospital.

 TOOLBOX

ambulance – *Rettungswagen*
assembly point – *Sammelplatz*
emergency services – *Einsatzkräfte, Rettungsdienste*
fire extinguisher – *Feuerlöscher*

first aid – *Erste Hilfe*
first-aider – *Sanitäter/in*
incident – *Vorfall, Ereignis*
to spread – *sich ausbreiten*

Communicating with colleagues **Unit 7**

3 The fire alarm went off at 19.58. I could see the flames in the Maintenance Workshop from my window. I called the fire brigade. At the Assembly Point, I administered first aid to two colleagues and called an ambulance. (time: 20.05). Tommy Atkins had burns on his hands and legs and Angela Thomson was in shock. The emergency services arrived at 20.15. Mr Atkins and Ms Thomson were taken to hospital. The fire was extinguished by 20.40.

4 I finished repairing a tank. When I reached over to unplug the soldering iron, I knocked over a bottle. I didn't know it was there. As soon as the bottle broke, I realized it was acetone. Someone else must have left it on the bench after a job. The acetone spilled on the floor. It trickled across to where Angela was welding and caught fire. I stomped on the flames and tried to put them out but it was no use. My hands and legs were burned so Mr Stewart put something on the burns and called the ambulance.

B Work with a partner. Put the events above in chronological order to make a record of the incident.

Tuesday 13.07.20..
Just before 8 o'clock: Angela Thomson was welding in the workshop; Tommy Atkins was repairing a tank. Tommy Atkins knocked over …

19.58: …

…
20.40: …

3 Writing an incident report

It is time to write the incident report for the Administration department.

Work with a partner. Write a formal report about the fire, using the record you produced in exercise 2B and the following structure.

Report on fire incident

Introduction: Say where and when the incident happened. Give the names and job titles of the people involved.

Background: Describe the situation just before the incident happened; give the starting time.

The fire incident: Describe the events that took place in the workshop.

Dealing with the emergency: Describe what happened at the Assembly Point, when the emergency services arrived and how the fire was dealt with.

> **Describing an incident**
>
> We **were working** in the workshop. Angela **was welding**. I **finished** repairing the tank. I **tried** to put the flames out, but they **were spreading** quickly.

› *Grammar: Simple past, page 158; Past progressive, page 158*

DAS KANN ICH (Unit 7)
- Eine Umfrage über Kommunikationsmittel im Betrieb durchführen. (Foundation)
- Ein Memo über das Aufstellen einer Maschine in einer Fabrik schreiben. (Part A)
- Meiner/m Vorgesetzten über ein Projekt auf Englisch mündlich berichten. (Part B)
- Einen kurzen Bericht über einen Vorfall in einer Fabrik schreiben. (Communication)

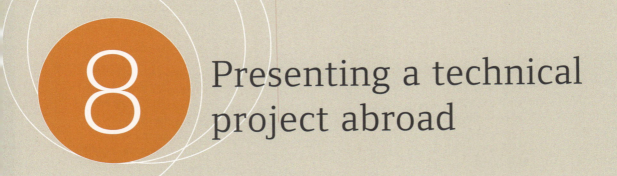

8 Presenting a technical project abroad

FOUNDATION: International standards

Situation: A Polish manufacturer is interested in buying equipment produced by your company and would like to know what international standards you use.
→ You make a list of the international standards you use for him.

1 Talking about standards in everyday life

You talk with other trainees about how almost everything is regulated by standards.

A 👥 Work in a group. Think about something you use every day and describe it in two or three sentences to the other people in your group. The first person who guesses what you are describing gets a point.

> I'm thinking of something which is made of plastic. It's black. It's the thing that keeps my phone working.

> It's your charging cable.

> ➡ **Defining things more closely**
>
> Do you know anybody **who** has an adaptor?
> Alexander Graham Bell, **who** invented the telephone, was born in Edinburgh.
> The aeroplane is a machine **which** flies.
> This is the only cable **that** fits all phones.
> This is the toolbox (**that**) Bob made.
>
> › *Grammar: Relative clauses, page 160*

B 👥 Make a list of everyday things in your life that are regulated by standards.

C 👥 Talk about why it is important for the consumer that the things on your list are regulated by standards. Make notes on these aspects and add your own ideas:

quality, safety, efficiency, …

Presenting a technical project abroad Unit 8

2 Reading about international standards in action

You check the internet for information on international standards and find the following text.

International standards help small businesses

The International Organization for Standardization (ISO) is a global organization responsible for developing new standards for products and services. The organization, which was founded in 1947, has its headquarters in Geneva, Switzerland. It currently works in 196 countries.

Two small-business owners in the Republic of Ireland explain how their companies use ISO standards.

Rod Garvey, Director, Heating Systems, Dublin

"We're one of the few small manufacturing companies in the heating field. We're a family business which employs 30 people. Most of our competitors are medium sized companies. In order to compete with them, Heating Systems has to offer more than the competition. It's not just the quality of our products but the speed with which we can get our systems on the market. We use ISO 9001 which is a quality management control standard for small businesses. We've been using this standard for 12 years. Since we started to use it, we've reduced our labour time in production and assembly and increased our output by 35%."

Elizabeth Rich, Director, Fire Safety, Cork

"Fire Safety makes and maintains fire safety equipment. We also provide fire risk assessment and consultancy services to small, medium-sized and large companies. We employ forty-two people. The first thing I did when I took over the business six years ago, was to set up standards for our services and products. The company had always worked to high standards, but when we started to sell equipment to larger companies, our clients required proof that our equipment was safe. For the last five years, we have been 13.220.20 Fire Protection Equipment certified. All our equipment is covered. Our customers are satisfied and so are we."

A Read the text and answer the following questions. Use your own words wherever possible.

1. What kind of business does Rod Garvey have?
2. Who are his competitors?
3. How does he compete with them?
4. What has happened in his company since it started using ISO standards?
5. What four things does Elizabeth Rich's company do?
6. Why does she insist on ISO standards?
7. How do the clients feel now that Elizabeth Rich's company is certified?

B Check the ISO standards mentioned in the text. Which, if any, of them are relevant for your company?

3 Researching international standards

Your supervisor asks you to draw up a list of international standards for the Polish manufacturer.

👥 Work in groups. Do internet research to find international standards relevant to your company. Make a list which your supervisor can show to the Polish manufacturer.

79

PART A: An automated washing system

Situation: You work for Hilmer Cleaning Systems in the UK and you have to plan an automated washing system for rubber mats for a customer in China.
→ You write a description of how the system works for the customer.

1 Thinking about the problem

Jinsibei Co., Ltd. is a waterjet cutting company located in Shenzhen, China. One of their biggest contracts is to cut rubber mats for a customer. The abrasive sand that is used in the waterjet has to be washed off the mats manually after cutting. The company is looking for an automated washing system to solve this problem.

A   Match the words in the list below with the pictures (a–f).

abrasive sand • air conditioning • conveyor • environmental legislation • palletizer • waterjet

B   Work with a partner. Discuss the roles that each item plays in the situation described above. Do you think they are part of the problem, or part of the solution?

> **→ Talking about possibilities**
>
> They **could** use the conveyor to transport the mats.
> The environmental legislation **might** be very strict.
>
> › Grammar: Modals and their substitutes, page 161

C   What other things do you think might be needed to solve the problem? Collect your ideas in groups.

2 Discussing the problem

You and Derek Ashborne, your supervisor, have a video conference with Liu Jinlong of Jinsibei, who describes exactly what they need.

A   21))) Listen to the video conference and answer these questions.

1. How are the mats cleaned after cutting?
2. What are the two disadvantages of the current cleaning process?
3. What three things should the mat-cleaning machine do?
4. What are the dimensions of the mats?
5. How do they want to get the sand out of the water?
6. What two reasons does Liu Jinlong give for wanting to filter the water out of the sand?
7. When will Derek send Jinsibei some ideas for the new system?

Presenting a technical project abroad   Unit 8

B Now use your answers to 2A to write a short memo in English about what Jinsibei Co., Ltd. needs.

> **Memo**
> To: John Goldsmith   Date: 03/08/20..
> From: Re: Rubber mats washing system Shenzen
> **Message:**
> Jinsibei Co., Ltd. in Shenzen, China is a …
> The company has problems because …
> They want us to produce a mat-cleaning system that …

3 Discussing the solution

You and Sheila Jones, another apprentice at Hilmer Cleaning Systems, discuss how you could solve the problem for Jinsibei.

A Put the following dialogue in the correct order. Sheila's part of the dialogue is in the correct order.

Sheila	You
1 We have to make sure that the whole system doesn't get too big and heavy because we have to transport it to Shenzhen in a container.	a That's no problem. It has to be a closed system anyway.
2 Do the mats have to be washed on the upper or on the lower side?	b No, they have to be dried with a hot air blower on both sides before they are palletized.
3 Can the mats be palletized when they are wet?	c OK. So to keep it light, it should be constructed from aluminium, maybe with plastic rollers.
4 OK, but if the mats are transported diagonally, upwards and downwards, most of the water will drip off anyway.	d OK, and I'll start thinking about the palletizer …
5 OK, and it must be possible to remove the filtered sand easily and quickly.	e Correct. It's important to save time and energy to reduce costs.
6 One thing we mustn't forget is that the washing system has to be set up right next to the waterjet cutter.	f They have to be washed on both sides, otherwise there will always be some sand left on them when they are palletized.
7 What about safety? The system should be easy and safe to operate.	g Yes, and the palletizer has to be positioned right behind it.
8 Good. I think I'll sketch a rough draft of the washing system and then we'll discuss the system again.	h That's right, but the water and sand mixture causes pollution in the conveyor, so the system must open easily for maintenance.

B Now practise the dialogue with your partner and prepare to perform it for the class.

TOOLBOX

abrasive – *scheuernd*
air conditioned – *klimatisiert*
diagonally – *diagonal*
draft – *Entwurf*

hot air – *Heißluft*
legislation – *Gesetzgebung*
manually – *von Hand*
palletizer – *Abstapeleinheit*

polluted – *verschmutzt*
reinforced – *verstärkt*
to sketch – *skizzieren*
water blaster – *Hochdruckreiniger*

4 Explaining the system

You and Sheila are in a meeting with Derek Ashborne. You discuss the construction drawing for the mat-washing system for Jinsibei.

A Match the words in the list to the numbers (1–7) on the construction drawing.

conveyor · filter · hot air blower · pallet · palletizer · rollers · water jets

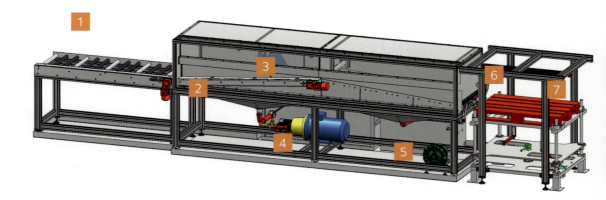

B Put the sentences in the correct order to describe how the mat-washing system works.

- **a** A forklift truck takes away the pallets.
- **b** A filter separates the sand from the water.
- **c** Water jets wash the mats clean of sand.
- **d** Hot-air blowers dry the mats.
- **e** The conveyor transports the mats upwards.
- **f** The operator puts the mats on the rollers.
- **g** The conveyor rolls the mats onto the palletizer.

C 👥 Now explain to your partner how the system works.

> **➔ Describing processes**
>
> Active: A forklift truck takes away the pallets.
> Passive: The pallets **are taken** away **by** a forklift truck.
>
> › *Grammar: Passive forms, page 159*

5 Talking about different applications

Derek Ashborne is pleased with the system that you have designed. He asks you to think of some other applications for the system.

👥 Work in small groups. Think of some other items that could be cleaned using a similar system. Use the photos below or your own ideas.

Make any changes to the system that you think are necessary and present it to the class.

Presenting a technical project abroad Unit 8

PART B: The presentation of the washing system

Situation: You work for Hilmer Cleaning Systems in the UK, and you have to plan an automated washing system for a customer in China. The system has now been constructed, and you fly to Shenzen to install and commission it and to train the operators.
→ You prepare a presentation to explain the system to the customers.

1 Describing the mat-feeding system

The first part of your presentation will deal with the mat-feeding system.

A Look at the diagram and read the description. Then answer the questions below.

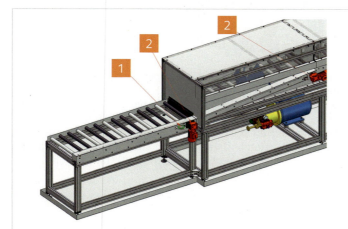

1: the mat-feeding system

After a worker has placed the mats onto the feeding system, he has to press the push-button (1). The motors of the feeding system and the interior transport system (2) start and the mat moves in the direction of the washing system. When the first ultrasonic sensor is activated by the mat, the pump starts and the washing system starts to wash the mats. Excess water drips into the floor tray.

1 How does the system start?
2 How does the mat move?
3 How does the pump start?
4 What's the purpose of the floor tray?

B Now complete these prompts to create the first slide for your presentation. You can label the diagram if you wish.

1: the mat-feeding system

- mats placed ▬
- push-button ▬
- motors of feeding system ▬
- mats move ▬
- ultrasonic sensor ▬
- pump and ▬
- excess water ▬

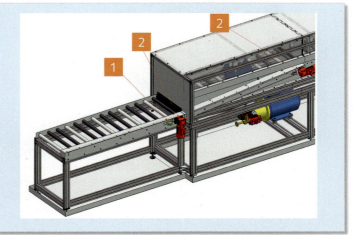

2 Explaining the washing system

You now prepare the next two slides for the presentation.

A   Complete the explanation of the washing system with the words from the list.

140 · alternating · chemicals · coupling · hoses · minute · nozzles · plunger · pressure · valve

2: the washing system and high-pressure nozzles

Water under high ▬¹ is used to clean the mats, to avoid the usage of ▬² during the washing process. The pressure is created by a ▬³ pump with a nominal pressure of ▬⁴ bar and a pump capacity of 48 litres per ▬⁵. The pump is driven by a 15 kW ▬⁶ current motor which is connected to the pump by a Rotex-▬⁷ to avoid knocks being transmitted from the pump to the motor. A pressure-limiting ▬⁸ is integrated in the water hose to avoid overloading the pump and the pressure ▬⁹. The mats are cleaned by three high-pressure ▬¹⁰ from both above and below as they are transported through the washing system.

B   Replace the German words in the text below with the correct English words from the list.

activates · blower · drying area · feed · light barrier · nozzles · switches off · time lag

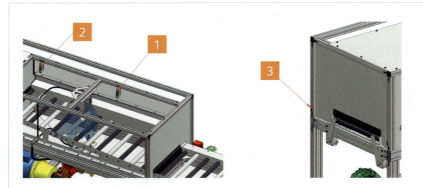

3: the washing process

The incoming mat ▬¹ (*betätigt*) the first ultrasonic sensor (1), the pump starts and the ▬² (*Düsen*) start the washing process. The second ultrasonic sensor (2) starts the ▬³ (*Gebläse*). When the mat is at least two-thirds in the ▬⁴ (*Trocknungsbereich*), the ultrasonic sensor (1) is no longer activated. The pump ▬⁵ (*schaltet ab*) automatically after a short ▬⁶ (*Zeitverzögerung*) to avoid wasting water. The mat activates the ▬⁷ (*Lichtschranke*) (3) but because the second ultrasonic sensor is no longer activated, the motor for the mat ▬⁸ (*Einzug*) switches off while the blower remains on.

C   Use words from the explanations to write prompts for the slides. Label the diagrams if you wish.

Presenting a technical project abroad Unit 8

3 Explaining the drying and stacking systems

The fourth and fifth slides of your presentation will describe the drying system and the stacking system.

Use the diagrams and descriptions to write prompts and label the diagrams for the remaining slides of the presentation.

4: the drying system

The blower, which has an air-flow rate of approximately 3,900 litres per minute, stands on vibration-cushioned feet. The air is sucked in, compressed and then distributed through PVC-hoses into the nozzles. The air is blown on both sides of the mats to provide the optimum drying process.

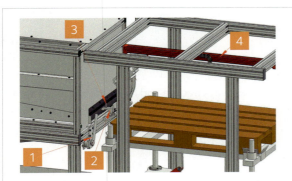

5: the stacking system

The endstops (1) are folded to the sides and the force of gravity pulls the mat into the gripper (2) of the palletizer. Both sensors (3) are activated, the gripper grabs the mat and pulls it slowly over the pallet. The end switch (4) of the linear unit is activated and the blower is switched off. The mat is placed on the pallet. The weight of the mats forces the pallet downwards.

4 Presenting the mat-washing system to Jinsibei

Now it is time to present the system to the customer.

A Work in groups of five. Each person in the group is responsible for creating one of the slides and explaining what it shows to the audience.

Slides:	Remember:
· mat-feeding system · washing system · washing process · drying system · stacking system	· give your presentation a suitable introduction and conclusion · don't fill the slide with text, just use short key words or prompts · don't read the text, use your own words · keep eye contact with the audience · be prepared to answer questions from the audience

B Practise your presentation in your groups, then give your presentation to the class. (You can give each other feedback using the feedback sheet on page 43.)   › *Useful phrases: Giving a presentation, page 149*

 TOOLBOX

air-flow rate – *Luftdurchsatz*   endstops – *Endanschläge*   gripper – *Greifer*
beat – *Schlag*   feed – *Einzug*   vibration-cushioned – *schwingungsgedämpft*
to compress – *verdichten*

COMMUNICATION: Business trips

Situation: Your company has won an award as one of the four best European start-ups of the year. You are going to the prize-giving ceremony in Amsterdam, where you will stay at the International Hotel.
→ You do internet research to find information about people from other cultures.

1 Checking in and checking out at a hotel

When you arrive at the hotel, there are four guests in front of you at reception. You listen to the receptionist talking to them.

1 Giovanni Rossi   2 Mary McGregor   3 Yusuf Zuabi   4 Akira Banerjee

A 22))) Copy the table. Listen to the first three guests as they check in and fill in the missing information.

	What questions do the guests ask?	What information does the receptionist give?
Giovanni Rossi	▬1	▬2
Mary McGregor	▬3	▬4
Yusuf Zuabi	▬5	▬6

B Akira Banerjee is checking out. Read what she says to the receptionist. What do you think the receptionist said to the guest?

1 Good morning. I'm very well, thank you.
2 I would like to check out.
3 I was in room 207.
4 It's been great. I love Amsterdam.
5 Yes, thank you. Everything was fine. I'll definitely be back.
6 Thank you. I'm flying GALE-M. They're very good.

C 23))) Now listen and check your answers.

2 Role-play: At reception

Work with a partner and role-play a conversation at a hotel reception desk.

Partner A: You are the hotel receptionist. Greet the guest, welcome him/her to the hotel and take down his/her details. You begin.
Partner B: You are a guest who has just arrived. Use your own personal details to check in and answer the receptionist's questions.

After that, do a second role-play and practise checking out.
› *Useful phrases: Checking in and out at a hotel, page 152*

Presenting a technical project abroad **Unit 8**

3 Chatting at breakfast

Next morning, the breakfast buffet is very full. You find a free seat at a table with another guest.

A Work with a partner. Put the dialogues in order to produce a conversation.

1. A Pleased to meet you, too. Where are you from?
   B I'm from … . What about you?
   A I'm from …
2. A I was here on holiday a few years ago.
   B Where are the best places to go?
   A If you have time, you should really go to …
3. A I'd better get ready to go now. Have a good day.
   B Thanks. See you later.
4. A Good morning. Is this seat taken?
   B No, it's not. You can sit here. Are you here for the prize-giving ceremony?
5. A Have you been to Amsterdam before?
   B No, I haven't. What about you?
6. A Yes, I am. My name's …
   B Pleased to meet you. I'm …

B Find a new partner. Add your own details then close your books and practise the dialogue.
› Unit 1, Communication, page 12

4 Cultural awareness

On the plane home, you read the following quiz about different cultures.

A Work with a partner. Complete each sentence with the best ending. When you have finished, ask your teacher for the answers and discuss which answers surprise you.

1. Many Japanese people …
   a always bow when they meet people for the first time.
   b bow when they meet each other, but they will shake hands with Westerners.
   c never shake hands with anyone.
2. A lot of Irish people respect people who are …
   a aggressive and dominant.
   b formal and quiet.
   c rich and powerful.
3. In Italy, you should never ask people about their …
   a families.
   b hobbies.
   c job or where they live.
4. In the Netherlands, some people will think you are rude if you …
   a eat cheese with a knife and fork.
   b leave a small amount of food on your plate when you've finished eating.
   c leave the table during a meal.
5. Soon after you've been introduced, many British people will …
   a invite you to visit them at home.
   b start to use first names.
   c want to know everything about you.
6. Many people from the Middle East may ask to take a break during meetings so that they can …
   a go for a walk.
   b phone home.
   c pray.

B Work in a group of four. Find information about people from other cultures on the internet. Use the information to make up a quiz like the one above. Pin your quiz on the wall and do a gallery walk with your partners. How highly does your team score on the other groups' quizzes?

DAS KANN ICH (Unit 8)
- Eine Liste von Normen erstellen, die meine Firma vertritt. (Foundation)
- Eine Beschreibung einer automatischen Waschanlage auf Englisch anfertigen. (Part A)
- Eine Präsentation der automatischen Waschanlage auf Englisch erstellen. (Part B)
- Quizfragen über kulturelle Unterschiede auf Englisch zusammenstellen. (Communication)

KMK Exam practice 4

1 Produktion: A2

Sie haben soeben Ihren Urlaubsantrag genehmigt bekommen. Da Ihr Ausbildungsbetrieb international tätig ist, muss die Abwesenheitsmitteilung auch in englischer Sprache erfolgen.

Danken Sie dem/der Absender/in der E-Mail für seine/ihre Mitteilung. Erwähnen Sie, dass diese nicht weitergeleitet wird und erst nach Rückkehr aus Ihrem Urlaub am 21. des nächsten Monats bearbeitet werden kann, da Sie bis dahin keinen Zugriff auf Ihre E-Mails haben. In dringenden Fällen möge man sich an David Fuller wenden.

2 Produktion: B1

Sie arbeiten in der Hamburger Filiale des britischen Unternehmens Xellent UK plc. Dieses ist spezialisiert u. a. auf die Herstellung von Gerüsten für Großbildleinwände sowie von Schienen für Fernsehkameras und Halterungen für Pyrotechnik. Die Firma hat weitere Filialen in Frankreich und den Niederlanden. Einmal im Jahr treffen sich alle Verantwortlichen aus den vier Ländern zur Besprechung von Verkaufsstrategien, um neue Produkte zu präsentieren.

In diesem Jahr soll die Tagung in Hamburg stattfinden. Aufgrund Ihrer Englischkenntnisse wurden Sie ausgewählt, um bei der Organisation mitzuwirken.

Formulieren Sie den Einladungstext auf Englisch. Verwenden Sie dafür die Notizen, die Ihnen Ihr Abteilungsleiter hinterlassen hat:

Betr.: Internationales Treffen vom 3.–6. Juli

- Jede Niederlassung soll bis zum 12. Juni maximal drei Personen benennen, die teilnehmen werden.
- Rückmeldung per Fax oder E-Mail: Auflistung von Namen, Telefonnummern und Zimmerwünschen (Einzel-/Doppelzimmer?). Hotelprospekt und Veranstaltungsplan „Hamburg Tipp" – beides in englischer Sprache – beilegen!
- Weisen Sie auf Folgendes hin: Auf der Tagung sollen neue, revolutionäre Produkte vorgestellt werden. In diesem Jahr stehen Metallkonstruktionen für Großveranstaltungen im Vordergrund, die leichter als bisherige zu transportieren und auf- und abzubauen sind.
- Daher handelt es sich hier um eine sehr wichtige Informationsveranstaltung, bei der in speziell vorbereiteten Räumen im Hauptgebäude der Niederlassung in Hamburg vorgestellt wird, wie diese Produkte funktionieren. Außerdem sollen Marketing-Strategien diskutiert werden.
- Zugleich soll das 25-jährige Bestehen der deutschen Tochterfirma auf einem Alsterdampfer gefeiert werden. Erfragen Sie, ob es Vegetarier gibt (oder jemand keinen Fisch mag).

3 Mediation: B1

Sie arbeiten für einen Zulieferer der Automobilindustrie. Zu einem Seminar mit dem Thema „Wie werden wir zukünftig Auto fahren?" werden Kunden und Geschäftspartner eingeladen. Ihr Chef hat Sie zu diesem Zweck gebeten, einen Kurzvortrag über autonomes Fahren zu halten.

Im Zuge Ihrer Recherche haben Sie folgenden Zeitungsartikel gefunden. Fassen Sie die technischen Fakten des Artikels für Ihren Vortrag auf Deutsch zusammen.

When in doubt, Sam intervenes

Nissan experiments with autonomous driving in their "Leaf"

The driver sits at the wheel of an electric Nissan Leaf - and does nothing at all. He does not even touch the steering wheel, or the brakes or the gas.

In this car almost everything is installed in order to facilitate autonomous driving: twelve cameras maintain an overview around the car and in the distance. Five radar systems and various laser scanners monitor the surrounding environment to the nearest millimeter – all connected to a map of the environment.

The goal is to be better and safer than a human driver – because human error is responsible for nine out of ten accidents.

However, when something unpredictable happens, often contrary to the rules of the road, man has to intervene: the imperfections of a road, for example, that require changing to the opposite lane, or being forced to use the emergency lane of a motorway because of an accident.

This is where Sam comes into play. This is an abbreviation for "Seamless Autonomous Mobility". If the computer does not know what to do, Sam can seamlessly intervene. If the camera on the roof detects a policeman, a human assistant in the data center quickly intervenes and is able to remotely steer the car.

But if something unexpected happens for which no computer can be programmed, for example in a tunnel without a mobile network, then Sam would not be able to help. This means that even in the future cars without a steering wheel and pedals will not be able to drive everywhere.

9 Enquiries and offers

FOUNDATION: A video conferencing system

Situation: You work for the German subsidiary of a Maltese firm that is interested in installing a video conferencing system.
→ You write a report on a suitable system for your supervisor.

1 Listening to a phone call

The owner of the firm in Malta would like to discuss the conferencing system with your supervisor, Claudia Weber. He has sent an email describing what he wants from the system.

A Work with a partner. Match the items in James Camilleri's email (1–4) with the list of suggestions Claudia Weber would like to make (a–f). There are two extra suggestions.

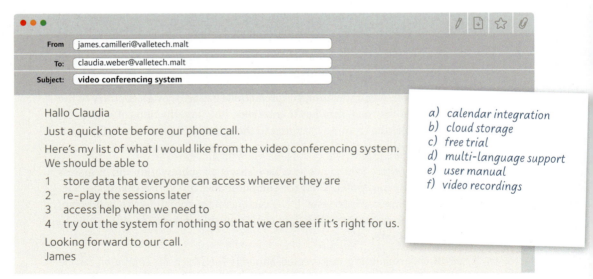

From: james.camilleri@valletech.malt
To: claudia.weber@valletech.malt
Subject: video conferencing system

Hallo Claudia
Just a quick note before our phone call.
Here's my list of what I would like from the video conferencing system. We should be able to
1 store data that everyone can access wherever they are
2 re-play the sessions later
3 access help when we need to
4 try out the system for nothing so that we can see if it's right for us.
Looking forward to our call.
James

a) calendar integration
b) cloud storage
c) free trial
d) multi-language support
e) user manual
f) video recordings

B 24 🎧 ▶ Listen to the telephone conversation and check your answers to exercise 1A. Does James Camilleri agree or disagree to the extra items Claudia Weber suggests?

→ **Comparing items**

This is **the cheapest** system.
This is **the most/least expensive** system.
good > **best**   bad > **worst**   little > **least**

› *Grammar: Comparatives and superlatives, page 160*

Enquiries and offers Unit 9

2 Comparing video conferencing systems

You find an overview of video conferencing systems online.

A Study the chart below and choose the system you think is best.

B 👥 Work with a partner. Compare your ideas and agree together on the system which is best for the company. Make notes on the advantages of the system you have chosen. Make notes on the other systems so that you can argue against them.

C 👥 Work with another pair. Discuss all the options and decide on the best system for the company.

www.TechMatters.com/review-of-video-conferencing-systems

	JOIN US	BUSINESS SCOPE	Let's Meet	TALK TO ME
	€15	€18.99	€12.99	€30
Free Trial	10 Days	14 Days	15 Days	30 Days
Operator-Assisted Meetings	✓	✗	✓	✗
Multi-Language Support	✓	✓	✗	✓
Calendar Integration	✗	✓	✗	✓
Phone Support	✓	✓	✗	✓
Cloud Storage	✓	✓	✓	✓
Audio Recordings	✓	✓	✓	✓
Video Recordings	✗	✓	✓	
Additional Support	Email, Forums, Chat	Email, Online Learning Centre, Webinars	Email, User Guide, FAQ	Online Help, Webinars

3 Writing a report

Now you write the report on the system you have chosen for Claudia Weber and James Camilleri.

👥 Work with a partner. Write your report on the video conferencing system using the following structure.

Introduction	– State the purpose of the report. – Give a short description of your research.	*This report will explain how we …* *We searched the internet and found …*
Main part	– Give the names of the systems. (The system you are going to suggest should come last on the list.) – Say which system you have chosen and explain why.	*We have chosen the … (name of the system) because …* *The system features …* *It does not feature …*
Conclusion	– Sum up and make recommendations.	*For these reasons, we believe that …* *In conclusion, we suggest …*

› Unit 7, Communication, page 76

PART A: An enquiry for linear drives

Situation: You work in the Quality Assurance department of Findlay Engineering in Glasgow, a company that supplies components for the automotive industry.
→ **You write an enquiry to a manufacturer of linear drives.**

1 Reading about precision measuring equipment

Your department needs a new, custom-made precision measuring system to accurately measure the HGV axles that Findlay Engineering produces. While you are doing reseach online, you find the following website. Some words are missing.

Read the website and complete the text with the words from the list.

accurate · contours · deviation · integrated · probe · repetitive · requirements · results · robust · stationary

Kuiso Measuring Instruments

Kuiso measuring systems can be used for simple or complex measuring tasks, for example measuring either the surface roughness of a production workpiece or the ▬¹ of a workpiece such as angles, radii, distances and coordinates. We provide mobile versions that work in separate measurement runs and ▬² models that measure in a single step using a high-precision ▬³.
Kuiso measuring systems are extremely precise and ▬⁴. They can detect even the smallest ▬⁵ from the standard, ensuring that your serially-produced components are of ▬⁶ high quality.

Flexible measuring systems
Kuiso measuring instruments are based on a versatile modular design, so they can easily be added to or ▬⁷ into existing measuring systems. You can configure your measuring station according to your own ▬⁸.

The measurement ▬⁹ can be compared on computer with the actual CAD profile. In this way, you can be sure that your production workpieces meet your specifications and are of the highest quality. Since the contour measurement systems are both compact and ▬¹⁰, they can be used both in production and in the measuring room.

 TOOLBOX

contour – *Umriss*
custom-made – *speziell angefertigt*
deviation – *Abweichung*
HGV (heavy goods vehicle) – *Lkw*
probe – *Sonde*
repetitive – *(sich) wiederholend*
stationary – *ortsfest*
versatile – *vielseitig verwendbar*

Enquiries and offers   Unit 9

2 Reading about linear drives

To measure the lorry axles accurately, you will need to mount the measuring device on a linear drive made up of a guiding rail and slides.

A Read the following website and find out what these expressions are in English. They are in the same order as in the text.

1 Kugeln
2 Präzisionsstahlschiene
3 Schlitten
4 Reibung
5 Steifigkeit
6 Führung
7 gehärtet
8 geschliffen
9 Abstreifer
10 Verschleiß

RACE linear drives

RACE linear drives achieve an extremely precise linear motion with the help of ball bearings between the precision steel rail and the slide. The coefficient of friction in our slides is only one-fiftieth of conventional slides. The slides can accommodate vertical and horizontal direction loads because of the extreme rigidity of the guidance of the slide on the rail.

RACE linear drives are extremely efficient and accurate and can be used in machining centres, lathes, grinding machines, heavy cutting machines and measurement systems. Industrial applications include industrial automation systems, laser engraving systems, packaging machines and even lifting equipment.

All our mechanical components are made of an aluminium-steel compound and are produced exclusively in our factory in Böblingen, Germany. The perfect gearing of all components ensures high flexibility, low costs and excellent work results.

Whether it is precision steel rails, drive units or slides, our components require only minor planning and minimal installation time.

Special features
- precision steel rails and slides, in sizes 20, 25, 30 and 35
- slides with four-row hardened and grounded roller bearings with wiper
- smooth running characteristics and low wear
- high accuracy and parallelism of the rails and slides
- standard length up to 4000 mm, special length on request

B Read the text again and answer the following questions.

1 Why is the friction of the linear drives so low?
2 Why can the slides accommodate vertical and horizontal loads?
3 Where are the components for the linear drives produced?
4 What materials are the components made of?
5 How are the ball bearings protected from wear?
6 What is the maximum length of the steel rail in metres?

TOOLBOX

to accommodate – *aufnehmen*   gearing – *Verzahnung*   slide – *Schlitten*

3 Understanding an online catalogue

You need to build three measuring systems for lorry axles with a length of 4.5 m. You check Race's online catalogue to get a rough idea of what the rails and slides cost.

A Work in a small group and discuss which of the following rails and slides are most suitable for a measuring system for lorry axles.

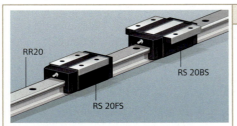

RACE linear drives: rail and slide combinations	
Characteristics	**Applications**
– two-point contact structure	– machine centres
– large permissible load	– CNC lathes
– high rigidity	– heavy cutting machines
– high precision (under 0 μ gap)	– automation devices
– can be pre-loaded	– measuring equipment

RACE LD20

Precision steel rail RR20	
length	3000 mm
width	20 mm
weight	2.5 kg
order code	RR20 3000
price:	€200.12
Slide RS 20FS	**Slide** RS 20BS
€ 33.18	€34.94

RACE LD25

Precision steel rail RR25	
length	4000 mm
width	25 mm
weight	2.5 kg
order code	RR25 4000
price:	€ 309.14
Slide RS 25FS	**Slide** RS 25BS
€40.24	€42.00

RACE LD30

Precision steel rail RR30	
length	4000 mm
width	30 mm
weight	5.1 kg
order code	RR30 4000
price:	€372.71
Slide RS 30FS	**Slide** RS 30BS
€50.82	€50.82

RACE LD35

Precision steel rail RR35	
length	5000 mm
width	35 mm
weight	5.8 kg
order code	RR35 5000
price:	€535.12
Slide RS 35FS	**Slide** RS 35BS
€81.00	€70.24

B Report your ideas to the class. Do you agree/disagree on the most suitable system? Explain your answers.

4 Writing an enquiry

Now it is time to write an enquiry for linear drives.

Work with a partner. Write an email to Race using the following prompts to help you.

– Use a suitable salutation and complimentary close.
– Use the addresses "sales@racegmbh.de" and "qadept@findlay.co.uk" and today's date.
– Ask for a quotation for three sets of the system you have chosen.
– As you are a regular customer, request a discount of 15%.
– Enquire about the date of delivery and the guarantee on the system.

› *Useful phrases: Writing enquiries, page 153*

Enquiries and offers   Unit 9

PART B: A desktop CNC milling machine

Situation: You work for H&P Ltd, a company in Sheffield that produces hydraulic power units and pneumatic controllers.
→ You search the internet for a desktop CNC milling machine and present it to your colleagues.

1 Talking about desktop machines

You and the other apprentices learn about all the large machines that H&P Ltd uses, but you sometimes wonder if smaller machines might also be useful.

A   Think of some jobs you could do in your company with a small desktop CNC milling machine. Make a list.

B   👥 Work with a partner from the same training company. Compare your lists. Do you have the same ideas?

C   👥 Work with another pair from a different company. Are there any items on their list that surprise you? Report your ideas to the class.

2 Producing labelling plates

The company is having problems with the labelling plates on its aggregates. Your supervisor, Sina Akrazi, is discussing the problem with the production manager, Harry Moore.

🔊 25 Listen to their conversation and answer the following questions.

1   What has just happened to the labelling plates on the aggregates?
2   What problems did they have when Bensons supplied the labelling plates?
3   What would be the advantage of producing their own labelling plates?
4   Which materials could they use for the plates?
5   Where do they start to look for a suitable machine?
6   What features does the machine that they find have?

3 Reading about a desktop CNC milling machine

Sina Akrazi asks you to find out more about the desktop CNC machine she has just come across. You find the text on page 96 on the company website.

A   Read the text, then say whether the following statements are true or false. Correct the false statements.

1   The CNC machine has its own CAD software.
2   You can machine S 135 steel with this model.
3   The electronics are designed to provide enough power to the stepper motors in case of heavy tasks.
4   You can only buy the CNC machine as a DIY kit.
5   You don't have to read a lot of text to complete the installation.
6   You have to use the manufacturer's tools with the CNC machine.
7   The maximum power for the spindles is 500 kW.
8   The machine is connected via a parallel interface to the computer.

TOOLBOX

---

aggregate – *Aggregat*
to engrave – *eingravieren*

gantry – *Portal*
labelling plate – *Typenschild*

model-maker – *Modellbauer/in*

Become an expert

Customize computer based workpieces to real models. With a suitable drawing program or a CAD-software, you can create a work file which can be processed by the Desktop CNC/3D System: Accurate, efficient and reproduced as often as you want. The workpiece materials are virtually unlimited: Wood, thermoplastics and non-ferrous metals like aluminium, brass or copper, can be processed.

Excellent quality at a fair price

The aluminium profile series has been developed in order to ensure sufficient accuracy and stability of the machine. It consists of two different linear track profiles and the cover profile. All other connecting elements consist of aluminium or stainless steel and together with the profiled structure they ensure the required rigidity. The stepper motors from Nanotec® have been carefully selected and specifically adapted to exactly fit the machine. The electronics have been specially designed to match the characteristics of the motors so that sufficient power for a reliable operation of the 3D system is ensured.

DIY kit or ready built machine

The machine is available as a DIY kit or as a directly operational system. If you opt for the kit, you save money. The construction of the machine is designed so that you can simply build up the machine within a few hours without any special tools. Only screw together – done! The EasyBuild installation instruction needs (almost) no text. The step-by-step instructions are based on chronologically numbered instruction steps with graphic images of all intermediate steps. The last section always shows the finished assembly so that you can easily check your own result.

Compatibility

Due to the 43 mm collar a wide range of tools can be used. With optional adapters, you can also use Proxxon or Dremel tools as drilling-/milling spindles directly. Other drilling-/milling spindles up to a power limit of 500 watts can also be used. Other system-guided tools, such as a drag knife, engraving needle or hot cutting system can be used optionally.

With the parallel interface of the 3D System many CNC softwares, such as EMC2, Mach 3 and more, can be used.

Source: Stepcraft GmbH & Co. KG

TOOLBOX

collar – *Spannhals*	durability – *Langlebigkeit*	rigidity – *Steifigkeit*
compatibility – *Kompatibilität*	engraving needle – *Graviernadel*	stepper motor – *Schrittmotor*
drag knife – *Schleppmesser*	hot cutting system – *Heißschneidesystem*	

Enquiries and offers Unit 9

B **Complete the gaps with suitable verbs from the list. Sometimes you have to change the form of the verbs.**

adapt · base · check · connect · control · ~~create~~ · operate · ~~process~~ · reproduce · use

Let me explain how this CNC milling machine works. First you *create*[1] a work file with a suitable CAD software on your computer and it is *processed*[2] by the machine's CNC/3D system. You can produce just one workpiece or you can ▬[3] it as often as you need. The aluminium profiles ensure that the machine is rigid and ▬[4] accurately and efficiently. The Nanotec® stepper motors have been specifically ▬[5] to fit the machine exactly and the electronics are designed to ▬[6] them precisely and reliably. The machine is available as a DIY kit or ready-assembled. The step-by-step assembly instructions are ▬[7] on numbered graphic images. At the end of each section you can ▬[8] your assembly against the pictures in the manual. Because of the large diameter of the toolholder, a wide range of tools can be ▬[9]. You can ▬[10] the CNC milling machine to your computer via a parallel interface.

› *Grammar: Passive forms, page 159*

4 Discussing technical specifications

Sina and Harry are discussing whether to buy the desktop CNC machine.

26))) **Listen to their conversation and answer the following questions.**

1 Which components are included in the package?
2 Why are the 6-point ball bearing cages necessary?
3 Why can the system be cleaned easily?
4 What is the minimum feed rate in mm/sec?
5 What's the maximum thickness of the processed materials?
6 What is necessary for the connection to the computer?
7 What is the operating voltage?
8 How long is the warranty?

5 Researching your personal CNC milling machine

Think about a project you have recently done at your company or at home, where a desktop CNC milling machine would have been helpful. If you have not done a project recently, you can use the workpiece below.

A Think about the sizes of the workpieces and decide which machine would be appropriate.

B Research details, sizes and prices of desktop CNC machines on the internet. (If you do not have the internet available, you can look at File 8 on page 137.)

C Present the model you have chosen to the class. Describe the project you need it for and explain why you have decided on that particular model.

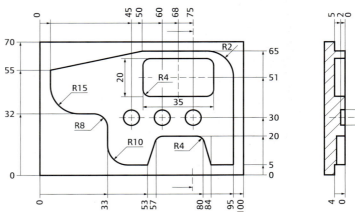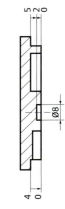

› *Useful phrases: Giving a presentation, page 149*

 TOOLBOX

3-phase current – *Drehstrom*
6-point ball bearing cage – *6-fach kugel-
    gelagerter Laufwagen*

to adjust – *einstellen*
assembly instruction – *Aufbauanleitung*
connecting cable – *Anschlusskabel*

to dismantle – *zerlegen*
feed rate – *Vorschub*
play-free – *spielfrei*

COMMUNICATION: The layout of business letters

Situation: You work at World Medical, a company that manufactures and repairs medical equipment. This week, you are helping out in the office.
→ You write an offer to a new customer in the UK.

1 Reading an English business letter

Your supervisor gives you a letter of enquiry from a new customer.

Study the layout and match the parts (1–11) of the letter on page 99 to the labels below (a–k).

- a address
- b body of the letter
- c complimentary close
- d copies
- e date
- f enclosure
- g inside address
- h reference initials
- i salutation
- j signature
- k subject line

2 Writing an English business letter

Your supervisor asks you to write an offer to Ms Lambert at the Dryden Medical Clinic.

A Complete the letter with suitable words and phrases from the list.

confirmation · deal with · delivery · discount · enclosing · enquiry · guaranteed · look forward to · offer · packed · price · this date

---

Thank you for your ▭¹ about surgery lights. We are pleased to send you the following ▭²:

One (1) ceiling light, WM 0076. ▭³: €2700.00.

We can deliver within two weeks of ▭⁴ of your order. Terms of ▭⁵ are DAP.

This offer lasts for two weeks from ▭⁶. If you place your order within one week, we can also offer a 2% ▭⁷. All of our lights are ▭⁸ for 2 years.

We will ▭⁹ your order carefully and quickly. The light will be ▭¹⁰ in a wooden packing crate.

I am ▭¹¹ a copy of our latest catalogue and price list and ▭¹² future orders.

› Useful phrases: Writing offers, page 153

B Write the complete offer, using the correct layout for a business letter, a suitable salutation and complimentary close, today's date, etc. Use the addresses from the letter on page 99.

› Useful phrases: Writing business letters, page 153

→ Salutation and complimentary closes in letters

	Salutation	Complimentary close
to a firm	Dear Sir or Madam	Yours faithfully (BE)
		Yours very truly / Cordially yours (AE)
to a person	Dear Mr Brown	Yours sincerely (BE)
	Dear Sharon	Sincerely yours / Best personal regards (AE)

TOOLBOX

confirmation of an order – *Auftragsbestätigung*
terms of delivery and payment – *Liefer- und Zahlungsbedingungen*

trade magazine – *Fachzeitschrift*
trial order – *Probebestellung*

Enquiries and offers **Unit 9**

| 1 | Dryden Medical Clinic
17 Dryden Street
London SE9 2BS
+44 (0)20 129546783
info@drydenclinic.com |

| 2 | 29 April 20.. |

| 3 | Our ref: LL/DC |

| 4 | World Medical
Rudower Straße 250
12489 BERLIN
GERMANY |

| 5 | Dear Sir or Madam |

| 6 | **Enquiry about surgery lights** |

| 7 | We have seen your advertisement in this month's editon of the trade magazine "Medical Business". We see that your company sells medical equipment.

We are an outpatient clinic in London. We are planning to add a new operating theatre and are interested in your surgery lights. We would like to place a trial order for one ceiling light. If the product is suitable, we will place a second order.

Please let us have details of your terms of delivery and payment. We would also like to know what type of packaging you use to protect the light during transport.

Barclay's Bank Head Office, London will be happy to supply references.

Many thanks for your attention to our enquiry.

We look forward to hearing from you soon. |

| 8 | Yours faithfully |

| 9 | *Linda Lambert*
Linda Lambert
Clinic Manager |

| 10 | cc Dr. Alice Black |

| 11 | Enc: Information pack "Dryden Medical Clinic" |

DAS KANN ICH (Unit 9)
– Einen Bericht über ein neues Videokonferenzsystem auf Englisch schreiben. (Foundation)
– Eine Anfrage für Linearantriebe an eine englische Firma verfassen. (Part A)
– Eine Desktop-CNC-Fräsmaschine im Internet suchen und auf Englisch präsentieren. (Part B)
– Ein Angebot für eine englische Firma erstellen. (Communication)

10 Ordering technical products

FOUNDATION: Aluminium containers

Situation: You are getting some work experience at a British company that makes aluminium containers.
→ **You call a customer and confirm his order by email.**

1 The product

The owner of a company that organizes events and festivals in Scotland, is interested in buying aluminium containers which he can use to transport electronic equipment to events. He has found this page on your company's website.

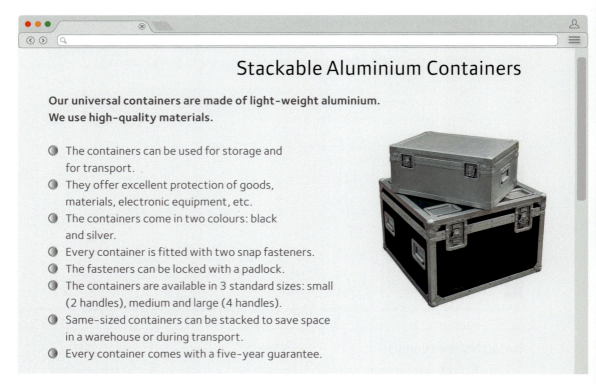

Stackable Aluminium Containers

Our universal containers are made of light-weight aluminium.
We use high-quality materials.

- The containers can be used for storage and for transport.
- They offer excellent protection of goods, materials, electronic equipment, etc.
- The containers come in two colours: black and silver.
- Every container is fitted with two snap fasteners.
- The fasteners can be locked with a padlock.
- The containers are available in 3 standard sizes: small (2 handles), medium and large (4 handles).
- Same-sized containers can be stacked to save space in a warehouse or during transport.
- Every container comes with a five-year guarantee.

 TOOLBOX

handle – *Griff* padlock – *Vorhängeschloss* snap fastener – *Schnappverschluss*

Ordering technical products   Unit 10

A Read the description of the product on page 100 and answer the following questions.

1 What are the containers made of?
2 What can they be used for?
3 What kinds of things can be stored in the containers?
4 How can the containers be carried?
5 How can the containers be closed?
6 How long is the guarantee period?

B Talk to partner. Discuss the advantages of the containers for transporting electronic equipment. Make notes that you can use when talking to the customer.

> **Describing objects**
>
> These containers **are made by** a British company. They **can be stacked** one on top of the other.

› *Grammar: Passive forms, page 159*

2 Role-play: A phone call with a customer

Your supervisor tells you that a prospective customer, Mr Young, would like some information before he places an order. He asks you to call Mr Young.

Work with a partner. **Partner A:** Look here. **Partner B:** Look at File 12 on page 139.

Read the website on page 100 again and prepare to answer Mr Young's questions.

– Ring Mr Young, introduce yourself and explain why you are calling.
– Answer Mr Young's questions using the information on the website.
– Suggest that he orders the medium-sized container (length: 800 mm; width: 600 mm; height: 610 mm).
– Say that you will confirm his order by email.

› *Useful phrases: Telephoning, page 149; Advising customers, page 151*

3 Confirming the order

Your supervisor asks you to confirm the order by email.

Work with the same partner as in exercise 2. Complete the email using words from the box.

catalogue · container · delivery · electronic equipment · guarantee · handles · list · medium · order · trial

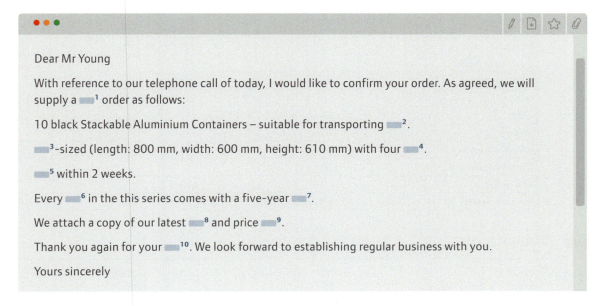

Dear Mr Young

With reference to our telephone call of today, I would like to confirm your order. As agreed, we will supply a ___¹ order as follows:

10 black Stackable Aluminium Containers – suitable for transporting ___².

___³-sized (length: 800 mm, width: 600 mm, height: 610 mm) with four ___⁴.

___⁵ within 2 weeks.

Every ___⁶ in the this series comes with a five-year ___⁷.

We attach a copy of our latest ___⁸ and price ___⁹.

Thank you again for your ___¹⁰. We look forward to establishing regular business with you.

Yours sincerely

101

PART A: A vintage car data sheet

Situation: You work for Wheeler Vintage Cars Ltd, a company in Lancaster that specializes in restoring vintage cars.
→ You order some spare parts by email from a specialist supplier.

1 Understanding a data sheet

Your supervisor asks you to make sure you know all about an extremely expensive car that the company is restoring. The owner of the car is going to sell it at an auction.

Read the data sheet below and label the numbers (1–7) in the picture.

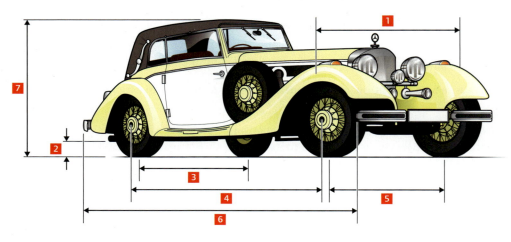

1936 MERCEDES-BENZ 540 K

	bodywork		
body type	4/5 seater convertible/cabriolet		
number of doors	2		
	dimensions & weights		
	mm	inches	
wheelbase	3290	129.5	
track/tread (front)	1511	59.5	
track/tread (rear)	1500	59.1	
length	5245	206.5	
width	1905	75	
height	1651	65	
ground clearance	203	8	
length/wheelbase ratio	1.59		
kerb weight	2286 kg	5040 lb	
fuel tank capacity	120.5 litres	26.5 UK Gal	31.8 US Gal

 TOOLBOX

body – *Karosserie*
ground clearance – *Bodenabstand*

kerb weight – *Leergewicht*
tread – *Spurweite*

vintage car – *Oldtimer*
wheelbase – *Radstand*

Ordering technical products   Unit 10

2 Completing a data sheet

Your supervisor describes the car to a customer who is interested in buying it at the auction.

27 🔊 **Listen to their conversation and complete the gaps in the data sheet.**

engine	
engine type	supercharged petrol
engine code	M 24 II
cylinders	▬1
capacity	▬2
bore × stroke	88 × 111 mm
bore/stroke ratio	0.79
valves	▬3
maximum power output	▬4
maximum torque	431 Nm at 2200 rpm
specific torque	79.8 Nm/litre
fuel system	petrol, carburettor
crankshaft bearings	9
engine coolant	▬5
compressor	▬6

performance	
acceleration 0–80 km/h	▬7
maximum speed	▬8
power-to-weight ratio	58.06 kW/g
weight-to-power ratio	17.22 kg/kW
fuel consumption	
litres per 100 km	▬9
chassis	
engine position	front
engine layout	longitudinal
drive wheels	rear wheel drive
steering	worm & nut
gearbox	▬10
top gear ratio	1
final drive ratio	3.08

3 Creating a handout

Your supervisor has a template in her computer which she uses to make information handouts for customers. She asks you to produce one for the 540 K.

Complete the template below with the correct numbers from the data sheets.

> Item number: WVC 7845
> Mercedes-Benz 540 K ▬1 door convertible/cabriolet.
> The body was designed by Friedrich Geiger with a front mounted engine powering the rear wheels. This is one of the W29 range of cars from Mercedes-Benz.
> The power is produced by a supercharged engine of ▬2 litre capacity. This unit features overhead valve gear, ▬3 cylinder layout, and ▬4 valves per cylinder. It produces ▬5 bhp (180 PS/133 kW) of power at ▬6 3500 rpm, and maximum torque of ▬7 Nm (318 lb·ft/44 kgm) at ▬8 rpm.
> The engine powers the wheels by means of a ▬9 speed manual gearbox. Its quoted weight at the kerb is ▬10 kg.
> The Mercedes-Benz 540 K is said to have a top speed of ▬11 km/h, or 120 mph.

4 Reading about superchargers

Before you order the spare parts you need, your supervisor wants to make sure that you know about superchargers.

A **Read the text on page 104 and do the tasks below.**

1 Say what a supercharger does.
2 Explain how it works.
3 Name three types of superchargers.
4 Describe the differences between the three types.

103

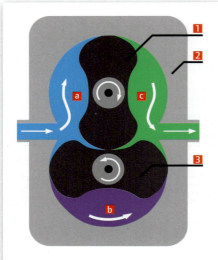

Roots superchargers

A supercharger increases the power of an engine by compressing air. This increases the pressure or density of the air which is pumped into an internal combustion engine. The compressed air feeds more oxygen in each cycle of the engine, which helps the engine to burn more fuel and do more work.

There are three different types of superchargers: Roots, twin-screw and centrifugal.

The main difference between them is how they move air and fluid to the intake manifold of the engine. Roots and twin-screw superchargers use different types of meshing lobes while a centrifugal supercharger uses an impeller, which draws air in. The Roots supercharger is the oldest. It was designed and patented by two American engineers, Philander and Francis Roots. They patented the design in 1859 as a machine that would help ventilate mine shafts. Later, Roots blowers were used in blast furnaces to blow combustion air to melt iron. In 1900, Gottlieb Daimler first included a Roots supercharger in a car engine.

B Match the following parts and work processes with the numbers (1–3) and letters (a–c) on the diagram.

- Forced air or air-fuel mixture into intake manifold
- Intake
- Pump body
- Pumping
- Rotary vane 1
- Rotary vane 2

5 Ordering the compressor

Your supervisor asks you to order the replacement vanes for the supercharger.

Study her sketch and her instructions then write an email to Mr Kelly (RobertKelly@carpartsdublin.com).

I've just spoken to Bob Kelly at Car Parts, Dublin. He has the vanes we need in stock. I told him we need them quickly and he's agreed to accept an order by email.

Cover the following points:
- *The telephone call*
- *Order the two vanes with two lobes – surface ground and polished*
- *Mention the attached diagram of an original part*
- *Ask for urgent delivery as agreed*
- *Mention the price we agreed (580 euros including VAT)*

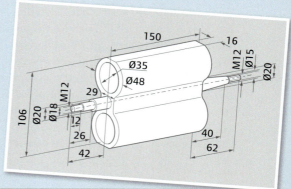

› *Useful phrases: Writing orders, page 154*

TOOLBOX

lobe – *Nocken*
Roots blower – *Roots-Gebläse, Drehkolbengebläse*

supercharger – *Turbolader*
vane – *Schaufel, Läufer*

PART B: An order for spare parts

> **Situation:** You work for Wheeler Vintage Cars Ltd, a company that specializes in restoring vintage cars.
> → You write an order for replacement parts from a specialist supplier.

1 Reading about the Mercedes-Benz 540 K Special Roadster

Your company is restoring a 1936 Mercedes-Benz 540 K Special Roadster for a client. Only 26 cars of this model were ever produced, of which only six examples still exist. It is one of the most expensive vintage cars in the world and Cathy Morrison, your supervisor, wants to make sure that you know all about it.

A Skim the text below and match the headlines (1–6) to the paragraphs (A–E). There is one headline more than you need.

1	The bodywork	3	The engine	5	The interior
2	The custom-made car	4	The frame	6	The suspension

The Mercedes-Benz 540 K Special Roadster

If the 540 K was the ultimate prewar Mercedes-Benz, then the Special Roadster was the ultimate 540 K. It was a racing car with a difference.

A Many parts of the car were the same as other Mercedes racing cars. The chassis layout was the same as the 540 K with a tube frame, the same style as was being used on the company's Silver Arrow racing cars at the time.

B The engine was closely related to one found in Mercedes racing cars. The 5.4-liter inline-8 engine is where the "540" in the car's name comes from, while the "K" stands for "Kompressor". The supercharger system, a Roots blower, was set up in a way that we'd think of today as odd. It could be either engaged manually for short periods by the driver or automatically at wide open throttle. The engine of the Special Roadster had two different power ratings as a result – 115 horsepower for normal conditions and 180 horsepower when the supercharger was used. Combined with the relatively low weight of the car, the power was enough to make the 540 K a fast machine, especially when it was used in smaller automobiles like the Special Roadster.

C The outside of the Special Roadster was beautifully designed. Even though the car is 17 feet long, it looks quite small. It is also very light when compared to other racing cars made by Mercedes' competitors at the time.

D On the other hand, the inside of the Special Roadster has room for only two people. Even though it was small inside, it was very comfortable to drive. It was also fitted out with fine leather and other expensive materials.

E In the 1930s, when Mercedes was first producing its 540 K range, the sedan cost more than $10,000. At the same time, the price of a Special Roadster was around $12,000. This was because each of them was custom-made for a specific person and each person wanted different things. For example, the one you see here has high doors, which were in line with the top of the hood. Other versions had doors that dipped down, or a shorter tail. Some were left-hand drive and a few were right-hand drive, depending on the country the car was going to be driven in.

 TOOLBOX

chassis – *Fahrwerk*	horsepower – *PS*	throttle – *Drosselklappe*
girder – *Träger*	sedan – *Limousine*	tube frame – *Rohrgestell*

B Match the German words to English expressions in the text. The German words are in the order they appear in English in the text.

1. Vorkriegs-
2. Fahrwerk
3. Rohrgestell
4. Turbolader
5. merkwürdig/seltsam
6. etw auslösen
7. Drosselklappe
8. Nennleistungen
9. PS
10. Sonderbestellung

C Answer the questions below to make notes on the text.

1. When was the Mercedes 540 K built?
2. What two parts were the same as in the other Mercedes racing cars?
3. What does the name 540 K stand for?
4. What is "odd" about the supercharger system?
5. What are the benefits of using this system?
6. How did the Special Roadster compare to other racing cars made at the time?
7. What is special about the interior of the Special Roadster?
8. Why was the Special Roadster so expensive?

2 Completing an online order form

Cathy calls Bob Kelly at Car Parts Dublin to order the spare parts. These parts are often custom-made.

A 28))) Listen to their conversation. Which parts from the list does Cathy need?

Item	Price per unit		Item	Price per unit	
wheel nut	€750		king pins	€1300	
water-pump shaft	€190		generator shaft	€240	
V-belt pulley	€650		fuel tap	€340	
servo-brake cylinder	€890		exhaust manifold	€430	
poppet valve	€160		eccentric adjuster for brake	€75	
petrol-non return valve	€260		brake shoes	€760	

Ordering technical products Unit 10

B **28 🔊 Copy the online order form, then listen to the phone call again and complete the order form.**

Order number: WCV 58598			
Item	necessary	in stock	to be produced
brakeshoes	4		

3 Preparing a written order

Cathy asks you to prepare the written order for Car Parts Dublin.

Use the information from exercise 2 and the prompts below to write the order.

– Start the order with the order number.
– Thank the supplier for their quotation of …
– Give details of quantity, product order number and price.
– State terms of delivery and discounts.
– Say how payment will be made (method of payment) and say when.

› *Useful phrases: Writing orders, page 154*

Mr Robert Kelly
Car Parts Ltd
Unit 23
Malahide Road Industrial Park
Dublin 17
Ireland

Wheeler Vintage Cars Ltd
33 Scotforth Road
Lancaster
LA1 5TQ

Order No.: …

Client number: 2339874

Dear Mr Kelly
…

Date: …

4 Talking about vintage cars

During a break at work, you talk to your colleagues about vintage cars.

👥 **Work in small groups. Talk about the following topics and report your ideas back to the class.**

– Have you or your friends ever worked on a vintage car? What was it and what did you have to repair?
– Would you like to repair or rebuild an old or vintage car? Say why / why not?
– If you could choose a vintage car to drive or work on, which car would it be? Explain your reasons.

 TOOLBOX

eccentric adjuster for brake – *Einsteller Exzenter Bremse*
exhaust manifold – *Auspuffkrümmer*
fuel tap – *Benzinhahn*
generator shaft – *Lichtmaschinenwelle*
king pin – *Achsschenkelbolzen*

petrol-non return valve – *Benzin-Rückhaltventil*
poppet valve – *Tellerventil*
servo-brake cylinder – *Servobremszylinder*
V-belt pulley – *Keilriemenscheibe*
water-pump shaft – *Wasserpumpenwelle*

107

COMMUNICATION: Enquiries, offers and orders

> **Situation:** You are helping out in the office at World Medical, a company that manufactures and repairs medical equipment.
> → You write an enquiry and an order to a supplier; then you write an offer to a customer.

1 Checking language for enquiries

You check that you know suitable English phrases for writing a letter of enquiry.

TIP
You will find similar phrases in the model letter on page 99.

Match the phrases and sentences from a German letter of enquiry (a–i) to the English equivalents (1–9).

a Wir haben Ihre Anzeige … gesehen.
b Wir sind ein/eine … in Deutschland.
c Wir haben vor, …
d Wir interessieren uns …
e Wir möchten eine Probebestellung … aufgeben.
f Wenn die Dienstleistungen Ihrer Firma unsere Voraussetzungen erfüllen, …
g Bitte nennen Sie uns Einzelheiten …
h Die … Bank wird Ihnen gerne Referenzen zukommen lassen.
i Wir freuen uns, bald von Ihnen zu hören.

1 If the product is suitable …
2 … (*name of bank*) will be happy to supply references.
3 Please let us have details …
4 We are a … (*type of firm*) in Germany.
5 We are interested in …
6 We are planning …
7 We have seen your advertisement …
8 We look forward to hearing from you soon.
9 We would like to place a trial order …

2 Writing an enquiry for calibration equipment

World Medical is looking for a supplier of calibration equipment. Jan Dube, the Quality Control Manager, asks you to write a letter of enquiry to a manufacturer. He gives you the following details.

👥 Work with a partner. Write a letter of enquiry to MCE using the notes on the right. Add today's date and your own reference numbers. Remember to use the correct salutation and complimentary close.

› *Useful phrases: Writing enquiries, page 153*

TIP
The letter on page 99 will help you with the layout.

Enquiry to MCE – Medical Calibration Equipment, Silverbank Industrial Estate, B5, Ferry Road, Edinburgh EH4 2EF
I found their details online.
· Tell them who we are and what we do.
· Say that we're extending the Quality Control Department and we need more calibration equipment.
· Ask about a trial order for one calibration machine.
· Say that if the trial order is OK, we'll place another order.
· Ask for terms of delivery / payment.
· Give the Triodod Bank, Berlin as a reference.
· Sign it with your name and let me have a copy.
Thanks, Jan

 TOOLBOX

calibration equipment – *Kalibriergerät(e)*

Ordering technical products Unit 10

3 Writing an order for calibration equipment

Neil McCain, the sales manager from Medical Calibration in Edinburgh, has replied to your enquiry. Jan Dube, your Quality Control Manager, is happy with the offer and asks you to write the order.

Write the complete order using Jan Dube's notes.

> - Thank Mr McCain for his reply to our letter of enquiry.
> - Confirm the trial order for one calibration machine.
> - The price we agreed is 352 euros including VAT.
> - Agree to the Terms of Delivery (Documentary Letter of Credit).
> - Thank Mr McCain for his attention to our order.
> - Say that if the product is suitable, we will place a second order.

Start like this and end with a suitable complimentary close.

Dear Mr McCain
Thank you for your reply to our letter of enquiry.
My supervisor, Jan Dube, has asked me to confirm our trial order for ...

› Useful phrases: Writing orders, page 154

4 Writing an offer for wheelchairs

Your supervisor took a call from a customer earlier today. She gives you her notes and asks you to write an offer.

Read your supervisor's notes then write the offer following the scheme below.

> Call from: Ms Smith, Administrator, Toll Road Hospital, Manchester M30
>
> Re. our product no. BP Chair 07
> Amount: 25 battery-powered wheelchairs
> Terms of delivery: EXW
> Delivery within one week of order
> Price: 232 euros per item. Discount for bulk order 0.5%
> Would like a price list

- Thank customer for the enquiry (give today's date).
- Thank for the interest in your company's products.
- Give details of terms of delivery and payment.
- Say that you are enclosing a price list as requested.
- Express hope that you will hear from Ms Smith soon.

› Useful phrases: Writing offers, page 153

DAS KANN ICH (Unit 10)
- Eine telefonische Bestellung per E-Mail auf Englisch bestätigen. (Foundation)
- Ersatzteile per E-Mail auf Englisch bestellen. (Part A)
- Eine schriftliche Bestellung für Ersatzteile auf Englisch aufgeben. (Part B)
- Eine Anfrage und ein Angebot auf Englisch verfassen. (Communication)

KMK Exam practice 5

1 Mediation: B1

Sie arbeiten bei einer freien Autowerkstatt, die auch Zubehörteile verkauft. Die Produktpalette soll um Diebstahlschutz-Geräte erweitert werden. Zunächst sollen vier Produkte eines britischen Zwischenhändlers für Kfz-Zubehör in Erwägung gezogen werden. Um sich einen Überblick zu verschaffen, bittet Ihr Vorgesetzter Sie, verschiedene Produkte zu beurteilen.

Fassen Sie die Besonderheiten und Einsatzgebiete der vier Produkte auf Seite 111 in einer Tabelle auf Deutsch zusammen.

	Stoplock Airbag 4x4 Steering Wheel Lock	Bulldog Euroclamp Security Wheel Clamp	Stronghold 14"–16" Wheel Clamp	Stronghold Sold Secure Protector Caravan Alloy Wheel Lock
Für welche Fahrzeuge?				
Schutz wovor?				
Installation				
Material, Ausführung				
Ausstattung				

2 Produktion: B1

Ihr Vorgesetzter bittet Sie, eine Probebestellung beim britischen Händler aufzugeben.

Verfassen Sie eine E-Mail auf Englisch und berücksichtigen Sie folgende Punkte:
- Informationen zum britischen Händler und seinen Produkten im Internet gefunden
- über die eigene Firma kurz informieren
- Grund der E-Mail: Probebestellung für Diebstahlschutz-Geräte
- Frage nach Lieferzeiten und -bedingungen
- Bitte nach einem günstigen Angebot
- höflicher Schluss

Mechanical car theft prevention

1. **Stoplock Airbag 4x4 Steering Wheel Lock**

   The Stoplock Airbag 4x4 Steering Wheel Lock has been specially developed for vehicles with bigger steering wheels, such as 4x4s or vans. It is made from high-grade steel and features a flashing LED warning light, providing additional security at night from pesky thieves.

   - Fits most vehicles
   - 10,000 key combinations
   - Highly visible
   - Flashing warning LED
   - Fits most vehicles
   - 5 year guarantee

2. **Bulldog Euroclamp Security Wheel Clamp**

   Lightweight and can be fitted in under 10 seconds, the Bulldog Euroclamp Security Wheel Clamp can fit most caravans, trailers and motorhomes to provide high level security.

   - Lightweight clamp with snap on fitting in less than 10 seconds.
   - TUV insurance approved- anti drill, anti-pick lock.
   - Fits most caravans, trailers and motorhomes.
   - Can be used hitched or un-hitched.

3. **Stronghold 14"–16" Wheel Clamp**

   The Wheel Clamp SH 5435 is part of the Stronghold range designed in the UK and manufactured to the highest standards. The range includes wheel clamps for securing caravans, motorhomes and trailers.

   - 14"–16" wheel clamp
   - Suitable for trailers, caravans and vehicles
   - Versatile heavy duty triangulation wheel clamp
   - Fully adjustable (set once only) for wheel diameter and width
   - Covers wheel nuts, wheel trims and alloy wheels
   - Electro plated arms for corrosion protection
   - High security lock, dust, water and corrosion proof
   - Robust heavy steel construction

4. **Stronghold Sold Secure Protector Caravan Alloy Wheel Lock**

   The Alloy Wheel Lock SH 5432 is part of the Stronghold range designed in the UK and manufactured to the highest standards. The range includes wheel clamps for securing caravans, motorhomes and trailers.

   - The ultimate lock for caravan alloy wheels, prevents tow-away theft and unauthorised wheel removal
   - Insurance approved protection for your caravan and trailers
   - Includes 1 x M12 x 30mm Allen key bolt and Allen key
   - Lightweight and compact design (under 3.4 kg)
   - Robust hardened steel construction
   - Foam protection to prevent damage to wheels
   - Yellow protective cap protects lock from dirt and water
   - For ease of fitting the locking arm can be passed through any convenient hole in the rim that allows the lock body to be fitted on the replacement wheel bolt

Source: Halfords Group PLC

11 Problems and complaints

FOUNDATION: Recycling

Situation: You work in the production department of an international smartphone manufacturer.
→ You reply to a comment on a web forum.

1 Reading about environmental issues

As smartphones contain many different chemical elements and compounds, you are attending a workshop on environmental issues. During the workshop, the trainer asks you to read the following text.

Reversing the damage done by mining

As studies show, mining can have a huge impact on the environment.

The most common environmental effects of mining are soil erosion, the formation of sinkholes and loss of biodiversity. Apart from these problems, chemicals from mining processes can contaminate soil, groundwater and surface water. In some cases, trees around mines are cut down to clear space for storage of soil and rocks from the mine.

Studies have discovered that these environmental problems are not only limited to the area directly beside the mine. The erosion of hillsides, water pollution and waste dumps can also have a negative effect on the surrounding areas.

In areas of wilderness, mining may cause the destruction of ecosystems and habitats. In farming areas, it may disturb or destroy grazing and croplands. In urban environments, mining may produce noise and dust, two elements which can affect people's health. Contamination resulting from leakage of chemicals used in some types of mining may also affect the health of the local population and of animals.

As a result of these studies, many governments around the world insist that mining companies follow environmental rules. Some governments also insist that, when mining is over, the companies clean up the mine and its surroundings and restore the environment for future use.

In many countries, before they are allowed to start mining, the mining companies have to pay a fixed amount of money into an account which is held by a third party until the land has been successfully cleaned up. Since 1978, the mining industry in the USA has reclaimed more than 2 million acres (8,000 km^2) of land. Vegetation is growing on this reclaimed land and wildlife has returned to live and breed there. Some of the land is being used for farming and ranching.

Do the following tasks using your own words as often as possible.

1. Explain why some governments have developed rules for mining companies.
2. Describe the rules and say what mining companies have to do.
3. Give examples from the text to show that the rules are working.

Problems and complaints   Unit 11

2 Understanding a presentation

The trainer talks about a study into environmental issues related to the production of smartphones.

A Before you listen, match the German words (1–8) to the English words in the list.

built-in battery · carbon footprint · dissolve · environment · glued · greenhouse gas · incinerator · toxic

1 Umwelt   3 CO₂-Fußabdruck   5 Müllverbrennungsanlage   7 eingebauter Akku
2 Treibhausgas   4 giftig   6 auflösen   8 verklebt

B 29))) ▶ Read the statements below. Then listen and complete the notes.

1 The organization that conducted the survey hoped that manufacturers would …
   a) clean up their products by eliminating hazardous ▬.   b) take back and ▬ old phones.
2 The study looked at three environmental areas:
   a) energy and ▬.   b) greener ▬.   c) the use of natural products and ▬.
3 Manufacturing a smartphone is estimated to cause ▬ kilogrammes of CO₂-equivalent emissions.
4 A smartphone contains heavy metals, including lead, mercury,
   a) ▬,   b) ▬ and   c) ▬.
5 One million phones contain …
   a) ▬ pounds of copper,   b) ▬ pounds of silver and   c) ▬ pounds of gold.
6 You can pay the phone company about ▬ euros for a new battery.

3 Suggesting improvements

The trainer asks you to discuss what smartphone manufacturers could do to improve their record on environmental issues. She writes some points on the board.

 Talk in groups. Expand on the suggestions for dealing with environmental issues related to the manufacture of smartphones above. Add your own ideas.

> recycle / extract and reuse components and metals
> change contract length / offer customers longer contracts
> greener / fewer materials / organic radical batteries (ORB)
> cut down on packaging / accessories

4 Replying to a comment on a forum

At the end of the workshop, the trainer points out the following comment on a forum. She asks you to write a reply.

> "So many people complain about the effects of technology on our surroundings. Why don't people understand that we can't produce technological equipment without damaging the environment?"

Give your opinion on the topic. Mention the pros and cons you have discovered and discussed on these pages to give examples to illustrate your opinion.

🧰 TOOLBOX

biodiversity – Artenvielfalt
cadmium – Cadmium
chromium – Chrom
circuit boards – Leiterplatten (PCBs)
ecosystem – Ökosystem

habitat – Lebensraum
leakage – Versickern; Leck
mercury – Quecksilber
tin – Zinn
water pollution – (Trink-)Wasserverschmutzung

113

PART A: A delivery of an assembly robot

Situation: You are doing work experience at KS Engineering, a British company that produces components for the automotive industry.
→ You write an email of complaint to the supplier about a delivery.

1 Discussing robots in industry

During your work, you often think about how widespread robots are in modern industrial applications.

A Work with a partner. Make a list of some of the tasks which robots perform in the automotive industry.

arc welding, assembly systems, cutting, heavy material handling, milling, …

B Compare your list with another pair.

C In your group, think of areas where humans and robots collaborate, and where there is robot-robot collaboration. Give examples, if possible, from your own training companies.

D Discuss in class: Do you think robots will replace humans in the workplace in the near future?

2 Reading a data sheet and a delivery note

Before you and your colleagues take delivery of a robot for mounting purposes, you read the data sheet and the delivery note.

A Match these definitions to words in the data sheet on this page and the delivery note on page 115.

1 amount a robot can carry
2 extent or distance
3 amount or quantity of heaviness or mass
4 overhead interior surface of a room
5 safety code against contact of water and dirt
6 number assigned for identification
7 insulated electrical conductor to provide electricity to a machine
8 hardware designed to communicate information between hardware and software devices

RobAG R500 SXJ	Data sheet
Payload	6 kg
Working envelope / max. reach	706.7 mm
Number of axes	6
Weight	52.5 kg
Mounting positions	Floor, ceiling, wall
Controller	CU555 compact
Protection class	IP 54

---

assembly system – *Montageanlage*
collaboration – *Zusammenarbeit*

complaint – *Beschwerde*
supplier – *Lieferant*

Problems and complaints **Unit 11**

				RobAG, Dortmund
Delivery note: Order no. 079819908				
Material no.	Name	Price per unit in €	Quantity in pcs	Total price in €
0021631003	**RobAG Robot R500 SXJ** Serial no. 282842	27,486.00	1	27,486.00
			1	
0003811085	**CU555 compact S55/X55/J55 Controller** Serial no. 506058		1	
0000302268	Power supply cable EU 3 m CEE 7 / VII		1	
0000205668	Set of labelling plates English – German		1	
0000591430	CONFIGURATION PROFITECH		1	
0000228319	PROFIBUS M/S		1	
0000739211	INTERFACE 24V PWR IN X55		1	
0000191987	CU555 Docs & parts standard		1	
0000174213	LMN 8.3 Software package		1	
0000842449	RobAG NetPro controller/device 3.2		1	
0000672135	RobAG Programming tools: TechExpert 3.2, GripExpert 3.2, VisualExpert 3.2		1	
			1	
0044167005	**Mobile teaching unit Activate V2** Serial no. 175348		1	
0000204433	Labelling plate Activate V2		1	
0000749382	**RobAG smartPAD cable 10 m** Serial no. 5137845		1	

B Find the following information in the data sheet and the delivery note:

1 the weight of the robot
2 the serial number of the robot controller
3 the length of the power supply cable
4 the voltage of the interface
5 the type number of the software package
6 the names of the tools for easy programming

3 Checking the delivery note

While your colleagues Andy and Ray are unpacking the robot, they check the contents against the delivery note.

30))) **Listen to their conversation and write down the problems with the delivery.**

Details on delivery note	Problems with delivery
RobAG Robot R500 SXJ Serial no. 282842	▭ 1
Power supply cable EU 3m CEE 7 / VII	▭ 2
RobAG NetPro controller/device 3.2	▭ 3
Mobile teaching unit Activate V2 Serial no. 175348	▭ 4
RobAG smartPAD cable 10 m Serial no. 5137845	▭ 5

TOOLBOX

data sheet – *Datenblatt*
delivery – *Lieferung*
delivery note – *Lieferschein*
payload – *Nutzlast*
protection class – *Schutzklasse*
type plate – *Typenschild*

115

4 Writing an email of complaint

Andy asks you to write an email of complaint to RobAG's UK sales department about the delivery.

Use your notes from exercise 3 to inform RobAG about the problems with the delivery and ask about the missing or wrong items.

› *Useful phrases: Making complaints, page 154*

To:	sales@robag.co.uk
From:	production@ks-engineering.co.uk
Subject:	Order no. 019908798

Dear Sir or Madam
We received our R500 SXJ today but when we unpacked the delivery, we found the following problems:
…

5 Role-play: A conversation with the sales representative

The day after you write the email, a RobAG sales representative calls your department.

Role-play the telephone conversation, using the German prompts below.

RobAG sales representative

Sagen Sie, dass Sie die E-Mail an RobAG weitergeleitet bekommen haben und dass Ihnen die Probleme sehr leid tun.

Antworten Sie, dass die Seriennummern im Lieferschein falsch sind und KS Engineering einen neuen Lieferschein erhalten wird.

Antworten Sie, dass dies ebenfalls ein Fehler von RobAG ist.

Antworten Sie, dass das Kabel für das neue smartPAD nur noch 5 m lang ist.

Antworten Sie, dass Sie so schnell wie möglich bei KS Engineering mit dem fehlenden Kabel vorbeikommen und dabei auch die neue Software für die Steuerung installieren wollen.

Antworten Sie, dass Sie kommen werden und entschuldigen Sie sich noch einmal für die Probleme.

Verabschieden Sie sich.

You

Fragen Sie, wie die Probleme gelöst werden könnten.

Fragen Sie, warum für die Steuerung eine falsche Software geliefert wurde.

Fragen Sie nach dem zu kurzen Kabel für das smartPAD.

Fragen Sie nach dem fehlenden Anschlusskabel.

Antworten Sie, dass Sie morgen nicht in der Firma sein werden, aber übermorgen um 9 Uhr ein guter Zeitpunkt wäre.

Antworten Sie, dass dies kein Problem sei und dass Sie übermorgen wieder in der Firma seien.

Verabschieden Sie sich.

Problems and complaints Unit 11

PART B: Problems with a 3D printer

Situation: You work in the Customer Services department of PrinTec, a manufacturer of 3D printers based in Leeds.
→ **You write a reply to an email of complaint from a customer.**

1 Identifying printer problems

To improve your English vocabulary, you check the names for printer problems by looking at the website below.

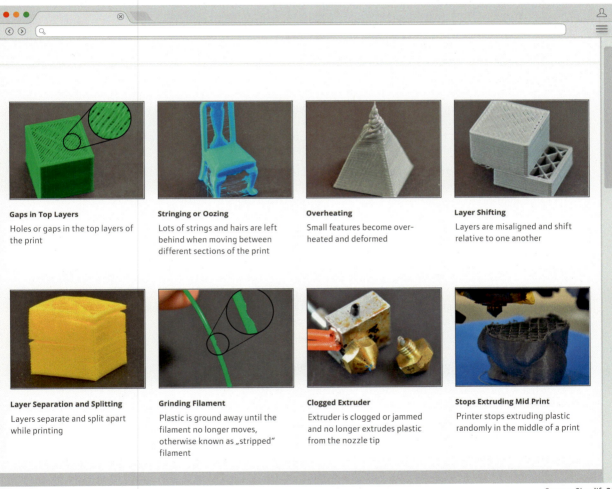

Gaps in Top Layers
Holes or gaps in the top layers of the print

Stringing or Oozing
Lots of strings and hairs are left behind when moving between different sections of the print

Overheating
Small features become overheated and deformed

Layer Shifting
Layers are misaligned and shift relative to one another

Layer Separation and Splitting
Layers separate and split apart while printing

Grinding Filament
Plastic is ground away until the filament no longer moves, otherwise known as „stripped" filament

Clogged Extruder
Extruder is clogged or jammed and no longer extrudes plastic from the nozzle tip

Stops Extruding Mid Print
Printer stops extruding plastic randomly in the middle of a print

Source: Simplify3D

Which English words from the website match these German words?

1 drahtförmige thermoplastische Kunststoffe (ABS und PLA)
2 Düse
3 etw. herauspressen, drücken
4 Fadenzug
5 falsch ausgerichtet
6 Schicht
7 Trennung
8 Überhitzung
9 verformt
10 verstopft

117

2 Reading about printer problems

You also read the following text about 3D printer problems.

Printer problems: Troubleshooting

Most 3D printers come equipped with a nozzle with a 0.4 mm diameter hole in the tip that allows accurate reproduction of very small features. The standard size nozzle works well for most parts, but may cause problems when trying to print extremely thin features that are smaller than the nozzle diameter. For example, the printer cannot accurately produce a 0.2 mm extrusion from a 0.4 mm nozzle. The extrusion width should always be equal to or greater than the nozzle diameter. Nozzles with a smaller diameter are usually available from the manufacturer.

The 3D printer and software interact constantly to make sure that the nozzle extrudes the correct amount of printer resin. If the extrusion settings are not configured properly, the printer may extrude more resin than programmed. This will result in excess resin that can distort the outer contours of your print. To resolve this issue, the settings need to be adjusted in the software. For example, the extrusion multiplier needs to be increased in cases of under-extrusion, or decreased for over-extrusion issues.

Oozing, or stringing, occurs when small strings of resin are deposited on a 3D printed model. This is typically due to resin oozing out of the nozzle while the extruder is moving to a new position. Before printing begins in a new location, the filament is pushed back into the nozzle so that resin can extrude from the tip. Ensure that the retraction option is enabled for each of your extruders (click on "Edit Process Settings" and select the Extruder tab). You can also increase the speed of your printer head, which reduces the amount of time that the extruder can ooze when moving between parts.

3D printers melt and extrude many kilograms of filament over the course of their working life. If the extruder is no longer able to push filament through the nozzle, a jam or clog occurs. This is usually due to something inside the nozzle that is blocking the resin from freely extruding. Heat the extruder to 100 °C and then manually pull the filament out, removing any foreign material jamming the nozzle. TIP: Use a thin wire to push the material back through the nozzle tip.

Ringing is a wavy pattern that may appear on the surface of a print due to printer vibrations or wobbles. This pattern may occur when the extruder makes a sudden change of direction, for example near a sharp corner. The inertia of the extruder can create vibrations when these sudden direction changes occur, which will be visible on the print itself. One reason might be that the printer is moving too fast, so reduce the print speed setting (click on "Edit Process Settings" and select the Print speed tab). A loose screw or a broken bracket might also cause excessive vibrations.

A Answer the questions on the different printer problems.

1 What is the diameter of the standard nozzle hole in most 3D printers?
2 What do you need to produce smaller features?
3 Why do the nozzles sometimes extrude too much resin?
4 How can you solve the problem of over-extrusion?
5 What should you do if your prints suffer from stringing?
6 How can you clean the nozzle if it is clogged?
7 Why may ringing appear on the surface of your workpiece?
8 How can you avoid the problem of ringing?

B Which two troubleshooting problems from the website on page 117 are also mentioned in the text above?

 TOOLBOX

---

bracket – *Halterung*
to configure – *einrichten*

printer resin – *geschmolzener Filamentkunststoff*
string – *Faden*

Problems and complaints Unit 11

3 Discussing a customer's problem

One day the Customer Services department receives the following email of complaint from a customer.

From: dave.holdenby@prime-engineering.co.uk
To: customerservice@printec.com
Subject: Printer fails on our PT2002 printer

Dear Sir or Madam

About six months ago we bought the PT2002 to produce special parts for our machine prototypes. At the beginning we were very satisfied with the printer but now, as you can see in the attached photo, the results are no longer satisfactory.

We would like to know what the cause of the problem is. The printer is still under warranty, so please inform us whether we should return it to you for inspection or if you can send a technician to carry out repairs on site.

Yours faithfully
Dave Holdenby
Head of Construction

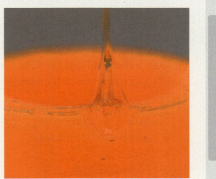

A Work with a partner. Read the email and explain the situation: Who is the customer, what is the problem, what does he want PrinTec to do?

B 31)) Wayne and Louise, two colleagues in the Production department, are discussing the problem. Listen to their conversation and answer the following questions.

1. Which two features of the print results are unsatisfactory?
2. Which feature of the printer hardly ever breaks?
3. Why does Louise think Prime Engineering might not be using the original filament?
4. What other problem might be a result of that?
5. What is the maximum workpiece height for this type of printer?
6. What is the temperature of the resin when it exits the extruder nozzle?
7. What do they think the main cause of Prime Engineering's problem might be?

4 Answering the email of complaint

Your supervisor in the Customer Services department asks you to write an email to Prime Engineering Ltd.

Answer Dave Holdenby's email from exercise 3. Use your answers to exercise 3 and mention these points:

- not the resin heating system because …
- original filament coils? cheap copies can cause …
- working height? maximum working height for PT2002 is …
- please check; otherwise 2-year on-site warranty

› Useful phrases: Writing emails, page 150; Dealing with complaints, page 155

> **Talking about consequences**
>
> If the filament **doesn't cool** quickly, it **loses** its shape.
> If you **use** the correct filament coil, you **won't have** any problems.

› Grammar: Conditional sentences, page 159

 TOOLBOX

to contaminate – *verschmutzen*
filament coil – *Filamentspule*

to harden – *aushärten*
to solidify – *fest werden*

COMMUNICATION: A telephone complaint

Situation: You work at World Medical, a company that manufactures medical equipment.
→ You deal with a telephone complaint.

1 Dealing with complaints on the telephone

Your supervisor gives you a list of phrases for dealing with complaints and tells you to keep it by the phone.

Match the headings (1–5) to the phrases (a–j). There are at least two phrases for every heading. Some phrases match more than one heading.

1 Apologizing
2 Asking for information
3 Reacting to information
4 Action
5 Ending the call

a Can I just check with you that I've understood everything?
b Could you tell me what it's about, please?
c Could you give me the order number, please?
d I'll have a replacement sent out as soon as possible.
e I'm sorry to hear that.
f Is there anything else I can do for you today?
g Just a moment while I write that down.
h Oh, no. That doesn't sound at all good.
i Thank you for your call. Once again, I'm sorry that there was a problem.
j We're prepared to replace the goods at our expense.

› *Useful phrases: Dealing with complaints, page 155*

2 Dealing politely with customers

A new customer, Jerzy Adamczyk, calls to complain about a trial order of X-ray machines. Your colleague, Melissa Wolf, takes the call. She is not very polite.

A 32))) With a partner, listen to the phone call and decide together how you would improve it. Make a list.

B 33))) Now listen to how Melissa should have dealt with the phone call with Jerzy Adamczyk. Which (if any) of your improvements does she make?

> **TIP**
>
> **Making / Dealing with complaints on the phone**
> Give your name clearly at the start of the call and write down the name of the person you are speaking to immediately. If necessary, check the spelling of the name.

3 Complaining to a supplier

World Medical ships their orders in special containers made by Sheffield Metal, a company in England. The latest consignment has not arrived, so your supervisor phones to complain about the delay in delivery. Jeanette Hogg answers the phone.

A Work with a partner. Look at the phrases (a–h) below and decide who says what – the caller or the person taking the call. (There are four phrases for each speaker.)

a delivery was promised
b How can I help you?
c I will do my best
d it's an order for
e the exact details
f the order number?
g to enquire about my order
h We can't fulfil our orders

Problems and complaints   Unit 11

B
When you have finished, match the phrases (a–h) with the gaps (1–8) in the text to complete the transcript of the phone call.

Jeanette Good morning. Sheffield Metal, Sales Department. Jeannette Hogg speaking.
Supervisor Good morning. This is Max Jahn from World Medical in Germany.
Jeanette Good morning, Mr Jahn. ▬¹
Supervisor I'm calling ▬² for containers for medical equipment. The order was sent almost one month ago, on 18 April, and ▬³ by 3 May but, so far, nothing has arrived.
Jeanette Oh. I'm sorry to hear that. Could you give me ▬⁴
Supervisor Yes. It's DF54736.
Jeanette DF54736. Just a moment, please. I'll check. I'm sorry, Mr Jahn. I don't seem to have any record of your order. Can I just check that I've understood everything? The order number is DF54736 and you ordered the containers on the 18th of April. Could you give me ▬⁵ of the order, please?
Supervisor Yes, ▬⁶ your aluminium containers for medical equipment.
Jeanette Aluminium containers for medical equipment. Mr Jahn, I'll have to speak to my colleague to find out what the problem is. Can I get back to you later?
Supervisor Well, yes. But I hope it won't take long. ▬⁷ until we have your containers.
Jeanette Yes. I realize that, Mr Jahn. I'm very sorry about this and ▬⁸ to get back to you as soon as possible.
Supervisor Many thanks for your help, Ms Hogg.

C
34)) Now listen and check your answers.

4 Role-play: Making a complaint by telephone

Now it is time to practise dealing with telephone complaints.

A
Work with a partner and role-play a telephone complaint using the prompts below.

PARTNER A	PARTNER B
You work for the supplier. You take a call from a customer who makes a complaint. Before you begin, refresh your knowledge of phrases for dealing with complaints (exercise 1).	You are the customer. Before you begin, make some notes as follows: – the name of your firm – the order number – the date of delivery – the problem (e.g. damaged/wrong goods, delay in delivery) – what you hope from Partner A

› *Useful phrases: Telephoning, page 149; Making complaints, page 154; Dealing with complaints, page 155*

B
When you have finished the phone call, change roles and do it again using different details.

DAS KANN ICH (Unit 11)
– Einen Kommentar zu einem Beitrag in einem Webforum auf Englisch schreiben. (Foundation)
– Eine Beschwerde per E-Mail auf Englisch verfassen. (Part A)
– Eine Antwort auf eine Beschwerde per E-Mail auf Englisch verfassen. (Part B)
– Mit telefonischen Beschwerden auf Englisch richtig umgehen. (Communication)

12 A job application

FOUNDATION: Where do I go from here?

Situation: You are thinking about applying for a work placement abroad. You start to think about what you have learned in your apprenticeship and where you might work when you have qualified.
→ You write a description of your apprenticeship for a European job agency.

1 Listening to newly-qualified technicians

You listen to an interview with three newly-qualified technicians. They are talking about the jobs they do and where they would like to find a permanent position.

1 Maren
Mechanical Engineering Technician

2 Garry
CAD Technician

3 Delon
Mechatronics Technician

A 35))) ▶ **Listen and say what the speakers liked best about their apprenticeship.**

1 Who enjoyed learning from experienced people?
2 Who liked the mixture of going to vocational college and doing practical work?
3 Who enjoyed making things in the workshop?

B 35))) ▶ **Listen again and complete the table with the missing information.**

Name	What I do at work	Sector?
Maren	▭¹ and ▭² machinery	▭³
Garry	fix ▭⁴ so that the ▭⁵ can go on with their work	▭⁶
Delon	install ▭⁷ equipment do ▭⁸ tasks such as checking or cleaning ▭⁹ the machine if there is a problem	▭¹⁰

A job application Unit 12

2 Thinking about your skills

You think about the skills you have learned during your apprenticeship.

A What do you enjoy most about your apprenticeship? What skills are you learning? How do you learn and develop these skills. First make notes on your own.

> **Talking about skills; thinking about possibilities**
>
> I **can** repair a motor.
> We**'re able to** fix the machines without any help.
> They **might be able to** get a job in the UK.
> You **could** look for work in the metal sector.

B 👥 Now talk to a partner about the skills you are learning.

C 👥 Now compare your ideas with another pair and make a list of the skills you are all learning, for example, soldering, welding, machine maintenance, etc. (Keep this list; you will need it for Part A, exercise 2, page 125.)

› *Grammar: Modals and their substitutes, page 161*

D Report your ideas to the class. In class, make a list in English of the different job titles in your field, e.g. mechanic. How can you use the skills you are learning in your preferred area of work?

3 Doing internet research

You search the internet for job opportunities in Europe.

A 👥 Work with a partner. Do internet research to find suitable career prospects in Europe. Make a poster showing job offers and companies in your sector. Present your ideas to the class.

B When you have finished, pin your poster to the wall and do a gallery walk. Rank the posters using the categories below. Give points from 1–5 for each category.

headline · design · photos/pictures · content · overall effect

4 Reading about the Europass

While you are doing your research online, you come across the European Skills Passport (Europass). You decide to use it to collect your own personal details for applications and your CV.

Download the Europass and start to complete it with your details. (Your teacher has the correct URL.)

> **INFO**
>
> **The European Skills Passport (Europass)**
> This is a standardized CV and language document that can be created online or on your own computer. Potential employers throughout Europe can clearly see your skills and qualifications.
>
> The following sections might be of particular interest to you:
> – **Language Passport** – a self-assessment tool for language skills and qualifications;
> – **Europass Mobility** – a record of skills acquired during a learning experience in a European country;
> – **Certificate Supplement** – a description of skills acquired by holders of vocational training certificates.

5 Describing your apprenticeship

You have contacted an EU job agency asking for help in looking for work experience in Europe. The agent for Germany asks you to write a short description of your apprenticeship in English for the agency file.

Write a short description of your apprenticeship. Before you begin, think about the aspects you should include, e.g. type of training, skills you learned, qualifications you gained, and make notes.

PART A: Job adverts and applications

Situation: You would like to gain some work experience abroad.
→ **You study some job adverts online and write an application for one of them.**

1 Analysing a job advertisement

You have found some information online about job opportunities abroad.

Study the advertisement below and say …

1. in which sector the employer is active.
2. what the company is looking for.
3. what the job requirements are.
4. what benefits are offered.
5. how to apply for the job.
6. what happens if the application is shortlisted.

TECHNICAL OPPORTUNITIES

Recruiter: Top-Tech Recruitment Agency

Fields: IT, mechatronics, metalwork, electrical engineering
Sector: Engineering

Region: London
Salary: Negotiable
Job Type: Renewable contracts

The UK is facing a chronic skills shortage in the engineering sector and trained workers from abroad are in high demand. We are a leading UK recruitment agency that is looking for suitably qualified technical personnel.
If you are interested in applying for a position, please complete our application form.

We are looking for:
- Reliability, commitment to the job and the willingness to work hard.
- The ability to work as part of a team.
- Strong personal drive and the ability to use your own initiative.
- The ability to work under pressure.
- Recognized qualifications and at least 2 years experience in your field.
- Good spoken and written English.

What's on offer:
- Contracts of 6 months, renewable.
- Starting salary £18 per hour minimum.
- Learning on the job from experienced staff.
- Opportunities for overtime.
- Starting date: Immediately.

If your application is shortlisted, you will be asked to send your CV together with a covering letter.

Initial interviews will be conducted by telephone.

TOOLBOX

commitment – *Engagement*
drive – *Tatendrang, Motivation*
in high demand – *sehr gefragt*
initial – *erste/r/s*

negotiable – *verhandelbar*
overtime – *Überstunden*
recognized qualifications – *anerkannte Qualifikationen*
renewable – *verlängerbar*

A job application Unit 12

2 Discussing job advertisements

You study some job advertisements and discuss them with your colleagues.

A Work in groups of three. **Partner A:** Look here. **Partner B:** Look at File 7 on page 137.
Partner C: Look at File 15 on page 141.

Read the job advertisement below and be ready to answer your partners' questions about it. Ask your partners questions about their job adverts. Find out about …

1 the type of employer.
2 what the job is.
3 what the requirements are.
4 the salary and benefits.
5 how to apply.
6 what happens if the application is shortlisted.

WELDER FABRICATOR

Markham Metals, Leeds, UK
We are a family business with vacancies for qualified metalworkers. We do all types of work, including general fabrication, handrails, gates and railings, sheet metal work, light structural work, and site installations and repairs.
We are looking for skilled welders or fabricators. Welding and general metalwork skills are essential. Driving licence required. The job will involve regular site work.

Job Type:
Full-time, starting at £9.36 per hour and rising annually
24 days paid holiday plus public holidays

Required education: Vocational College Certificate or equivalent
Required experience: Welding, general metalwork, workshop experience

Use this link to apply with your CV.
If your application is shortlisted, we will arrange a time for a telephone interview.

B Discuss the job offers in your group. Say which position interests you. Explain why you are (or are not) qualified for the position. Use the list of skills that you developed in Foundation, exercise 2 (page 123) to support your answer.

> **Expressing your wishes**
>
> **I'd** (= I would) **like** a job as a CAD technician.
> **I'd** (= I would) **love** to work for … (company) / to work in … (sector).

3 Writing an application

You are going to apply to one of the advertisements you read in exercise 2 above. Choose the one which you think suits you best.

A Read the tips for writing a CV on page 128. Then write your own CV, using the model on page 129 and any appropriate words and phrases from the model.

› *Unit 12, Communication, page 128*

B Read the tips for writing a covering letter on page 130. Then write a covering letter for the job advertisement you have chosen, using the model on page 131 and any appropriate words and phrases.

› *Unit 12, Communication, page 128; Useful phrases: Writing a covering letter, page 156*

PART B: Job interviews

> **Situation:** You have been shortlisted for a job in the UK.
> → You prepare for and practise a telephone interview and a face-to-face interview.

1 Handling telephone interviews

You and a colleague have decided to practise telephone interviews together.

A With your partner, read the text below and decide which sentences (1–8) fit the gaps (A–F) in the text. There are two more sentences than you need.

YOUR TELEPHONE INTERVIEW

One short phone call is all it takes to get you to the next level in your job application process – or not. Here are some tips to help you get that job.

Be prepared!
Gather the following documents and lists the day before the interview:
• a copy of the job description;
• a copy of your letter of application, your CV and your references;
• a list of questions you want to ask the interviewer;
• a list of your strengths and weaknesses.
So that the interviewer doesn't get irritated by the sound of you flicking through papers, **A** .

On the day of the call
• Place a notebook and a couple of pens beside the phone **B** .
• Make sure the room you are in is quiet.
• Switch off your computer and disconnect all social media.
• If possible, use a landline. If you use your mobile phone, make sure it is fully charged **C** .
• Get the interviewer's phone number in case you get disconnected.

Dress for the job
You should dress as you would for a face-to-face interview. Strange as it sounds, **D** . Remember to smile. You can't sound bored or uninterested if you have a smile on your face. To keep your voice sounding good, **E** .

During the call
Concentrate and stay focused. Listen carefully and reply to the interviewer appropriately. Be professional and polite. At the end of the call, you can ask, "Do my qualifications meet the company's needs?" However the interview goes, always end with "Thank you for your call." The last few words of a conversation are often the ones that people remember **F** .

---

1 and that you take the call in a place where reception is good
2 ask the interviewer how many candidates he/she has spoken to today
3 pin these documents and lists to the wall so that you can check them during the call
4 please hang on while I think of the answer
5 so always leave a good impression at the end
6 so that you can take notes during the interview
7 swallow a teaspoon of honey just before the call
8 you're more likely to feel and sound professional if you look the part

A job application Unit 12

2 Practising a telephone interview

You and your colleague decide to practise a telephone interview together.

A Work with a partner. Do internet research to find suitable career prospects in Europe. Make a poster showing job offers and companies in your sector. Present your ideas to the class.

B With your partner, prepare a dialogue and role-play a telephone interview.

> **Asking for clarification**
> I'm sorry, could you say that again?
> So, if I understand you correctly …
> I don't quite understand what you mean by …

› *Useful phrases: Telephoning, page 149*

3 Preparing for a face-to-face interview

You listen to a podcast in which an expert gives tips about how to handle face-to-face job interviews.

A What is the expert likely to say? With a partner, brainstorm a list of expressions you might hear and make notes under the headings below.

Here are a few expressions from the podcast to start you off.

Stage 1: Greetings and introductions
arrive at the interview on time

Stage 2: Small talk
talk about the weather

Stage 3: The main part of the interview
talk about yourself

Stage 4: Questions from the candidate
do background research into the company before the interview

Stage 5: Further arrangements and the end of the interview
ask when you can expect to hear from the company again

B 36)) Now listen and check. How many of your expressions did you hear?

4 Practising for an interview

You and your colleague decide to practise the main part of an interview together.

A First of all, study the list of common interview questions (File 16 on page 142) and how to answer them.

B Work with a partner.

Partner A: Choose one of the job advertisements you read in Part A (page 125, File 7 on page 137 or File 15 on page 141) and tell your partner which one you have chosen. Think about the questions the interviewer might ask and how you might answer. Make notes.

Partner B: Study the job advertisement your partner has chosen. Make a list of questions you might ask.

C When you are both ready, role-play the job interview. When you have finished, change roles if you wish.

127

COMMUNICATION: A CV and a covering letter

Situation: You find out online about the documents which you will need for job applications.
→ You study an English CV and covering letter, and tips on how to prepare them.

1 Reading a website about CVs

You find an interesting website with tips, but the headings have got mixed up.

Work with a partner. Read the tips, (1–9) and match them to the headings (a–i).

- a Education and training
- b Hobbies and interests
- c Personal statement
- d Personal details
- e References
- f Key skills
- g Work experience
- h Contact details
- i Further skills

→ TIPS for writing your CV

www.internationalCVs_Technical

Your CV is a summary of your abilities, work experience, education and qualifications. There is no set format for a British CV but you should keep it short, using clear headings to guide the reader.

1 Give your name and address, telephone number(s) (home/mobile) and email address.

2 This should be a short message that grabs the attention of the reader. Use note form. This helps to keep your CV focused and direct, for example: *Motivated precision mechanic with experience in German engineering industry.*

3 Here you can summarize your skills and experience which are relevant to the job for which you are applying.

4 As a general rule, CVs should be in reverse chronological order, listing the most recent position first. For each position held you should provide the dates of the start and end of employment, the employer's name and address, the job title, the main duties and responsibilities and achievements.

5 Give a brief description of qualifications (school, academic and/or professional). Give the names of schools or colleges in reverse chronological order.

6 Here you should write about common skills gained throughout your education and work experience, such as languages, IT skills, good maths skills or a full, clean driving licence. These skills are of interest for any employer.

7 This feature is optional, but could provide something more personal to discuss at an interview. Be careful about what you write; a dangerous sport or *socializing with friends* may not be what an employer wants to hear!

8 Write your date of birth and nationality under this heading.

9 Due to data protection laws, candidates should not provide referees' names, addresses or any other contact details on CVs, but should state that details are available on request. Always ask your referees' permission before you give someone their contact details.

2 Analysing a CV

You also find an example of a British-style CV online.

Study the CV below. What differences can you find between this CV and a German CV?

MARTIN BIENEK
Am Kattenkamp 236, 33611 Bielefeld, Germany
Landline: (+49) 521 394677
Mobile: (+49) 176 3628419
Email: martin.bienek43@gmx.com

PERSONAL STATEMENT
Mobile and flexible apprentice metal worker, in final year of 3-year course, seeking position abroad.

KEY SKILLS
Turning, CNC milling, panel beating and welding
Machine maintenance and repair
Excellent spoken and written English
Good spoken and written Polish

WORK EXPERIENCE

Since 20..	Experience during apprenticeship of turning, grinding, CNC milling and waterjet cutting
20..	5-day placement at Hagen Maschinenbau GmbH (local engineering company) doing maintenance and repairs of workshop machinery

EDUCATION AND TRAINING

Since 20..	3-year apprenticeship at Hagen Maschinenbau GmbH and Vocational Training College for Metalwork and Electrical Engineering in Bielefeld, Germany
June 20..	Mittlerer Schulabschluss (School Leaving Certificate) Main subjects: Mathematics, Physics, Computer Studies
20.. – 20..	Realschule Bielefeld (secondary school)

FURTHER SKILLS
MS Office and database management
Full driving licence
First aid certificate

HOBBIES AND INTERESTS
Athletics, football
Training local junior football team

PERSONAL DETAILS
Date of birth: 06 April 20..
Nationality: German

REFERENCES
Available on request

3 Analysing a covering letter

Martin has applied for a job as a machinist in a domestic appliances manufacturer in Ireland.

Read Martin's covering letter on the opposite page and match the parts (1–5) with explanations from the list.

a asking the employer to invite you for an interview
b reference to details on your CV
c reference to the position
d saying why the applicant is applying for the position
e stating why the applicant is the best person for the job

4 Mediation: Writing a covering letter

Your supervisor gives you the following text and asks you to make notes on the contents in German for the apprentice file.

Read the text and make notes in German for the file.

Writing your covering letter

A covering letter is a formal letter with a standard structure. Do not use the same letter for all companies and all jobs but include a different covering letter with your CV for each job you are applying for. Your covering letter should be one page long. Try to avoid having too many sentences beginning with "I".
In the letter you should …

1. refer to the position for which you are applying; give the source of the employer's address;

2. give details of your education and training; explain what you are doing at the moment;

3. explain why you are applying for the position;

4. explain what you can offer the employer;

5. close politely, referring to enclosures (attachments in the case of online applications) and asking the employer to invite you for an interview.

Here are some things to remember:
» After "Dear …" all letters and emails then start with a capital letter.
» If you start a letter / an email with a personal name (*Dear Anne, Dear Ms Green*), you finish it with "Yours sincerely".
» If you begin a letter / email with no personal name (*Dear Sir/Madam*), you always finish it with "Yours faithfully".

› *Useful phrases: Writing a covering letter, page 156*

Am Kattenkamp 236, 33611 Bielefeld, Germany
Phone: (+49) 521 394677, Mobile: (+49) 176 3628419
Email: martin.bienek43@gmx.com

20 April 20..

Scott Domestic Appliances Ltd
Silverbank Industrial Estate
DUBLIN
D11 F4E2
IRELAND

Attn. Mr Haig, Human Resources Director

Dear Mr Haig

Machinist

1 With reference to your advertisement Ref. No. 17673 on the internet, I would like to apply for the post as machinist.

2 I am very interested in the job you are offering as I feel sure it will give me the opportunity to develop both personally and professionally. I am particularly keen to work where I can apply my skills on a daily basis.

3 As you can see from the enclosed CV, I am coming to the end of my three-year training as a metalworker. I have been studying at a German vocational college and learning on the job at a German company that manufactures industrial machines. My duties include turning and milling as well as the maintenance and repair of our machines.

4 As I have practical skills and experience, am flexible and mobile and speak fluent English, German and Polish, I believe I will be a strong member of any team I join and will benefit your company.

5 My CV is enclosed and I am available for an interview at short notice.

I would very much appreciate it if you would consider my application and hope that you will grant me an interview.

I look forward to hearing from you soon.

Yours sincerely

M. Bienek

Martin Bienek

Encl.

DAS KANN ICH (Unit 12)

- Eine Beschreibung meiner Ausbildung auf Englisch verfassen. (Foundation)
- Englische Stellenanzeigen analysieren und mich darauf bewerben. (Part A)
- Mich auf ein Bewerbungsgespräch auf Englisch gut vorbereiten. (Part B)
- Bewerbungsunterlagen auf Englisch richtig verfassen und gestalten. (Communication)

KMK Exam practice 6

1 Produktion: B1

Sie arbeiten für einen Betrieb, der Produkte für Angebotswochen von Discounter-Ketten zusammenstellt. Heute geht es um eine Themenwoche, die mit Küchenutensilien zu tun hat. Bevor Sie die Anzeigenabteilung informieren können, benötigen Sie Warenproben zur Demonstration. Einige Muster wurden jedoch nicht, fälschlich oder beschädigt geliefert.

Schreiben Sie eine Beschwerde an den Lieferanten in Wales anhand folgender Vorgaben:

- Die für letzte Woche angekündigte Lieferung erfolgte erst gestern.
- Geordert waren fünf Kochtöpfe der Serie Steel 100 und zehn schmiedeeiserne Bratpfannen der Serie 200, geliefert wurden jedoch zehn Kochtöpfe und fünf Bratpfannen.
- Eine Kiste mit Wasserkochern ist beschädigt. Einige davon sind zerkratzt.
- Die bestellten Backbleche fehlen.
- Als Demonstration können die Wasserkocher genutzt werden; die fehlenden Bratpfannen und Backbleche werden jedoch dringend benötigt.
- Bitte um sofortige Regelung dieser Angelegenheiten.

2 Interaktion: A2/B1

Sie haben sich für ein Praktikum in England beworben und wurden nun zu einem Vorstellungsgespräch eingeladen.

Diskutieren Sie auf Englisch mit Ihrem/r Gesprächspartner/in folgende Fragen:

- You can choose between a job interview at 8.30 a.m. or 2 p.m. What time would you choose and why?
- How would you dress?
- What would be the first words you say when you enter the room?
- What would be your motivation for wanting an internship in the UK?
- What could you do to stop yourself being nervous?
- How would you prepare yourself for the interview?
- How would you deal with questions you cannot answer?
- How important is it to mention personal interests and hobbies in a job interview?

3 Produktion: B1

Sie planen ein Praktikum in einem metallverarbeitenden Betrieb in Großbritannien, um auch Ihre Sprachkenntnisse zu erweitern. Sie haben folgende Stellenanzeige gefunden:

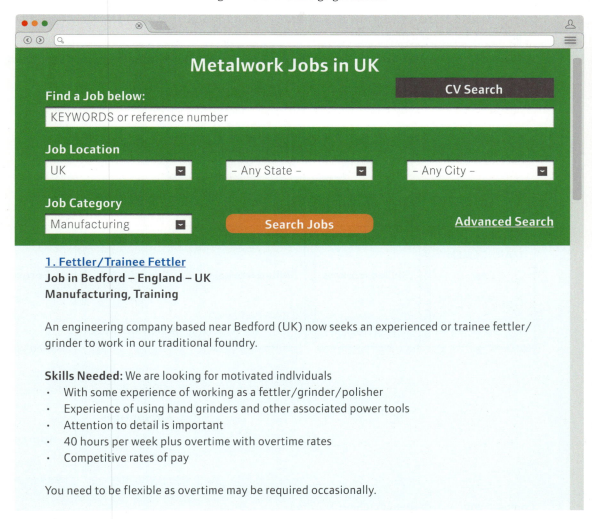

Sie entschließen sich zu einer Bewerbung.

Schreiben Sie den Text eines Bewerbungsschreibens (ohne Nennung Ihres Namens, Ihrer Adresse, des Datums und ohne Unterschrift). Schildern Sie Ihre fachlichen Erfahrungen in zwei Bereichen. Erwähnen Sie, dass Sie im Anhang einen Lebenslauf mitschicken.

Verwenden Sie für Ihren Text diese Checkliste:

– Anrede
– Bezug auf Internetseite
– Interesse / Grund für Bewerbung
– Dauer: drei Monate
– Erfahrungen auf zwei Fachgebieten
– Anlagen: Lebenslauf
– Schlusssatz

P Partner files

FILE 1: Unit 1, Part B, exercise 3

Partner A

A Answer Martin Foster's (= Partner B's) questions about the organization chart below. Spell all the names that are not familiar to you.

B Some of the information in the chart is missing, so ask Partner B questions to complete the chart.

What does Lukas Hanitzsch do?
Who works in the Construction department?
What's the name of the supervisor in … ?

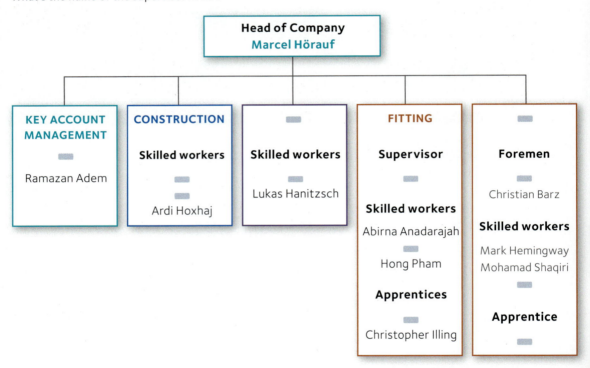

C Compare your charts when you have finished.

FILE 2: Unit 3, Communication, exercise 1C

Partner A

Dictate these email addresses to Partner B. Check B's answers.

1 DavidMcCarthy+list@net.us
2 sergei-nikitin@com.ru
3 your own email address
4 the email address of your firm or another email address you often write to

FILE 3: Unit 2, Communication, exercise 5

Partner A and Partner B

Partner A: You work for your training company. (Use your own name and the name of your company.)
Partner B: You work for Trent Electrical Equipment Ltd in Stoke. (Make up an English name for yourself.)

Role-play a telephone call and taking a message. Partner A starts:
Good morning, (name of company). (Your name) speaking. ...

Partner A

Answer the phone. Introduce yourself and ask how you can help.

Say that Mr Schmidt is out of the office at the moment.

Say that Frau Wendlinger is in a meeting. Ask if the caller would like to leave a message.

Ask the caller for his/her contact details.

Say that you will pass on the message.

Thank Partner B for calling.

Partner B

Introduce yourself and ask to speak to Mr Schmidt in the Production department.

Ask to speak to Frau Wendlinger.

Say that the electric drills the company ordered are not available. Ask for somebody to call you back to discuss an alternative.

Give your contact details.

Thank Partner A and end the call politely.

FILE 4: Unit 5, Foundation, exercise 1B

Partner B

Read out these mathematical equations. Partner A will write them down. When you have finished, check that Partner A has written them correctly.

1. $13^2 = 169$
2. $579 \div 26 = 22.26923$
3. $1.234 + 56,789 = 58,023$
4. $70° < 180°$
5. $a2 \approx b2$
6. $48,571,053 - 27,640,598 = 20,930,455$

FILE 5: Unit 5, Communication, exercise 1C

> **Describing graphs**
> The graph/chart shows …
> The horizontal/vertical axis is divided into … units/sections each representing …
> The x axis / The y axis has a scale from … to …

Partner B

Describe this line graph to Partner A. Partner A will draw it. Check Partner A's graph when you have finished.

FILE 6: Unit 4, Part B, exercise 4B

Partner A

Describe the two workpieces from the turning machine to Partner B. Answer any questions your partner has.

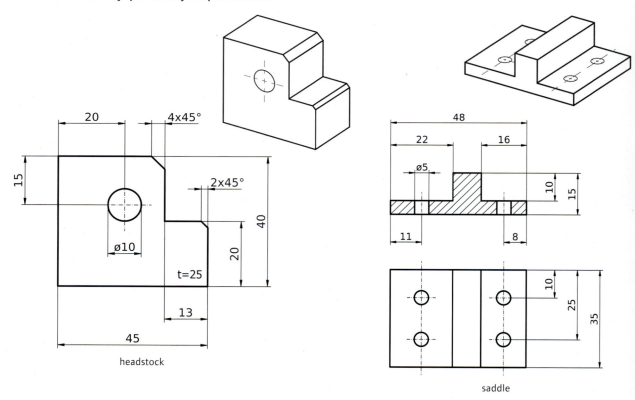

Which parts (1–5) of the turning machine on page 41 do the drawings match?

FILE 7: Unit 12, Part A, exercise 2A

Partner B

Read the job advertisement below and be ready to answer your partners' questions about it. Ask your partners questions about their job adverts. Find out about …

1 the type of employer.
2 what the job is.
3 what the requirements are.
4 the salary and benefits.
5 how to apply.
6 what happens if the application is shortlisted.

Sheet Metal Worker/Fabricator

DESC Fabrications Ltd – Oxford, England

We are a large sheet metal company, established in 1986. We are looking for workers for all types of sheet metal fabrication to work with stainless steel, aluminium and mild steel.
Ability to weld would be an advantage but not essential.

Hours of work are Monday–Thursday 8.00–4.30 and Friday 8.00–1.15.
Salary is dependent on experience.
The ideal candidate needs to be reliable, show they have a good initiative, able to work as part of a team or on their own.
Good working conditions.
Use of company van.

If you feel you are suitable for this role, please apply with your CV and a covering letter to Oxford Fabrications Ltd. Unit 7, Oxford Industrial Estate, OX22 7JY, UK.
Successful candiates will be invited to a preliminary interview at a local assessment centre.

Job type: Full-time
Pay: starts at £10.44 per hour; 25 days paid holiday
Job location: Oxford, UK
Required education: Vocational Technical School qualification

FILE 8: Unit 9, Part B, exercise 5B

In the table below you can find the different prices (excl. VAT = value added tax) for CNC milling machines.

Type	Clamping Surface (X Y)	Working Space (X Y Z)	Overall Size (L x W x H)	Weight (kg)	Price Construction Kit (€)	Price Ready to Run System (€)
1-210	210 x 290	210 x 210 x 40	320 x 342 x 350	11	729	1078
2-300	232 x 380	210 x 300 x 105	430 x 345 x 410	13	829	1178
2-240	312 x 500	300 x 420 x 140	552 x 440 x 510	15	979	1328
2-600	432 x 680	420 x 600 x 140	737 x 558 x 510	19	1279	1728
2-840	615 x 920	600 x 840 x 140	968 x 745 x 510	31	1499	1948

FILE 9: Unit 1, Part B, exercise 3

Partner B

A   You are Martin Foster. You want to know about the structure of the head office in Nuremberg. Ask Partner A questions about the organization chart:

What does Julia Schreiber do?
Who works in the Production department?
What are the names of the skilled workers in … ?

B   Some of the information in Partner A's chart is missing, so answer Partner A's questions. Spell all the names that are not familiar to you.

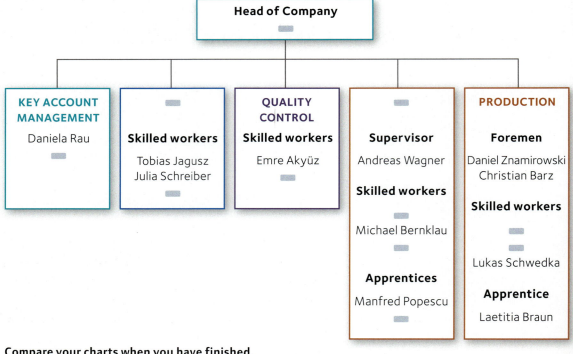

C   Compare your charts when you have finished.

FILE 10: Unit 3, Communication, exercise 1C

Partner B

Dictate these email addresses to Partner A. Check A's answers.

1   beatrice-kuhn@berlin_tools.de
2   Hamish.MacPherson@net.uk
3   your own email address
4   the email address of your firm or another email address you often write to

FILE 11: Unit 5, Foundation, exercise 3

Partner B

You have received an email from Metall Wagner GmbH with information about a platform trolley you are interested in. Unfortunately, some of the information is incorrect. The company calls you to correct the information.

Take the call from Partner A (Metall Wagner GmbH) and ask about the correct information.

> **Clarifying details**
>
> **Asking about and giving dimensions**
> What are the dimensions of the … ?
> It says here that the … measures … by …
>
> **Confirming information**
> The trolley is made of …
> The castors are made of …
> Could you repeat that, please?

PLATFORM TROLLEY
Platform trolley / aluminum
1500 x 700 x 670 mm

Other information: Four castors on the bottom made of steel.
They measure approximately 170 mm in diameter and 65 mm in width.
All wheels are fitted with wheel brakes.

FILE 12: Unit 10, Foundation, exercise 2

Partner B

You are Tom Young. You organize festivals in Scotland. An employee at AluBox (Partner A) is going to phone you to give you information about aluminium containers. You are not sure about what you want so you may need to ask the caller to repeat information.

Before you start, read the prompts below carefully. You start the conversation by answering the phone:

Hello, Tom Young speaking. …

- Explain that you would like some information about aluminium containers for transporting electronic equipment, such as lights, microphones, cables, speakers, etc.
- You would like the following information:
    - How big is the medium-sized container?
    - Can the storage containers also be used for transport?
    - Can the containers be locked in any way?
    - Are the containers suitable for transporting goods that might break?
- Say that you would like to place a trial order for 2 containers.
- Ask for a copy of the latest catalogue and price list.
- Thank the caller for his/her help and say you look forward to receiving confirmation of the order.
- End the phone call politely.

FILE 13: Unit 6, Foundation, exercise 2

Partner B

You are a GP (general practitioner = *Hausarzt*) visiting the trade fair. You go to the World Medical stand to enquire about portable X-ray equipment.

Before you start, read the instructions below and prepare to take notes.

Explain that you often deal with accidents on construction sites and need portable X-ray equipment. Ask Partner A …

… for general information about the equipment
… if the equipment can be used outdoors
… about specifications
… the price
… the delivery details
… the packaging details

Make notes as Partner A answers your questions.

Change roles if you want. Prepare to perform your role-play for the class.

FILE 14: Unit 4, Part B, exercise 4B

Partner B

Describe the two workpieces from the turning machine to Partner A. Answer any questions your partner has.

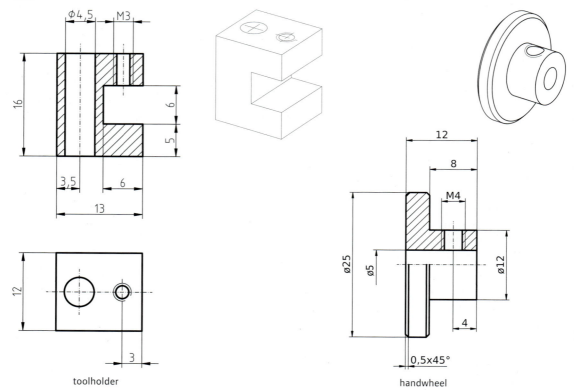

toolholder

handwheel

Which parts (1–5) of the turning machine on page 41 do the drawings match?

FILE 15: Unit 12, Part A, exercise 2A

Partner C

Read the job advertisement below and be ready to answer your partners' questions about it. Ask your partners questions about their job adverts. Find out about …

1 the type of employer.
2 what the job is.
3 what the requirements are.
4 the salary and benefits.
5 how to apply.
6 what happens if the application is shortlisted.

Machinist

Jet Parts, 22 Ferry Road Park, Birmingham B24 7XS

Jet Parts is a leading manufacturer of metal parts for the automobile industry. The company has factories at 6 sites in the UK.

We are continually looking for qualified machinists to join our team.

Candidates must be able to …
- understand and work from engineering drawings.
- use manual milling machines.
- use manual lathe machines.
- use hand tools.
- work to close tolerances.

A good understanding of general workshop practice is a must.

Vocational School Certificate or equivalent required.

Starting salary: £10.00/hour
Day shift with plenty of opportunities for paid overtime
Subsidized canteen
25 days holidays + bank holidays

Please apply with your CV to HR Department, Jet Parts, 22 Ferry Road Park, Birmingham B24 7XS.

Please note: If you have not heard from us within 28 days, please assume you have been unsuccessful on this occasion. However, we will keep you CV on file for 6 months in case any suitable positions should arise.

FILE 16: Unit 12, Section B, exercise 4

Common interview questions	Tips
… about yourself – Tell us about yourself. / How would you describe yourself? – What are your strengths and weaknesses? – What are your hobbies? – Tell us about a mistake you made in the past and how you handled it. – What question would you not like us to ask you?	– Be honest. Show that you are able to use your strengths and indicate that you are working on your "weaknesses". – Always keep in mind that you are applying for a position. – Be positive. Even if a mistake was made, remember to say that you learned from it. – Say that you hope they do not ask you about a particular department / task as you do not yet have much experience in that department/area. Keep it simple and say something positive.
… about your education, work experience and skills – Why did you choose to train at vocational college? – What responsibilities did you have / do you have during the work placement? / at work? – Please tell me about your present job. – What have you learned in your present job that you think would help you in the position you're applying for with us?	– Talk about the aspects of your education, work experience and skills that are relevant for the job in question. – Be honest. Don't say you know MS Office if you only learned Word, PowerPoint and Excel. – Talk about a particular project or task which you did successfully.
… about what you know – What languages do you speak? – What computer software are you familiar with?	– Answer honestly.
… about your motivation – Why did you apply for this job? – Why do you want to work for this company? – Why do you think you would be a good candidate for this job? – What would you like to achieve in the next five/ten years?	– Show that you have researched the company and know what the job is about. – Stress the positive aspects of the company and the job. – Talk about realistic goals and describe how you would like to progress with your career.
Questions you can ask the interviewer	
– I would like to continue improving my skills. What courses does the company give? – What kind of training is given to new employees? – Who would I report to? – What are the prospects for promotion? – What are the next stages of the selection process? – When could I start?	

Mock exam: B1

Schriftliche Prüfung

Zeit: 90 Minuten
Hilfsmittel: allgemeines zweisprachiges Wörterbuch
Maximale Punktzahl: 100 Punkte

Im Rahmen der schriftlichen Prüfung werden die Aufgabenanteile für die drei Kompetenzbereiche wie folgt gewichtet:
Rezeption 40 %
Produktion 30 %
Mediation 30 %

Im Folgenden werden vier Aufgaben vorgelegt, die Sie bearbeiten sollen. Die erste und die zweite Aufgabe beziehen sich auf Ihre Fähigkeit, englische Texte (gesprochene und geschriebene) zu verstehen = **Rezeption**. In der dritten Aufgabe sollen Sie ein Schriftstück erstellen = **Produktion** eines englischen Textes. Bei der vierten Aufgabe wird von Ihnen erwartet, dass Sie Texte von der deutschen oder englischen in die jeweils andere Sprache übertragen = **Mediation**.

Die Prüfung beginnt mit der Hörverständnisaufgabe. Alle weiteren Aufgaben können in beliebiger Reihenfolge bearbeitet werden.

Rezeption I: Hörverstehen   20 Punkte

Sie arbeiten für einen Großhändler für Baumaschinen. Ihr Vorgesetzter bittet Sie, auf einer internationalen Messe mit anderen Experten Kontakte aufzunehmen und Informationen bzgl. potenzieller Geschäftspartner zu sammeln. Sie haben die Möglichkeit, die Aussagen einiger interessanter Teilnehmer über sich und ihre Firmen aufzuzeichnen.

37)) Im Hotelzimmer hören Sie sich die Aufzeichnungen von Clive, Fiona und Keith zwei Mal an. Füllen Sie dabei die untenstehenden Tabellen aus, indem Sie pro Aufzählungspunkt stichwortartige Notizen machen.

Name and position	Clive Hancourt	export manager	Fiona	intern	Keith Wallace	mechanical engineer
company	name	location	name	location	name	location
	ManuMetal	▬	Henderson Bros.	▬	MetLab Ltd	▬
how long in business	▬		▬		▬	
kind of business	▬ ▬		▬		▬	
machinery / tools produced or worked with	▬		▬ ▬		▬	
customers	▬ ▬		▬		▬	
employees	▬ ▬		▬		▬	

Rezeption II: Leseverstehen   **20 Punkte**

Ihrem Betrieb liegt eine Bewerbung eines potenziellen neuen Mitarbeiters, John Conniff, vor. Da der Meister nur über geringe Englischkenntnisse verfügt, gibt er Ihnen einen Vordruck und bittet Sie, diesen auf Deutsch auszufüllen.

Entnehmen Sie die entsprechenden Informationen dem folgenden Bewerbungsschreiben und ergänzen Sie die fehlenden Informationen im Vordruck auf Seite 145.

Dear Mr Wunderlich,

My name is John Conniff and I live in Dublin, Ireland. During the last few years I have travelled to most European countries, but I fell in love with Germany, even if my knowledge of the German language is limited (still). In fact, I am writing to you about your firm's offer for skilled English workers and learners to work in your country for three months. I am very interested in the opportunity to improve my qualifications and get work experience while I am still young.

At present I am training at Metalworks in Dublin to become a lathe operator. I am in the first year of my apprenticeship.

In the first weeks of my employment I gained skills in working on and shaping easier metal workpieces with hand tools. Then, I was introduced to smaller machines first, like column drills, metal shears, bandsaws, and later on, to bigger machine tools like grinding machines, milling machines and lathes. I even learned to operate the latter with CNC equipment. After all, I found out that my favourite kind of machines are the lathes.

I was lucky to have been given several jobs which had to do with lathes in the last half year.

Such jobs included:

– unloading a packed new lathe from a truck
– unpacking and commissioning the machine
– installing the electrical supply
– learning what the main parts of the machine are, the chuck, apron etc.
– getting to know the main turning operations like boring, threading or facing
– processing easier workpieces with the help of engineering drawings, e.g. several kinds of shafts, how to make grooves, chamfers, threads, shoulders and so on.

During the last three weeks, I even experienced work with CNC lathes and had a little insight into this exciting field of manufacturing. I especially hope to deepen my knowledge in this area in Germany.

I hope to hear from you soon. I could travel anytime to come to an interview.

Yours sincerely,

John Conniff

Auswertung der Bewerbung von:

Name:	*Conniff*		
Vorname:	*John*		
Nationalität:	*Irisch*		
Beschäftigt bei:	▬	Ausbildungsberuf:	▬
Bewerbung für die Dauer von:	▬	Ausbildungsjahr:	▬
Erfahrung mit folgenden Maschinen (max. 5):	▬ ▬	▬ ▬	▬
Art der Erzeugnisse:	▬	▬	
Erfahrung mit einer Drehmaschine:	▬		
Tätigkeiten bei der Inbetriebnahme einer Drehmaschine (max. 4):	▬ ▬	▬ ▬	
Besonderes Interesse an:	▬		
Wünsche für den Einsatzbereich:	▬	▬	▬

Produktion   30 Punkte

Sie arbeiten in einem international operierenden Unternehmen, das Haushaltsbatterien herstellt. Die Produkte werden unter verschiedenen Namen vorrangig bei Discountern angeboten.

Für eine Messe soll ein Flyer in englischer Sprache angefertigt werden. Entwerfen Sie den Text, der wichtige Ereignisse in der Firmengeschichte beinhaltet.

K&S BATTERIES GERMANY: A SUCCESS STORY	
1950:	Gründung (Karl und Siegfried Mertens), Erfolg durch Batterien für Transistorradios, Erweiterung der Produktpalette (Akkus, Knopfzellen), bekannt in der Bevölkerung als „Kraft und Saft"
In den 80ern:	Krise, verursacht durch Zunahme der Anzahl von Mitbewerbern
1990:	Gründung von Filialen in den neuen Bundesländern, in Frankreich und Großbritannien
2000:	Änderung der Absatzstrategie (Produktion für Discounter)
Zukunft:	Weiterhin positiver Trend erwartet

Mediation (Sprachmittlung)   30 Punkte

Die deutschen Berufsgenossenschaften schreiben Betriebsanweisungen für Maschinen und Anlagen vor. Da in Ihrem Betrieb zunehmend Mitarbeiterinnen und Mitarbeiter aus anderen Ländern beschäftigt sind, soll ein solches Dokument zur Arbeitssicherheit auch in englischer Sprache erstellt werden.

Erarbeiten Sie Anweisungen und Angaben auf Englisch, die sich auf die Beurteilung möglicher Gefahren, den Schutz der Mitarbeiterinnen und Mitarbeiter und den reibungslosen Ablauf des Betriebes der Maschine beziehen. Tragen Sie diese Anweisungen in eine „Operating Directive" ein. Es genügen stichwortartige Formulierungen. Orientieren Sie sich dabei an der deutschen Betriebsanweisung auf Seite 146.

BETRIEBSANWEISUNG
für die Bedienung von CNC-Drehmaschinen

GEFAHREN FÜR MENSCH UND UMWELT

- Während des Werkzeug- und Werkstückwechsels besteht die Gefahr von Quetsch- und Schnittverletzungen.
- Durch sich bewegende Werkstücke und wegfliegende Teile können schwere Verletzungen entstehen.
- Hautkontakt mit Kühlschmierstoffen kann Hautschäden und allergische Reaktionen verursachen.

SCHUTZMASSNAHMEN UND VERHALTENSREGELN

- Die Maschine darf nicht unbefugt betrieben werden.
- Überprüfen Sie Schutzhauben oder andere Sicherheitsvorrichtungen, bevor Sie die Maschine einschalten.
- Spannen Sie die Werkstücke immer fest ein.
- Wechseln Sie Werkzeuge und Werkstücke nur im Stillstand.
- Entfernen Sie Späne mit einem Spanhaken oder einer Bürste.

VERHALTEN BEI STÖRUNGEN

- Betätigen Sie den Not-Aus-Schalter.
- Stellen Sie die Maschine sofort aus und beheben Sie die Störung im Stillstand.
- Melden Sie die Störung Ihrem Vorgesetzten.

INSTANDHALTUNG

- Setzen Sie Ihren Vorgesetzten von Unregelmäßigkeiten der Maschine in Kenntnis.
- Bei der Instandhaltung die Betriebsanleitung des Herstellers beachten.
- Reparaturen dürfen nur durch befähigte Personen ausgeführt werden.
- Sichern Sie die Maschinen gegen unbeabsichtigtes Wiedereinschalten.

Mündliche Prüfung

Die mündliche Prüfung ist eine Gruppenprüfung, bei der Sie Gespräche persönlichen und fachlichen Inhalts in der Fremdsprache führen sollen. Sie dauert pro Kandidat/in ca. 15 min. Die Zeit, in der beide miteinander kommunizieren, zählt für beide gleichermaßen. D. h., die gesamte Prüfungsdauer zum Kompetenzbereich „Interaktion" kann 20–25 Minuten dauern. Zur Vorbereitung haben Sie 20 Minuten Zeit.

Phase I: Sie werden gebeten, sich zu persönlichen oder beruflichen Themen zu äußern. Die Kandidaten/Kandidatinnen werden im Wechsel befragt.

Phase II: Im zweiten Teil sollen Sie zusammen mit einem/einer anderen Kandidaten/Kandidatin ein Rollenspiel durchführen. Dazu erhalten Sie vom Prüfer / von der Prüferin Rollenkarten, auf denen eine Situation beschrieben ist, die Sie vorspielen sollen.

Phase III: Eventuell nehmen Sie in einem dritten Teil zu einer vorgegebenen Situation Stellung.

Hilfsmittel: allgemeines zweisprachiges Wörterbuch.

Interaktion   30 Punkte

Ihre Aufgaben für Phase I könnten wie folgt lauten:
Geben Sie Auskünfte über sich und Ihren beruflichen Werdegang anhand folgender Stichworte:

- Your professional career:
  - Training, qualifications, internships etc.
  - Reasons why you chose this job / career path
- The company you work for:
  - General / field of specialization
  - Number of employees, working conditions
- Your experiences / daily routine in the company:
  - Administrative tasks (give examples)
  - Machines you use (give examples)
  - Your likes/dislikes

Ihre Aufgaben für Phase II könnten wie folgt lauten:
Sie werden gebeten, an der Planung des Tags der offenen Tür in Ihrem Ausbildungsbetrieb mitzuwirken. Sie besprechen mit einem Kollegen / einer Kollegin die unten aufgeführten Themen. Diese können auch durch andere Ideen erweitert werden.

Fassen Sie zum Schluss der Diskussion abwechselnd die wichtigsten Ergebnisse zusammen, um sie der Abteilungsleitung vorzustellen.

- target group(s)
- catering
- PR activities / campaigns
- weekday(s) to choose, opening hours
- give-aways, samples
- information material
- involvement of staff
- budget required

Ihre Aufgabe für Phase III könnte wie folgt lauten:
Sie arbeiten in einer Autowerkstätte. Da eine zusätzliche Hebevorrichtung angeschafft werden soll, informieren Sie sich in einem Onlinekatalog.

Diskutieren Sie anhand des Fotos mit Ihrem/Ihrer Partner/in, ob sich das abgebildete Gerät eignen würde.

Technical data	
Lifting capacity	3,500 kg
Lifting height	1,780 mm
Working height	1,920 - 1,980 mm
Cylinder diameter	123 mm
Lifting / lowering time	app. 30 Sec.
Foundation depth	2,400 mm
Pump unit	3.0 kW
Ecological hydraulic fluid	12 l
Voltage	230/400 V - 50 Hz - 16 A

Electro-hydraulic single-ram lift, 3,5 t capacity, superstructure with arms

Steel cassette:
- ☐ Waterproof steel cassette (WHG)
- ☐ Self-carrying

Hydraulic unit:
- ☐ Hard-chrome plated cylinder
- ☐ Integrated anti-rotation device
- ☐ Corrosion-free guiding elements
- ☐ Hydraulic unit with immersed motor for fitting in floor
- ☐ Ecological hydraulic fluid
- ☐ Pneumatic emergency lowering
- ☐ Pushbutton control unit

Superstructure:
- ☐ Single telescopic arms
- ☐ Internal arm locking system
- ☐ Low minimum height

Standard colours
- ☐ Base plate: Grey RAL 7016
- ☐ Arms: Red RAL 3020

Source: Autopstenhoj

U Useful phrases

Describing your company	Unit 1
– We are a small family business / medium-sized company in the automotive sector. – The company is based in … – We manufacture components for the … industry. – We supply/produce machines for customers in the … sector. – Our products are used in … – We install/manufacture/export … – The company maintains / carries out …	– *Wir sind ein kleiner Familienbetrieb / ein mittelständisches Unternehmen in der Automobilbranche.* – *Das Unternehmen hat seinen Sitz in …* – *Wir fertigen Bauteile für die …-Industrie.* – *Wir liefern/produzieren Maschinen für Kunden in der …-Branche.* – *Unsere Produkte werden in … eingesetzt.* – *Wir installieren/fertigen/exportieren …* – *Das Unternehmen hält … instand / führt … aus.*

Making introductions	Unit 1
Greeting people you do not know – Good morning/afternoon/evening. I'm … – How do you do? My name is … – Nice/Pleased to meet you. – Nice to meet you, too. – Excuse me. Are you … ? – Yes, I am. / No, I'm not. I'm … – Welcome to … – Thank you. It's nice to be here. **Introducing people** – This is … . / These are my colleagues, John and Mary. – I'd like to introduce … from the … department.	– *Guten Morgen/Tag/Abend. Ich bin …* – *Freut mich. Mein Name ist …* – *Es freut mich, Sie kennenzulernen.* – *Ganz meinerseits.* – *Entschuldigung. Sind Sie … ?* – *Ja, das bin ich. / Nein, das bin ich nicht. Ich heiße …* – *Herzlich willkommen in/bei …* – *Dankeschön. Es ist schön, hier zu sein.* – *Das ist … / Das sind meine Kollegen, John und Mary.* – *Darf ich Ihnen … aus der …-Abteilung vorstellen?*

Showing visitors around the company	Unit 1
Giving a tour of the company – Let's start by visiting … – Here we have the … department. – On the left/right, you can see … – This is where we make/assemble … **Asking for and giving directions** – Could you tell me the way to …, please? – Yes, certainly. – Go down the corridor until you get to … – Turn left at the first/second/last door on your right. – Turn right at the end of the corridor. **Offering help/refreshments** – Can I take your coat? – Would you like something to drink? – Would you like some tea/coffee/water?	– *Lassen Sie uns mit dem Besuch der/des … beginnen.* – *Hier haben wir die Abteilung …* – *Zu Ihrer Linken/Rechten sehen Sie …* – *Hier stellen wir … her / bauen wir … zusammen.* – *Könnten Sie mir bitte sagen, wie ich nach / zu/r/m … komme?* – *Ja, selbstverständlich.* – *Gehen Sie den Flur entlang, bis Sie zu/r/m … kommen.* – *Nehmen Sie die erste/zweite/letzte Tür rechts.* – *Biegen Sie am Ende des Flures rechts ab.* – *Möchten Sie Ihren Mantel ablegen?* – *Darf ich Ihnen etwas zu trinken anbieten?* – *Möchten Sie Tee/Kaffee/Wasser?*

Describing your job	Unit 2
– I work in a workshop/factory. – I install/test/replace/inspect … – I maintain/repair machines. – I diagnose problems/faults. – I advise customers.	– *Ich arbeite in einer Werkstatt/Fabrik.* – *Ich installiere/teste/ersetze/kontrolliere …* – *Ich warte/repariere Maschinen.* – *Ich stelle Probleme/Fehler fest.* – *Ich berate Kunden/Kundinnen.*

– I follow technical drawings.	– *Ich halte mich an die technischen Zeichnungen.*
– I work fixed hours / a 39-hour week / shifts.	– *Ich habe feste Arbeitszeiten / eine 39-Stunden-Woche / arbeite Schicht.*
– I do a lot of overtime.	– *Ich mache viele Überstunden.*

Giving a presentation — Unit 2

Introduction

– My name is … and this is my partner, …	– *Mein Name ist … und das ist meine/e Partner/in, …*
– We are apprentices at … in Germany.	– *Wir sind Auszubildende bei … in Deutschland.*
– This morning, I'm / we're going to talk about …	– *Heute Morgen werde(n) ich / wir über … sprechen.*
– Our topic today is …	– *Das heutige Thema lautet …*

Structure

– I've divided my presentation into three main parts, as follows: …	– *Ich habe meine Präsentation in drei Hauptteile unterteilt, und zwar …*
– First/Firstly, … ; Second/Secondly, … ; After that / Then …	– *Erstens, … ; Zweitens, … ; Anschließend/dann …*

Signposts

– To begin with, …; Next, …; Now …	– *Zuerst, …; Als Nächstes, …; Jetzt …*
– The next topic I'm going to talk about is …	– *Das nächste Thema, das ich behandeln möchte, lautet …*
– Now I'd like to move on to …	– *Jetzt möchte ich zum Thema … übergehen.*

Handouts

– I've prepared a few things/handouts for you to take away.	– *Ich habe etwas/Handouts für Sie zum Mitnehmen vorbereitet.*
– I hope you'll find these copies of the graphics useful.	– *Ich hoffe, dass Sie diese Ausdrucke der Grafiken nützlich finden.*

Conclusion

– Before I finish my presentation, I'd just like to mention …	– *Bevor ich meinen Vortrag beende, möchte ich kurz … erwähnen.*
– I'd like to go over the main points again.	– *Ich möchte die Hauptpunkte nochmals kurz darlegen.*
– Finally / In conclusion / In summary, …	– *Zum Schluss / Abschließend / Zusammenfassend …*

Questions / Thanking the audience

– Are there any questions?	– *Gibt es / Haben Sie noch Fragen?*
– We have time for a few questions / one last question.	– *Wir haben noch Zeit für ein paar Fragen / eine letzte Frage.*
– Well, that's the end of my presentation.	– *Damit bin ich am Ende meiner Präsentation angelangt.*
– Thank you for your attention / for listening.	– *Vielen Dank für Ihre Aufmerksamkeit / fürs Zuhören.*

Telephoning — Unit 2

Identifying yourself

– Good morning. My name's …	– *Guten Morgen. Ich heiße …*
– Good afternoon. This is … from … (company).	– *Guten Tag. Hier spricht … von … (Firma).*
– Good evening. I work for …	– *Guten Abend. Ich arbeite bei …*

Explaining the reason for your call

– I'm enquiring about …	– *Ich wollte mich nach … erkundigen.*
– I'd like some information on …	– *Ich hätte gern nähere Informationen zu …*

Asking for a person/department

– I'd like to speak to Mr/Ms …	– *Ich hätte gern (mit) Herrn/Frau … gesprochen.*
– Could you put me through to the … department, please?	– *Könnten Sie mich bitte zur …-Abteilung durchstellen?*

Saying what you want to do
- Can I leave a message?
- I'll call again later.
- Could you ask Mr/Ms ... to call me back?

- *Kann ich eine Nachricht hinterlassen?*
- *Ich rufe später noch einmal an.*
- *Könnten Sie Herrn/Frau ... bitten, mich zurückzurufen?*

Ending the call
- Thank you for your help/assistance.
- You're welcome.
- Goodbye.
- Have a nice day/evening.

- *Vielen Dank für Ihre Hilfe/Unterstützung.*
- *Gern geschehen. / Bitte sehr.*
- *Auf Wiederhören.*
- *Einen schönen Tag/Abend noch.*

Taking telephone calls — Unit 2

- Who's calling, please?
- Could you spell your name, please?
- I'm sorry, I didn't understand. Could you repeat that, please?
- I'll put you through.
- I'm trying to connect you.
- Please hold the line.
- I'm afraid the line is engaged.
- I'm sorry, ... (name) is unavailable at the moment.
- Would you like to speak to someone else?
- Would you like to leave a message?

- *Wie ist Ihr Name bitte?*
- *Könnten Sie bitte Ihren Namen buchstabieren?*
- *Ich habe das nicht verstanden. Könnten Sie das bitte wiederholen?*
- *Ich stelle Sie durch.*
- *Ich versuche, Sie zu verbinden.*
- *Bleiben Sie bitte dran.*
- *Der Anschluss ist leider besetzt.*
- *Es tut mir leid, ... (Name) ist im Moment nicht da.*
- *Möchten Sie mit jemand anderem sprechen?*
- *Möchten Sie eine Nachricht hinterlassen?*

Writing emails — Unit 3

Salutation
- Dear Sir/Madam (*formal*)
- Dear Mr/Ms Smith (*formal*)
- Dear Paul (and Paula)
- Good morning, Paul (*less formal*)
- Hi/Hello Paula (*less formal*)

- *Sehr geehrte Damen und Herren,*
- *Sehr geehrter Herr / Sehr geehrte Frau Schmidt,*
- *Lieber Paul, (Liebe Paula,)*
- *Guten Morgen Paul,*
- *Hallo Paula,*

Complimentary close
- Yours faithfully (*formal*)
- Regards / Best regards / Best wishes / Yours sincerely (*formal*)
- Regards / Best regards / Best wishes
- All the best (*less formal*)

- *Mit freundlichen Grüßen*
- *Mit freundlichen Grüßen / Freundliche Grüße*
- *Schöne/Viele Grüße*
- *Alles Gute / Herzliche Grüße*

Opening sentence
- I'm just writing to ... (*formal*)
- Just a quick note/message to ... (*less formal*)

- *Ich schreibe Ihnen, um zu ...*
- *Nur eine kurze Mitteilung/Nachricht, um zu ...*

Conclusion
- I look forward to your reply / to hearing from you. (*formal*)
- Many thanks in advance. (*formal*)
- I hope to hear from you soon. (*less formal*)

- *Ich freue mich auf Ihre Antwort.*
- *Vielen Dank im Voraus.*
- *Ich freue mich, bald von Ihnen/Dir zu hören.*

Useful phrases

Describing size and dimensions — Unit 4

– How long is it?	– Wie lang ist es?
– It's 000 cm long. / The length is 000 cm.	– Es ist 000 cm lang. / Die Länge beträgt 000 cm.
– How wide is it?	– Wie breit ist es?
– It's 000 cm wide. / The width is 000 cm.	– Es ist 000 cm breit. / Die Breite beträgt 000 cm.
– How thick is it?	– Wie dick ist es?
– It's 000 cm thick. / The thickness is 000 cm.	– Es ist 000 cm dick. / Die Dicke beträgt 000 cm.
– How high is it?	– Wie hoch ist es?
– It's 000 cm high. / The height is 000 cm.	– Es ist 000 cm hoch. / Die Höhe beträgt 000 cm.
– How big is the television?	– Wie groß ist der Fernseher?
– It's 00 by 00 by 00.	– Die Maße sind 00 mal 00 mal 00.

Talking about health and safety — Unit 5

Describing safety measures

– Make sure that …	– Stellen Sie sicher, dass …
– Check that …	– Überprüfen Sie, ob …
– Disconnect …	– Lösen/Unterbrechen Sie die Verbindung … / Ziehen Sie den Stecker …
– Warn people that …	– Warnen Sie die Leute vor …
– Be careful not to …	– Achten Sie darauf, nicht zu …
– You mustn't …	– Sie dürfen nicht …

Explaining potential risks

– You could get an electric shock / be seriously injured.	– Sie könnten einen Stromschlag bekommen / sich schwer verletzen.
– You could electrocute / seriously injure …	– Sie könnten … durch einen Stromschlag töten / schwer verletzen.
– Death or serious injury may result from failure to …	– Das Unterlassen von … könnte den Tod oder schwere Verletzungen zur Folge haben.

Describing graphs — Unit 5

– The graph/chart shows/presents …	– Die Grafik / Das Diagramm zeigt … / stellt … dar.
– The horizontal/vertical axis has a scale from … to …	– Die waagerechte/senkrechte Achse hat eine Skala von … bis …
– The x axis / The y axis is divided into … units/sections each representing …	– Die X-Achse / Die Y-Achse ist unterteilt in … Einheiten/Abschnitte, die … darstellen.

Advising customers — Unit 6

Greeting

– Good morning/afternoon. How can I help you?	– Guten Morgen/Tag. Wie kann ich Ihnen helfen?

Showing the product

– This is our latest model.	– Das ist unser neuestes Modell.
– How about this one?	– Wie wäre es hiermit?
– This one has some interesting features.	– Dieses (Modell) hat interessante Funktionen.
– There's a five-year guarantee.	– Es gibt fünf Jahre Garantie.

Making suggestions

– I wouldn't recommend that one.	– Ich würde dieses dort nicht empfehlen.
– You could try this one instead.	– Sie könnten stattdessen dieses hier ausprobieren.
– It might be better to take this model.	– Vermutlich wäre es besser, dieses Modell zu nehmen.

Asking for advice	Unit 6
Explaining what you need	
– I'm looking for a(n) …	– Ich suche ein/e(n) …
– I need a(n) … for my …	– Ich brauche ein/e(n) … für mein/e(n) …
Asking about the product	
– How much does it weigh?	– Wie viel wiegt es?
– How many batteries will I need?	– Wie viele Batterien brauche ich?
Accepting/Rejecting suggestions	
– Yes, I think that's the right one for me.	– Ja, ich denke, dass dies das Richtige für mich ist.
– Good. I'll take it/them.	– Gut, ich nehme ihn/sie/es.
– Sorry, I don't think that's what I had in mind.	– Das ist leider nicht das, was ich mir vorgestellt habe.
– I'm afraid that's not really what I'm looking for.	– Ich fürchte, das ist nicht das, wonach ich suche.

Making arrangements	Unit 6
Inviting sb to a meeting	
– Ms Smith would like to invite you to a meeting on … (day) at … (time).	– Frau Smith möchte Sie zu einem Treffen am … (Tag) um … (Uhrzeit) Uhr einladen.
– I would like to invite you to lunch/dinner.	– Ich möchte Sie zum Essen/Abendessen einladen.
– The meeting will take place at my office / our premises in … (town/city).	– Das Treffen findet in meinem Büro / in unseren Räumlichkeiten in … (Ort/Stadt) statt.
Accepting/Declining the invitation	
– Thank you for your invitation to meet you at … (place).	– Vielen Dank für Ihre Einladung für das Treffen in … (Ort).
– I am pleased / We are delighted to accept your invitation/offer.	– Gern nehme(n) ich/wir Ihre Einladung / Ihr Angebot an.
– I'm sorry, but I'm … (reason) on that date / at that time.	– Es tut mir leid, aber ich kann an diesem Tag / zu dieser Zeit nicht, da … (Grund).
Making an alternative suggestion	
– How about meeting on … (day) at … (time) instead?	– Wie wäre es, wenn wir uns stattdessen am … (Tag) um … (Uhrzeit) treffen?
Conclusion	
– I look forward to your reply. (*formal*)	– Ich freue mich auf Ihre Antwort.
– I hope to hear from you soon. Many thanks.	– Ich hoffe, von Ihnen bald zu hören. Besten Dank.

Checking in and out at a hotel	Unit 8
Checking in	
– Good morning. My name is … . I have a reservation.	– Guten Morgen. Mein Name ist … . Ich habe reserviert.
– The reservation may be under the name of my company, …	– Die Reservierung kann unter dem Namen meiner Firma … sein.
– I would like to check in. I booked a room on the ground floor, with wheelchair access.	– Ich würde gerne einchecken. Ich habe ein barrierefreies Zimmer im Erdgeschoss gebucht.
– Where can I park my car?	– Wo kann ich mein Auto parken?
– What time is breakfast?	– Wann gibt es Frühstück?
Checking in	
– I'm going home today so I would like to check out.	– Ich reise heute ab und würde gerne auschecken.
– Could I have the bill, please?	– Könnte ich bitte die Rechnung bekommen?
– The bill is being paid by / should be sent to …	– Die Rechnung wird beglichen von … / sollte an … gesandt werden.

Useful phrases

Writing business letters	Unit 9
Salutation	
– Dear Sir or Madam (*to a firm*)	– *Sehr geehrte Damen und Herren,*
– Dear Mr Brown	– *Sehr geehrter Herr Brown,*
– Dear Sharon	– *Liebe Sharon,*
Complimentary close	
– Yours faithfully (*BE: to a firm*)	– *Mit freundlichen Grüßen*
– Yours very truly / Cordially yours (*AE: to a firm*)	– *Mit freundlichen Grüßen*
– Yours sincerely (*BE*)	– *Mit freundlichen Grüßen*
– Sincerely yours / Best personal regards (*AE*)	– *Mit freundlichen Grüßen / Beste Grüße*

Writing enquiries	Unit 9
Source of address	
– We saw your advertisement/brochure/catalogue in …	– *Wir haben Ihre/n Anzeige/Prospekt/Katalog in … gesehen.*
– We visited your stand/presentation at the trade fair in …	– *Wir haben Ihren Stand / Ihre Präsentation auf der Messe in … besucht.*
About your firm	
– We are a small/medium-sized company in the … sector.	– *Wir sind ein kleiner/mittelständischer Betrieb in der …-Branche.*
– We are interested in your … (products).	– *Wir interessieren uns für Ihre … (Produkte).*
What you require	
– Please send us samples of your … / your latest catalogue.	– *Bitte schicken Sie uns Muster/Proben Ihrer … / aus Ihrem aktuellen Katalog.*
– Please give us / let us have a quotation for … / details of all discounts.	– *Bitte schicken Sie uns / machen Sie uns ein Angebot für … / informieren Sie uns zu allen Einzelheiten Ihrer Rabatte.*
– Full details of your terms of delivery and payment would be appreciated.	– *Wir würden uns freuen, genaue Informationen zu Ihren Versand- und Zahlungsbedingungen zu erhalten.*
References	
– References can be obtained from … (name of bank/company).	– *Referenzen können von … (Name der Bank/Firma) angefordert werden.*
Polite ending	
– If your products find our customers' approval, …	– *Wenn Ihre Produkte unseren Kunden zusagen, …*
– … we will be able to place a sizeable order very soon.	– *… werden wir in naher Zukunft eine größere Bestellung in Auftrag geben.*
– We look forward to hearing from you soon / receiving your offer within the next few days.	– *Wir würden uns freuen, bald von Ihnen zu hören / Ihr Angebot in den nächsten Tagen zu erhalten.*

Writing offers	Unit 9, Unit 10
Reference to enquiry	
– Many thanks for your letter of … (date) enquiring about … (*general enquiry*)	– *Vielen Dank für Ihren Brief vom … (Datum) mit Ihrer Anfrage bzgl. …*
– We refer to your enquiry of … (date) for … (*specific enquiry*)	– *Wir beziehen uns auf Ihre Anfrage vom … (Datum) bzgl. …*
Reference to information, samples, etc.	
– Enclosed (please find) our latest brochure / catalogue / price list.	– *Anbei finden Sie unsere(n) aktuelle(n) Prospekt/Katalog/Preisliste.*
– We are sending you a selection of samples.	– *Wir übersenden Ihnen eine Auswahl an Mustern/Proben.*

Terms

- We would like to point out that our prices are quoted DAP / EXW / …
- We draw your attention to the fact that our guarantee/warranty period extends over … / is valid for …
- Terms of payment: we offer a …% cash discount for payment within … days.
- For orders over … we offer a discount of …%.

Further information

- Our delivery date is approximately … days/weeks after receipt of your order.
- Delivery time is about … weeks/months.
- We can guarantee immediate delivery.

Polite ending

- We look forward to receiving your order and assure you that we will give it our prompt and careful attention.

- *Wir möchten darauf hinweisen, dass sich unsere Preise DAP / EXW / … verstehen.*
- *Wir möchten Sie darauf hinweisen, dass unser Garantie-/Haftungszeitraum … beträgt.*
- *Zahlungsbedingungen: Bei Zahlung innerhalb von … Tagen gewähren wir … % Skonto.*
- *Für Bestellungen über … räumen wir einen (Mengen-) Rabatt von … % ein.*

- *Die Lieferung erfolgt etwa … Tage/Wochen nach Eingang Ihrer Bestellung.*
- *Der Lieferzeitraum beträgt etwa … Wochen/Monate.*
- *Wir können Ihnen eine sofortige Lieferung garantieren.*

- *Wir freuen uns auf Ihre Bestellung und sichern Ihnen eine zügige und gewissenhafte Abwicklung zu.*

Writing orders — Unit 10

- Thank you for your quotation of …
- Many thanks for your quotation.
- We agree to your terms and are pleased to give you an order for …
- We enclose / are enclosing order no. …
- We understand that all prices are DAP / EXW / … / include VAT.
- Payment will be made by … (method of payment) on delivery of the goods.
- Payment will be made within … days of receipt of the goods.
- Please acknowledge this order by return of post.
- We look forward to receiving the goods as soon as possible.
- We trust you will give this order your prompt/careful attention.

- *Vielen Dank für Ihr Angebot für …*
- *Vielen Dank für Ihr Angebot.*
- *Wir stimmen Ihren Bedingungen zu und freuen uns, Sie mit einer Bestellung über … zu beauftragen.*
- *Wir fügen Bestellnr. … bei.*
- *Wir sind uns bewusst, dass sich alle Preise DAP / EXW / … / inklusive Mehrwertsteuer verstehen.*
- *Die Zahlung erfolgt durch … (Zahlungsmethode) bei Lieferung der Ware(n).*
- *Die Zahlung erfolgt innerhalb von … Tagen nach Eingang der Ware(n).*
- *Bitte bestätigen Sie diese Bestellung postwendend.*
- *Wir würden uns freuen, die Ware(n) sobald wie möglich zu erhalten.*
- *Wir erwarten eine zügige/gewissenhafte Abwicklung dieser Bestellung.*

Making complaints — Unit 11

Situation

- With reference to our order number … which arrived / was due on … (date), …
- I'm sorry to have to inform you that …
- When we opened the containers/boxes, we discovered/saw that …
- … some/all of the items/parts were broken/damaged/missing.
- While testing the equipment, we saw that it was not working properly / it became apparent that it was not up to standard.

- *Mit Bezug auf unsere Bestellnummer …, die am … (Datum) eingetroffen ist / fällig war, …*
- *Leider müssen wir Ihnen mitteilen, dass …*
- *Beim Öffnen der Behälter/Container bemerkten/sahen wir, dass …*
- *… einige der / alle Artikel/Teile kaputt/beschädigt waren / fehlten.*
- *Beim Testen des Geräts / der Geräte stellten wir fest / stellte sich heraus, dass es/sie nicht funktionierte(n) / es/sie den Anforderungen nicht entsprach(en).*

Useful phrases

Request
- Please investigate the matter as soon as possible.
- Please let us know what can be done to solve this problem.
- Could you please explain (why) … ?

Reason
- We have a large order from a regular customer, which we have to fill quickly.
- We are unable to continue production until we have the equipment.
- If we do not receive the goods within the next … days, we will have to stop production.

Polite ending
- We hope to receive your answer / an explanation immediately / without delay / by … (date).
- We must point out that our further business relationship will depend on a satisfactory solution to the problem.

— *Bitte untersuchen Sie diese Angelegenheit so schnell wie möglich.*
— *Bitte teilen Sie uns mit, welche Maßnahmen getroffen werden können, um dieses Problem zu beheben.*
— *Könnten Sie bitte erklären (warum) … ?*

— *Wir haben eine große Bestellung eines Stammkunden, die wir schnell ausführen müssen.*
— *Wir können mit der Produktion nicht fortfahren, solange die Geräte nicht da sind.*
— *Wenn wir die Ware nicht innerhalb der nächsten … Tage erhalten, müssen wir die Produktion einstellen.*

— *Wir hoffen auf Ihre sofortige Antwort/Erklärung / bis zum … (Datum).*
— *Wir müssen darauf hinweisen, dass unsere weitere Zusammenarbeit von einer zufriedenstellenden Lösung des Problems abhängt.*

Dealing with complaints — Unit 11

Polite opening
- We are very sorry (to hear) that the goods arrived damaged/broken/late.
- We are very sorry (to learn) that you have received faulty/damaged / the wrong goods.
- Please accept our sincere apologies.
- We apologize for the inconvenience caused.

Reason
- Unfortunately, there was a mix-up in our sales department.
- We are sorry to say that one of our staff was ill and could not complete the order.
- The damage was caused by bad handling in transit / a problem with the packing.
- We have had some problems with new software but these have now been solved.

Action taken
- We have sent a replacement consignment by courier / by express delivery which you will receive by … at the latest.

Polite ending
- We hope that we can continue our successful business relationship, despite this problem.
- We assure you that we will make every effort to ensure there are no problems in the future.
- We hope that this solution solves the problem to your satisfaction.
- Don't hesitate to contact us again if you have any further difficulties.

— *Wir bedauern sehr, dass die Ware bei Ihnen beschädigt/kaputt/verspätet eingetroffen ist.*
— *Es tut uns sehr leid, dass Sie mangelhafte/ schadhafte / die falsche Ware erhalten haben.*
— *Wir bitten vielmals um Entschuldigung.*
— *Wir entschuldigen uns vielmals für die entstandenen Unannehmlichkeiten.*

— *Leider ist es in unserer Vertriebsabteilung zu einer Verwechslung gekommen.*
— *Leider war einer unserer Mitarbeiter krank und konnte daher die Bestellung nicht bearbeiten.*
— *Der Schaden ist durch mangelhafte Abfertigung während des Transports / ein Problem bei der Verpackung entstanden.*
— *Wir hatten einige Probleme mit der neuen Software, aber diese konnten behoben werden.*

— *Wir haben Ihnen per Kurierdienst/Expressversand eine Ersatzlieferung geschickt, die Sie spätestens bis … erhalten werden.*

— *Wir hoffen sehr, dass wir trotz dieses Problems unsere erfolgreiche Zusammenarbeit fortsetzen können.*
— *Wir versichern Ihnen, dass wir alles tun werden, um derartige Probleme in Zukunft zu vermeiden.*
— *Wir hoffen, dass diese Lösung das Problem zu Ihrer Zufriedenheit behebt.*
— *Bitte kontaktieren Sie uns, sollten Sie weitere Schwierigkeiten haben.*

Writing a covering letter — Unit 12

Opening phrases
- With reference to your advertisement in … (newspaper) of … (date), …
- I would like / wish to apply for the above-mentioned position/post of … (job).

- Bezugnehmend auf Ihre Ausschreibung in … (Zeitung) vom … (Datum), …
- Hiermit möchte ich mich für die oben genannte Stelle als … (Berufsbezeichnung) bewerben.

Education/Training / Present employment
- I attended … (school/college) for … (length of time).
- I studied … (subjects) at vocational school in … (town/city) from … (date) to … (date).
- At present I am working for a(n) … (type of company) as a(n) … (job).
- I will complete my period of training on … (date).

- Von … bis … (Jahr) besuchte ich (Schule/Hochschule).
- An der Berufs(fach)schule in … (Ort) lernte/belegte ich … (Fächer) von … (Datum) bis … (Datum).
- Zurzeit arbeite ich für eine / bei einer … (Firmenbezeichnung) als … (Berufsbezeichnung).
- Am … (Datum) werde ich meine Ausbildung abschließen.

Closing paragraph
- I enclose / Enclosed is my CV/résumé / a list of my qualifications and experience.
- I am available for interview at your earliest convenience.
- I hope you will consider my application favourably and …
- … (I) look forward to hearing from you in the near future.

- Anbei finden Sie meinen Lebenslauf / eine Übersicht meiner Qualifikationen und Erfahrungen.
- Für ein Vorstellungsgespräch stehe ich Ihnen jederzeit gern zur Verfügung.
- Über eine positive Antwort freue ich mich sehr und …
- … (ich) freue mich darauf, von Ihnen bald zu hören.

G Grammar

Simple present

1. I **work** for an engineering company. I **maintain** and **repair** machines.
2. The company **produces** components for the automobile industry.
3. The new milling machine **doesn't work** when you switch on the power.

 - Das *simple present* wird für wiederholte, oft regelmäßige Handlungen in der Gegenwart verwendet.
 - Signalwörter: *regularly, sometimes, often, always, normally* usw.
 - Manche Verben, die keine Handlung, sondern einen Zustand ausdrücken (*need, like, want, hate, love, know, believe*), stehen (fast) ausschließlich im *simple present*.
 - In der 3. Person (*he, she, it, Peter, the firm* usw.) wird ein *-s* angefügt (2).
 - Verneinungen werden mit *doesn't/don't* gebildet (3).

Present progressive

1. One of our customers **is** currently **having** a problem with a waterjet cutting machine.
2. The project managers **are looking** at the plans on their laptop.

 - Das *present progressive* wird gebraucht, wenn man gerade ablaufende oder noch nicht abgeschlossene Handlungen beschreibt.
 - Signalwörter: *at the moment, (right) now, just, currently* usw.

Questions and short answers

1. **Do** you **use** vernier callipers often? – Yes, I **do**. / No, I **don't**.
2. **Did** you **make** the hole punch yourself? – Yes, I **did**. / No, I **didn't**.
3. **Can** you **carry** it in your pocket? – Yes, you **can**. / No, you **can't**.
4. **Is** it small? – Yes, it **is**. / No, it **isn't**.
5. **When/Why/How did** you **change** the fuse?

 - Fragen im *simple present* werden mit *do/does* gebildet (1).
 - Fragen im *simple past* werden mit *did* gebildet (2, 5).
 - In Sätzen mit Hilfsverben (*is/have/can/will/should/…*) bildet man Fragen, indem man das Hilfsverb des Aussagesatzes vor das Subjekt stellt (3, 4).
 - Kurzantworten bestehen aus *yes/no* + Personalpronomen + Hilfsverb (+ *n't*) (1–4).
 - Fragewörter stehen immer am Anfang des Fragesatzes (5).

Imperatives

1. **Do not / Don't block** emergency exits.
2. **Keep** emergency stop buttons free.
3. **Switch off** machinery before you remove the safety cover.
4. **Never touch** a live power cable.

 - Man verwendet den Imperativ für Hinweise, Befehle, Warnungen und Erklärungen.
 - Der Imperativ ist die Grundform (= Infinitiv) des Verbs. Man verwendet die gleiche Form, wenn man zu einer oder mehreren Personen spricht (2, 3).
 - Negativformen werden mit *do not* bzw. *don't* gebildet (1).
 - Bei Negativformen mit *never* entfällt *don't* (4).

Simple past

1. I **talked** to my supervisor about the job last week.
2. Yesterday I **made** a workpiece on a milling machine.
3. I **didn't finish** it until late in the afternoon.
4. What time **did** you **start** work?
5. My first day at work **was** a disaster.

- Das *simple past* verwendet man, um zu sagen, wann etwas geschehen ist (1, 2, 3), oder um über Vergangenes zu berichten.
- Signalwörter: *yesterday, last week, two days ago, in 1998, When …?* usw.
- Bei den regelmäßigen Verben wird im *simple past* in allen Personen *-(e)d* angehängt.
- Verneinungen und Fragen werden in allen Personen mit *did/didn't* gebildet.
- Eine Liste der unregelmäßigen Verben befindet sich auf S. 223.

Past progressive

1. I **was working** in a factory last week.
2. I **was standing** on a ladder when a colleague **bumped** into it and I **fell** off.

- Mit dem *past progressive* drückt man aus, dass eine Handlung oder ein Vorgang zu einer bestimmten Zeit in der Vergangenheit gerade im Verlauf war (1).
- Es beschreibt oft eine Handlung, die gerade im Verlauf war, als eine zweite Handlung einsetzte. Die zweite Handlung steht im *simple past* (2).

Present perfect

1. He **has worked** here for six months.
2. They **haven't found** the cause of the problem yet.
3. I**'ve talked** to her twice today.
4. **Have** you **been able to** repair the motor?

- Mit dem *present perfect* sagt man, dass (nicht: wann!) etwas geschehen ist. Man drückt damit auch aus, seit wann oder wie lange ein Zustand schon andauert.
- Signalwörter (Zeitadverbien): *for two years, this week, since 2017, already, yet* usw. Sie benennen einen Zeitraum, auf den sich der Satz bezieht und der bis in die Gegenwart reicht.

Future with *will* and *going to*

1. I think the installation **will take** about two days.
2. I**'ll (will) order** the spare parts this afternoon.
3. We **won't (will not) need** the spare parts until next week.
4. We**'re going to replace** the toolholder tomorrow.
5. This old motor **is going to break down** soon.

- *Will* wird verwendet, um Vorhersagen zu machen oder Vermutungen über die Zukunft auszudrücken (1).
- *Will* wird für spontane Entscheidungen, Angebote und Versprechen verwendet (2).
- Im gesprochenen Englisch lautet die Verneinung *won't*, ansonsten *will not* (3).
- *Be going to* (+ Infinitiv des Verbs) wird verwendet, um über Pläne oder Absichten zu sprechen (4), oder wenn die Gewissheit (oder ein Anzeichen dafür) besteht, dass etwas geschehen wird (5).

Passive forms

1. The machine **is bolted** to the floor.
2. The resin recycler **was installed** on Tuesday morning.
3. The cables **have** already **been laid**.
4. The distribution board **could be bought** from a local supplier.
5. The control unit **will be installed by** us as part of our service.

- Das Passiv wird oft verwendet, wenn man auf eher unpersönliche Art und Weise über Fakten, Vorgänge und Zahlen berichtet.
- Das Passiv wird mit der entsprechenden Form von *be* + Partizip Perfekt (3. Verbform) gebildet. Es können alle Zeiten gebildet werden.
- Passivsätze mit modalen Hilfsverben werden mit einem modalen Hilfsverb + *be* + Partizip Perfekt (3. Verbform) gebildet (4).
- „Von" und „durch" werden in Passivsätzen durch *by* ausgedrückt (5).

Conditional sentences

1. Type 0: If it **trips** the switch, it **turns on** the alarm.
2. Type 1: If you **touch** the overhead power cable, you **will get** an electric shock.

- Bedingungen, die allgemeingültig sind bzw. die immer eintreffen, werden mit einem *if*-Satz des Typs 0 ausgedrückt. Hier sind beide Satzteile im *simple present*.
- Ein *if*-Satz des Typs 1 drückt eine Bedingung aus, die der Sprecher für durchaus möglich oder wahrscheinlich hält. Der damit verbundene Hauptsatz drückt eine Vorhersage aus, die je nach Situation als Warnung, Versprechen o. ä. zu verstehen ist (2).
- Steht der *if*-Nebensatz an erster Stelle, wird er durch ein Komma vom Hauptsatz abgetrennt (1, 2).

Verb + *to*-infinitive or *-ing* form

1. I enjoy **working** in a team.
2. I expect **to qualify** as a CAD technician in June.
3. I love **repairing / to repair** old cars.
4. I'd love **to have** the chance to work on that vintage Mercedes.
5. I'm interested in **getting** some work experience abroad.

- Auf eine Gruppe von Verben folgt immer die *-ing*-Form (1). Zu diesen Verben gehören *dislike, enjoy, finish, give up, imagine, involve, keep, mind, miss, practise, risk, stop, suggest*.
- Auf eine zweite Gruppe von Verben folgt immer ein *to*-Infinitiv (2). Zu diesen Verben gehören *agree, arrange, choose, decide, expect, hope, learn, offer, plan, promise, want*.
- Auf eine dritte Gruppe von Verben kann sowohl die *-ing*-Form als auch ein *to*-Infinitiv folgen (3). Zu diesen Verben gehören *begin, continue, hate, like, love, prefer, start*.
- Nach *would hate, would like, would love* and *would prefer* (Kurzform *'d like* usw.) steht nur der *to*-Infinitiv. (4)
- Nach einer Präposition kommt immer die *-ing*-Form (5).

Relative clauses

1 Trading standards are doorways **which/that enable goods to enter other countries**.
2 The ISO is the body **which/that creates international standards**.
3 The workpiece **(that) they made** was deformed.
4 Manufacturers are the ones **who have to follow these regulations**.
5 The IEC, **which was created in 1906**, has harmonized the rules worldwide.

- Relativpronomen leiten Relativsätze ein.
- Es gibt den notwendigen und den nicht notwendigen Relativsatz. Notwendige Relativsätze sind für das Verständnis des Satzes unbedingt erforderlich (1, 2, 3, 4) und stehen ohne Komma. Nicht notwendige Relativsätze geben lediglich Zusatzinformationen und werden durch Kommata getrennt (5).
- In notwendigen Relativsätzen kann das Relativpronomen wegfallen, wenn es Objekt ist, d. h. wenn im Relativsatz ein Subjekt steht (3).

Adjectives and adverbs

1 Repairing the turning machine is an **easy** job.
2 We need it to be fixed **quickly**.
3 It's **really** hard to get the settings right.
4 Can it be fixed **easily**?
5 I don't speak German very **well**.

- Man verwendet Adjektive, um Personen oder Sachen näher zu beschreiben (1).
- Adverbien beziehen sich auf Verben (2, 4, 5) oder Adjektive (3).
- Adverbien haben in der Regel eine andere Form als Adjektive. Man fügt normalerweise die Endung *-ly* an das Adjektiv an (2, 3). Endet das Adjektiv auf *-y*, wird die Endung zu *-ily* (4).
- Das Adverb von *good* lautet *well* (5).

Comparatives and superlatives

1 The new model is **harder/easier** to use.
2 It's **more expensive than** the other machines.
3 It's the **simplest** and **cheapest** machine, but not the **best**.
4 It's the **most flexible** solution.
5 You spend **less** money on software.
6 It is**n't as easy** to manage **as** the other machines.

- Adjektive steigert man mit *-er/-est* oder *more/most* (1, 4).
- Unregelmäßig sind: *good – better – best, bad – worse – worst, little* (wenig) *– less – least, far – farther/further – farthest/furthest* (3, 5).
- Vergleiche bildet man mit *than* und *(not) as ... as* (2, 6).

Much, many, a lot (of)

1 How **much** time do you spend answering emails?
2 How **many** text messages do you get at work every day?
3 I get **a lot of** text messages. **Lots of** them are instructions from my supervisor.
4 We have **too many** meetings at work. We waste **too much** time on them.

- *Much* verwendet man nur bei nicht-zählbaren Nomen, z.B. *time*. (1)
- *Many* verwendet man nur bei Nomen im Plural. (2)
- *Much* und *many* werden meist in verneinten Aussagesätzen und in Fragen verwendet. In bejahten Aussagesätzen ist *a lot of* bzw. *lots of* gebräuchlicher. (3)
- Nach *too, so, as, very* und *how* werden immer *much* und *many* verwendet. (4)

Modals and their substitutes

1 Currents of 1–4 amps **can** cause nerve damage.
2 A shock of this strength **could** even cause cardiac arrest.
3 This machine **must** be turned on manually.
4 You **will be able to** make the workpiece with the turning machine.
5 We **won't be allowed to** install the new machine on our own.
6 We **should** compare the costs of both machines.
7 The cutting tools were broken and **had to** be replaced.
8 You **mustn't** switch this machine back on again.
9 I **would** like a job as a CAD technician.

- Modale Hilfsverben wie *can, could, may, would* usw. drücken eine Fähigkeit, eine Erlaubnis, eine Empfehlung, ein Verbot oder einen Wunsch aus.
- Modale Hilfsverben haben in allen Personen die gleiche Form; bei der Verneinung gibt es zusammengezogene Kurzformen.
- Modale Hilfsverben stehen normalerweise in der Gegenwartsform, manche auch in der Vergangenheit. Ersatzverben (*substitutes*) werden benutzt, um alle übrigen Zeiten zu bilden.

Hilfsverb	Ersatzverb
can	*be able to*
could	
may	*be allowed to*
might	
must	*have to*
need not	*don't have to*
shall	
should/ought to	
must not	*not be allowed to*

Transcripts

Track 2: Unit 1, Foundation, exercise 2

1. OK. I'll start. The company I work for is called BCC Electronics. We manufacture electronic equipment. The head office is in London. It's a medium-sized company.
2. I'm a trainee at International Solutions. It's an IT company. The head office is in Berlin. It's a start-up.
3. I'm an apprentice at Nilsson Construction. It's a Swedish building company. The head office is in Stockholm, in Sweden. You've probably heard of it. It's a big multinational.
4. I work for a company called Han Gao. It's a metal dealer. The Head office is in Hong Kong. It's a global company.
5. Right. I'm doing an apprenticeship at Jahn Services. We're in the automotive sector. The head office is in Minden. It's a large company.
6. The name of my company is Aikon. We manufacture medical equipment. The head office is in Stuttgart. It's a small firm.

Track 3: Unit 1, Part A, exercise 2B

Martin Foster   Ah. Good. You're all here. Good morning. I'm Martin Foster. I'll be your supervisor while you're here. Welcome to Newcastle.
Apprentice 2   Thank you, Mr Foster. Nice to meet you.
Apprentice 1   Good morning.
Martin Foster   Nice to meet you, too. Well, we have a lot to cover this morning, so let's get started. Erm. Before we go onto the factory floor, the first doors here, on the right, are the offices. The head of the company and his secretary are in the first rooms on the right and, next door to their offices is the Finance department. The Finance department is also next to Marketing.
Apprentice 2   Secretary's office … head of company … finance … marketing …
Apprentice 1   So, all of the offices are in this corridor?
Martin Foster   Not all of them. There are more offices on the first floor. We'll be going up the stairs to the first floor after we've had a look around down here. Now, the next area is Dispatch, where all the finished products leave Mech-On.
Apprentice 2   Dispatch. That's a pretty big area.
Martin Foster   Well, yes. We produce a lot of goods at Mech-On. If you look over here, where the factory opens out, you'll see where all that production happens.
Apprentice 1   Wow! It's big.
Martin Foster   Yes, I know. Oh. By the way, before we go onto the factory floor, these are the toilets and the locker rooms. I'll give you the keys for your lockers later … Right then, let's just start here and go round the factory floor. This is the stores for materials and tools and next to it is the waterjet cutting area. It's usually loud and it spills a lot of water around.
Apprentice 1   I know about waterjet cutting. It really is loud. What goes on next door?
Martin Foster   The room next door to the waterjet cutting is the measuring room.
Apprentice 1   OK. Stores, waterjet cutting, measuring room. I think I've got it! And there are two CNC milling machines in the middle of the factory floor.
Martin Foster   That's correct. This one here is a standard 4-axis and the one behind it is a 5-axis ultrasonic milling machine. The ultrasonic milling machine is new. OK. Let's go on round the factory floor. Here's where the milling and drilling get done.
Apprentice 2   You've only got one drilling machine?
Martin Foster   Yes, because most of our drilling work is done on the CNC-centres. Good. Well, we're almost finished. Here, at the end of this section, we have controlled turning machines, there are the workbenches for mounting. Finally, over there, we have the grinding machines.
Apprentice 1   The grinding machines are on the left when you come into the factory …
Apprentice 2   … And the toilets and the locker rooms are on the right.
Martin Foster   That's correct. Very good. So, as you see, we've done a complete round of the factory floor and we're back in the corridor leading to reception. We're now going to go up to my office on the first floor where we'll go on with the rest of your introduction to Mech-On.

Track 4: Unit 1, Part B, exercise 1B

Right, then. I'd like to go on with my introduction to the Newcastle branch of Mech-On by looking at the organization chart of the company. Please look at the screen while I talk you through the different departments. As you can see, there are five departments. All of these departments are under the Head of Division, David Stevens. Mr Stevens supervises all the processes here. As the Head of Mech-On UK, he's in charge of all of the five departments you see listed below his name.

Now, the first department you can see on the left is Sales and Purchasing. This department is run by two colleagues, Emma Smith and Hazel Jones. They sell all our products, and they buy materials, tools and so on.

The second department is Construction. Trevor Spencer and Susan Morley are in charge of that department. They're both CAD engineers.

Now we come to Production. That's where you'll be working while you're here. You know me, I'm the Supervisor, and Tanja Thomson is the Line Manager. Tanja is in charge of two skilled workers, Joan Tennant and Steven Blake, and she's also in charge of you. Please remember that. The Line Manager is the person in charge of the skilled workers and the apprentices.

Fitting is next. Eric Gilderdale is the Foreman in the Fitting department. As you see, he is in charge of the Fitters and Turners, James Mason and Mary Brown, as well as several other apprentices. Last but not least, we come to Quality Control. Now, Quality Control is a very important part of our business. We have to keep up our good reputation for manufacturing the best products. Malcolm Bradbury is the Quality Control Manager and he's in charge of three Test Technicians, Robert Shipley, Martha Hine and Jane Lucas. These three technicians do a really important job and …

Track 5: Unit 1, Communication, exercise 1A

Martyna   Hello. I'm Martyna Nowak. I'm 42. I was born in Poland. I'm a line manager.
Halil   Good morning. My name is Halil Özdemir. I'm 29 years old. I was born in Germany. I'm a training supervisor.
Deema   Good afternoon. My name is Deema Mansour. I'm 19. I was born in Syria. I'm an apprentice.

Robert	Hallo. I'm Robert Klein. I'm 21. I was born in Austria. I'm a skilled worker.
Canan	Hallo. I'm Canan Tolon. I'm 25 years old. I was born in Turkey. I'm a CAD engineer.
Alexei	Good morning. My name is Alexei Melnyk. I'm 39 years old. I was born in Ukraine. I'm an electrical engineer.

Track 6: Unit 2, Foundation, exercise 1A

Welding, panel beating, paint spraying – these are just three of the jobs you might be doing in the workshop. We all enjoy being there, but there could be some dangers attached to the work. Not using eye protection when welding could result in "arc eye" or you could have problems with your breathing. Not wearing ear protection when panel beating could result in permanent or temporary deafness. Safety in the workshop is very important.

Now, the first thing I want to talk about is what you wear in the workshop. I'm talking about protective clothing – hard hats or overalls, for example. Now, I know that safety shoes might not look very cool, but you're given them for a reason – to keep you safe. Wear them!

Now, here are a few problems that might lead to accidents in your workshop. Sometimes, messiness can lead to minor accidents. I don't know how many times I've walked into a workshop and seen dirt and rubbish on the floor. Have a good look around your workshop and clean it up. Make sure everything is in the right place. Another thing which is very dangerous – and I've seen this a few times, too – is when emergency cut out switches are covered or hidden by piles of boxes. If there's an emergency in the workshop, you need to be able to switch everything off quickly, so, the safety rule for emergency switches is: Keep them free!

Top-heavy shelving, now that's another dangerous thing. When you fill a shelf, put the heavy stuff at the bottom and light stuff at the top. It's a matter of common sense, really.

One of the biggest dangers I see is poor ventilation. Don't block the ventilators and open the windows, even in winter.

Now, as far as machinery or equipment is concerned, not using guards or screens or using damaged guards or screens or the wrong guards or screens can also cause trouble. And please, please, please, use the right tool for the job. Do not use a wrench as a hammer.

As I say, these are just a few of the problems. I'd like you now to work in groups and brainstorm a list of other things that might make your workshop a dangerous place.

Track 7: Unit 2, Communication, exercise 4

Julie	HUM Machines Ltd. Julie Matthews speaking.
Liam	Can I speak to Martin Brown in the workshop, please?
Julie	Who's calling please?
Liam	This is Liam Donnelly.
Julie	I'm sorry, could you spell your name, please?
Liam	It's L I A M D O double-N E double-L Y. I'm calling from Machine Tools in Manchester. It's about the drills Mr Brown ordered.
Julie	Thank you, Mr Donnelly. I'll try Mr Brown for you. Please hold the line.
Liam	Thank you.
Julie	Mr Donnelly. I'm sorry, Mr Brown is unavailable at the moment. Would you like to speak to someone else?
Liam	Yes. All right. Anyone in the workshop will do.
Julie	Thank you. I'll put you through.
	…
Julie	I'm sorry, Mr Donnelly. I'm afraid the line is engaged. Would you like to leave a message for Mr Brown?
Liam	Yes, please. Would you tell Mr Brown that the drills he ordered aren't available and ask him to call me to discuss an alternative. My telephone number is 161 839 5005 and the extension is 822.
Julie	I'm sorry. I didn't understand. Could you repeat that, please?
Liam	Sure. It's 161 839 5005, extension 822.
Julie	Thank you, Mr Donnelly. I'll make sure that Mr Brown gets the message.

Track 8: KMK Exam practice 1: exercise 1, Hörverstehen

A very good morning, ladies and gentlemen. Welcome to our manufacturing facility here in Gloucester. I hope you had a pleasant journey. I also hope you will benefit from your internship during the next few weeks.

Unfortunately Mr Brady, our Managing Director, can't be with us today as he and the head of Sales and Purchasing, Ms Lawrence, are having an important meeting in Birmingham right now. My name is Fred McKenzie. I am in charge of the Personnel department. Before showing you our plant, let me begin with a short introduction to our company.

We are proud to be able to offer our customers flexibility and quality. Providing the best possible quality means producing powerchairs and scooters for the disabled without any defects throughout all stages of production.

In our company each individual employee is responsible for eliminating defects where they arise or where they are discovered immediately. Each of you is one of the team now. If you have an idea where and how to improve our production, feel free to talk to your head of department!

Let me now turn to your schedule for the next couple of weeks. One of the highlights this week will be our celebration on Friday. It's the 25th anniversary of our production of the best-selling powerchair throughout Europe. Besides, we will also celebrate our 250,000th mobility scooter for the disabled this month. Mr Bird, our head of production will tell you more about it later on. He is responsible for the assembly lines, your first place of work in this company.

During the following week you will have a look into the Research and Development department, led by Walter Bright. Your final stage will be the Quality Assurance department.

I am sure you will get on with all our colleagues easily. If there are any problems, contact Barbara Collins. She is a member of the works council and responsible for our trainees. Now – let's start our tour. Please follow me …

Track 9: Unit 3, Foundation, exercise 1A

a   I enjoy working with my vernier callipers. They're used for measuring thicknesses, inside diameters, outside diameters and depth. It's the best measuring tool ever. It's much more accurate than a normal ruler. That can only measure down to 1 millimetre, or maybe 0.5 millimetres if you have a good one. Good vernier callipers can measure within 0.1 millimetres. The second tool I like is my inspection mirror. I use it when I'm working on machines to check for screws and things that might have become loose during vibration testing. This is the most useful tool a mechatronics technician like me can have.

b   I spend a lot of time on the factory floor, checking and repairing machinery and devices. If something's not working properly, I have to diagnose the problem – find out what's wrong – then I have to fix it. In this case, I use a multimeter that measures voltage, current and resistance or one that can measure the capacitance, inductance and current gain of transistors. That one's a very advanced, high-tech tool. At the other end of the scale, I often have to use a soldering iron which is a very simple tool. My father taught me how to use a soldering iron when I was a kid. He was a machine builder, too.

c   I like working with the centre punch I made myself. Basically, you use a centre punch to mark the centre of a hole when drilling holes. A drill can wander if it doesn't start in a hole so you use the punch to form a dent to guide the tip of the drill. You place the tip on the point where you want the hole, then hit it hard with a hammer. An automatic centre punch operates without the need for a hammer, but I really prefer the one I made. It's just a metal rod with a shaped tip on the end that has been hardened. I always use it when I need to drill holes in metal sheets.

Track 12: Unit 3, Communication, exercise 1B

Supervisor	I'll just give you my email address. It's t m dot martin at technical underscore tools dot de.
Mary-Anne	Sorry, could you repeat that, please?
Supervisor	No problem. t m dot martin at technical underscore tools dot de. You can reach me directly with that address.
Mary-Anne	Thank you. Well, my email address is mary hyphen anne hyphen brown at five plus five services dot net. The fives are written as numbers. Oh, and my first name, Mary-Anne – Anne is written with an e.
Supervisor	OK. I'll just read that back to you. Mary hyphen anne hyphen brown at five plus five services dot net. Mary-Anne with a hyphen, the fives written as numbers and Mary-Anne written with an e at the end of Anne.
Mary-Anne	Yes. That's correct.

Track 13: Unit 4, Part B, exercise 1

Börne	Wilsberg Metall. Börne am Apparat. Wie kann ich Ihnen helfen?
Supervisor	Good morning, Mr Börne. Julia Saunders here.
Börne	Good morning, Ms Saunders.
Supervisor	I got your message about the workpiece. I'm sorry, I don't understand why some information is missing, but maybe we can sort it out now on the phone.
Börne	Thanks. That would be great. Maybe you could just talk me through the whole thing.
Supervisor	Fine. OK … It's an almost square plate with a side length of 120 mm.
Börne	OK, square, 120 mm. I've got that.
Supervisor	On the left side on the top there's a chamfer of 10 by 10 mm.
Börne	Yes, got it. OK.
Supervisor	On the top at the right there's a convex semicircle with a radius of 20 mm …
Börne	Aha …
Supervisor	… followed by a concave semicircle of another 20 mm.
Börne	OK. Top right, a convex semicircle with a radius of 20 mm, followed by a concave semicircle of another 20 mm.
Supervisor	That's right. So, now, on the base line, there's a groove that's 15 mm deep topped by a semicircle with a radius of 15 mm.
Börne	Where is that on the base line?
Supervisor	Sorry. It's exactly in the middle.
Börne	Ah, OK.
Supervisor	Now, there are 4 boreholes with a diameter of 6 mm. Number 1 is 30 mm from the bottom line and 25 mm from the left side.
Börne	Does it have a thread?
Supervisor	No, just a bore. The next one is 85 mm from the bottom and 15 mm from the left.
Börne	OK.
Supervisor	Then 60 mm from the bottom and 60 mm from the left and 85 mm from the bottom and 60 mm from the left.
Börne	Got it. Anything else?
Supervisor	The last feature is a 24 mm hole at 60 mm from the bottom and 25 mm from the left. And that's all.
Börne	OK. That's clear now. What material do you want it in?

Track 14: Unit 5, Foundation, exercise 1A

1   is approximately equal to
2   degree
3   divided by
4   is equal to / equals
5   is greater than
6   is less than
7   minus
8   multiplied by / times
9   per cent
10 squared
11 plus or minus
12 is not equal to

Track 15: Unit 5, Part A, exercise 2B

Fitter	OK, before we start the turning machine for the first time, we have to pay special attention to all the relevant sections of this operating manual here.
Apprentice	You mean things like cleaning the machine and so on?
Fitter	That's right. Cleaning the machine, the electrical connection of the machine to the line, and all the instructions for lubrication.
Apprentice	OK. What does it say about the electricity supply?
Fitter	It says you have to connect the electric system of the machine to line voltage by turning the main switch on the control cabinet.
Apprentice	What's the line voltage?
Fitter	It's 3-phase current, 400 volts.
Apprentice	My boss told me that we ordered a few extras for the machine. Are they already all connected in the machine?
Fitter	Yes. All our turning machines are delivered with the electric drives already connected. So, this means the motors, as well as all switching devices required for operating the machine, have been installed and wired.

Apprentice	That's good. I see that there's a seal over this screw. Does that mean that I'm not allowed to open the machine?
Fitter	That's right. You're not allowed to modify or disassemble the machine yourself. You must contact someone from our service staff if there is a problem. According to the warranty regulations, only one of our trained staff is allowed to disassemble the machine.
Apprentice	OK. I understand. I'm not allowed to take the machine apart.
Fitter	Good. So, the last thing we need to do is to measure the sound level. It's measured during no-load running without chip removal, and with the movable hood closed.
Apprentice	And what's the maximum sound level?
Fitter	It's 80 decibels.
Apprentice	Oh. OK. Will we do a test run after that?
Fitter	Yes. I'll do a test run with you this afternoon. There shouldn't be any problems, so we'll be finished by three o'clock.
Apprentice	Great. I'll be able to start working with the machine first thing tomorrow morning.
Fitter	That's right … OK, so let's check the sound level. What do we have to do first … ?

Track 16: Unit 5, Communication, exercise 2A

I'd like to move on now to this table. As you can see, this company's sales in the UK were at 10.3 million euros in the first quarter of the financial year and, in the second quarter, sales rose rapidly to 11.4 million euros. However, when we look at the third quarter, we can see that sales dropped drastically to 8.2 million euros. By the end of the year, things had recovered and sales rose to 10.3 million euros, reaching the same volume of sales as in the first quarter.
Now, you can see at a glance that sales figures for Germany over the same period were much lower. We start off with …

Track 17: Unit 6, Foundation, exercise 1

Supervisor	Guten Morgen. Kann ich Ihnen helfen?
Customer	Erm. Sorry. Do you speak English?
Supervisor	Yes, of course. How can I help you?
Customer	Well, I'm interested in buying some pulse monitors. The kind you can hold in your hand.
Supervisor	Hand pulse monitors. Yes, we produce quite a few models. Most of them measure blood pressure and pulse.
Customer	Blood pressure and pulse? Oh, that's useful.
Supervisor	Can you give me some information so I can show you the most suitable model? For example, who will be using the equipment?
Customer	I'm in charge of a team of pool attendants at a swimming pool complex and I'd like to buy them for my team.
Supervisor	Right. That's a good start. Swimming pools. So, you'll need waterproof equipment. Now, you say it's a swimming pool complex. So, the pools are indoors and outdoors?
Customer	That's right. Indoors, there's a 50-metre pool for swimming laps and a small pool for babies and small children, and outdoors we have a 25-metre pool and playground, with another small pool for children.
Supervisor	Right, then. That means you'll need monitors with adjustable screens that can be used in bright sunlight. Good. I think that's all I need to know. I have just the right model for you. Here you are. This is our WM 206: Pulse and Blood Pressure Monitor.
Customer	Oh. That looks good. Is it easy to operate?
Supervisor	Yes. It's very easy to operate.
Customer	And how accurate is it?
Supervisor	We guarantee that they are accurate to plus/minus 2 bpm.
Customer	Bpm?
Supervisor	Sorry, beats per minute.
Customer	OK. It's a nice size. It's not too heavy.
Supervisor	Yes. If you'd like to know the exact details, it's 11.6 by 6.5 by 2.8 centimetres with a 6.1 by 3.3 centimetre touch screen. It comes with a slip-on, waterproof cover measuring 12 by 7.5 by 3 centimetres and, without batteries, it weighs 150 grammes.
Customer	What batteries does it use?
Supervisor	6-volt batteries. We supply three rechargeable batteries with every pulse monitor.
Customer	That all sounds very impressive. How much does it cost?
Supervisor	It's not expensive. It costs one hundred and thirteen euros.
Customer	A hundred and thirteen euros. Hmm. And how soon can the equipment be delivered after I've placed an order?
Supervisor	We can usually deliver within three days after payment. Each pulse monitor is packaged individually in a small plastic case, by the way, to protect them from damage.
Customer	Well, that all sounds very good to me. Could you let me have a list of the details to take with me? I'll have to discuss everything with my boss before I can place an order.
Supervisor	Of course. If you'd just like to wait a moment, I'll …

Track 18: Unit 6, Part A, exercise 1

Stevens	Morning, Martin. Do you remember I was telling you the other day that Brooks want to increase their order? They've asked if we can produce about 10,000 shafts a year, which means around 50 a day.
Foster	Yes, well, that's really good news, of course. But I still think that we'll never be able to meet an order of this size with the machines we have at the moment. For this kind of serial production we need something like an NEF from DMG MORI.
Stevens	Yes. I know. But there are quite a few different models, aren't there? What do we actually need?
Foster	Well, the shafts we have to produce for Brooks have a diameter of 80 mm and a length of 100.
Stevens	OK. 80 mm diameter by 100 mm length.
Foster	That's right … but we should really buy a machine that can cope with bigger parts as well.
Stevens	So, something like 500 mm by 1000 length?
Foster	No, not that big. I'd say that the maximum is 300 mm diameter by 700.

Stevens OK. 300 mm diameter by 700 mm length. Do we need a special control unit?
Foster Well most of our machines have Siemens control units. It would make a lot of sense to stick with them.
Stevens What about the extra options? Is there anything we really need?
Foster Well, it would save a lot of time to order a chip conveyor to get rid of chips.
Stevens Ah, yes. That's a good idea. Let's see what they cost. I'm rather busy right now … could you call the DMG MORI representative and ask for some information. Maybe they can give us some advice.
Foster Right. I'll get one of the apprentices on to that right now.
Stevens Good. When you have all the information, let me have a written report. OK?
Foster OK. No problem.

Track 19: Unit 7, Foundation, exercise 2

1: Making a quick decision

David OK. The supervisor is going to a meeting about improving internal communication in the company and he'd like us to tell him what internal communication we use, what we use it for, what we like, what we don't like and so on. Where are we going to start? Marta, you always have good ideas …
Marta Well, it might be a good idea to think about situations where we need internal communication and start from there. Hmm? … Come on, you guys. Janek, what do you think?
Janek Right. What about when we have to make a quick decision on something?
Marta OK. Well, I think a face-to-face meeting is good when you want to make a quick decision. And when you need to sort out a problem, a face-to-face meeting is always best.
David Yes, but if the other person isn't around, you can't have a face-to-face meeting. When I'm out on a job and I need a quick decision from my supervisor, I phone him.
Janek I agree with David, the phone's good for a quick decision. There are some situations when I want to have my supervisor's decision in writing, though, so I'd say that when you want a quick decision in writing, it's better to send a message.
Marta Uh-hu. I see what you're getting at, Janek.
David Yes. So, what are we going to say, then? When we need to make a quick decision, a face-to-face meeting is a good option. Other good options for making a quick decision are using the telephone for a phone call or a text. Is that what we're going to say?

2: Sharing information

David Is that what we're going to say?
Marta Yes. I think that's fine. What next? What about sharing information? I use emails a lot of the time. I like emails because you can write them in a couple of minutes and send them in a second. Sometimes my emails just contain text, but a lot of the time I attach documents or drawings. The really big advantage for me, though, is that I can copy in so many people, so I only have to write the email once.
Janek Yes, but one of the things I really dislike about emails is that you get so many of them. My personal favourite is the intranet. The big advantage over email is that an intranet is structured, so it's easy to find the information you're looking for.
David Sorry, but I have the same problem with the intranet as I have with face-to-face meetings. You need to be at work to access the intranet. I work all over the place so I need to have access to information wherever I am. I think cloud storage is better. You can access cloud storage from anywhere and, it's not just that you can share information, you can also synchronize files. I wish we used cloud storage here.
Marta You can share selected information with clients on the cloud, too, can't you? Maybe we should mention that to the supervisor.
Janek Hey. That's a good idea. Let's tell the supervisor that we use emails and the intranet, but we feel that using the cloud might be more useful. Yes? And, of course, the advantage of using the cloud is that the company can share information with clients. He can bring that up at the meeting.

3: Discussing a project

Janek He can bring that up at the meeting.
David Oh, yes. The meeting. That's another type of internal communication, isn't it? In this case, they're discussing the project. I'm glad I don't have to go to a lot of meetings. Meetings take up too much time. I'd rather be out doing my job.
Marta Me, too. I hate meetings. Especially when somebody stands up and reads things from slides.
Janek I can only agree with you there. When they're full of writing, slides are a real waste of time. When it's written information, a hand-out is always better.
David Right, well, I think we have enough now. Face-to-face meeting, phone calls and text messages for making quick decisions; emails and intranet for sharing information, and a suggestion that the company might consider cloud storage.
Marta And, don't forget to mention that, at meetings, slides should only be used for graphic images and not for a lot of text. If it's written information, we'd rather have a hand-out.

Track 20: Unit 7, Part A, exercise 2B/C

Kate Good morning, Mr Meesang. How are you today?
Surat Fine, thank you. I hope you're well, too, Ms O'Brien.
Kate Yes, I'm fine, thanks. But, please, call me Kate.
Surat Thank you. My first name is Surat.
Kate Surat. OK … Listen, my colleague and I will arrive in Bangkok on the 30th of November so I'd just like to check a few things with you before we arrive. Has the resin-sealing unit arrived at the factory yet?
Surat Not yet, but I've been told that it's already in Bangkok port and should be delivered to our factory on the 29th November. It will be waiting for you when you arrive in Bangkok the next day.
Kate OK. That's excellent. One important thing, though, Surat. Please, don't unpack the machine before my colleague and I arrive. Please leave it in the crate. The resin-sealer must be handled very carefully.
Surat Don't worry. I understand. I'll tell my colleagues to leave the machine in the crate until you are here. I expect it's very heavy.

Transcripts

Kate	Yes, it weighs 4 tons. Do you have a forklift truck that can carry that weight?
Surat	Well, we have a DFG 435. I think that is strong enough for transportation within the factory building.
Kate	Sorry, Surat, but I don't think it is. We really need a more powerful one, like a TFG 540. Can you get a TFG 540?
Surat	Er … yes, I think so. I don't think that will be a problem. There's a factory nearby that has a TFG 540. My cousin works there. He'll help us with that. … What do you need to fix the machine on the floor? Nuts and bolts?
Kate	Yes. Sixteen bolts – M18x150 – and the nuts as well.
Surat	Right, no problem.
Kate	And we'll need a drill and some 18 millimetre drill bits. We'll also need glue to fix the bolts to the floor.
Surat	Drills, drill bits, glue. You don't have to worry, Kate, our electricians have all of these things.
Kate	Yes. I know, but I just want to be sure. Now, how about the electricity supply? We need to lay data cables and power cables. Do we have to lay cable trunks?
Surat	No, that's not necessary. There's enough space for cables under the flooring.
Kate	And the pneumatics? Can the cables and the pneumatic hose be laid under the floor, too?
Surat	No problem, we can lay a pneumatic hose under the flooring, too.
Kate	Fine. I think that's it. Or, do you have any questions about the installation?
Surat	No, no. Everything will be fine.
Kate	I'm sure it will. If possible, I'd like to have everything up and running by the 3rd of December so that you can start production the following week.
Surat	No problem at all, Kate. My men and I will work hard to get the job done on time.
Kate	Thank you, Surat. I'm looking forward to meeting you soon.
Surat	You, too, Kate. Have a good flight.

Track 21: Unit 8, Part A, exercise 2A

Liu	… one of our contracts is cutting rubber mats for an important customer.
Derek	So what exactly is the problem?
Liu	The thing is, we cut these rubber mats with our water-jet cutter, of course, but there is also abrasive sand mixed in with the water.
Derek	OK …
Liu	This sand helps to cut the rubber, but some sand remains on the rubber mats and we have to wash it off after cutting. So … we have to wash down the mats manually, and we can't do that within the air-conditioned plant, so we have to do it outside in the heat.
Derek	And that also takes a lot of time probably.
Liu	That's true. It's actually about four minutes per mat.
Derek	Oh, that's a lot. OK, how can we help?
Liu	What we need is a kind of washing machine for these mats.
Derek	All right, do you have an idea of how that could work?
Liu	Yes, well, we thought about a kind of conveyor that cleans the mats on both sides, dries them and palletizes them.
Derek	OK. I think we can come up with something like that … let me just write this down: cleans mats on both sides … dries and palletizes them …
Liu	That's right.
Derek	First of all, what are the dimensions of the mats?
Liu	Length 1000 mm, width 500 mm and 20 mm thick.
Derek	OK. 1000 mm, width 500 mm and 20 mm thick. And how about the water? It's polluted with sand after the cleaning process …
Liu	That's another problem. Could we filter the sand out, so that we can reuse both the sand and the water? You know, the environmental legislation in Shenzhen is rather strict.
Derek	We'll try our best. filter sand out of water … and then you want the system to dry the mats before palletizing them?
Liu	That's right. That will save us lots of time and money.
Derek	Well, OK. I have all the information I need now. Give me two weeks and then I think I can send you some ideas about what we could do.
Liu	Fine, thank you. I look forward to …

Track 22: Unit 8, Communication, exercise 1A

1

Receptionist	Good morning. Welcome to the International Hotel.
Giovanni	Good morning. My name is Rossi – Giovanni Rossi. I have a reservation.
Receptionist	Here we are. Giovanni Rossi.
Giovanni	Yes. From Rossi Technology, Rome.
Receptionist	Thank you. You're in room 303, on the third floor.
Giovanni	What time is breakfast served?
Receptionist	We serve a buffet breakfast in the dining room between 8 and 10 a.m.
Giovanni	Eight till 10? Can I have a swim before breakfast?
Receptionist	Yes, of course. The swimming pool is open from 6 a.m. till 10 p.m.
Giovanni	That's great. Thank you.
Receptionist	You're welcome. Enjoy your stay, Mr Rossi.

2

Receptionist	Good morning. Welcome to the International Hotel.
Mary	Good morning. I have a reservation under McGregor, McGregor Robotics.
Receptionist	Mary McGregor, from Glasgow.
Mary	Yes. That's right. I booked a room on the ground floor, with wheelchair access.
Receptionist	Yes, that's correct. You're in room 15, on this floor.
Mary	Does the dining room have wheelchair access?
Receptionist	Yes. it does. All of our rooms and facilites have wheelchair access.
Mary	Good. Thank you.
Receptionist	Let me know if you need any extra towels or pillows.
Mary	That's very kind of you.
Receptionist	My pleasure. Have a good stay, Ms McGregor.

3

Receptionist	Good morning. Welcome to the International Hotel.
Yusuf	Thank you. I would like to check in.
Receptionist	Of course. What name is the reservation under?
Yusuf	My name is Yusuf Zuabi.
Receptionist	Could you spell your surname, please?
Yusuf	Yes. It's Z U A B I, "Zuabi", with a Z. The reservation may be under the name of my company, Tech Solutions.
Receptionist	Thank you. Ah, yes, here it is, Tech Solutions, Berlin, Mr Yusuf Zuabi. You're in room 201, on the second floor. Here's your key. The buffet breakfast is served in the dining room between 8 and 10 a.m.

Yusuf	Thank you. I have a question. Where can I park my car?
Receptionist	There's a secure car park at the back of the hotel. The man at the gate will let you in.
Yusuf	Good. Thank you.
Receptionist	No problem. Enjoy your stay.

Track 23: Unit 8, Communication, exercise 1C

Receptionist	Good morning, Ms Banerjee. How are you this morning?
Akira	Good morning. I'm very well, thank you.
Receptionist	How can I help you?
Akira	I'm going home today so I would like to check out.
Receptionist	Of course. What room were you in?
Akira	I was in room 207.
Receptionist	Did you have a nice time in Amsterdam?
Akira	It's been great. I love Amsterdam.
Receptionist	Was everything OK for you in the hotel?
Akira	Yes, thank you. Everything was fine. I'll definitely be back.
Receptionist	I'm pleased to hear that. Have a good trip home.
Akira	Thank you. I'm flying GALE-M. They're very good.

Track 24: Unit 9, Foundation, exercise 1B

Claudia	Good morning, Mr Camilleri. It's Claudia here. You wanted to talk about the video conferencing system?
James	Ah. Hallo there, Claudia. Thanks for calling. How's the weather there in Berlin? It's a beautiful day here in Valletta.
Claudia	You're lucky. It's raining here.
James	Oh, dear. Well, never mind. Perhaps it will be nice tomorrow. Do you have my email there?
Claudia	Yes, I do.
James	Good. Let's start. First of all, I'd like to be able to store data that everyone can access wherever they are. What do you think of that idea?
Claudia	It's a good idea. We'll need cloud storage.
James	Cloud storage? Oh, yes. I've heard of that. Fine. And I'd like the system to let us re-play the sessions later.
Claudia	So, we'll need a video recording function.
James	Right. That makes sense. It's a video conferencing system, so it should be able to make video recordings.
Claudia	Yes. That's right.
James	Of course. Right, well, only two more things. Will the makers supply a guide that helps us to use the system?
Claudia	A user manual? Yes. Probably. If not, there will be some other kind of help available.
James	Oh. All right. Then, the last thing is, will they let us try out the system for nothing so that we know if it is the right one for us?
Claudia	Sure. Most of them offer a free trial.
James	Good. Well, I think that's it. I'd like you to get started on that today.
Claudia	I'll do that, Mr Camilleri, but I wanted to suggest two other functions.
James	Oh. All right. You're the expert. What else do you suggest?
Claudia	Hmm. I wondered about multi-language support.
James	Why would we need that?
Claudia	Hmm. Just in case someone doesn't speak good English?
James	Oh, no. I don't think we need that. What was the other thing?
Claudia	Well, some video conferencing systems have calendar integration so that you can schedule more meetings. I think you'll want to arrange more meetings.
James	Well, yes, but my secretary, Maria, does that for me.
Claudia	Oh, of course. I just thought it might be useful.
James	All right. I'll probably never use it but you can add the calendar thing to the other items we discussed.
Claudia	Very well, Mr Camilleri. I'll get on with it right away.
James	Thanks, Claudia. Goodbye.

Track 25: Unit 9, Part B, exercise 2

Harry	Hi, Sina. How are things going?
Sina	Hi, Harry. Not so good at the moment. We have a problem with one of our aggregates again.
Harry	Oh, what is it?
Sina	You can't read the numbers we engraved on the labelling plates any more. The colour came off.
Harry	Oh, no. Not again.
Sina	Maybe we should order our labelling plates from Bensons again. They're more expensive, but the plates at least keep their colour.
Harry	You're right. But we had a few problems with Bensons as well in the past. That's why we stopped using them.
Sina	I know. Some plates were delivered late for one of our orders and two were missing.
Harry	… so we couldn't dispatch that aggregate to Norway on time. … But what can we do now?
Sina	Maybe we could produce our labelling plates ourselves?
Harry	Hmm. That's a good idea. That would make us a lot more independent. But you know what a CNC machine for that kind of job costs, don't you?
Sina	I do … but maybe we could find a smaller machine, you know, the type that model-makers use? We only need a relatively small machine.
Harry	Yeah … one we could use to produce our labelling plates from metal and plastics.
Sina	Right. Let me look on the internet. Maybe we can find something suitable.
Harry	Yeah, go ahead. … Ah, what's that?
Sina	OK … This looks interesting. A kind of desktop CNC machine …
Harry	… desktop gantry CNC machine … with linear drives …
Sina	Could be just what we need …

Track 26: Unit 9, Part B, exercise 4

Sina	… then we can decide whether we want to buy it.
Harry	We need to find out first whether there are any optional extras for the 2-240 model that we need.
Sina	I don't think there are. It says here: "Complete DIY kit including all mechanical and electronic components". It also says that there are easy-to-follow assembly instructions with pictures, so the assembly only takes a couple of hours.
Harry	OK, that sounds good.
Sina	Now there's one thing in the list of features which I think is really important. It's the 6-point ball bearing cage in all the linear profiles … and the play-free movement of the carriages

Harry	Well that's absolutely necessary, of course. We need maximum precision … especially for the smaller plates.
Sina	And look what it says here: "The carriages can be continuously adjusted and are freely accessible externally without disassembly."
Harry	That's a real advantage if you don't have to dismantle the whole system for cleaning or any other purposes. What's the minimum feed rate?
Sina	Er … let me see … It says the feed rate is at least 3000 mm/min … divided by 60 seconds
Harry	So 50 mm/sec?
Sina	Yes, 50 mm/sec.
Harry	Have you found anything on the thickness of the materials we can machine on it?
Sina	Yes, it's 15 mm.
Harry	Great. That's perfect for our purposes. By the way, is there an additional box for the electronic controller?
Sina	No, there isn't. The control electronics are integrated in the machine housing and there is only one connecting cable from the machine to the computer.
Harry	Do we need 3-phase current to operate it?
Sina	No, it works between 100 and 240 V.
Harry	That sounds good. Now, one final question: Does it come with a warranty?
Sina	Yes, there's a 2-year warranty. But surely the most important question is: How much does it cost?
Harry	Yes, go on then. How much does it cost?
Sina	It says here the 2-240 costs …

Track 27: Unit 10, Part A, exercise 2

Morrison	Good morning. Can I help you?
Brown	Good morning. My name is George Brown. I have an appointment with Ms Morrison to see the Mercedes 540 K.
Morrison	Hello, Mr Brown. Nice to meet you. How are you today?
Brown	Fine thanks. I'm looking forward to seeing the car.
Morrison	Yes, of course. It's a lovely car. It's over here.
Brown	Wow. It's beautiful. It's in very good condition.
Morrison	Yes, the owner treated it with great care.
Brown	Can I have a look at the engine?
Morrison	Certainly.
Brown	Ah-ha, 8 cylinders.
Morrison	Yes, 8 cylinders with a capacity of 5.4 litres.
Brown	And how many valves does it have?
Morrison	16 overhead valves; 2 on each cylinder.
Brown	And what's the maximum power output?
Morrison	It's 178 brake horsepower or, today, 133 kilowatts at 3500 revolutions per minute.
Brown	That's very impressive for a car built in 1936.
Morrison	It is, isn't it?
Brown	How is the engine cooled?
Morrison	It's water-cooled.
Brown	And what about the maximum speed?
Morrison	A hundred and ninety-three kilometres per hour with an acceleration of 11.7 seconds from zero to 80 kilometres per hour.
Brown	Wow, that's excellent for 1936. So … how many gears does it have?
Morrison	It's a 4 speed manual gearbox. There's no reverse gear, of course.
Brown	No, they didn't have reverse gear then, did they? Oh … What's missing here?
Morrison	The compressor vanes were broken. We've dismantled them and we're going to order new ones.
Brown	OK. What type of compressor is it?
Morrison	It's a Roots supercharger.
Brown	Uh-hu. What's the fuel consumption?
Morrison	It's about 30 litres per 100 kilometres.
Brown	Oh. That's a lot.
Morrison	Well, compared with today's cars, yes. But in the old days, nobody cared about things like that.
Brown	Yes. I know.
Morrison	Is there anything else you would like to know?
Brown	Well, the main question for me is: will the car be in good running order? I would like to take it out on the road every now and then.
Morrison	Oh, yes. Of course! You'll be able to drive it, no problem at all.
Brown	Well, thank you, Ms Morrison. You've been very helpful.
Morrison	Not at all. Here's a hand-out with the specific information on it. And, good luck at the auction.
Brown	Thanks. I'll probably need it.

Track 28: Unit 10, Part B, exercise 2

Kelly	Car Parts Dublin. Bob Kelly speaking.
Morrison	Hi Bob. It's Cathy Morrison from Wheeler Vintage Cars here.
Kelly	Hi Cathy. What can I do for you?
Morrison	I've got a Mercedes 540 K Special Roadster here which needs a few spare parts.
Kelly	A Special Roadster? Amazing! There aren't a lot of them about.
Morrison	No, you're right. There are only six of them left.
Kelly	Wow! I hope you're looking after it. So, what do you need from me?
Morrison	Well, first of all, I need 4 completely new brakeshoes.
Kelly	Let me check. No problem. I've got 15 in stock. What else?
Morrison	You know the adjusters for the brakes?
Kelly	You mean the eccentric ones?
Morrison	Yes. We need four of them.
Kelly	Oooh. Sorry, we only have two left. But, you're in luck. We're going to produce another ten of them later this week.
Morrison	Then we need 2 wheelnuts. The ones with the huge single thread in the middle.
Kelly	They're in stock, no problem.
Morrison	Then there's this poppet valve. I'd better replace all 8 of them.
Kelly	I can let you have 6 now, but I can produce another two in a few days.
Morrison	And the V-belt pulley is also broken, so I need one of them, too.
Kelly	V-belt pulley … in stock. That's quite a list you're giving me, Cathy. Anything else?
Morrison	I'm afraid so. Two of the king pins are broken.
Kelly	I've got king pins in stock. I'd actually recommend that you replace all four of them.
Morrison	OK. I suppose you're right. OK. Just one more thing. The fuel tap.

Kelly	Oh, yes. There's always a problem with the fuel tap in the 540 Ks. I'm sorry, though, I have to disappoint you here. We don't have any. But, as it's you, I'll get our CNC miller to produce one. You'll have it within the next two weeks. Was there anything else?
Morrison	Not for now, but can you send me what you have in stock immediately so that we can get started on the job?
Kelly	Sure. Just fill in the order sheet online and we'll deliver what we can. The rest will be produced as soon as possible. You can send a written order later.
Morrison	That's great, Bob. Thanks. I'll get the online order over to you today and you'll get the written order this week.
Kelly	Great. All the best with that Special Roadster. I'd love to pop over and see it.
Morrison	Well, why don't you do that? It'd be nice to see you again.

Track 29: Unit 11, Foundation, exercise 2B

Good morning, everyone. Thank you. I'd like to talk this morning about some of the environmental issues related to the production of smartphones.

Right. There was a study recently, which aimed to find out the answer to the question: How well do manufacturers of smartphones protect the environment?

The aim of the study was to gather information that would help persuade phone manufacturers to reduce emissions of greenhouse gases. The organization that conducted the survey also hoped that they would clean up their products by eliminating hazardous substances and that they would take back and recycle old phones. The organizers of the study looked at three environmental areas: one, energy and climate, two, greener products and, three, the use of natural products and energy in a way that does not harm the environment.

The study looked at the carbon footprint of a mobile phone and saw that the main problem lies in the manufacturing processes. Basically, more carbon is used to make and put together smartphones than consumers ever use after buying them. According to the study, manufacturing a smartphone is estimated to cause 16 kg of CO_2-equivalent emissions.

Now, apart from using huge amounts of energy and materials, manufacturing smartphones requires using toxic chemicals. Toxic, hazardous, poisonous materials – call them what you will – it's easy to forget that your sexy new smartphone contains heavy metals, including lead, mercury, tin, cadmium and chromium. All of these are very dangerous for the environment.

Some of you are probably thinking, "Why does it matter? We don't come into direct contact with these toxic materials." The thing is, these hazardous substances don't just disappear when you throw your phone away. When they aren't recycled, phones often end up in landfills or incinerators and they can release heavy metals into groundwater and air. Contaminated groundwater is linked to several diseases.

Of course, there are also precious metals in electronics. One million phones contain 35,000 pounds of copper, 772 pounds of silver, and 75 pounds of gold, so the phones are worth recycling. In a lot of African countries where old phones are sent to be dumped, workers dissolve or burn circuit boards to get at the precious metals. This may be profitable, but it can cause serious health problems.

Batteries are another problem. Some phones contain built-in batteries that you can't change so, once the batteries are dead, the phone is useless and it gets thrown away. Sure, you can pay the company about 70 euros for a new battery but …

Yes, I know there are guides on the internet showing you how to do it yourself, but it's not easy. A lot of phones are glued so they can't be opened or they have special screws …

OK. OK. Let's take a break there. When we come back, we'll have a look at some improvements that the manufacturers of smartphones and other electronic equipment might make.

Track 30: Unit 11, Part A, exercise 3

Ray	Oof! It's pretty heavy, isn't it?
Andy	Yes, it weighs over 50 kilos according to the data sheet. I think we'll need a gantry crane to install it. But let's check the contents of the package with the delivery note first.
Ray	OK, … Well here on the type plate it says R500 SXJ.
Andy	Yes, that's correct.
Ray	… and the serial number is 282824.
Andy	Hold on. Say that again.
Ray	282824.
Andy	There's something wrong here. It should be 282842 according to the delivery note. I think we need to check that with the supplier. I'll make a note of that.
Ray	So, what's next on the list?
Andy	OK. The next item is the robot controller, the CU555 compact.
Ray	Yes, that must be this grey box here.
Andy	Then it says here: power supply cable EU 3m CEE 7 / VII.
Ray	Hmmm. Can't find that anywhere.
Andy	OK, so we'll have to add that to the email, too.
Ray	Yeah, but let's check the other things first.
Andy	Right. What about the interface 24V PWR IN X55?
Ray	Yes, that's OK. It's here on the back of the controller.
Andy	Is there a handbook with it, too?
Ray	Yes, this looks like the handbook and documentation.
Andy	OK. Then it says LMN 8.3 … That's the software package which should be installed on the controller already.
Ray	Well, we can't check that before the robot is up and running.
Andy	No, OK. And what's that? Is it the controller device?
Ray	Yes, it says: NetPro 3.1 on the package.
Andy	Uh-o. Another error. It should be version 3.2 according to the delivery note. We'd better check that with the supplier as well. Now, what about TechExpert 3.2? That's a software tool for easy programming, as well as GripExpert 3.2 and VisualExpert 3.2.
Ray	Yes, they seem to be here in among the handbook and documentation.
Andy	OK, the next item is the mobile teaching unit.
Ray	Yes, got that here. Let's just check the serial number … here it is: 175384.
Andy	Wrong again. It says here 175348. Let's just make a note of that … 175348.
Ray	Now, here's the smartPAD cable …
Andy	… that should be 10 metres.
Ray	No, it doesn't look like 10 metres to me. Let me check. 2, 4, … it's only 5 metres.
Andy	OK, we'll have to mention that in the email as well.
Ray	I think that's everything. So, are you going to write the email to RobAG?
Andy	No, I have a meeting right now, but I know somebody who can do it for me …

Transcripts

Track 31: Unit 11, Part B, exercise 3B

Louise Have you seen this email from Prime Engineering that Customer Services forwarded to us?

Wayne Yes, that print looks really terrible. Look at it: the top looks like a piece of chewing gum.

Louise Yeah, very funny. But it's not just the form, the surface also looks so rough. The surface is not as smooth as our printer resin usually is after it hardens.

Wayne Do you think the resin might be overheating?

Louise It looks a bit like that, doesn't it. But so far we've only ever had one broken heating element … and that one was completely broken. I've never heard of a case of overheating, unless they are printing with the heat settings too high.

Wayne But what surprises me most is the strange colour. I'm not sure whether they're using our original filament coils. They might have bought cheap copies which work at first, but now they might be contaminating or even clogging the nozzle.

Louise Yes, it looks a bit like that, doesn't it? That could be the problem. By the way which printer model are they using?

Wayne The PT2002.

Louise OK. The PT2002 has a maximum working height of 200 mm. What is the height of this workpiece, do you think?

Wayne I can't tell from the photo, but to me it looks more than that … Do you think that could be the problem?

Louise I'm pretty certain it is. They must have ignored the software warning and started printing anyway. When the height of the printed workpiece reached the maximum working height, the machine stopped printing and the hot nozzle prevented the filament from cooling and solidifying quickly.

Wayne That makes sense.

Louise The filament may be anywhere between 190 to 240 degrees Celsius when it exits the extruder nozzle. When filament cools, it quickly hardens so that it retains the correct shape. You need to achieve the correct distance between the nozzle and the top of the workpiece, so that the filament can quickly solidify to produce the exact dimensions of your 3D printed part. In this photo, it looks like the filament extruded at the top of the workpiece was not able to cool quickly enough to retain its shape.

Wayne I think you're right. OK, so what do we do now?

Louise Can you ask Customer Services to write them a reply? They should tell them that we believe that they have either used different filament coils … ones which are not our originals … or the maximum working height has been exceeded.

Wayne OK, I'll get on to it now …

Track 32: Unit 11, Communication, exercise 2A

Melissa Wolf.

Jerzy Oh. Hello. Erm. Do you speak English?

Melissa Yes.

Jerzy Oh. Good. This is Jerzy Adamczyk calling from the Denta Dental Clinic in Warsaw. Is that the sales department?

Melissa Yes.

Jerzy And, erm, who am I speaking to, please?

Melissa Wolf.

Jerzy Ah. Mrs Wolf. Erm. Is, erm, are you the correct person to take a complaint about a delivery?

Melissa What's the problem?

Jerzy It's about my order for X-ray machines. Both of the X-ray machines were damaged. One of them – the glass on one of the machines is scratched and the other machine is dented. I mean, the metal casing is dented. I think that …

Melissa What's the order number?

Jerzy 942761.

Melissa OK. I can't do anything at the moment. I'll get it sorted after lunch.

Jerzy So, will you phone me back? My phone number is …

Melissa It's here on the display.

Jerzy 0048 129 546 783?

Melissa Yes.

Jerzy And my name is Adamczyk. You will be sure to look into this? Well, thank you very much.

Track 33: Unit 11, Communication, exercise 2B

Melissa *Guten Morgen. Verkaufsabteilung.* Melissa Wolf *am Apparat.*

Jerzy Oh. Hello. Erm. Do you speak English?

Melissa Yes, of course. How can I help you?

Jerzy Oh. Good. This is Jerzy Adamczyk calling from the Denta Dental Clinic in Warsaw. Is that the sales department?

Melissa Yes, this is the sales department. My name's Melissa Wolf.

Jerzy Ah. Mrs, erm, Ms Wolf. Hmm. Is, erm, are you the correct person to take a complaint about a delivery?

Melissa It depends on what it's about. Could you give me some details?

Jerzy It's about my order for X-ray machines. Both of the X-ray machines were damaged. One of them – the glass on one of the machines is scratched and the other machine is dented. I mean, the metal casing is dented. I think that there was a problem during transport.

Melissa Oh, I'm sorry to hear that. Could you give me the order number, please?

Jerzy It's 942761.

Melissa Just a moment, please. Right. 942761. I have it here. Two X-ray machines. And you say that both of them are damaged?

Jerzy That is correct. I am sorry, but I have to say that I am disappointed about this business. This is a trial order but I had to complain last week because the equipment did not arrive on the date we agreed. Now the machines are here and I can't use them.

Melissa Oh, dear. I'm extremely sorry to hear that you've had so much trouble. I'm sure my superior would like to discuss this with you. Can I ask her to phone you when she comes in to work tomorrow?

Jerzy Yes. All right. I'll be at home all day tomorrow so she should call me there. The number is 0048 129 546 993.

Melissa 0048 129 546 993. Yes. You'll get a call from my superior tomorrow, Mr Adamczyk.

Jerzy Could you tell me her name, please?

Melissa It's Mia Richter.

Jerzy Mia Richter. Good. Thank you very much, Ms Wolf.

Melissa You're welcome, Mr Adamczyk. Thank you for calling.

Jerzy Goodbye.

Track 34: Unit 11, Communication, exercise 3C

Jeanette — Good morning. Sheffield Metal, Sales Department, Jeannette Hogg speaking.
Supervisor — Good morning. This is Max Jahn from World Medical in Germany.
Jeanette — Good morning, Mr Jahn. How can I help you?
Supervisor — I'm calling to enquire about my order for containers for medical equipment. The order was sent almost one month ago, on the 18th of April, and delivery was promised by the 3rd of May but, so far, nothing has arrived.
Jeanette — Oh. I'm sorry to hear that. Could you give me the order number?
Supervisor — Yes. It's DF54736.
Jeanette — DF54736. Just a moment, please. I'll check. I'm sorry, Mr Jahn. I don't seem to have any record of your order. Can I just check that I've understood everything? The order number is DF54736 and you ordered the containers on the 18th of April. Could you give me the exact details of the order, please?
Supervisor — Yes, it's an order for your aluminium containers for medical equipment.
Jeanette — Aluminium containers for medical equipment. Mr Jahn, I'll have to speak to my colleague to find out what the problem is. Can I get back to you later?
Supervisor — Well, yes. But I hope it won't take long. We can't fulfil our orders until we have your containers.
Jeanette — Yes. I realize that, Mr Jahn. I'm very sorry about this and I will do my best to get back to you as soon as possible.
Supervisor — Many thanks for your help, Ms Hogg.

Track 35: Unit 12, Foundation, exercise 1

1 Maren
Presenter — Hallo, and welcome to this week's podcast. This week, we're talking to a group of people who have recently gained their technical qualifications. Let's start with you, Maren. Would you like to introduce yourself?
Maren — Sure. I'm Maren and I've just completed my apprenticeship as a Mechanical Engineering Technician.
Presenter — What did you like best about your apprenticeship?
Maren — I enjoy making things, so the best time for me was when we were in the workshop.
Presenter — Apart from making things, what else do you do at work?
Maren — Well, I install and service machinery.
Presenter — Right. Hmm. A last question, Maren. Now that you're qualified, where would you like to work?
Maren — Definitely in the automotive sector. A job at BMW would be great.

2 Garry
Presenter — Hi. What's your name and what do you do?
Garry — My name's Garry and I'm a CAD Technician.
Presenter — Just in case any of our listeners don't know, what does CAD stand for?
Garry — CAD stands for computer aided design.
Presenter — OK. What did you enjoy most about your apprenticeship, Garry?
Garry — I enjoyed learning from experienced people.
Presenter — Nice. What do you do as a CAD Technician?
Garry — Well, I work with computers, of course. I work with engineers who create drawings on computers. Sometimes there's a problem, then I have to fix the software so that the engineers can go on with their work.
Presenter — That sounds interesting. What sector would you like to work in?
Garry — I'd like to work in construction – Hochtief, for example. Everybody needs somewhere to live, and every country needs offices, factories, hospitals, and so there will always be work for people like me.

3 Delon
Presenter — Hello. Can you tell us your name and something about your apprenticeship?
Delon — Yes. My name's Delon and I've just qualified as a Mechatronics Technician.
Presenter — What did you like best during your apprenticeship?
Delon — I liked the mixture of going to vocational college and doing practical work in the factory.
Presenter — What do you do at work?
Delon — Basically, I install electronic equipment; transmitters, antennas, that kind of thing. Then, I do regular maintenance tasks such as checking and cleaning so that we don't have any problems with the equipment. If we do have a problem, I repair the machine.
Presenter — It sounds as if you have a lot of different things to do. What about the future? Where would you like to work?
Delon — I'd like to work in the steel industry. I did my apprenticeship at Thyssenkrupp, so, ideally, I'd like to stay on there.

Track 36: Unit 12, Part B, exercise 3B

Presenter — Thanks for coming along to talk to us today, Pat.
Pat — My pleasure. It's nice to be here.
Presenter — Good. Now, today you're going to give us advice about how to prepare for an interview.
Pat — Correct. I'm going to go through each of the five stages of a job interview and talk about how candidates can prepare themselves. So, stage one, greetings and introductions. That's perhaps the easiest part of the interview but it still needs some preparation. First of all, you should find out where the interview location is and how to get there so that you arrive in good time. Try to give yourself enough time to relax and calm down. You should also make sure that you're wearing appropriate clothes.
Presenter — First impressions count. Would you advise people to buy new clothes specially for the interview?
Pat — No, not particularly. Your clothes need to be appropriate for the job, clean and smart, that's all. They don't have to be new.
Presenter — Right. What about body language at the start of the interview?
Pat — Body language is important. Walk into the room as confidently as possible, shake hands and make eye contact. Don't be shy. Look directly at the interviewer or interviewers. You'll be asked to take a seat, and there will be a bit of small talk.

Presenter	Talking about the weather, your journey, that kind of thing?
Pat	That's right. There might also be a question about where you live or your hobbies.
Presenter	Some people find it difficult to make small talk, even in their own language. What advice can you give us there, Pat?
Pat	I think the best thing to do is to simply get into the habit of making small talk in English with a colleague or a friend.
Presenter	That's a good idea. Practise making small talk whenever you can.
Pat	That's it. Now, let's move on to the main part of the interview. You'll be asked questions by one or more interviewers.
Presenter	The interview might be conducted by more than one person?
Pat	That's correct. Sometimes there's a panel of interviewers. Now, preparation for this part is extremely important. Think about the questions you might be asked and make a list. You'll definitely be asked to talk about yourself. Perhaps the interviewer will ask you about your strengths and weaknesses. Write down the questions – and think about how you're going to answer. And always remember to relate your answers to the job on offer.
Presenter	Yes, that's important. Keep focused on the job. What should a candidate do if he or she doesn't understand a question?
Pat	If you don't understand a question, ask the interviewer to clarify. You can say: "Could you explain what you mean by … ?" – whatever it is. A good interviewer will ask the question again in a slightly different way.
Presenter	Hmm. I hope so. Now, earlier you mentioned questions from the candidate. I remember my very first interview. I had no idea what to ask.
Pat	Oh, dear. Some preparation would have helped. It's important to do some background research into the company before you go for the interview. Find out about the company's most recent developments and the future prospects of the company you hope to work for. Go to the firm's home page on the internet, read the business section of your newspaper, or look through business magazines. As you're doing your research, note down any questions that occur to you concerning the company. You should also, of course, prepare some questions about the job itself. Then, when you're asked if you have any questions, this is your chance to show your interest in the company and the job.
Presenter	Right. Be prepared with questions about the company and the job! And that's the end of the interview and you can say goodbye.
Pat	Well, not quite. Before the interview comes to an end, the interviewer usually says when the candidate can expect to hear from the company or if there's to be a further interview or a test – hmm – say, in the form of an assessment centre evaluation. So, only after these arrangements have been made, then your last task as a candidate is to say thank you and goodbye. Again, a good, firm handshake and a smile, and that's it.
Presenter	Well, thank you, Pat, for these very helpful interviewing tips. I'm sure our listeners have learned a lot today and that they'll be able to put your tips to good use in their interviews. Now, next week's podcast is about …

Track 37: KMK Mock exam: Rezeption I, Hörverstehen

Clive	Hello. I'm Clive Hancourt. I'm the export manager for ManuMetal. The company was founded in the 1970s and we're based in Manchester. We manufacture a wide range of metal-working tools. We also offer repair services for tools with original coatings, which make them like-new. Recycling is another important field for us – we recycle tools that can't be repaired professionally any more. The tools we manufacture can be used for turning, milling and drilling. Our customers work in the machine tool industry or they're active in the transportation or energy industries. Our company motto is: "Employees are the key to our future success". In manufacturing we employ certified metal-cutting professionals, machine tool operators, CNC programmers, engine fitters and many other skilled workers.
Fiona	Hello. My name is Fiona, I'm an intern with Henderson Bros. My company has developed from a one-man operation in London in 1953 to a large manufacturer of arc welding products. That's why "Knowing what takes you forward" is our company motto. Our basic products are welders but we also offer plasma cutters and automation systems with integrated robots to increase our customers' productivity. Guns and torches as well as instruments for your gas management, such as flow meters, complete our product range. In manufacturing we employ machinists, coil winders, testers, and assemblers. All in all, the company has about 450 employees.
Keith	Hi. I work for MetLab Ltd, and we don't actually produce anything … our business is material testing using chemical or mechanical analysis … Oh, yes, sorry … my name is Keith Wallace and I'm a mechanical engineer. MatLab is the third biggest laboratory in the UK. The company was founded in 2004 and we have been in Sheffield, South Yorkshire, ever since then. If quality is an important factor, we are the ideal partner for anyone working with metal. And this means all kinds of metal. "Always in safe hands" is our company's slogan. MetLab has a well-equipped machine shop with electromechanical and hydraulic machines to perform tests, for example compression or bending tests on metallic materials. The work is mainly done by lab technicians.

1–12 Unit word list

Dieses Wörterverzeichnis enthält alle neuen Wörter aus *Metal Matters – 3rd Edition* in der Reihenfolge ihres Erscheinens (Seitenzahlen sind angegeben). Nicht angeführt sind die Wörter aus dem Grundwortschatz (vgl. **Handreichungen für den Unterricht**). Wörter aus den Hörverständnisübungen sind mit einem **T** (Transkript) und Wörter aus den *Partner files* mit einem **P** gekennzeichnet. Die Zahl am linken Rand gibt die Seitenzahl an.

Abkürzungen	AE = amerikanisches Englisch	jdm = jemandem	pl = plural noun
	BE = britisches Englisch	jdn = jemanden	sb = somebody
	etw = etwas	jds = jemandes	sth = something

UNIT 1

6	foundation [faʊnˈdeɪʃn]	Grundlage	
	profile [ˈprəʊfaɪl]	Porträt, Beschreibung, Profil	
	apprentice [əˈprentɪs]	Auszubildende/r, Lehrling	
	trainee [treɪˈniː]	Auszubildende/r, Praktikant/in	
	global player [ˌgləʊbl ˈpleɪə]	international agierendes Unternehmen	
	producer [prəˈdjuːsə]	Hersteller, Produzent	
	cable [ˈkeɪbl]	Kabel	
	connector [kəˈnektə]	Verbinder, Stecker	
	head office [ˌhed ˈɒfɪs]	Zentrale, Sitz	
	to found [faʊnd]	gründen	
	to run [rʌn]	(Unternehmen usw.) führen	
	structure [ˈstrʌktʃə]	Aufbau, Struktur	
	chairman [ˈtʃeəmən]	Vorsitzende/r	
	board [bɔːd]	Aufsichtsrat	
	finance [ˈfaɪnæns]	Finanz, Finanzen	
	purchasing [ˈpɜːtʃəsɪŋ]	Einkauf	
	partner [ˈpɑːtnə]	Gesellschafter/in	
	sales [seɪlz]	Verkauf, Vertrieb	
	to employ sb [ɪmˈplɔɪ]	jdn beschäftigen	
	including [ɪnˈkluːdɪŋ]	einschließlich	
	research [rɪˈsɜːtʃ]	Forschung	
	scientist [ˈsaɪəntɪst]	Wissenschaftler/in	
	to develop [dɪˈveləp]	entwickeln	
	to manufacture [ˌmænjuˈfæktʃə]	fertigen, herstellen	
	mechanical engineering [mɪˌkænɪkl ˌendʒɪˈnɪərɪŋ]	Maschinenbau	
	factory [ˈfæktəri]	Fabrik, Werk	
	automation [ˌɔːtəˈmeɪʃn]	Automatisierung, Automation	
	power generation [ˈpaʊə dʒenəreɪʃn]	Stromerzeugung	
	power distribution [ˈpaʊə dɪstrɪbjuːʃn]	Stromverteilung	
	industrial electronics [ɪnˌdʌstriəl ɪlekˈtrɒnɪks]	Industrieelektronik	
	telecommunication [ˌtelɪkəˌmjuːnɪˈkeɪʃn]	Fernmeldetechnik, Telekommunikation	
	vocational training [vəʊˌkeɪʃənl ˈtreɪnɪŋ]	Berufsausbildung	
	apprenticeship [əˈprentɪʃɪp]	Lehre, Ausbildung	
	role [rəʊl]	Rolle	
	headline [ˈhedlaɪn]	Überschrift	
7	according to [əˈkɔːdɪŋ tə]	gemäß, entsprechend, zufolge	
	multinational (company) [ˌmʌltiˈnæʃnəl]	internationaler Konzern	
	well known [ˌwel ˈnəʊn]	bekannt	
	works [wɜːks]	Fabrik, Werk	
	production [prəˈdʌkʃn]	Produktion, Fertigung, Herstellung	
	sector [ˈsektə]	Bereich, Branche, Sektor	
	grid [grɪd]	Raster	
	size [saɪz]	Größe	
	medium-sized [ˈmiːdiəm saɪzd]	mittelgroß, mittelständisch	
	solution [səˈluːʃn]	Lösung	
	construction [kənˈstrʌkʃn]	Bau	
	building [ˈbɪldɪŋ]	Bauwesen	
	service [ˈsɜːvɪs]	Dienst, Dienstleistung	
T	equipment [ɪˈkwɪpmənt]	Geräte, Ausstattung	
	dealer [ˈdiːlə]	Händler/in	
	training [ˈtreɪnɪŋ]	Ausbildung	
	automotive [ɔːˈtəmətɪv]	Automobil-	
	medical [ˈmedɪkl]	medizinisch	
	to cover [ˈkʌvə]	(Thema) behandeln	
	employee [ɪmˈplɔɪiː]	Angestellte/r, Beschäftigte/r	
	target group [ˈtɑːgɪt gruːp]	Zielgruppe	
	competitor [kəmˈpetɪtə]	Wettbewerber/in, Konkurrent/in	
	on one's own [ɒn wʌnz ˈəʊn]	alleine	
	to structure [ˈstrʌktʃə]	aufbauen, strukturieren	
	prepared [prɪˈpeəd]	bereit, vorbereitet	
	audience [ˈɔːdiəns]	Publikum	
8	layout [ˈleɪaʊt]	Raumaufteilung, Plan	

Unit word list

	firm [fɜːm]	Firma
	based in ... ['beɪst ɪn]	mit Sitz in ...
	subsidiary [səb'sɪdiəri]	Niederlassung
	workplace ['wɜːkpleɪs]	Arbeitsplatz
	training company ['treɪnɪŋ kʌmpəni]	Ausbildungsbetrieb
	reception [rɪ'sepʃn]	Empfang, Rezeption
	supervisor ['suːpəvaɪzə]	Ausbildungsleiter/in, Abteilungsleiter/in, Vorgesetzte/r
	to refresh [rɪ'freʃ]	auffrischen
	department [dɪ'pɑːtmənt]	Abteilung
	CNC milling [ˌsiː en 'siː mɪlɪŋ]	CNC-Fräsen
	construction [kən'strʌkʃn]	Konstruktion(sabteilung)
	dispatch [dɪ'spætʃ]	Versand(abteilung)
	drilling ['drɪlɪŋ]	Bohren, Bohrabteilung
	grinding ['graɪndɪŋ]	Schleifen, Schleiferei
	locker rooms pl ['lɒkə ruːmz]	Umkleideräume
	measuring room ['meʒərɪŋ ruːm]	Messraum
	turning ['tɜːnɪŋ]	Drehen, Dreherei
	waterjet ['wɔːtədʒet]	Wasserstrahl
	waterjet cutting ['wɔːtədʒet kʌtɪŋ]	Wasserstrahlschneiden
9	tour [tʊə]	Rundgang
	factory floor ['fæktəri flɔː]	Fertigungsbereich, Werkshalle
T	Nice to meet you. [ˌnaɪs tə 'miːt ju]	Schön, dich/euch/Sie kennenzulernen.
	to get started [get 'stɑːtɪd]	loslegen, anfangen
	head [hed]	Leiter/in, Chef/in
	to connect (sth to sth) [kə'nekt]	(etw mit etw) verbinden, (etw an etw) anschließen
	corridor ['kɒrɪdɔː]	Flur, Gang
	stairs pl [steəz]	Treppe
	to have a look around [həv ə ˌlʊk ə'raʊnd]	sich umsehen
	finished product [ˌfɪnɪʃt 'prɒdʌkt]	Fertigware, Fertigprodukt
	pretty ['prɪti]	ziemlich
	goods pl [gʊdz]	Ware(n)
	to open out [ˌəʊpən 'aʊt]	sich öffnen, sich verbreitern
	by the way [ˌbaɪ ðə 'weɪ]	übrigens, à propos
	locker ['lɒkə]	Schließfach, Spind
	to share sth [ʃeə]	sich etw teilen
	to worry ['wʌri]	Bedenken haben, sich Sorgen machen
	separate ['seprət]	getrennt
	section ['sekʃn]	Bereich
	material [mə'tɪəriəl]	Werkstoff, Material
	tool [tuːl]	Werkzeug
	to spill [spɪl]	(Wasser) verschütten, verspritzen
	CNC milling machine [ˌsiː en ˌsiː 'mɪlɪŋ məʃiːn]	CNC-Fräse
	axis, axes ['æksɪs, 'æksiːz]	Achse, Achsen
	four-axis [ˌfɔːr 'æksɪs]	vierachsig
	ultrasonic [ˌʌltrə'sɒnɪk]	Ultraschall-
	drilling machine ['drɪlɪŋ məʃiːn]	Bohrmaschine
	finished ['fɪnɪʃt]	fertig
	controlled [kən'trəʊld]	gesteuert
	turning machine ['tɜːnɪŋ məʃiːn]	Drehmaschine
	workbench ['wɜːkbentʃ]	Werkbank
	mounting ['maʊntɪŋ]	Montage
	grinding machine ['graɪndɪŋ məʃiːn]	Schleifmaschine
	beside [bɪ'saɪd]	neben
	round [raʊnd]	Runde
	to lead (to sth) [liːd]	(zu etw) führen
	to go on with sth [ˌgəʊ 'ɒn wɪθ]	mit etw weitermachen
	directions pl [də'rekʃnz]	Wegbeschreibung
	to give directions [ˌgɪv də'rekʃnz]	den Weg beschreiben
	floor plan ['flɔː plæn]	Grundriss, Lageplan
	to take turns [ˌteɪk 'tɜːnz]	sich abwechseln
	along [ə'lɒŋ]	entlang
	past sth [pɑːst]	an etw vorbei, hinter etw
	straight ahead [ˌstreɪt ə'hed]	geradeaus
	till [tɪl]	bis
	rough [rʌf]	grob
	sketch [sketʃ]	Skizze
	starting point ['stɑːtɪŋ pɔɪnt]	Ausgangspunkt
	entrance ['entrəns]	Eingang
10	branch [brɑːntʃ]	Niederlassung
	chart [tʃɑːt]	Diagramm, Tabelle
	organization chart [ˌɔːgənaɪ'zeɪʃn tʃɑːt]	Organigramm
	first of all [ˌfɜːst əv 'ɔːl]	zunächst, zuallererst
	CAD engineer [ˌsiː eɪ 'diː endʒɪnɪə]	Technische/r Zeichner/in
	fitting ['fɪtɪŋ]	Montage
	fitter ['fɪtə]	Monteur/in
	turner ['tɜːnə]	Dreher/in
	foreman/-woman ['fɔːmən, 'fɔːwʊmən]	Vorarbeiter/in, Meister/in
	division [dɪ'vɪʒn]	Geschäftsbereich, Division, Sparte
	head of division [ˌhed əv dɪ'vɪʒn]	Bereichsleiter/in
	line manager [laɪn 'mænɪdʒə]	direkte/r Vorgesetzte/r
	quality control ['kwɒləti kəntrəʊl]	Qualitätskontrolle

	skilled worker [ˌskɪld 'wɜːkə]	Facharbeiter/in		to go on [ˌgəʊ 'ɒn]	währen, dauern
	test technician ['test teknɪʃn]	Prüftechniker/in	P	key account management [kiː əˌkaʊnt 'mænɪdʒmənt]	Großkundenbetreuung
T	screen [skriːn]	Leinwand, Bildschirm		to include [ɪn'kluːd]	einbeziehen, aufnehmen
	to supervise ['suːpəvaɪz]	überwachen, beaufsichtigen	12	introductions pl [ˌɪntrə'dʌkʃnz]	Bekanntmachen, Vorstellen
	process ['prəʊses]	Ablauf, Prozess, Verfahren		Human Resources (HR) [ˌhjuːmən rɪ'sɔːsɪz]	Personalabteilung
	to be in charge of sth [bi ɪn 'tʃɑːdʒ əv]	für etw zuständig/verantwortlich sein		computerized [kəm'pjuːtəraɪzd]	Computer-
	to list [lɪst]	(in einer Liste) aufführen		personnel [ˌpɜːsə'nel]	Personal
	colleague ['kɒliːg]	Kollege/Kollegin		personnel file [ˌpɜːsə'nel faɪl]	Personalakte
	and so on [ənd 'səʊ ɒn]	und so weiter			
	last but not least [ˌlɑːst bʌt nɒt 'liːst]	zu guter Letzt	T	electrical engineer [ɪˌlektrɪkl ˌendʒɪ'nɪə]	Elektroingenieur/in, Elektrotechniker/in
	to keep up sth [ˌkiːp 'ʌp]	etw aufrecht erhalten		place of birth [ˌpleɪs əv 'bɜːθ]	Geburtsort
	reputation [ˌrepju'teɪʃn]	Ruf		job description ['dʒɒb dɪskrɪpʃn]	Stellenbeschreibung
11	understanding [ˌʌndə'stændɪŋ]	Verständnis	13	formal ['fɔːml]	formell, förmlich
	excerpt ['eksɜːpt]	Auszug		refreshment [rɪ'freʃmənt]	Erfrischung
	shaft [ʃɑːft]	Welle		suitable ['suːtəbl]	geeignet, passend
	micrometre ['mʌɪkrəˌmiːtə]	Mikrometer		to avoid [ə'vɔɪd]	vermeiden
	diameter [daɪ'æmɪtə]	Durchmesser		illness ['ɪlnəs]	Krankheit
	batch [bætʃ]	Charge, Los		politics ['pɒlətɪks]	Politik
	label ['leɪbl]	Etikett, Siegel		journey ['dʒɜːni]	Fahrt, Anreise
	tolerance ['tɒlərəns]	Toleranz		pay [peɪ]	Bezahlung, Gehalt
	out of tolerance [ˌaʊt əf 'tɒlərəns]	außerhalb der Toleranz		response [rɪ'spɒns]	Antwort, Reaktion
	flywheel ['flaɪwiːl]	Schwungrad		to be based in ... [bi 'beɪst ɪn]	seinen Sitz in ... haben, in ... sein
	to drill [drɪl]	bohren		view [vjuː]	Aussicht
	outer ring [ˌaʊtə 'rɪŋ]	Außenring		in fact [ɪn 'fækt]	tatsächlich, eigentlich
	to reduce [rɪ'djuːs]	senken, reduzieren, verringern		Excuse me. [ɪk'skjuːz mi]	Verzeihung. Entschuldigung.
	weight [weɪt]	Gewicht		to hold up sb [ˌhəʊld 'ʌp]	jdn aufhalten
	to make changes [ˌmeɪk 'tʃeɪndʒɪz]	Änderungen vornehmen		to keep sb waiting [ˌkiːp 'weɪtɪŋ]	jdn warten lassen
	lifting system ['lɪftɪŋ sɪstəm]	Hubsystem			

UNIT 2

hydraulic [haɪ'drɔːlɪk]	hydraulisch, Hydraulik-	
piston ['pɪstən]	Kolben	
to fit [fɪt]	passen	
to mention ['menʃn]	erwähnen, nennen	
lift cabin ['lɪft kæbɪn]	Aufzugskabine	
screw [skruː]	Schraube (zur Befestigung von Teilen mit Innengewinde)	

			14	health [helθ]	Gesundheit
				safety ['seɪfti]	Sicherheit
				health and safety [ˌhelθ ənd 'seɪfti]	Arbeitssicherheit, Sicherheit am Arbeitsplatz
				training course ['treɪnɪŋ kɔːs]	Lehrgang, Schulung
	purpose ['pɜːpəs]	Zweck, Absicht		poster ['pəʊstə]	Plakat
	to tighten ['taɪtn]	(Schraube) festziehen		workshop ['wɜːkʃɒp]	Werkstatt
	lift shaft ['lɪft ʃɑːft]	Aufzugsschacht		hazard ['hæzəd]	Gefahr
	connecting pipe [kəˌnektɪŋ 'paɪp]	Verbindungsrohr, -leitung		trainer ['treɪnə]	Ausbilder/in, Dozent/in
	flange [flændʒ]	Flansch		talk [tɔːk]	Vortrag
	as far as [əz 'fɑːr əz]	soweit		to discuss [dɪ'skʌs]	diskutieren, besprechen, (über etw) sprechen
	to concern sth [kən'sɜːn]	etw betreffen			
	supplier [sə'plaɪə]	Zulieferer, Lieferant/in		welding ['weldɪŋ]	Schweißen
	cooperation [kəʊˌɒpə'reɪʃn]	Zusammenarbeit		panel beating ['pænl biːtɪŋ]	Spenglerarbeiten
				paint spraying ['peɪnt spreɪɪŋ]	Spritzlackieren

Unit word list

to **be attached to sth** [bɪ əˈtætʃt tə]	mit etw verbunden sein	to **shut down sth** [ˌʃʌt ˈdaʊn]	etw ausschalten
protection [prəˈtekʃn]	Schutz	to **distract** [dɪˈstrækt]	ablenken
eye protection [ˈaɪ prətekʃn]	Augenschutz, Schutzbrille	to **smoke** [sməʊk]	rauchen
to **weld** [weld]	schweißen	**jewellery** [ˈdʒuːəlri]	Schmuck
to **result in sth** [rɪˈzʌlt ɪn]	etw zur Folge haben	**electrical appliance** [ɪˌlektrɪkl əˈplaɪəns]	Elektrogerät
arc eye [ˈɑːk aɪ]	verblitztes Auge	to **plug in** [ˌplʌg ˈɪn]	einstecken
breathing [ˈbriːðɪŋ]	Atmung	**maintenance** [ˈmeɪntənəns]	Wartung, Instandhaltung
ear protection [ˌɪə prəˈtekʃn]	Gehörschutz	**instruction** [ɪnˈstrʌkʃn]	Anweisung
permanent [ˈpɜːmənənt]	dauerhaft	**emergency exit** [ɪˈmɜːdʒənsi eksɪt]	Notausgang
temporary [ˈtemprəri]	vorübergehend	**emergency stop button** [ɪˈmɜːdʒənsi stɒp bʌtn]	Not-Aus-Taster
deafness [ˈdefnəs]	Taubheit	to **remove** [rɪˈmuːv]	entfernen, abheben
protective clothing [prəˌtektɪv ˈkləʊðɪŋ]	Schutzkleidung	**safety cover** [ˈseɪfti kʌvə]	Sicherheitsabdeckung
hard hat [ˌhɑːd ˈhæt]	Schutzhelm	**due to** [ˈdjuː tə]	aufgrund von, wegen
overall [ˌəʊvərˈɔːl]	Schutzanzug	**ladder** [ˈlædə]	Leiter
safety shoes pl [ˈseɪfti ʃuːz]	Sicherheitsschuhe	to **bump into sth** [ˈbʌmp ɪntə]	gegen etw stoßen
to **keep sb safe** [ˌkiːp ˈseɪf]	jdn schützen	to **fall off** [ˌfɔːl ˈɒf]	herunterfallen
messiness [ˈmesinəs]	Unordnung, Unsauberkeit	to **recognize** [ˈrekəgnaɪz]	erkennen
minor [ˈmaɪnə]	klein(er/e/s), geringfügig	**safety sign** [ˈseɪfti saɪn]	Sicherheitsschild, Hinweisschild
dirt [dɜːt]	Schmutz, Dreck	**fire exit** [ˈfaɪər eksɪt]	Notausgang
rubbish [ˈrʌbɪʃ]	Abfall, Müll	**high voltage** [ˌhaɪ ˈvəʊltɪdʒ]	Hochspannung
emergency [ɪˈmɜːdʒənsi]	Notfall	**fire extinguisher** [ˈfaɪər ɪkstɪŋgwɪʃə]	Feuerlöscher
switch [swɪtʃ]	Schalter	**gloves** pl [glʌvz]	Handschuhe
emergency cut out switch [ɪˌmɜːdʒənsi ˈkʌt aʊt swɪtʃ]	Not-Aus-Schalter	**acid** [ˈæsɪd]	Säure
to **cover** [ˈkʌvə]	verdecken, abdecken	**highly flammable** [ˌhaɪli ˈflæməbl]	leicht entzündlich
pile [paɪl]	Stapel	**no entry** [ˌnəʊ ˈentri]	Einfahrt/Zutritt verboten
to **switch on/off** [ˌswɪtʃ ˈɒn, ˈɒf]	ein-/ausschalten	**naked lights** pl [ˌneɪkɪd ˈlaɪts]	offene Flammen
rule [ruːl]	Vorschrift, Regel	**first aid** [ˌfɜːst ˈeɪd]	Erste Hilfe
top-heavy [ˌtɒp ˈhevi]	kopflastig	**safety goggles** pl [ˈseɪfti gɒglz]	Schutzbrille
shelving [ˈʃelvɪŋ]	Regale	to **pin** [pɪn]	(mit einer Nadel) befestigen, anheften
to **fill** [fɪl]	(Regal) befüllen	**gallery walk** [ˈgæləri wɔːk]	Galerierundgang
shelf, shelves [ʃelf, ʃelvz]	Regal, Regale	to **rank** [ræŋk]	einstufen, (in einer Rangliste) bewerten
stuff [stʌf]	Sachen, Zeug	**category** [ˈkætəgəri]	Kategorie
common sense [ˌkɒmən ˈsens]	gesunder Menschenverstand	**design** [dɪˈzaɪn]	Gestaltung, Design
ventilation [ˌventɪˈleɪʃn]	Belüftung	**overall effect** [ˌəʊvərˌɔːl ɪˈfekt]	Gesamteindruck, Gesamtwirkung
to **block** [blɒk]	versperren, blockieren	16 **engineering** [ˌendʒɪˈnɪərɪŋ]	Technik, Ingenieurwissenschaft, Maschinenbau
ventilator [ˈventɪleɪtə]	Abzug, Ventilator	**job title** [ˈdʒɒb taɪtl]	Berufsbezeichnung
machinery [məˈʃiːnəri]	Maschinen	**heating** [ˈhiːtɪŋ]	Heizung
guard [gɑːd]	Schutzvorrichtung	**technical drawing** [ˌteknɪkl ˈdrɔːɪŋ]	technische Zeichnung
screen [skriːn]	Schutzschirm		
damaged [ˈdæmɪdʒd]	beschädigt, defekt		
wrench [rentʃ]	Schraubenschlüssel		
hammer [ˈhæmə]	Hammer		
to **brainstorm** [ˈbreɪnstɔːm]	Ideen sammeln		
related to sth [rɪˈleɪtɪd tə]	bezüglich etw		
15 **guideline** [ˈgaɪdlaɪn]	Richtlinie		

Mechanical Design Engineer [mɪˌkænɪkl dɪˈzaɪn endʒɪnɪə]	Konstruktionsmechaniker/in	power plant [ˈpaʊə plɑːnt]	Kraftwerk
Maintenance Technician [ˈmeɪntənəns teknɪʃn]	Wartungstechniker/in	refrigeration [rɪˌfrɪdʒəˈreɪʃn]	Kühlung, Kühl-
Mechanical Fitter [mɪˌkænɪkl ˈfɪtə]	Maschinenmonteur/in	to turn [tɜːn]	sich drehen
Project Manager [ˌprɒdʒekt ˈmænɪdʒə]	Projektleiter/in	workpiece [ˈwɜːkpiːs]	Werkstück
mainly [ˈmeɪnli]	hauptsächlich	turning tool [ˈtɜːnɪŋ tuːl]	Drehwerkzeug
part [pɑːt]	Bauteil	milling cutter [ˌmɪlɪŋ ˈkʌtə]	Fräser
template [ˈtempleɪt]	Vorlage, Schablone	precise [prɪˈsaɪs]	präzis, genau
precision [prɪˈsɪʒn]	Präzision, Genauigkeit	production system [prəˈdʌkʃn sɪstəm]	Fertigungssystem, Produktionssystem
accurate(ly) [ˈækjərət]	genau	data pl [ˈdeɪtə]	Daten, Angaben
millimetre [ˈmɪlimiːtə]	Millimeter	cutting speed [ˈkʌtɪŋ spiːd]	Schnitt-, Schneidegeschwindigkeit
challenge [ˈtʃælɪndʒ]	schwierige Aufgabe, Herausforderung	feed rate [ˈfiːd reɪt]	Vorschubgeschwindigkeit
to assemble [əˈsembl]	zusammenbauen, montieren	production process [prəˈdʌkʃn ˈprəʊses]	Fertigungsablauf, Produktionsprozess
water supply [ˈwɔːtə səplaɪ]	Wasserversorgung	to program [ˈprəʊɡræm]	programmieren
condition [kənˈdɪʃn]	Zustand	industrial [ɪnˈdʌstrɪəl]	industriell, Industrie-
responsibility [rɪˌspɒnsəˈbɪləti]	Aufgabe, Zuständigkeit, Verantwortlichkeit	smooth(ly) [smuːð]	reibungslos
pre-planning [priːˈplænɪŋ]	Vorausplanung	production plant [prəˈdʌkʃn plɑːnt]	Produktionsanlage, Fertigungsbetrieb
relating to [rɪˈleɪtɪŋ tə]	bezüglich, betreffend	wear [weə]	Abnutzung, Verschleiß
17 duty [ˈdjuːti]	Pflicht, Aufgabe	to prevent [prɪˈvent]	verhindern
to train [treɪn]	ausbilden, eine Ausbildung machen	breakdown [ˈbreɪkdaʊn]	Ausfall, Störfall
		servicing [ˈsɜːvɪsɪŋ]	Wartung, (routinemäßige) Überprüfung
pliers pl [ˈplaɪəz]	Zange	selection [sɪˈlekʃn]	Auswahl
screwdriver [ˈskruːdraɪvə]	Schraubendreher, Schraubenzieher	electrician / electrical engineer [ɪˌlekˈtrɪʃn, ɪˌlektrɪkl ˌendʒɪˈnɪə]	Elektriker/in
special tool [ˌspeʃl ˈtuːl]	Spezialwerkzeug	precision mechanic [prɪˈsɪʒn mɪkænɪk]	Feinwerkmechaniker/in
mass production [ˌmæs prəˈdʌkʃn]	Massenproduktion	machine builder [məˈʃiːn bɪldə]	Maschinenbauer/in
mould [məʊld]	Gussform	cutting tool mechanic [ˈkʌtɪŋ tuːl mɪkænɪk]	Schneidwerkzeugmechaniker/in
to mount [maʊnt]	montieren	tool maker [ˈtuːl meɪkə]	Werkzeugmacher/in
function [ˈfʌŋkʃn]	Funktion	mechatronic systems engineer [mekəˌtrɒnɪk ˌsɪstəmz endʒɪˈnɪə]	Mechatroniker/in
to commission [kəˈmɪʃn]	in Betrieb nehmen		
specialist [ˈspeʃəlɪst]	Fachmann/-frau, Spezialist/in	industrial mechanic [ɪnˌdʌstrɪəl mɪˈkænɪk]	Industriemechaniker/in
automotive [ˌɔːtəˈməʊtɪv]	Automobil-	steel [stiːl]	Stahl
passenger car [ˈpæsɪndʒə kɑː]	Pkw	plastics [ˈplæstɪks]	Kunststoff
lorry BE [ˈlɒri]	Lkw	18 dual system [ˌdjuːəl ˈsɪstəm]	duales System
vehicle [ˈviːəkl]	Fahrzeug	presentation [ˌpreznˈteɪʃn]	Vortrag, Präsentation
to install [ɪnˈstɔːl]	installieren		
accessories pl [əkˈsesəriz]	Zubehör	to enter sth [ˈentə]	etw (Ausbildung usw.) beginnen, mit etw anfangen
gas [ɡæs]	Gas		
liquid [ˈlɪkwɪd]	Flüssigkeit	scheme [skiːm]	Programm, Plan
compressed air [kəmˌprest ˈeə]	Druckluft	vocational college [vəʊˌkeɪʃənl ˈkɒlɪdʒ]	Berufsschule
vessel [ˈvesl]	Gefäß, Behälter		
pipe [paɪp]	Rohr, Röhre	to combine [kəmˈbaɪn]	verknüpfen, kombinieren
pipeline [ˈpaɪplaɪn]	(Rohr-)Leitung	hands-on [ˌhændz ˈɒn]	praktisch
refinery [rɪˈfaɪnəri]	Raffinerie		

Unit word list

job experience [ˌdʒɒb ɪkˈspɪəriəns]	Berufserfahrung	on behalf of sb [ɒn bɪˈhɑːf əv]	für jdn, in jds Namen
deep [diːp]	tief, vertieft	to confirm [kənˈfɜːm]	bestätigen
trade [treɪd]	Gewerbe, Branche	service check [ˈsɜːvɪs tʃek]	Wartung, (routinemäßige) Überprüfung, Inspektion
mechanics [mɪˈkænɪks]	Mechanik	lathe [leɪð]	Drehbank
mechatronics [mekəˈtrɒnɪks]	Mechatronik	factory manager [ˈfæktəri mænɪdʒə]	Betriebsleiter/in, Werksleiter/in
to gain [geɪn]	erwerben	mobile [ˈməʊbaɪl]	Handy, Mobiltelefon
qualification [ˌkwɒlɪfɪˈkeɪʃn]	Abschluss, Qualifikation	to represent [ˌreprɪˈzent]	darstellen, vertreten
degree [dɪˈgriː]	Abschluss	equivalent [ɪˈkwɪvələnt]	Entsprechung, Übersetzung
to recognize [ˈrekəgnaɪz]	anerkennen	engaged [ɪnˈgeɪdʒd]	(Telefon:) besetzt
to take on sb [ˌteɪk ˈɒn]	jdn einstellen	to be unavailable [bɪ ˌʌnəˈveɪləbl]	(Telefon:) nicht zu sprechen sein
at the end of the day [ət ði end əv ðə ˈdeɪ]	letzten Endes	to hold the line [ˌhəʊld ðə ˈlaɪn]	(Telefon:) am Apparat bleiben
to benefit [ˈbenɪfɪt]	(davon) profitieren	to put sb through [ˌpʊt ˈθruː]	(Telefon:) jdn durchstellen
expert staff [ˌekspɜːt ˈstɑːf]	Fachpersonal		
generation [ˌdʒenəˈreɪʃn]	Generation	21 Speaking. [ˈspiːkɪŋ]	(Telefon:) Am Apparat.
permanent [ˈpɜːmənənt]	unbefristet	drill [drɪl]	Bohrer
to keep on sb [ˌkiːp ˈɒn]	jdn behalten	available [əˈveɪləbl]	lieferbar, verfügbar
recruitment [rɪˈkruːtmənt]	Einstellung, Anwerbung (von Personal)	alternative [ɔːlˈtɜːnətɪv]	Alternative
		extension [ɪkˈstenʃn]	Durchwahl
education system [ˌedʒuˈkeɪʃn sɪstəm]	Bildungssystem, Schulsystem	digit [ˈdɪdʒɪt]	Ziffer
		except for [ɪkˈsept fə]	außer
workshop manager [ˌwɜːkʃɒp ˈmænɪdʒə]	Werkstattleiter/in	P to make up sth [ˌmeɪk ˈʌp]	sich etw ausdenken
qualified [ˈkwɒlɪfaɪd]	Fach-, mit Abschluss, qualifiziert		
to attend [əˈtend]	(Schule) besuchen	**UNIT 3**	
19 to pass an exam [ˌpɑːs ən ɪgˈzæm]	eine Prüfung bestehen	24 vernier callipers pl [ˈvɜːniə kælɪpəz]	Messschieber
particular [pəˈtɪkjələ]	speziell	to measure [ˈmeʒə]	messen
long-time [ˌlɒŋ ˈtaɪm]	langfristig	thickness [ˈθɪknəs]	Stärke, Dicke
to join a company [ˌdʒɔɪn ə ˈkʌmpəni]	bei einem Unternehmen anfangen	inside diameter [ˌɪnsaɪd daɪˈæmɪtə]	Innendurchmesser
mind map [ˈmaɪndmæp]	Mindmap	outside diameter [ˌaʊtsaɪd daɪˈæmɪtə]	Außendurchmesser
to continue to do sth [kənˈtɪnjuː tə]	mit etw weitermachen	depth [depθ]	Tiefe
canteen [kænˈtiːn]	Kantine	measuring tool [ˈmeʒərɪŋ tuːl]	Messwerkzeug
noise [nɔɪz]	Lärm	ruler [ˈruːlə]	Lineal
overtime work [ˈəʊvətaɪm wɜːk]	Überstunden	inspection mirror [ɪnˈspekʃn mɪrə]	Kontrollspiegel
supervised [ˈsuːpəvaɪzd]	unter Aufsicht	loose [luːs]	locker
to work overtime [ˌwɜːk ˈəʊvətaɪm]	Überstunden machen	vibration testing [vaɪˈbreɪʃn testɪŋ]	Schwingprüfung, Vibrationsprüfung
branch [brɑːntʃ]	Ast, Zweig	device [dɪˈvaɪs]	Gerät
working hours pl [ˌwɜːkɪŋ ˈaʊəz]	Arbeitszeiten	to diagnose [ˈdaɪəgnəʊz]	diagnostizieren, feststellen
to write up sth [ˌraɪt ˈʌp]	etw (Text) ausarbeiten	multimeter [ˌmʌltiˈmiːtə]	Multimeter
		voltage [ˈvəʊltɪdʒ]	Spannung
20 client [ˈklaɪənt]	Kunde/Kundin	current [ˈkʌrənt]	Strom
to leave a message [ˌliːv ə ˈmesɪdʒ]	eine Nachricht hinterlassen	resistance [rɪˈzɪstəns]	Widerstand
voicemail [ˈvɔɪsmeɪl]	Mailbox	capacitance [kəˈpæsɪtəns]	Kapazität
to take a message [ˌteɪk ə ˈmesɪdʒ]	etw ausrichten	inductance [ɪnˈdʌktəns]	Induktivität
		current gain [ˈkʌrənt geɪn]	Stromverstärkung
to call back [ˌkɔːl ˈbæk]	zurückrufen	transistor [trænˈzɪstə]	Transistor

advanced	[əd'vɑːnst]	fortschrittlich, modern
scale	[skeɪl]	Skala
soldering iron	['səʊldərɪŋ aɪən]	Lötkolben
centre punch	['sentə pʌntʃ]	Körner
to mark	[mɑːk]	kennzeichnen, markieren
to wander	['wɒndə]	wandern
to form	[fɔːm]	formen, bilden
dent	[dent]	Vertiefung
to guide	[gaɪd]	leiten, führen
tip	[tɪp]	Spitze
to operate	['ɒpəreɪt]	funktionieren, arbeiten
rod	[rɒd]	Stab
shaped	[ʃeɪpt]	geformt
to harden	['hɑːdn]	härten

25
close-up photo	[kləʊs ˌʌp 'fəʊtəʊ]	Nahaufnahme
column	['kɒləm]	(Text:) Spalte
hand tool	['hænd tuːl]	Handwerkzeug
toolbox	['tuːlbɒks]	Werkzeugkasten
to carry sth	['kæri]	etw mit sich führen

26
work experience	['wɜːk ɪkspɪəriəns]	Praktikum
tool trolley	['tuːl trɒli]	Werkzeugwagen
to identify	[aɪ'dentɪfaɪ]	identifizieren, bestimmen
to enter sth	['entə]	etw betreten
electric drill	[ɪ'lektrɪk drɪl]	Elektrobohrmaschine
handfile	['hændfaɪl]	Handfeile
hacksaw	['hæksɔː]	Bügelsäge
jigsaw	['dʒɪgsɔː]	Stichsäge
ratchet	['rætʃɪt]	Ratschenschlüssel

27
adjustable spanner	[əˌdʒʌstəbl 'spænə]	Rollgabelschlüssel
Allen head wrench	['ælən hed rentʃ]	Innensechskantschlüssel, Inbusschlüssel
angle	[æŋgl]	Winkel
set	[set]	Satz
chisel	['tʃɪzl]	Meißel
engineer's hammer	[ˌendʒɪnɪəz 'hæmə]	Schlosserhammer
side cutting pliers pl	[ˌsaɪd kʌtɪŋ 'plaɪəz]	Seitenschneider
socket wrench	['sɒkɪt rentʃ]	Steckschlüssel
double ended ring spanner	[ˌdʌbl endɪd 'rɪŋ spænə]	Doppelringschlüssel
double open ended spanner	[ˌdʌbl ˌəʊpən endɪd 'spænə]	Doppelmaulschlüssel
soft faced hammer	[ˌsɒft feɪst 'hæmə]	Schonhammer
three corner scraper	[ˌθriː kɔːnə 'skreɪpə]	Schabeisen mit dreieckiger Ziehklinge
flat file	['flæt faɪl]	Flachfeile
vice	[vaɪs]	Schraubstock

waterpump pliers pl	['wɔːtəpʌmp plaɪəz]	Wasserpumpenzange
pump	[pʌmp]	Pumpe
assembly	[ə'sembli]	Montage
assembly line	[ə'sembli laɪn]	Fertigungsstraße, Montageband
to service	['sɜːvɪs]	warten, überprüfen
to mark out	[ˌmɑːk 'aʊt]	anreißen, anzeichnen
die plate	['daɪ pleɪt]	Formplatte
hardly ever	[ˌhɑːdli 'evə]	kaum, fast nie
nut	[nʌt]	Mutter
bolt	[bəʊlt]	Schraube (zur Befestigung von Muttern)
washer	['wɒʃə]	Unterlegscheibe
fastener	['fɑːsnə]	Verbindungselement
cross slot / Phillips screw	['krɒs slɒt skruː, 'fɪlɪps skruː]	Kreuzschlitzschraube
hexagon screw	['heksəgən skruː]	Sechskantschraube
Pozidriv screw	['pɒzɪdrɪv skruː]	Pozidriv-Kreuzschlitzschraube
Security T screw	[sɪ'kjʊərəti tiː skruː]	Torx-TR-Schraube
slotted screw	['slɒtɪd skruː]	Schlitzschraube
Torx screw	['tɔːks skruː]	Torxschraube

28
cap nut	['kæp nʌt]	Überwurfmutter, Hutmutter
hex nut	['heks nʌt]	Sechskantmutter
nylon insert lock nut	[ˌnaɪlɒn ɪnsɜːt 'lɒk nʌt]	Sicherungsmutter mit Nylon-Einsatz
square nut	['skweə nʌt]	Vierkantmutter
hex bolt	['heks bəʊlt]	Sechskantschraube
machine bolt	[mə'ʃiːn bəʊlt]	Maschinenschraube
sheet metal	['ʃiːt metl]	Blech
sheet metal screw	['ʃiːt metl skruː]	Blechschraube
thread	[θred]	Gewinde
thread cutting machine screw	[ˌθred kʌtɪŋ mə'ʃiːn skruː]	gewindeschneidende Maschinenschraube
external tooth lock washer	[ɪkstɜːnl ˌtuːθ 'lɒk wɒʃə]	außengezahnte Zahnscheibe
flat washer	[flæt 'wɒʃə]	Unterlegscheibe
internal tooth lock washer	[ɪntɜːnl ˌtuːθ 'lɒk wɒʃə]	innengezahnte Zahnscheibe
split lock washer	[splɪt ˌlɒk 'wɒʃə]	Federring, Federscheibe
drawer	[drɔː]	Schublade, Schubfach
power tool	['paʊə tuːl]	Elektrowerkzeug

29
machine tool	[mə'ʃiːn tuːl]	Werkzeugmaschine
bandsaw	['bændsɔː]	Bandsäge
milling machine	['mɪlɪŋ məʃiːn]	Fräsmaschine

Unit word list

off-hand grinder [ˌɒfhænd 'graɪndə]	Handschleifmaschine	compound slide [ˌkɒmpaʊnd 'slaɪd]	Kreuzschlitten
power hacksaw ['paʊə hæksɔː]	Maschinenbügelsäge	control unit [kən'trəʊl juːnɪt]	Steuergerät
column ['kɒləm]	Säule	headstock ['hedstɒk]	Spindelkasten
chuck [tʃʌk]	Spannfutter, Bohrfutter	protective hood [prə,tektɪv 'hʊd]	Schutzhaube
dial ['daɪəl]	Anzeige, Regler	rack [ræk]	Zahnstange
motor ['məʊtə]	Motor	tool holder ['tuːl həʊldə]	Werkzeughalter
to swivel ['swɪvl]	schwenken	to serve [sɜːv]	dienen
to be composed of sth [bi kəm'pəʊzd əv]	aus etw bestehen	housing ['haʊzɪŋ]	Gehäuse
base [beɪs]	Basis, Sockel	driving pulley ['draɪvɪŋ pʊli]	Antriebsscheibe
to support [sə'pɔːt]	tragen, halten, stützen	back gear [ˌbæk 'gɪə]	(Räder-)Vorgelege
in turn [ɪn 'tɜːn]	wiederum, seiner-/ihrerseits	live centre [ˌlaɪv 'sentə]	verfahrbare Führungsspitze
hold down clamp [ˌhəʊld daʊn 'klæmp]	Niederhalter	feed reverse gear [fiːd rɪ,vɜːs 'gɪə]	Vorschub rückwärts
to contain [kən'teɪn]	enthalten	to feed [fiːd]	vorschieben
to turn [tɜːn]	drehen	operation [ˌɒpə'reɪʃn]	Betrieb
spindle ['spɪndl]	Spindel	lathe operator [leɪð 'ɒpəreɪtə]	Dreher/in
control dial [kən'trəʊl daɪəl]	Drehregler	flying chips [ˌflaɪɪŋ 'tʃɪps]	herumfliegende Späne
to hold [həʊld]	halten	coolant ['kuːlənt]	Kühlmittel
cutting tool ['kʌtɪŋ tuːl]	Schneidwerkzeug	to slide [slaɪd]	gleiten
30 frequently ['friːkwəntli]	oft, häufig	to accommodate [ə'kɒmədeɪt]	aufnehmen, unterbringen
to machine [mə'ʃiːn]	(maschinell) bearbeiten	length [leŋθ]	Länge
flat [flæt]	eben	to fasten sth to sth ['fɑːsn tə]	etw an etw befestigen
surface ['sɜːfɪs]	Oberfläche, Fläche	to house [haʊz]	beherbergen
irregular [ɪ'regjələ]	uneben	gears pl [gɪəz]	Gangschaltung
to bore [bɔː]	innendrehen	clutch [klʌtʃ]	Kupplung
swivelling head ['swɪvlɪŋ hed]	Schwenkkopf	lever ['liːvə]	Hebel
to remove [rɪ'muːv]	entfernen, abtragen	cross slide ['krɒs slaɪd]	Querschlitten
to rotate [rəʊ'teɪt]	rotieren, sich drehen	rugged ['rʌgɪd]	robust, stabil
multi-toothed cutter [ˌmʌlti tuːθt 'kʌtə]	mehrzahniges Fräswerkzeug	casting ['kɑːstɪŋ]	Gussstück
equipped with sth [ɪ'kwɪpt wɪð]	mit etw ausgestattet	carriage assembly ['kærɪdʒ əsembli]	Werkzeugschlitten
power feed ['paʊə fiːd]	automatischer Vorschub	gear [gɪə]	Zahnrad
smooth [smuːð]	glatt, ruhig	rotation [rəʊ'teɪʃn]	Rotation, Drehung
manual feed [ˌmænjʊəl 'fiːd]	manueller Vorschub	compound rest ['kɒmpaʊnd rest]	Kreuzschlitten
surface finish [ˌsɜːfɪs 'fɪnɪʃ]	Oberfläche(nbeschaffenheit)	rigid(ly) ['rɪdʒɪd]	starr, fest
to fabricate ['fæbrɪkeɪt]	fertigen, herstellen	to clamp [klæmp]	einspannen
feature ['fiːtʃə]	Teil, Sonderanfertigung	height [haɪt]	Höhe
circular ['sɜːkjələ]	kreisförmig	support [sə'pɔːt]	Träger, Halter
cross section [ˌkrɒs 'sekʃn]	Querschnitt	32 to take care of sth [ˌteɪk 'keər əv]	sich um etw kümmern, etw bearbeiten, etw erledigen
to drive [draɪv]	antreiben	enquiry [ɪn'kwaɪəri]	Anfrage
gear train ['gɪə treɪn]	Getriebe	to appear [ə'pɪə]	erscheinen, auftreten, vorkommen
tailstock ['teɪlstɒk]	Reitstock	dot [dɒt]	Punkt
centre ['sentə]	Reitstockspitze	hyphen ['haɪfn]	Bindestrich
to ream [riːm]	reiben	underscore ['ʌndəskɔː]	Unterstrich
to thread [θred]	Gewinde schneiden	to dictate [dɪk'teɪt]	diktieren
taper ['teɪpə]	Kegel	subject line ['sʌbdʒɪkt laɪn]	Betreffzeile
31 apron ['eɪprən]	Schlosskasten	indication [ˌɪndɪ'keɪʃn]	Hinweis, Anzeichen
bed slideways ['bed slaɪdweɪz]	Maschinenbett	to state [steɪt]	angeben, erklären, sagen

181

	request (for sth) [rɪˈkwest]	Bitte (um etw)	aluminium BE [ˌæljəˈmɪniəm]	Aluminium
	assistance [əˈsɪstəns]	Hilfe, Unterstützung	aluminum AE [əˈluːmɪnəm]	Aluminium
	to announce [əˈnaʊns]	ankündigen	stress [stres]	Betonung
	covering letter [ˈkʌvərɪŋ letə]	Anschreiben, Begleit- schreiben	syllable [ˈsɪləbl]	Silbe
	brochure [ˈbrəʊʃə]	Broschüre	ferrous metals pl [ˌferəs ˈmetlz]	Eisenmetalle
	venue [ˈvenjuː]	Veranstaltungsort	e.g. [ˌiː ˈdʒiː]	z.B.
	event [ɪˈvent]	Veranstaltung	non-ferrous metals pl [nɒn ˌferəs ˈmetlz]	Buntmetalle
	flyer [ˈflaɪə]	Faltblatt	heavy metals pl [ˌhevi ˈmetlz]	Schwermetalle
	to attach [əˈtætʃ]	(E-Mail:) anhängen	copper [ˈkɒpə]	Kupfer
	update (on sth) [ˈʌpdeɪt]	aktuelle Informationen (zu etw)	light metals pl [ˌlaɪt ˈmetlz]	Leichtmetalle
	agenda [əˈdʒendə]	Tagesordnung	non-metals pl [ˌnɒn ˈmetlz]	Nichtmetalle, Steine und Erden
	application [ˌæplɪˈkeɪʃn]	Antrag, Bewerbung	natural [ˈnætʃrəl]	natürlich
	stand [stænd]	(Messe-)Stand	artificial [ˌɑːtɪˈfɪʃl]	künstlich
	fair [feə]	Messe	compounds pl [ˈkɒmpaʊndz]	Verbundwerkstoffe
	to interview sb [ˈɪntəvjuː]	mit jdm ein Vorstellungs- gespräch führen		
33	reply [rɪˈplaɪ]	Antwort	35 mechanical(ly) [mɪˈkænɪkl]	mechanisch
	to reply [rɪˈplaɪ]	antworten	property [ˈprɒpəti]	Eigenschaft
	catalogue [ˈkætəlɒg]	Katalog	elastic(ally) [ɪˈlæstɪk]	elastisch
	item [ˈaɪtəm]	Artikel	flexible [ˈfleksəbl]	biegsam
	in stock [ɪn ˈstɒk]	auf Lager, verfügbar	hard-wearing [ˌhɑːd ˈweərɪŋ]	strapazierfähig, verschleiß- fest
	Yours faithfully [ˌjɔːz ˈfeɪθfəli]	... und verbleiben mit freundlichen Grüßen	light-weight [ˈlaɪtweɪt]	leicht
	Ltd [ˈlɪmɪtɪd]	GmbH	malleable [ˈmæliəbl]	formbar
	to dispatch [dɪˈspætʃ]	versenden	resilient [rɪˈzɪliənt]	federelastisch
	to do business with sb [du ˈbɪznəs wɪð]	mit jdm Geschäfte machen	tough [tʌf]	zäh
	complimentary close [ˌkɒmplɪˌmentri ˈkləʊz]	(Brief:) Schlussformel	to absorb [əbˈsɔːb]	absorbieren, aufnehmen
	polite(ly) [pəˈlaɪt]	höflich	to deform [dɪˈfɔːm]	verformen
	salutation [ˌsæljuˈteɪʃn]	(Brief:) Anrede	to bend [bend]	biegen
	sir [sɜː]	Herr	in response to [ɪn rɪˈspɒns tə]	als Reaktion auf
	madam [ˈmædəm]	Dame	to apply sth [əˈplaɪ]	etw anwenden
	unknown [ˌʌnˈnəʊn]	unbekannt	force [fɔːs]	Kraft
	Best regards / Regards [rɪˈgɑːdz]	Mit freundlichen Grüßen	stress [stres]	Belastung
	Best wishes [best ˈwɪʃɪz]	Mit freundlichen Grüßen	compressive stress [kəmˌpresɪv ˈstres]	Druckbelastung, Druck- spannung
	Yours sincerely [ˌjɔːz sɪnˈsɪəli]	Mit freundlichen Grüßen	defect [ˈdiːfekt]	Schaden, Fehler
			to withstand sth [wɪðˈstænd]	etw aushalten, einer Sache widerstehen
	UNIT 4		shock [ʃɒk]	Stoß, Stöße
34	trade fair [ˈtreɪd feə]	(Branchen-, Handels-)Messe	plastic(ally) [ˈplæstɪk]	plastisch
	to classify [ˈklæsɪfaɪ]	klassifizieren	to fracture [ˈfræktʃə]	brechen, zerbrechen
	overview [ˈəʊvəvjuː]	Übersicht	to rupture [ˈrʌptʃə]	reißen, zerreißen
	carbon fibre [ˌkɑːbən ˈfaɪbə]	Kohlefaser	indentation [ˌɪndenˈteɪʃn]	Eindruck, Einkerbung
	iron [ˈaɪən]	Eisen	scratching [ˈskrætʃɪŋ]	Verkratzen
	cast iron [ˌkɑːst ˈaɪən]	Gusseisen	to resist [rɪˈzɪst]	einer Sache widerstehen
	glass fibre [ˌglɑːs ˈfaɪbə]	Glasfaser	distorting [dɪˈstɔːtɪŋ]	verformend, deformierend
	lead [led]	Blei	shape [ʃeɪp]	Form
	stone [stəʊn]	Stein	silvery-grey [ˌsɪlvəri ˈgreɪ]	silbrig-grau
	titanium [tɪˈteɪniəm]	Titan		
	zinc [zɪŋk]	Zink		

Unit word list

	crash helmet ['kræʃ helmɪt]	Sturzhelm	
	household goods *pl* ['haʊshəʊld gʊdz]	Haushaltsartikel	
	rough [rʌf]	rau	
	hand-out ['hændaʊt]	Arbeitsblatt, Informationsblatt, Merkblatt	
	to **distribute** [dɪ'strɪbjuːt]	verteilen	
	to **refer to sth** [rɪ'fɜː tə]	auf etw verweisen, sich auf etw beziehen	
	conclusion [kən'kluːʒn]	Schluss	
36	**engine** ['endʒɪn]	Motor	
	Stirling engine ['stɜːlɪŋ endʒɪn]	Stirlingmotor	
	base [beɪs]	Grundkörper	
	cooler ['kuːlə]	Kühlkörper	
	motion link ['məʊʃn lɪŋk]	Kulisse, Kulissenführung	
	stand [stænd]	Ständer	
	physical ['fɪzɪkl]	physikalisch	
	density ['densəti]	Dichte	
	elasticity [ˌiːlæ'stɪsəti]	Elastizität	
	thermal expansion [ˌθɜːml ɪk'spænʃn]	Wärmeausdehnung	
	thermal conductivity [ˌθɜːml kɒndʌk'tɪvəti]	Wärmeleitfähigkeit	
	dense [dens]	dicht	
	to **expand** [ɪk'spænd]	sich ausdehnen	
37	**user manual** [ˌjuːzə 'mænjuəl]	Benutzerhandbuch, Betriebsanleitung	
	axle ['æksl]	Achse	
	displacement axle [dɪs'pleɪsmənt æksl]	Verdrängerachse	
	crankshaft ['kræŋkʃɑːft]	Kurbelwelle	
	ready-assembly model [ˌredi ə'sembli mɒdl]	Fertigmodell	
	to **lubricate** ['luːbrɪkeɪt]	schmieren	
	self-assembled [ˌself ə'sembld]	selbst zusammengebaut	
	as follows [əz 'fɒləʊz]	folgendermaßen, wie folgt	
	warranty ['wɒrənti]	Garantie	
	void [vɔɪd]	unwirksam, ungültig	
	lubricant ['luːbrɪkənt]	Schmiermittel	
	excess ['ekses]	überschüssig	
	ceramic paste [səˌræmɪk 'peɪst]	Keramikpaste	
	working piston ['wɜːkɪŋ pɪstən]	Arbeitskolben	
	partially ['pɑːʃəli]	teilweise	
	to **disassemble** [ˌdɪsə'sembl]	auseinanderbauen, demontieren	
	thoroughly ['θʌrəli]	gründlich	
	to **apply** [ə'plaɪ]	(Flüssigkeit usw.) auftragen	
	trial run ['traɪəl rʌn]	Probelauf	
	droplet ['drɒplət]	Tröpfchen	
	to **regrease** [ˌriː'griːs]	nachfetten	
	bearing ['beərɪŋ]	Lager	
	drop [drɒp]	Tropfen	
	prolonged [prə'lɒŋd]	(lang) anhaltend	
	cleaning ['kliːnɪŋ]	Reinigung	
	to **relubricate** [ˌriː'luːbrɪkeɪt]	nachschmieren	
	not unless [nɒt ən'les]	nicht bevor; nur (dann) wenn	
	to **rebuild** [ˌriː'bɪld]	neu aufbauen	
	dust [dʌst]	Staub	
	abrasion dust [ə'breɪʒn dʌst]	Abriebstaub	
	to **build up** [ˌbɪld 'ʌp]	sich anreichern, sich bilden	
	friction bearing ['frɪkʃn beərɪŋ]	Gleitlager, Gleitlagerung	
	cylinder ['sɪlɪndə]	Zylinder	
	to **settle** ['setl]	sich ablagern, sich festsetzen	
	to **cause sth do to sth** [kɔːz]	dazu führen, dass etw etw tut	
	standstill ['stændstɪl]	Stillstand	
	inside [ɪn'saɪd]	Innenseite, das Innere	
	sliding surface [ˌslaɪdɪŋ 'sɜːfɪs]	Gleitfläche	
	cloth [klɒθ]	Tuch	
	brass [brɑːs]	Messing	
	to **reassemble** [ˌriːə'sembl]	wieder zusammenbauen	
	as a rule [əz ə 'ruːl]	in der Regel	
	oxidation [ˌɒksɪ'deɪʃn]	Oxidation	
	ageing ['eɪdʒɪŋ]	Alterung	
	to **be subject to sth** [bi 'sʌbdʒekt tə]	einer Sache unterliegen	
	intended [ɪn'tendɪd]	vorgesehen, beabsichtigt	
	to **tarnish** ['tɑːnɪʃ]	anlaufen	
	patina ['pætɪnə]	Patina	
	fingerprint ['fɪŋgəprɪnt]	Fingerabdruck	
	to **darken** ['dɑːkən]	nachdunkeln	
	sweaty palms *pl* [ˌsweti 'pɑːmz]	verschwitzte Handflächen	
	moisture ['mɔɪstʃə]	Feuchtigkeit	
	to **polish** ['pɒlɪʃ]	polieren	
	polish ['pɒlɪʃ]	Politur	
	to **age** [eɪdʒ]	altern	
	desired [dɪ'zaɪəd]	gewünscht	
	source [sɔːs]	Quelle	
38	to **oil** [ɔɪl]	ölen	
	to **rust** [rʌst]	rosten	
	kit [kɪt]	Bausatz	
	assembly instructions *pl* [ə'sembli ɪnstrʌkʃnz]	Montageanleitung	
	powder ['paʊdə]	Pulver	
	to **slow down sth** [ˌsləʊ 'daʊn]	etw (ab)bremsen	
39	**specific** [spə'sɪfɪk]	speziell, bestimmt, konkret	
	specifications *pl* [ˌspesɪfɪ'keɪʃnz]	technische Daten, Spezifikationen	
	dimensions *pl* [dɪ'menʃnz]	Abmessungen, Dimensionen	
T	to **sort out sth** [ˌsɔːt 'aʊt]	etw klären	
	to **talk sb through sth** [ˌtɔːk 'θruː]	etw mit jdm durchgehen	

	plate [pleɪt]	Platte
	chamfer ['tʃæmfə]	Fase
	convex ['kɒnveks]	konvex
	semicircle ['semisɜːkl]	Halbkreis
	radius, radii ['reɪdɪəs, 'reɪdɪaɪ]	Radius, Radien
	concave [kɒn'keɪv]	konkav
	base line ['beɪs laɪn]	Grundlinie
	groove [gruːv]	Nut
	borehole ['bɔːhəʊl]	Bohrloch
	bore [bɔː]	Bohrung
	feature ['fiːtʃə]	technisches Merkmal
	continuous line [kən,tɪnjuəs 'laɪn]	durchgezogene Linie
	chain-dotted line ['tʃeɪn dɒtɪd laɪn]	strichpunktierte Linie
	dimension line [dɪ'menʃn laɪn]	Bemaßungslinie
	to label ['leɪbl]	bezeichnen, etikettieren
	circumference [sə'kʌmfərəns]	Umfang
40	rectangle ['rektæŋgl]	Rechteck
	triangle ['traɪæŋgl]	Dreieck
	circle ['sɜːkl]	Kreis
	cube [kjuːb]	Würfel
	cubical ['kjuːbɪkl]	würfelförmig
	solid ['sɒlɪd]	(dreidimensionaler) Körper
	rectangular solid [rek,tæŋgjələ 'sɒlɪd]	Quader
	sphere [sfɪə]	Kugel
	hemisphere ['hemɪsfɪə]	Halbkugel
	hemispherical [,hemɪ'sferɪkl]	halbkugelförmig
	cone [kəʊn]	Kegel, Konus
	bar [bɑː]	Barren
	block [blɒk]	Klotz, Block
	film [fɪlm]	Folie
	sheet [ʃiːt]	Blech
	strip [strɪp]	Leiste, Streifen
	tube [tjuːb]	Rohr
	wire ['waɪə]	Draht
41	rolled [rəʊld]	gewalzt, Walz-
	cylindrical(ly) [sə'lɪndrɪkl]	zylindrisch
	conical ['kɒnɪkl]	konisch, kegelförmig
	L-shaped ['el ʃeɪpt]	L-förmig
	symmetrical [sɪ'metrɪkl]	symmetrisch
	edge [edʒ]	Kante
	back to back [,bæk tə 'bæk]	Rücken an Rücken
P	saddle ['sædl]	Sattel
	handwheel ['hændwiːl]	Handrad
42	signpost ['saɪnpəʊst]	Hinweise zur Orientierung der Zuhörer in einer Präsentation
	to invite sth [ɪn'vaɪt]	zu etw auffordern
	clarity ['klærəti]	Klarheit, Deutlichkeit
	correctness [kə'rektnəs]	Richtigkeit
	spelling ['spelɪŋ]	Rechtschreibung
	prompt card ['prɒmt kɑːd]	Moderationskarte
	either ['aɪðə]	eines (von mehreren)
	index card ['ɪndeks kɑːd]	Karteikarte
	to divide [dɪ'vaɪd]	teilen, unterteilen
43	feedback ['fiːdbæk]	Rückmeldung(en)
	to be one's turn [bi wʌnz 'tɜːn]	an der Reihe sein
	improvement [ɪm'pruːvmənt]	Verbesserung
	to support [sə'pɔːt]	(Argumentation) untermauern
	to deal with sth ['diːl wɪð]	sich mit etw befassen
	manner ['mænə]	Art (und Weise)
	overall score [əʊvər,ɔːl 'skɔː]	Gesamtpunktzahl

UNIT 5

46	manual ['mænjuəl]	Handbuch
	safety instructions pl ['seɪfti ɪnstrʌkʃnz]	Sicherheitshinweise
	measurement ['meʒəmənt]	Maß, Maßangabe, Messung
	trolley ['trɒli]	Wagen
	scaffold ['skæfəʊld]	Gerüst
	term [tɜːm]	Begriff
	mathematical operation [mæθə,mætɪkl ,ɒpə'reɪʃn]	Rechenoperation
	approximate(ly) [ə'prɒksɪmət]	ungefähr, zirka
	degree [dɪ'griː]	Grad
	to read out sth [,riːd 'aʊt]	etw vorlesen
47	rectilinear solid [rektɪ,lɪnɪə 'sɒlɪd]	geradkantiger Körper
	reverse order [rɪ,vɜːs 'ɔːdə]	umgekehrte Reihenfolge
	alphabetical [,ælfə'betɪkl]	alphabetisch
	platform trolley ['plætfɔːm trɒli]	Plattformwagen, Transportwagen
	castor ['kɑːstə]	Rolle
	rubber ['rʌbə]	Gummi
	to fit sth with sth [fɪt]	etw mit etw ausstatten
	brake [breɪk]	Bremse
48	safety precautions pl ['seɪfti prɪkɔːʃnz]	Sicherheitsvorkehrungen, Sicherheitsmaßnahmen
	decal ['diːkæl]	Aufkleber
	to stick [stɪk]	kleben
	improperly [ɪm'prɒpəli]	nicht richtig
	to grease [griːs]	einfetten, schmieren
	to eject [i'dʒekt]	auswerfen, herausschleudern
	deadly ['dedli]	tödlich
	chuck jaw ['tʃʌk dʒɔː]	Futterbacke, Klemmbacke
	to protrude [prə'truːd]	vorstehen, herausragen
	beyond [bɪ'jɒnd]	über, jenseits
	securely [sɪ'kjʊəli]	fest, sicher
	distortion [dɪ'stɔːʃn]	Verzug

	to press [pres]	drücken		to take sth apart [ˌteɪk əˈpɑːt]	etw auseinandernehmen
	to power up [ˌpaʊər ˈʌp]	einschalten, hochfahren		chip removal [ˈtʃɪp rɪmuːvl]	Späneförderung
	to restart [ˌriːˈstɑːt]	neu starten		moveable [ˈmuːvəbl]	beweglich
	control panel [kənˈtrəʊl pænl]	Steuerkonsole		hood [hʊd]	Schutzhaube
	severe(ly) [sɪˈvɪə]	stark, schwer		decibel [ˈdesɪbel]	Dezibel
	immediately [ɪˈmiːdiətli]	sofort, unverzüglich	50	visuals pl [ˈvɪʒuəlz]	visuelle Hilfsmittel
	hydraulic pressure [haɪˌdrɔːlɪk ˈpreʃə]	Hydraulikdruck		to attract sb's attention [əˌtrækt əˈtenʃn]	jds Aufmerksamkeit wecken
	to set [set]	einstellen		to remove [rɪˈmuːv]	(Kleidung usw.) ausziehen
	to unplug [ˌʌnˈplʌg]	ausstecken, vom Stromnetz trennen		to do one's job [duː wʌnz ˈdʒɒb]	jds Aufgabe erfüllen
49	warning [ˈwɔːnɪŋ]	Hinweis, Warnhinweis	51	to set up [ˌset ˈʌp]	aufbauen, einrichten
	electrocution [ɪlektrəˈkjuːʃn]	(Tötung durch) Stromschlag		to align [əˈlaɪn]	ausrichten
	to lock [lɒk]	abschließen, verschließen		maintenance instructions pl [ˈmeɪntənəns ɪnstrʌkʃnz]	Wartungsanleitung
	main switch [ˌmeɪn ˈswɪtʃ]	Hauptschalter		regular maintenance routines pl [ˌregjələ ˈmeɪntənəns ruːtiːnz]	regelmäßige Wartung(sarbeiten)
	moving parts pl [ˌmuːvɪŋ ˈpɑːts]	bewegliche Teile		central lubrication [ˌsentrəl luːbrɪˈkeɪʃn]	Zentralschmierung
	to crush [krʌʃ]	zerquetschen		chafing [ˈtʃeɪfɪŋ]	Abscheuerung
	to entangle [ɪnˈtæŋgl]	(sich/etw) verfangen		clamping force [ˈklæmpɪŋ fɔːs]	Spannkraft
	to trap [træp]	einklemmen		connection terminal [kəˈnekʃn tɜːmɪnl]	Verbindungsklemme
	injury [ˈɪndʒəri]	Verletzung(en)		hose [həʊz]	Schlauch
	risk of fire [ˌrɪsk əf ˈfaɪə]	Brandgefahr		humidity [hjuːˈmɪdəti]	Feuchtigkeit
	risk of explosion [ˌrɪsk əv ɪkˈspləʊʒn]	Explosionsgefahr		leakage [ˈliːkɪdʒ]	Leck, undichte Stelle
	control cabinet [kənˌtrəʊl ˈkæbɪnət]	Steuerungskasten		V-belt [ˈviː belt]	Keilriemen
	drive [draɪv]	Antrieb	52	working space [ˈwɜːkɪŋ speɪs]	Arbeitsbereich
	line voltage [ˈlaɪn vəʊltɪdʒ]	Netzspannung		level [ˈlevl]	Stand, Pegel
	no-load running [nəʊ ˌləʊd ˈrʌnɪŋ]	Leerlaufbetrieb		to top up [ˌtɒp ˈʌp]	nachfüllen
	sound level [ˈsaʊnd levl]	Lärmpegel, Geräuschpegel		visual inspection [ˌvɪʒuəl ɪnˈspekʃn]	Sichtprüfung
	switching device [ˈswɪtʃɪŋ dɪvaɪs]	Schaltgerät		damage [ˈdæmɪdʒ]	Schaden
	warranty regulations pl [ˈwɒrənti regjuleɪʃnz]	Garantiebedingungen		deformation [ˌdiːfɔːˈmeɪʃn]	Verformung
T	to pay (special) attention to sth [ˌpeɪ əˈtenʃn tə]	(besonders) auf etw achten		wiring [ˈwaɪərɪŋ]	Verkabelung
	relevant [ˈreləvənt]	relevant, wichtig, entsprechend		to dismount [dɪsˈmaʊnt]	abmontieren
	section [ˈsekʃn]	Abschnitt		wiper [ˈwaɪpə]	Abstreifer
	operating manual [ˌɒpəreɪtɪŋ ˈmænjuəl]	Betriebsanleitung		filter insert [ˈfɪltər ɪnsɜːt]	Filtereinsatz
	connection [kəˈnekʃn]	Anschluss		power chuck [ˈpaʊə tʃʌk]	Kraftspannfutter
	to turn sth [tɜːn]	etw drehen		tension [ˈtenʃn]	Spannung
	three phase current [ˌθriː feɪz ˈkʌrənt]	Drehstrom		cross drive [ˈkrɒs draɪv]	Querantrieb
	extra [ˈekstrə]	Sonderzubehör, Zusatzausstattung, Extra		guideway [ˈgaɪdweɪ]	Führungsschiene
	to wire [ˈwaɪə]	verkabeln, anschließen		window shield [ˈwɪndəʊ ʃiːld]	Schutzscheibe
	seal [siːl]	Siegel		crack [kræk]	Riss
	to modify [ˈmɒdɪfaɪ]	verändern, modifizieren		air conditioning system [ˈeə kəndɪʃnɪŋ sɪstəm]	Klimasteuerung, Klimaanlage
	trained staff [ˌtreɪnd ˈstɑːf]	Fachpersonal		fan [fæn]	Ventilator
				tank [tæŋk]	Tank

sealing point ['siːlɪŋ pɔɪnt]	Dichtstelle	teething problems pl ['tiːðɪŋ prɒbləmz]	Kinderkrankheiten, Anlaufschwierigkeiten
to renew [rɪ'njuː]	erneuern	54 graph [grɑːf]	Diagramm, Grafik
to gather ['gæðə]	sich sammeln	union ['juːnɪən]	Gewerkschaft
lube system ['luːb sɪstəm]	Schmierung	union representative [ˌjuːnɪən reprɪ'zentətɪv]	Gewerkschaftsvertreter/in
piping ['paɪpɪŋ]	Rohrleitungen	conference ['kɒnfərəns]	Tagung, Konferenz
tight [taɪt]	eng, fest, knapp	bar chart ['bɑː tʃɑːt]	Säulendiagramm
plug connector ['plʌg kənektə]	Stecker, Steckverbinder	line graph ['laɪn grɑːf]	Liniendiagramm
corrosion [kə'rəʊʒn]	Korrosion	pie chart ['paɪ tʃɑːt]	Tortendiagramm
switch cabinet [ˌswɪtʃ 'kæbɪnət]	Schaltschrank	table ['teɪbl]	Tabelle
		to go up [ˌgəʊ 'ʌp]	steigen
tight fit [taɪt 'fɪt]	enger Sitz	to go down [ˌgəʊ 'daʊn]	sinken
to readjust [riːə'dʒʌst]	nachjustieren	to increase [ɪn'kriːs]	zunehmen, ansteigen
clearance ['klɪərəns]	Spiel	increase ['ɪŋkriːs]	Zunahme, Anstieg
required [rɪ'kwaɪəd]	erforderlich	to flatten out [ˌflætn 'aʊt]	sich stabilisieren, sich einpendeln (bei)
power supply ['paʊə səplaɪ]	Stromversorgung	to level off [ˌlevl 'ɒf]	sich stabilisieren, sich einpendeln (bei)
power supply chain ['paʊə səplaɪ tʃeɪn]	Stromversorgungskette	to decrease [dɪ'kriːs]	abnehmen, sinken
power feed ['paʊə fiːd]	Stromzuführung	decrease ['diːkriːs]	Abnahme, Sinken
troubleshooting ['trʌblʃuːtɪŋ]	Fehlersuche	to drop [drɒp]	sinken, fallen
		drop [drɒp]	Fall, Sinken
to smear [smɪə]	beschmieren	to rise [raɪz]	ansteigen
to occur [ə'kɜː]	auftreten, vorkommen	rise [raɪz]	Anstieg
to solve [sɒlv]	lösen	to fluctuate ['flʌktʃueɪt]	schwanken, sich ständig verändern
cross slide taper ['krɒs slaɪd teɪpə]	Keilleiste des Planschlittens	fluctuation [ˌflʌktʃu'eɪʃn]	Schwankung(en), ständige Veränderung
main bearing [ˌmeɪn 'beərɪŋ]	Hauptlager(ung)	to fall [fɔːl]	abstürzen
quill [kwɪl]	Pinole	fall [fɔːl]	Absturz
steady rest ['stedi rest]	Lünette	to climb [klaɪm]	steigen
overhung [əʊvə'hʌŋ]	auskragend, hervorstehend	climb [klaɪm]	Anstieg
centre line ['sentə laɪn]	Mittellinie, Achse	to peak [piːk]	einen Spitzenwert erreichen
to re-align [riːə'laɪn]	neu ausrichten, nachjustieren	peak [piːk]	Spitzenwert
		horizontal [ˌhɒrɪ'zɒntl]	waagrecht, horizontal
to displace [dɪs'pleɪs]	verschieben	vertical ['vɜːtɪkl]	senkrecht, vertikal
unsteady [ʌn'stedi]	wackelig	unit ['juːnɪt]	Einheit
constraint [kən'streɪnt]	Auflage	55 figures pl ['fɪgəz]	Zahlen, Ziffern
cutting section ['kʌtɪŋ sekʃn]	Spanquerschnitt	sales pl [seɪlz]	Umsatz, Umsätze, Verkaufszahlen
if appropriate [ɪf ə'prəʊprɪət]	gegebenenfalls	financial year [faɪˌnænʃl 'jɪə]	Geschäftsjahr
quill force ['kwɪl fɔːs]	Pinolenanstellkraft	quarterly ['kwɔːtəli]	vierteljährlich, Quartals-
53 exactly faced [ɪgˌzæktli 'feɪst]	genau bearbeitet	quarter ['kwɔːtə]	Quartal
right angle [ˌraɪt 'æŋgl]	rechter Winkel	T drastic(ally) ['dræstɪk]	drastisch
leeway ['liːweɪ]	Abdrift	to recover [rɪ'kʌvə]	sich erholen
gib [dʒɪb]	Bolzen	volume ['vɒljuːm]	Volumen
face [feɪs]	Fläche	at a glance [ət ə 'glɑːns]	auf einen Blick
imperfect [ɪm'pɜːfɪkt]	mangelhaft	to contrast [kən'trɑːst]	gegenüberstellen, vergleichen
slide [slaɪd]	Schlitten		
to project [prə'dʒekt]	ausladen, vorstehen	condition [kən'dɪʃn]	Bedingung
projection [prə'dʒekʃn]	Ausladung	blue collar workers pl [ˌbluː kɒlə 'wɜːkəz]	Arbeiter/innen
to be unsupported [bi ˌʌnsə'pɔːtɪd]	keine Unterstützung haben	white collar workers pl [ˌwaɪt kɒlə 'wɜːkəz]	Angestellte
excessive [ɪk'sesɪv]	übermäßig		
incorrect [ˌɪnkə'rekt]	fehlerhaft		

Unit word list

UNIT 6

56	to **advise** [əd'vaɪz]	beraten
	medical equipment [ˌmedɪkl ɪ'kwɪpmənt]	medizinische Geräte, Medizintechnik
	portable ['pɔːtəbl]	tragbar, mobil
	swimming pool attendant ['swɪmɪŋ puːl ətendənt]	Bademeister/in
	to **enquire about sth** [ɪn'kwaɪər əbaʊt]	sich nach etw erkundigen
	pulse and blood pressure monitor [ˌpʌls ənd 'blʌd preʃə mɒnɪtə]	Puls- und Blutdruckmessgerät
T	**swimming pool complex** ['swɪmɪŋ puːl kɒmpleks]	Bäderlandschaft, Schwimmbadanlage
	waterproof ['wɔːtəpruːf]	wasserdicht
	lap [læp]	Bahn (im Schwimmbecken)
	adjustable [ə'dʒʌstəbl]	regelbar, einstellbar
	bright [braɪt]	(Licht:) hell, gleißend
	sunlight ['sʌnlaɪt]	Sonnenlicht
	to **operate sth** ['ɒpəreɪt]	etw bedienen, etw betreiben
	beat per minute [ˌbiːt pɜː 'mɪnɪt]	Schlag pro Minute
	by [baɪ]	(Abmessungen:) mal
	cover ['kʌvə]	Hülle, Tasche
	slip-on cover [ˌslɪp ɒn 'kʌvə]	Einstecktasche
	to **weigh** [weɪ]	wiegen
	gramme BE [græm]	Gramm
	battery ['bætəri]	Batterie, Akku
	rechargeable battery [ˌriːˈtʃɑːdʒəbl 'bætəri]	wiederaufladbare Batterie, Akku
	to **supply** [sə'plaɪ]	liefern
	impressive [ɪm'presɪv]	beeindruckend, eindrucksvoll
	to **place an order** [ˌpleɪs ən 'ɔːdə]	einen Auftrag erteilen, eine Bestellung aufgeben
	delivery terms pl [dɪ'lɪvəri tɜːmz]	Lieferbedingungen
	to **package** ['pækɪdʒ]	verpacken
	individual(ly) [ˌɪndɪ'vɪdʒuəl]	einzeln
	to **adjust** [ə'dʒʌst]	regeln, einstellen
	accuracy ['ækjərəsi]	Genauigkeit
	packaging ['pækɪdʒɪŋ]	Verpackung
	case [keɪs]	Gehäuse
57	**X-ray** ['eksreɪ]	Röntgen
	darkroom ['dɑːkruːm]	Dunkelkammer
	radiation [ˌreɪdi'eɪʃn]	Strahlung
	dose [dəʊs]	Dosis
	power consumption [ˌpaʊə kən'sʌmpʃn]	Stromverbrauch
	net [net]	netto
	gross [grəʊs]	brutto
P	**general practitioner (GP)** [ˌdʒenrəl præk'tɪʃənə]	Allgemeinarzt/-ärztin, Hausarzt/-ärztin
	to **deal with sth** ['diːl wɪð]	sich um etw kümmern
	construction site [kən'strʌkʃn saɪt]	Baustelle
	to **perform sth** [pə'fɔːm]	(Theater usw.:) etw aufführen, etw spielen
	latest ['leɪtɪst]	neueste/r/s
	feature ['fiːtʃə]	Merkmal, Funktion
	if I were you [ɪf ˌaɪ wə 'juː]	an deiner/eurer/Ihrer Stelle
	salesperson ['seɪlzpɜːsn]	Verkäufer/in
	to **reject** [rɪ'dʒekt]	ablehnen, zurückweisen
	to **have sth in mind** [həv ɪn 'maɪnd]	an etw denken, sich etw vorstellen
58	**serial production** [ˌsɪəriəl prə'dʌkʃn]	Serienfertigung, Serienproduktion
	requirement [rɪ'kwaɪəmənt]	Anforderung, Voraussetzung
T	**the other day** [ði ˌʌðə 'deɪ]	neulich
	to **cope with sth** ['kəʊp wɪð]	mit etw zurechtkommen
	to **make sense** [meɪk 'sens]	vernünftig sein, sinnvoll sein, einleuchten
	to **stick with sth** ['stɪk wɪð]	bei etw bleiben, sich an etw halten
	option ['ɒpʃn]	Möglichkeit, Alternative, Option
	chip conveyor ['tʃɪp kənveɪə]	Späneförderer
	to **get rid of sth** [get 'rɪd əv]	etw loswerden
	bulk production ['bʌlk prədʌkʃn]	Massenfertigung
59	**representative** [ˌreprɪ'zentətɪv]	Vertreter/in
	component [kəm'pəʊnənt]	Bauelement
	to **customize** ['kʌstəmaɪz]	nach Kundenwunsch fertigen
	performance [pə'fɔːməns]	Leistung
	productivity [ˌprɒdʌk'tɪvəti]	Produktivität
	series ['sɪəriːz]	Serie, Baureihe
	single workpiece [ˌsɪŋgl 'wɜːkpiːs]	Einzelteil
	user ['juːzə]	Anwender/in
	unbeatable [ʌn'biːtəbl]	unschlagbar
	benchmark ['bentʃmɑːk]	Maßstab
	flexibility [ˌfleksə'bɪləti]	Flexibilität
	outstanding [aʊt'stændɪŋ]	herausragend, außergewöhnlich
	to **achieve** [ə'tʃiːv]	erreichen
	efficient [ɪ'fɪʃnt]	leistungsfähig, effizient
	capabilities pl [ˌkeɪpə'bɪlətiz]	Möglichkeiten, (Leistungs-)Vermögen
	to **make sth available** [ˌmeɪk ə'veɪləbl]	etw zur Verfügung stellen
	entry-level user [ˌentri levl 'juːzə]	Einsteiger/in

English	IPA	German
(machine) operator	[ˈɒpəreɪtə]	Maschinenbediener/in, Maschinenführer/in
to benefit from sth	[ˈbenɪfɪt frəm]	von etw profitieren
dynamics	[daɪˈnæmɪks]	Dynamik
numerous	[ˈnjuːmərəs]	zahlreich
configuration	[kənˌfɪgəˈreɪʃn]	Einstellung, Konfiguration
small series manufacturing	[smɔːl ˌsɪəriːz mænjuˈfæktʃərɪŋ]	Kleinserienfertigung
to ensure	[ɪnˈʃʊə]	garantieren, sicherstellen
to open up new opportunities	[əʊpən ˌʌp njuː ɒpəˈtjuːnətiz]	neue Möglichkeiten/Chancen eröffnen
marketplace	[ˈmɑːkɪtpleɪs]	Markt, Marktplatz

60
English	IPA	German
to analyse	[ˈænəlaɪz]	analysieren
universal	[ˌjuːnɪˈvɜːsl]	universell, Universal-
turning length	[ˈtɜːnɪŋ leŋθ]	Drehlänge
integrated	[ˈɪntɪgreɪtɪd]	integriert
drive power	[ˈdraɪv paʊə]	Antriebsleistung
12-station disc turret reception	[twelv ˌsteɪʃn ˈdɪsk tʌrɪt rɪsepʃn]	12-fach-Revolverscheiben-Werkzeugaufnahme
reception	[rɪˈsepʃn]	Aufnahme
chip tank	[ˈtʃɪp tæŋk]	Spänebehälter
tool drive	[ˈtuːl draɪv]	Werkzeugantrieb
spindle brake	[ˈspɪndl breɪk]	Spindelbremse
discharge	[ˈdɪstʃɑːdʒ]	Auswurf
commissioning	[kəˈmɪʃnɪŋ]	Inbetriebnahme
instruction	[ɪnˈstrʌkʃn]	Einweisung
tool cart	[ˈtuːl kɑːt]	Werkzeugwagen
at a single grasp	[ət ə ˌsɪŋgl ˈgrɑːsp]	mit einem Griff
training package	[ˈtreɪnɪŋ pækɪdʒ]	Schulungspaket
participant	[pɑːˈtɪsɪpənt]	Teilnehmer/in
means of transport	[ˌmiːnz əf ˈtrænspɔːt]	Transportmittel
transport locks pl	[ˈtrænspɔːt lɒks]	Transportsicherungen
freight	[freɪt]	Fracht, Beförderung
package	[ˈpækɪdʒ]	Paket, Sendung
on request	[ɒn rɪˈkwest]	auf Anfrage
sufficient	[səˈfɪʃnt]	ausreichend, genügend
investment	[ɪnˈvestmənt]	Investition
addition	[əˈdɪʃn]	Ergänzung, Erweiterung

61
English	IPA	German
to estimate	[ˈestɪmeɪt]	schätzen
control centre	[kənˈtrəʊl sentə]	Steuerzentrale
to compress	[kəmˈpres]	verdichten, komprimieren
to pump	[pʌmp]	pumpen
distance	[ˈdɪstəns]	Abstand
pneumatic	[njuːˈmætɪk]	pneumatisch

62
English	IPA	German
operating voltage	[ˌɒpəreɪtɪŋ ˈvəʊltɪdʒ]	Betriebsspannung
phase	[feɪz]	Phase
protective earth	[prəˌtektɪv ˈɜːθ]	Schutzleiter, Schutzerde
fuse	[fjuːz]	Sicherung
slow-blow fuse	[ˌsləʊ bləʊ ˈfjuːz]	träge Sicherung
nominal current	[ˌnɒmɪnl ˈkʌrənt]	Nennstrom
frequency	[ˈfriːkwənsi]	Frequenz
nominal apparent power	[nɒmɪnl əˌpærənt ˈpaʊə]	Nennscheinleistung
conductor cross-section	[kənˌdʌktə ˈkrɒs sekʃn]	Leiterquerschnitt
increased	[ɪnˈkriːst]	gesteigert
exclusive	[ɪkˈskluːsɪv]	exklusiv
cycle	[ˈsaɪkl]	Zyklus
monitoring	[ˈmɒnɪtərɪŋ]	Überwachung, Kontrolle
tool load	[ˈtuːl ləʊd]	Antriebslast der Werkzeuge
alternating	[ˈɔːltəneɪtɪŋ]	wechselnd
vibration-critical	[vaɪˈbreɪʃn krɪtɪkl]	schwingungskritisch
set-up	[ˈsetʌp]	Aufspannung
modification	[ˌmɒdɪfɪˈkeɪʃn]	Änderung, Modifikation
multi-thread cycle	[ˌmʌlti θred ˈsaɪkl]	Mehrgewindezyklus
interface	[ˈɪntəfeɪs]	Schnittstelle, (Bedien-)Oberfläche
to enter	[ˈentə]	(Daten) eingeben
contour	[ˈkɒntʊə]	Kontur
parameter	[pəˈræmɪtə]	Parameter
graphical	[ˈgræfɪkl]	grafisch
context menu	[ˈkɒntekst menjuː]	Kontextmenü
predefined	[ˌpriːdɪˈfaɪnd]	vordefiniert
input screen	[ˈɪnpʊt skriːn]	Eingabemaske
programming	[ˈprəʊgræmɪŋ]	Programmieren
generation	[ˌdʒenəˈreɪʃn]	Erzeugung
complicated	[ˈkɒmplɪkeɪtɪd]	kompliziert
power transmission thread	[ˈpaʊə trænsmɪʃn θred]	Bewegungsgewinde

64
English	IPA	German
arrangement	[əˈreɪndʒmənt]	(Termin-)Vereinbarung, Vorbereitung
ecological	[ˌiːkəˈlɒdʒɪkl]	ökologisch, Öko-
to set up sth	[ˌset ˈʌp]	etw (Treffen usw.) vereinbaren
to get in touch with sb	[get ɪn ˈtʌtʃ wɪð]	sich mit jdm in Verbindung setzen
waste water	[ˌweɪst ˈwɔːtə]	Abwasser
filter press	[ˈfɪltə pres]	Filterpresse
to book	[bʊk]	reservieren, buchen
noon	[nuːn]	Mittag

Unit word list

	timetable ['taɪmteɪbl]	Programm, Fahrplan, Flugplan
	by tomorrow [baɪ tə'mɒrəʊ]	bis morgen
65	appointment [ə'pɔɪntmənt]	Termin
	to reserve [rɪ'zɜːv]	reservieren
	with a room attached [wɪð ə ˌruːm ə'tætʃt]	mit einem Nebenraum
	to postpone [pə'spəʊn]	(nach hinten) verschieben
	business partner ['bɪznəs pɑːtnə]	Geschäftspartner/in
	itinerary [aɪ'tɪnərəri]	Reiseplan

UNIT 7

68	internal [ɪn'tɜːnl]	intern
	to carry out sth [ˌkæri 'aʊt]	etw durchführen
	measures pl ['meʒəz]	Maßnahmen
	survey ['sɜːveɪ]	Umfrage
	means of communication [ˌmiːnz əf kəmjuːnɪ'keɪʃn]	Kommunikationsmittel
	method ['meθəd]	Art (und Weise), Weg
	energy engineer ['enədʒi endʒɪnɪə]	Energieingenieur/in, Energietechniker/in
69	face-to-face [ˌfeɪs tə 'feɪs]	persönlich
T	in writing [ɪn 'raɪtɪŋ]	schriftlich
	to get at sth ['get ət]	auf etw hinauswollen
	to copy in sb [ˌkɒpi 'ɪn]	jdn auf CC / in den Verteiler setzen
	to access sth ['ækses]	auf etw zugreifen
	access (to sth) ['ækses]	Zugriff (auf etw)
	storage ['stɔːrɪdʒ]	(Daten-)Speicherung
	to synchronize ['sɪŋkrənaɪz]	abgleichen, synchronisieren
	to select [sɪ'lekt]	auswählen
	to bring up sth [ˌbrɪŋ 'ʌp]	etw zur Sprache bringen
	to take up time [ˌteɪk 'ʌp taɪm]	Zeit beanspruchen
	slide [slaɪd]	(Präsentation:) Folie
	waste of time [ˌweɪst əf 'taɪm]	Zeitverschwendung
	to consider sth [kən'sɪdə]	etw in Betracht ziehen, über etw nachdenken
	graphic image [ˌgræfɪk 'ɪmɪdʒ]	Grafik, Schaubild
	quantity ['kwɒntəti]	Menge
	amount [ə'maʊnt]	Menge, Betrag
	degree [dɪ'griː]	Grad, Maß
	attachment [ə'tætʃmənt]	(E-Mail:) Anhang
70	relocation [ˌriːləʊ'keɪʃn]	Verlegung, Verlagerung
	to relocate sth [riːləʊ'keɪt]	etw verlegen, etw verlagern
	thermal (cutoff) fuse [ˌθɜːml 'fjuːz]	Thermosicherung

memo ['meməʊ]	Notiz, Kurzmitteilung, Aktenvermerk
thermal cutoff [ˌθɜːml 'kʌtɒf]	thermische Abschaltung
to skim [skɪm]	(Text) überfliegen
application [ˌæplɪ'keɪʃn]	Anwendung
to integrate ['ɪntɪgreɪt]	integrieren, einbauen
circuit board ['sɜːkɪt bɔːd]	Leiterplatte, Platine
to overheat [ˌəʊvə'hiːt]	sich überhitzen, zu heiß werden
to catch fire [ˌkætʃ 'faɪə]	in Brand geraten, Feuer fangen
thermal pellet [ˌθɜːml 'pelɪt]	thermisch geschütztes Gehäuse
fusible alloy [ˌfjuːzɪbl 'æloɪ]	Schmelzlegierung
hermetic sealing [həˌmetɪk 'siːlɪŋ]	hermetische Abdichtung
resin ['rezɪn]	Harz
resin-sealed ['rezɪn siːld]	mit Gießharz vergossen
ambient temperature [ˌæmbɪənt 'temprətʃə]	Umgebungstemperatur
to melt [melt]	schmelzen, zum Schmelzen bringen
to interrupt [ˌɪntə'rʌpt]	unterbrechen
a broad range of [ə ˌbrɔːd 'reɪndʒ əv]	eine große Auswahl von
to suit sth [suːt]	für etw passen
operating temperature [ˌɒpəreɪtɪŋ 'temprətʃə]	Betriebstemperatur
rated current [ˌreɪtɪd 'kʌrənt]	Nennstrom
to conform to sth [kən'fɔːm tə]	einer Sache entsprechen
environmental standard [ɪnvaɪrənˌmentl 'stændəd]	Umweltnorm
regulations pl [ˌregju'leɪʃnz]	Vorschriften
to be sensitive to sth [bi 'sensətɪv tə]	empfindlich auf etw reagieren
abnormal [æb'nɔːml]	ungewöhnlich, anormal
range [reɪndʒ]	Bereich, Umfang
version ['vɜːʃn]	Ausführung, Modell
resin-seal ['rezɪn siːl]	Gießharzverguss
reliability [rɪˌlaɪə'bɪləti]	Zuverlässigkeit
domestic [də'mestɪk]	Haushalts-
commercial [kə'mɜːʃl]	gewerblich
iron ['aɪən]	Bügeleisen
air conditioner ['eə kəndɪʃnə]	Klimaanlage
ventilation fan [ˌventɪ'leɪʃn fæn]	Ventilator
gas boiler ['gæs bɔɪlə]	Gaskessel
transformer [trænsˈfɔːmə]	Transformator
adaptor [ə'dæptə]	Adapter
charger ['tʃɑːdʒə]	Ladegerät

	battery pack ['bætəri pæk]	Akku	74	on site [ɒn 'saɪt]	vor Ort
	photocopier ['fəʊtəʊkɒpiə]	Kopiergerät		to lift [lɪft]	heben, anheben
	laser beam printer ['leɪzə biːm prɪntə]	Laserdrucker		to take care [teɪk 'keə]	aufpassen
				to overhaul [ˌəʊvə'hɔːl]	überholen, wieder instandsetzen
71	airtight ['eətaɪt]	luftdicht		headquarters pl [ˌhed'kwɔːtəz]	Zentrale, Hauptsitz
	resin-sealing unit ['rezɪn siːlɪŋ juːnɪt]	Versiegelungsanlage		to keep in touch [ˌkiːp ɪn 'tʌtʃ]	in Verbindung bleiben, Kontakt halten
	crate [kreɪt]	Kiste	75	fitting piece ['fɪtɪŋ piːs]	Anschlussstück
	forklift truck [ˌfɔːklɪft 'trʌk]	Gabelstapler		sharp bend [ˌʃɑːp 'bend]	Knick, enge Kurve
	drill bit ['drɪl bɪt]	Bohrer, Bohrspitze		straight [streɪt]	gerade
	glue [gluː]	Klebstoff		piping ['paɪpɪŋ]	Leitung, Schlauch
	data cable ['deɪtə keɪbl]	Datenkabel, Datenleitung		tight bending [ˌtaɪt 'bendɪŋ]	starke Krümmung
	power cable ['paʊə keɪbl]	Stromkabel, Stromleitung		tight hose [ˌtaɪt 'həʊz]	gespannter Schlauch
	cable trunk ['keɪbl trʌŋk]	Kabelkanal		to hold up sth [ˌhəʊld 'ʌp]	etw aufhalten
	flooring ['flɔːrɪŋ]	Fußboden		to fix [fɪks]	(Problem:) lösen
	pneumatic hose [njuːˌmætɪk 'həʊz]	Druckluftschlauch, Pneumatikschlauch		oral ['ɔːrəl]	mündlich
	temperature detection ['temprətʃə dɪtekʃn]	Temperaturmessung, -erfassung	76	incident ['ɪnsɪdənt]	Vorfall
				notice ['nəʊtɪs]	Warnhinweis, Hinweisschild
				fire damage ['faɪə dæmɪdʒ]	Brandschaden
T	to unpack [ʌn'pæk]	auspacken		to report to sb [rɪ'pɔːt tə]	sich bei jdm melden
	to handle sth ['hændl]	etw behandeln		statement ['steɪtmənt]	Aussage, Schilderung
	transportation [ˌtrænspɔː'teɪʃn]	Beförderung, Transport		first-aider [ˌfɜːst 'eɪdə]	Sanitäter/in
	nearby ['nɪəbaɪ]	in der Nähe		welder ['weldə]	Schweißer/in
	to fix [fɪks]	befestigen		shouting ['ʃaʊtɪŋ]	Geschrei
	to lay cables [ˌleɪ 'keɪblz]	Kabel/Leitungen verlegen		next door [ˌnekst 'dɔː]	nebenan
	up and running [ˌʌp ən 'rʌnɪŋ]	betriebsbereit		to put out a fire [pʊt ˌaʊt ə 'faɪə]	einen Brand löschen
	on time [ɒn 'taɪm]	rechtzeitig, pünktlich		to spread [spred]	sich ausbreiten
				to set off the alarm [set ˌɒf ði ə'lɑːm]	Alarm auslösen
72	specifically [spə'sɪfɪkli]	ausdrücklich		assembly point [ə'sembli pɔɪnt]	Sammelplatz
	resin-sealer ['rezɪn siːlə]	Versiegelungsanlage		crash [kræʃ]	Krach, Schlag, Rums
	report update [rɪ'pɔːt ʌpdeɪt]	aktueller Bericht		acetone ['æsɪtəʊn]	Aceton
73	status ['steɪtəs]	Stand, Zustand, Status		flash [flæʃ]	Stichflamme
	customs ['kʌstəmz]	Zoll		to stomp [stɒmp]	trampeln, treten
	customs inspector ['kʌstəmz ɪnspektə]	Zollinspektor/in		flame [fleɪm]	Flamme
	contact ['kɒntækt]	Kontaktperson		to light [laɪt]	sich entzünden
	safety officer ['seɪfti ɒfɪsə]	Sicherheitsbeauftragte/r	77	to go off [ˌgəʊ 'ɒf]	(Alarm:) losgehen
	underneath [ˌʌndə'niːθ]	unter, unterhalb		fire brigade ['faɪə brɪgeɪd]	Feuerwehr
	to hang [hæŋ]	hängen		to administer sth [əd'mɪnɪstə]	etw geben, etw erteilen
	fuse box ['fjuːz bɒks]	Sicherungskasten		ambulance ['æmbjələns]	Rettungswagen
	appropriate [ə'prəʊpriət]	entsprechend, passend, geeignet		burn [bɜːn]	Verbrennung
	distribution board [ˌdɪstrɪ'bjuːʃn bɔːd]	Stromverteilung		to be in shock [bi ɪn 'ʃɒk]	unter Schock stehen
	NH-fusage [ˌen 'eɪtʃ fjuːzɪdʒ]	NH-Sicherungen		emergency services pl [ɪ'mɜːdʒənsi sɜːvɪsɪz]	Einsatzkräfte, Rettungsdienste
	residual current circuit breaker (RCCB) [rɪˌzɪdjʊəl kʌrənt 'sɜːkɪt breɪkə]	FI-Schutzschalter, Fehlerstromschutzschalter		to extinguish [ɪk'stɪŋgwɪʃ]	löschen
				to reach (over) [riːtʃ]	greifen
				to knock over sth [ˌnɒk 'əʊvə]	etw umstoßen
	finishing date ['fɪnɪʃɪŋ deɪt]	Fertigstellungstermin		to realize sth ['rɪəlaɪz]	etw (be)merken

Unit word list

bench [bentʃ]	Werkbank	
to spill [spɪl]	(Flüssigkeit:) laufen, auslaufen	
to trickle ['trɪkl]	rinnen, (in einem Rinnsal) laufen	
chronological(ly) [ˌkrɒnə'lɒdʒɪkl]	chronologisch	
administration [ədˌmɪnɪ'streɪʃn]	Verwaltung	
record ['rekɔːd]	Aufzeichnung(en)	
involved (in sth) [ɪn'vɒlvd]	(an etw) beteiligt	
background ['bækgraʊnd]	Hintergrund	
to deal with sth ['diːl wɪð]	mit etw umgehen	

UNIT 8

78 to regulate ['regjuleɪt] — regeln
charging cable ['tʃɑːdʒɪŋ keɪbl] — Ladekabel
to define [dɪ'faɪn] — definieren
more closely [ˌmɔː 'kləʊsli] — näher, genauer
to invent [ɪn'vent] — erfinden
everyday ['evrɪdeɪ] — Alltags-
aspect ['æspekt] — Gesichtspunkt, Aspekt
efficiency [ɪ'fɪʃnsi] — Effizienz
79 standardization [ˌstændədaɪ'zeɪʃn] — Normung
currently ['kʌrəntli] — zurzeit, gegenwärtig, momentan
manufacturing company [ˌmænjʊ'fæktʃərɪŋ kʌmpəni] — Fertigungsbetrieb, Produktionsunternehmen
field [fiːld] — Bereich, Gebiet
to compete [kəm'piːt] — konkurrieren
competition [ˌkɒmpə'tɪʃn] — Konkurrenz
quality management ['kwɒləti mænɪdʒmənt] — Qualitätsmanagement, Qualitätssicherung
labour ['leɪbə] — Arbeit
output ['aʊtpʊt] — Produktion
to maintain [meɪn'teɪn] — warten, instand halten
fire safety ['faɪə seɪfti] — Brandschutz
fire risk assessment ['faɪə rɪsk əsesmənt] — Brandrisikobewertung, -analyse
consultancy [kən'sʌltənsi] — Beratung
to take over sth [ˌteɪk 'əʊvə] — etw übernehmen
to set up standards [set ˌʌp 'stændədz] — Normen aufstellen
proof [pruːf] — Nachweis(e), Beleg(e)
fire protection ['faɪə prətekʃn] — Brandschutz
certified ['sɜːtɪfaɪd] — geprüft, zertifiziert
to cover ['kʌvə] — absichern, erfassen
satisfied ['sætɪsfaɪd] — zufrieden

to insist on sth [ɪn'sɪst ɒn] — auf etw bestehen
to research sth [rɪ'sɜːtʃ] — etw recherchieren, sich über etw informieren
to draw up [ˌdrɔː 'ʌp] — (Text) erstellen, (Liste) aufstellen
80 automated ['ɔːtəmeɪtɪd] — automatisch
washing system ['wɒʃɪŋ sɪstəm] — Waschanlage
mat [mæt] — Matte
abrasive sand [əˌbreɪsɪv 'sænd] — Abrasivsand
to wash off sth [ˌwɒʃ 'ɒf] — etw abwaschen
manually ['mænjuəli] — von Hand
conveyor [kən'veɪə] — Förderband, Förderer, Fördersystem
legislation [ˌledʒɪs'leɪʃn] — Gesetze, Gesetzgebung
palletizer ['pælɪtaɪzə] — Palettierer
item ['aɪtəm] — Gegenstand
to transport [træn'spɔːt] — befördern, transportieren
strict [strɪkt] — streng

T contract ['kɒntrækt] — Vertrag
to mix [mɪks] — mischen
to wash down sth [ˌwɒʃ 'daʊn] — etw abwaschen
plant [plɑːnt] — Werk, Betrieb
heat [hiːt] — Hitze
washing machine ['wɒʃɪŋ məʃiːn] — Waschmaschine
to palletize ['pælɪtaɪz] — palettieren
to come up with sth [ˌkʌm 'ʌp wɪð] — sich etw ausdenken, sich etw einfallen lassen
to pollute [pə'luːt] — verschmutzen
to filter ['fɪltə] — filtern
to reuse [ˌriː'juːs] — wiederverwenden

81 hot air blower [hɒt 'eə bləʊə] — Heißluftgebläse
to construct [kən'strʌkt] — bauen, konstruieren
roller ['rəʊlə] — Rolle, Walze
upwards ['ʌpwədz] — aufwärts, nach oben
downwards ['daʊnwədz] — abwärts, nach unten
to drip off [ˌdrɪp 'ɒf] — abtropfen
to position [pə'zɪʃn] — platzieren
to sketch [sketʃ] — skizzieren
draft [drɑːft] — Entwurf
mixture ['mɪkstʃə] — Mischung, Gemisch
82 to separate ['sepəreɪt] — trennen
83 to train sb [treɪn] — jdn schulen
feeding system ['fiːdɪŋ sɪstəm] — Einzug
push-button ['pʊʃbʌtn] — Drucktaster, Taster
interior [ɪn'tɪəriə] — Innen-
ultrasonic sensor [ˌʌltrəˌsɒnɪk 'sensə] — Ultraschallsensor
to activate ['æktɪveɪt] — aktivieren, betätigen
floor tray ['flɔː treɪ] — Bodenwanne
84 nozzle ['nɒzl] — Düse

	high-pressure nozzle [ˌhaɪ preʃə 'nɒzl]	Hochdruckdüse
	pressure ['preʃə]	Druck
	usage ['juːsɪdʒ]	Verwendung
	nominal pressure [ˌnɒmɪnl 'preʃə]	Nenndruck
	capacity [kə'pæsəti]	Leistung
	knock [nɒk]	Stoß, Schlag
	to transmit [trænsˈmɪt]	übertragen
	to limit ['lɪmɪt]	begrenzen, beschränken
	to overload [ˌəʊvəˈləʊd]	überlasten
	alternating current (AC) [ˌɔːltəneɪtɪŋ 'kʌrənt]	Wechselstrom
	chemicals pl ['kemɪklz]	Chemikalien
	coupling ['kʌplɪŋ]	Kupplung
	plunger pump ['plʌndʒə pʌmp]	Kolbenpumpe, Plunger-pumpe
	valve [vælv]	Ventil
	feed [fiːd]	Einzug
	light barrier ['laɪt bæriə]	Lichtschranke
	time lag ['taɪm læg]	Zeitverzögerung
	to waste [weɪst]	verschwenden, vergeuden
	prompt [prɒmpt]	Stichwort
85	stacking system ['stækɪŋ sɪstəm]	Stapeleinheit
	air-flow rate ['eə fləʊ reɪt]	Luftdurchsatz
	vibration-cushioned [vaɪˈbreɪʃn kʊʃnd]	schwingungsgedämpft
	to suck in [ˌsʌk 'ɪn]	ansaugen
	to blow [bləʊ]	blasen
	optimum ['ɒptɪməm]	optimal
	endstop [endstɒp]	Endanschlag
	to fold [fəʊld]	klappen
	force of gravity [ˌfɔːs əv 'grævəti]	Schwerkraft
	gripper ['grɪpə]	Greifer
	to grab [græb]	greifen
	end switch ['end swɪtʃ]	Endschalter
	linear unit ['lɪniə juːnɪt]	Lineareinheit
	to force [fɔːs]	zwingen, hier: drücken
	key word ['kiː wɜːd]	Schlagwort, Stichwort
	eye contact ['aɪ kɒntækt]	Blickkontakt
	to be prepared to do sth [bɪ prɪˈpeəd tə duː]	bereit sein, etw zu tun
86	award [əˈwɔːd]	Auszeichnung, Preis
	prize-giving ceremony [ˌpraɪz gɪvɪŋ 'serəməni]	Preisverleihung
	receptionist [rɪˈsepʃənɪst]	Empfangsmitarbeiter/in
	to check in [ˌtʃek 'ɪn]	sich anmelden, einchecken
T	reservation [ˌrezəˈveɪʃn]	Reservierung
	to serve [sɜːv]	servieren
	buffet breakfast ['bʌfeɪ brekfəst]	Frühstücksbüfett
	dining room ['daɪnɪŋ ruːm]	(Hotel:) Speisesaal
	ground floor [ˌgraʊnd 'flɔː]	Erdgeschoss
	wheelchair ['wiːltʃeə]	Rollstuhl
	access ['ækses]	Zugang
	facilities pl [fəˈsɪlətiz]	Einrichtungen
	secure [sɪˈkjʊə]	sicher, bewacht
	gate [geɪt]	Tor, Einfahrt
	to check out [ˌtʃek 'aʊt]	sich abmelden, auschecken
87	Pleased to meet you. [ˌpliːzd tə 'miːt ju]	Schön, Sie kennen zu lernen.
	to get ready [get 'redi]	sich bereit machen, sich fertig machen
	Is this seat taken? [ɪz ðɪs ˌsiːt 'teɪkən]	Ist hier besetzt?
	cultural awareness [ˌkʌltʃərəl əˈweənəs]	Kulturbewusstsein, kulturelle Sensibilität
	to bow [baʊ]	sich verbeugen
	to shake hands with sb [ˌʃeɪk 'hændz wɪð]	jdm die Hand geben
	to respect [rɪˈspekt]	respektieren, achten
	aggressive [əˈgresɪv]	aggressiv
	dominant ['dɒmɪnənt]	dominant
	powerful ['paʊəfl]	mächtig
	to pin sth to sth [pɪn]	etw an etw befestigen

UNIT 9

90	video conferencing ['vɪdiəʊ kɒnfərənsɪŋ]	Videokonferenz
	item ['aɪtəm]	Punkt
	to re-play [ˌriːˈpleɪ]	erneut abspielen
	session ['seʃn]	Sitzung
	integration [ˌɪntɪˈgreɪʃn]	Einbindung, Integrierung
	cloud storage ['klaʊd stɔːrɪdʒ]	Datenspeicherung in der Cloud
	trial ['traɪəl]	Test, Probe
	support [səˈpɔːt]	Unterstützung
	recording [rɪˈkɔːdɪŋ]	Aufzeichnung, Aufnahme
T	Never mind. [ˌnevə 'maɪnd]	Macht nichts.
	to supply sth [səˈplaɪ]	etw zur Verfügung stellen, etw liefern
	to schedule [ˈʃedjuːl]	planen, (Termin) ansetzen
91	to argue against/for sth [ˈɑːgjuː əgenst/fə]	sich gegen/für etw aussprechen, gegen/für etw argumentieren
	to assist [əˈsɪst]	assistieren, helfen, unterstützen
	research [rɪˈsɜːtʃ]	Recherche
	to feature ['fiːtʃə]	(Merkmal) aufweisen
	to sum up [ˌsʌm 'ʌp]	zusammenfassen
	recommendation [ˌrekəmenˈdeɪʃn]	Empfehlung
	in conclusion [ɪn kənˈkluːʒn]	abschließend
92	linear drive ['lɪniə draɪv]	Linearantrieb
	quality assurance ['kwɒləti əʃʊərəns]	Qualitätssicherung

Unit word list

	measuring equipment ['meʒərɪŋ ɪkwɪpmənt]	Messgerät(e)	
	custom-made ['kʌstəm meɪd]	speziell angefertigt, individuell gefertigt	
	HGV (heavy goods vehicle) [,eɪtʃ dʒiː 'viː]	Lkw	
	deviation [,diːvi'eɪʃn]	Abweichung	
	probe [prəʊb]	Sonde	
	repetitive [rɪ'petətɪv]	(sich) wiederholend	
	stationary ['steɪʃənri]	ortsfest, stationär	
	surface roughness ['sɜːfɪs rʌfnəs]	Oberflächenrauigkeit	
	coordinates pl [kəʊ'ɔːdɪnəts]	Koordinaten	
	measurement run ['meʒəmənt rʌn]	Messfahrt	
	to detect [dɪ'tekt]	erfassen	
	versatile ['vɜːsətaɪl]	vielseitig verwendbar	
	to configure [kən'fɪgə]	einrichten, konfigurieren	
	measuring station ['meʒərɪŋ steɪʃn]	Messplatz, Messstation	
	to meet [miːt]	(Anforderungen usw.) erfüllen	
93	guiding rail ['gaɪdɪŋ reɪl]	Führungsschiene	
	motion ['məʊʃn]	Bewegung	
	ball bearing [,bɔːl 'beərɪŋ]	Kugellager	
	rail [reɪl]	Schiene	
	coefficient [,kəʊɪ'fɪʃnt]	Koeffizient	
	friction ['frɪkʃn]	Reibung	
	conventional [kən'venʃnl]	herkömmlich, konventionell	
	rigidity [rɪ'dʒɪtəti]	Steifigkeit	
	guidance ['gaɪdəns]	Führung	
	automation system [,ɔːtə'meɪʃn sɪstəm]	Automatisierungssystem, -anlage	
	laser engraving ['leɪzər ɪngreɪvɪŋ]	Lasergravur	
	lifting equipment ['lɪftɪŋ ɪkwɪpmənt]	Hebegeräte, Hebezeuge	
	compound ['kɒmpaʊnd]	Verbindung, Verbundwerkstoff	
	gearing ['gɪərɪŋ]	Verzahnung	
	drive unit ['draɪv juːnɪt]	Antriebseinheit, -aggregat	
94	permissible load [pə,mɪsɪbl 'ləʊd]	zulässige Last	
	to pre-load [,priː 'ləʊd]	vorspannen	
	order code ['ɔːdə kəʊd]	Bestellcode, Bestellschlüssel	
	quotation [kwəʊ'teɪʃn]	Preisangebot, Kostenvoranschlag	
	regular customer [,regjələ 'kʌstəmə]	Stammkunde/-kundin	
	to request sth [rɪ'kwest]	um etw bitten	
	discount ['dɪskaʊnt]	Rabatt	
	date of delivery [,deɪt əv dɪ'lɪvəri]	Lieferdatum	
95	desktop machine ['desktɒp məʃiːn]	Tischgerät	
	hydraulic power unit [haɪ,drɔːlɪk 'paʊə juːnɪt]	Hydraulikaggregat	
	pneumatic controller [njuː,mætɪk kən'trəʊlə]	pneumatischer Regler	
	labelling plate ['leɪbəlɪŋ pleɪt]	Typenschild	
	aggregate ['ægrɪgət]	Aggregat	
T	to engrave [ɪn'greɪv]	(ein)gravieren	
	to come off [,kʌm 'ɒf]	sich lösen, abgehen	
	independent [,ɪndɪ'pendənt]	unabhängig	
	model-maker ['mɒdlmeɪkə]	Modellbauer/in	
	gantry ['gæntri]	Portal	
	stepper motor ['stepə məʊtə]	Schrittmotor	
	DIY kit [,diː aɪ 'waɪ kɪt]	Bausatz	
	parallel interface [,pærəlel 'ɪntəfeɪs]	Parallel-Schnittstelle	
96	to customize ['kʌstəmaɪz]	individuell anpassen	
	to create [kri'eɪt]	(Datei) anlegen	
	work file ['wɜːk faɪl]	Arbeitsdatei	
	to process ['prəʊses]	verarbeiten	
	to reproduce [,riːprə'djuːs]	kopieren, reproduzieren	
	virtually ['vɜːtʃuəli]	praktisch	
	unlimited [ʌn'lɪmɪtɪd]	unbegrenzt	
	thermoplastic pl [,θɜːməʊ'plæstɪk]	Thermoplaste	
	stability [stə'bɪləti]	Stabilität	
	to consist of sth [kən'sɪst əv]	aus etw bestehen	
	linear track profile [,lɪniə 'træk prəʊfaɪl]	Linearachsprofil	
	cover profile ['kʌvə prəʊfaɪl]	Abdeckungsprofil	
	stainless steel [,steɪnləs 'stiːl]	Edelstahl	
	profiled ['prəʊfaɪld]	profiliert	
	specifically [spə'sɪfɪkli]	eigens, speziell	
	to adapt [ə'dæpt]	anpassen	
	characteristics pl [,kærəktə'rɪstɪks]	Merkmale, Eigenschaften	
	reliable [rɪ'laɪəbl]	zuverlässig	
	ready built ['redi bɪlt]	fertig montiert	
	directly operational [də,rektli ɒpə'reɪʃənl]	direkt einsatzbereit	
	to opt for sth ['ɒpt fə]	sich für etw entscheiden	
	to screw [skruː]	schrauben	
	installation instruction [,ɪnstə'leɪʃn ɪnstrʌkʃn]	Montageanleitung	
	to base [beɪs]	basieren, fußen	
	intermediate [,ɪntə'miːdiət]	Zwischen-	
	compatibility [kəm,pætə'bɪləti]	Kompatibilität	

	collar [ˈkɒlə]	Spannhals		to guarantee [ˌgærənˈtiː]	garantieren
	power limit [ˈpaʊə lɪmɪt]	Leistungsobergrenze		to pack [pæk]	verpacken
	system-guided [ˈsɪstəm gaɪdɪd]	systemgeführt		wooden [ˈwʊdn]	Holz-
				packing crate [ˈpækɪŋ kreɪt]	Packkiste
	drag knife [ˈdræg naɪf]	Schleppmesser		price list [ˈpraɪs lɪst]	Preisliste
	engraving needle [ɪnˈgreɪvɪŋ niːdl]	Graviernadel			
	hot cutting system [ˈhɒt kʌtɪŋ sɪstəm]	Heißschneidesystem			

UNIT 10

97	6-point ball bearing cage [ˌsɪks pɔɪnt ˈbɔːl beərɪŋ keɪdʒ]	sechsfach kugelgelagerter Laufwagen	100	to clarify [ˈklærəfaɪ]	klären, abklären
				container [kənˈteɪnə]	Behälter, Box, Container
				stackable [ˈstækəbl]	stapelbar
T	play-free [ˈpleɪ friː]	spielfrei		storage [ˈstɔːrɪdʒ]	Aufbewahrung, Lagerung
	carriage [ˈkærɪdʒ]	Schlitten		fitted with [ˈfɪtɪd wɪð]	ausgestattet mit
	continuously [kənˈtɪnjuəsli]	fortwährend, ständig, kontinuierlich		snap fastener [ˈsnæp fɑːsnə]	Schnappverschluss
	freely accessible [ˌfriːli əkˈsesəbl]	frei zugänglich		padlock [ˈpædlɒk]	Vorhängeschloss
				handle [ˈhændl]	Griff
	disassembly [ˌdɪsəˈsembli]	Zerlegen, Demontage		to stack [stæk]	stapeln
				warehouse [ˈweəhaʊs]	Lagerhalle, Lager
	to dismantle [dɪsˈmæntl]	demontieren, zerlegen	101	guarantee period [ˌgærənˈtiː pɪərɪəd]	Garantiezeit
	feed rate [ˈfiːd reɪt]	Vorschub			
	connecting cable [kəˈnektɪŋ keɪbl]	Anschlusskabel		prospective customer [prəˌspektɪv ˈkʌstəmə]	potenzielle/r Kunde/Kundin
P	clamping surface [ˈklæmpɪŋ sɜːfɪs]	Aufspannfläche	P	light [laɪt]	Scheinwerfer
				microphone [ˈmaɪkrəfəʊn]	Mikrofon
	working space [ˈwɜːkɪŋ speɪs]	Arbeitsraum		speaker [ˈspiːkə]	Lautsprecher
	overall size [ˌəʊvərˌɔːl ˈsaɪz]	Gesamtmaße		with reference to [wɪð ˈrefrəns tə]	mit Bezug auf, bezüglich
				to establish [ɪˈstæblɪʃ]	etablieren, schaffen, aufbauen
98	body [ˈbɒdi]	(Brief:) Haupttext	102	vintage car [ˌvɪntɪdʒ ˈkɑː]	Oldtimer
	enclosure [ɪnˈkləʊʒə]	(Brief:) Anlage		data sheet [ˈdeɪtə ʃiːt]	Datenblatt
	inside address [ˌɪnsaɪd əˈdres]	Innenadresse		to restore [rɪˈstɔː]	restaurieren
				spare part [ˌspeə ˈpɑːt]	Ersatzteil
	reference initials pl [ˈrefərəns ɪnɪʃlz]	(Brief:) Zeichen		specialist supplier [ˌspeʃəlɪst səˈplaɪə]	Fachhändler/in
	signature [ˈsɪgnətʃə]	Unterschrift		auction [ˈɔːkʃn]	Versteigerung, Auktion
	surgery light [ˈsɜːdʒəri laɪt]	Operationslampe, -leuchte		to sell at auction [ˌsel ət ˈɔːkʃn]	versteigern
	edition [ɪˈdɪʃn]	(Zeitschrift etc.:) Ausgabe		body [ˈbɒdi]	(Auto:) Karosserie
	trade magazine [ˈtreɪd mægəziːn]	Fachzeitschrift		4 seater [ˌfɔː ˈsiːtə]	Viersitzer
				convertible [kənˈvɜːtəbl]	Cabriolet
	outpatient clinic [ˈaʊtpeɪʃnt klɪnɪk]	Ambulanz		inch [ɪntʃ]	Zoll
				wheelbase [ˈwiːlbeɪs]	Radstand
	operating theatre [ˈɒpəreɪtɪŋ θɪətə]	Operationssaal		track [træk]	Spurweite
				tread [tred]	Spurweite
	trial order [ˌtraɪəl ˈɔːdə]	Probebestellung		ground clearance [ˈgraʊnd klɪərəns]	Bodenabstand
	ceiling [ˈsiːlɪŋ]	(Zimmer-)Decke			
	payment [ˈpeɪmənt]	Zahlung		ratio [ˈreɪʃiəʊ]	Verhältnis
	terms pl of payment [ˌtɜːmz əf ˈpeɪmənt]	Zahlungsbedingungen		kerb weight [ˈkɜːb weɪt]	Leergewicht
				fuel [ˈfjuːəl]	Kraftstoff
	to protect [prəˈtekt]	schützen		tank capacity [ˈtæŋk kəpæsəti]	Tankinhalt
	reference [ˈrefərəns]	Referenz			
	attention [əˈtenʃn]	Aufmerksamkeit		gallon [ˈgælən]	Gallone (UK = 4,45l; US = 3,78l)
	confirmation [ˌkɒnfəˈmeɪʃn]	Bestätigung			
	to enclose [ɪnˈkləʊz]	(Brief:) beifügen			

Unit word list

103 to **buy** sth at **auction** [ˌbaɪ ət 'ɔːkʃn] — etw ersteigern
supercharged engine [ˌsuːpətʃɑːdʒd 'endʒɪn] — Kompressormotor
petrol BE ['petrəl] — Benzin
capacity [kə'pæsəti] — Hubraum
stroke [strəʊk] — Hub
power output ['paʊər aʊtpʊt] — Leistung
torque [tɔːk] — Drehmoment
specific torque [spə,sɪfɪk 'tɔːk] — spezifisches Drehmoment
carburettor [ˌkɑːbə'retə] — Vergaser
acceleration [əkˌselə'reɪʃn] — Beschleunigung
maximum speed [ˌmæksɪməm 'spiːd] — Höchstgeschwindigkeit
fuel consumption ['fjuːəl kənsʌmpʃn] — Krafstoffverbrauch
chassis ['ʃæsi] — Fahrgestell
engine layout ['endʒɪn leɪaʊt] — Motoranordnung
longitudinal [ˌlɒndʒɪ'tjuːdɪnl] — längs
rear wheel drive [ˌrɪə wiːl 'draɪv] — Hinterradantrieb
steering ['stɪərɪŋ] — Lenkung
worm-and-nut steering [ˌwɜːm ənd nʌt 'stɪərɪŋ] — Zahnstangenlenkung
gearbox ['gɪəbɒks] — Schaltgetriebe
top gear [ˌtɒp 'gɪə] — höchster Gang
gear ratio ['gɪə reɪʃiəʊ] — Übersetzung
final drive ratio [ˌfaɪnl draɪv 'reɪʃiəʊ] — Achsübersetzung

T to **treat** [triːt] — behandeln
care [keə] — Sorgfalt
overhead valve [ˌəʊvəhed 'vælv] — obenliegendes Ventil
brake horsepower ['breɪk hɔːspaʊə] — *Pferdestärken-Einheit in UK und USA*
revolution [ˌrevə'luːʃn] — Umdrehung
to **cool** [kuːl] — kühlen
gear [gɪə] — Gang
4-speed manual gearbox [ˌfɔː spiːd ˌmænjuəl 'gɪəbɒks] — Viergang-Handschaltgetriebe
reverse gear [rɪˌvɜːs 'gɪə] — Rückwärtsgang
vane [veɪn] — Schaufel, Läufer
supercharger ['suːpətʃɑːdʒə] — Kompressor, Turbolader
in good running order [ɪn gʊd ˌrʌnɪŋ 'ɔːdə] — in gutem Zustand, in Schuss

front-mounted engine [ˌfrʌnt maʊntɪd 'endʒɪn] — Frontmotor
to **power** ['paʊə] — antreiben
rear wheel ['rɪə wiːl] — Hinterrad
range [reɪndʒ] — Reihe, Produktlinie

valve gear ['vælv gɪə] — Ventile
rpm [ˌɑː piː 'em] — U/min
quoted ['kwəʊtɪd] — angegeben
kerb [kɜːb] — Bordstein
104 internal combustion engine [ɪnˌtɜːnl kəm'bʌstʃən endʒɪn] — Verbrennungsmotor
to **feed** [fiːd] — zuführen
oxygen ['ɒksɪdʒən] — Sauerstoff
twin-screw supercharger [ˌtwɪn skruː 'suːpətʃɑːdʒə] — Doppelschnecken-Turbolader
centrifugal [sen'trɪfjʊgl] — zentrifugal, Zentrifugal-
fluid ['fluːɪd] — Flüssigkeit
intake manifold [ˌɪnteɪk 'mænɪfəʊld] — Ansaugkrümmer
meshing ['meʃɪŋ] — ineinandergreifend
lobe [ləʊb] — Nocken
impeller [ɪm'pelə] — Flügelrad, Impeller
to **draw in** sth [ˌdrɔː 'ɪn] — etw einziehen
to **patent** ['peɪtnt] — patentieren
to **ventilate** ['ventɪleɪt] — belüften
mine [maɪn] — Bergwerk, Grube, Mine
mine shaft ['maɪn ʃɑːft] — Schacht, Stollen
Roots blower ['ruːts bləʊə] — Roots-Gebläse, Drehkolbengebläse
blast furnace ['blɑːst fɜːnɪs] — Hochofen
combustion air [kəm'bʌstʃn eə] — Verbrennungsluft
to **include** sth in sth [ɪn'kluːd] — etw in etw einbauen
forced air [ˌfɔːst 'eə] — Zwangsluft
intake ['ɪnteɪk] — Zufuhr, Ansaugung
pump body ['pʌmp bɒdi] — Pumpengehäuse
rotary vane [ˌrəʊtəri 'veɪn] — Drehkolben
replacement [rɪ'pleɪsmənt] — Ersatz
to **grind** [graɪnd] — schleifen
urgent ['ɜːdʒənt] — eilig, dringend
VAT (value added tax) [ˌvæljuː 'ædɪd tæks] — MwSt (Mehrwertsteuer)
105 to **exist** [ɪg'zɪst] — existieren
bodywork ['bɒdiwɜːk] — Wagenaufbau, Karosserie
frame [freɪm] — Gestell
interior [ɪn'tɪəriə] — Innenausstattung
suspension [sə'spenʃn] — Aufhängung
ultimate ['ʌltɪmət] — vollendet, ultimativ
prewar [ˌpriː 'wɔː] — Vorkriegs-
racing car ['reɪsɪŋ kɑː] — Rennwagen
tube frame ['tjuːb freɪm] — Rohrgestell
arrow ['ærəʊ] — Pfeil
closely related to [ˌkləʊsli rɪ'leɪtɪd tə] — eng verwandt mit
8 inline engine [ˌeɪt 'ɪnlaɪn endʒɪn] — Achtzylinder-Reihenmotor
odd [ɒd] — merkwürdig, seltsam

	to engage [ɪnˈgeɪdʒ]	einschalten	
	throttle [ˈθrɒtl]	Drosselklappe, Gaspedal	
	power rating [ˈpaʊə ˌreɪtɪŋ]	Nennleistung	
	to fit out sth [ˌfɪt ˈaʊt]	etw ausstatten	
	leather [ˈleðə]	Leder	
	sedan [sɪˈdæn]	Limousine	
	hood [hʊd]	Motorhaube	
	to dip [dɪp]	senken	
	left-hand drive [ˌleft hænd ˈdraɪv]	Linkslenker, Linkslenkung	
	tail [teɪl]	Heck	
	horsepower [ˈhɔːspaʊə]	PS	
106	price per unit [ˌpraɪs pɜː ˈjuːnɪt]	Stückpreis, Einzelpreis	
	wheel nut [ˈwiːl nʌt]	Radmutter	
	water-pump shaft [ˈwɔːtə pʌmp ʃɑːft]	Wasserpumpenwelle	
	V-belt pulley [ˌviː belt ˈpʊli]	Keilriemenscheibe	
	servo-brake cylinder [ˌsɜːvəʊ breɪk ˈsɪlɪndə]	Servobremszylinder	
	poppet valve [ˈpɒpɪt vælv]	Tellerventil	
	petrol-non return valve [ˌpetrəl nɒn rɪˈtɜːn vælv]	Benzin-Rückhalteventil	
	king pin [ˈkɪŋ pɪn]	Achsschenkelbolzen	
	generator shaft [ˈdʒenəreɪtə ʃɑːft]	Lichtmaschinenwelle	
	fuel tap [ˈfjuːəl tæp]	Benzinhahn	
	exhaust manifold [ɪgˌzɔːst ˈmænɪfəʊld]	Auspuffkrümmer	
	eccentric adjuster for brake [ɪkˌsentrɪk əˌdʒʌstə fə ˈbreɪk]	Einsteller Exzenter Bremse	
	brake shoes pl [ˈbreɪk ʃuːz]	Bremsbacken	
T	to suppose [səˈpəʊz]	vermuten, glauben	
	to disappoint [ˌdɪsəˈpɔɪnt]	enttäuschen	
	miller [ˈmɪlə]	Fräser/in	
	order sheet [ˈɔːdə ʃiːt]	Bestellschein	
	to pop over [ˌpɒp ˈəʊvə]	vorbeikommen	
107	method of payment [ˌmeθəd əf ˈpeɪmənt]	Zahlungsweise	
	to rebuild [ˌriːˈbɪld]	erneuern, umbauen	
108	calibration equipment [kalɪˈbreɪʃn ɪkwɪpmənt]	Kalibriergerät(e)	
	to extend [ɪkˈstend]	erweitern	
109	Documentary Letter of Credit [dɒkjuˌmentri ˌletər əf ˈkredɪt]	Dokumentenakkreditiv	
	scheme [skiːm]	Schema	
	re [riː]	bezüglich, betreffs	
	battery-powered [ˈbætəri paʊəd]	batteriebetrieben	
	bulk order [ˌbʌlk ˈɔːdə]	Großbestellung, Großauftrag	
	to express sth [ɪkˈspres]	etw zum Ausdruck bringen	
	as requested [əz rɪˈkwestɪd]	wie gewünscht	

UNIT 11

112	complaint [kəmˈpleɪnt]	Beschwerde, Reklamation	
	issue [ˈɪʃuː]	Frage, Problem	
	to attend sth [əˈtend]	an etw teilnehmen	
	to reverse [rɪˈvɜːs]	umkehren, rückgängig machen	
	mining [ˈmaɪnɪŋ]	Bergbau, Abbau, Förderung	
	study [ˈstʌdi]	Untersuchung, Studie	
	impact [ˈɪmpækt]	Auswirkung(en), Folge(n)	
	soil erosion [ˌsɔɪl ɪˈrəʊʒn]	Bodenerosion	
	formation [fɔːˈmeɪʃn]	Bildung	
	sinkhole [ˈsɪŋkhəʊl]	Erdfall, Doline	
	loss [lɒs]	Verlust	
	biodiversity [ˌbaɪədaɪˈvɜːsɪti]	Artenvielfalt	
	to contaminate [kənˈtæmɪneɪt]	verunreinigen, kontaminieren	
	groundwater [ˈgraʊndwɔːtə]	Grundwasser	
	surface water [ˈsɜːfɪs wɔːtə]	Oberflächenwasser	
	to cut down [ˌkʌt ˈdaʊn]	(Baum) fällen	
	to clear space [ˌklɪə ˈspeɪs]	Platz schaffen	
	rock [rɒk]	Fels, Stein	
	hillside [ˈhɪlsaɪd]	Hang	
	pollution [pəˈluːʃn]	Verschmutzung	
	waste dump [ˈweɪst dʌmp]	Müllhalde	
	surrounding area [səˌraʊndɪŋ ˈeərɪə]	Umgebung	
	wilderness [ˈwɪldənəs]	Wildnis	
	destruction [dɪˈstrʌkʃn]	Zerstörung	
	ecosystem [ˈiːkəʊsɪstəm]	Ökosystem	
	habitat [ˈhæbɪtæt]	(natürlicher) Lebensraum	
	farming area [ˈfɑːmɪŋ eərɪə]	Landwirtschaftsfläche(n)	
	to disturb [dɪˈstɜːb]	stören	
	to destroy [dɪˈstrɔɪ]	zerstören	
	grazing [ˈgreɪzɪŋ]	Weideland	
	cropland [ˈkrɒplænd]	Anbaufläche	
	urban environment [ˌɜːbən ɪnˈvaɪrənmənt]	städtischer Raum	
	to affect sb/sth [əˈfekt]	sich auf jdn/etw auswirken, negative Auswirkungen auf jdn/etw haben	
	contamination [kənˌtæmɪˈneɪʃn]	Verunreinigung, Kontamination	
	leakage [ˈliːkɪdʒ]	Austreten, Versickern	
	population [ˌpɒpjuˈleɪʃn]	Bevölkerung	
	government [ˈgʌvənmənt]	Regierung	
	to clean up [ˌkliːn ˈʌp]	reinigen, saubermachen, aufräumen	

Unit word list

surroundings *pl* [səˈraʊndɪŋz]	Umgebung	
to restore [rɪˈstɔː]	wiederherstellen, wieder in den ursprünglichen Zustand versetzen	
fixed amount [ˌfɪkst əˈmaʊnt]	Pauschalbetrag	
account [əˈkaʊnt]	Konto	
third party [ˌθɜːd ˈpɑːti]	Dritte/r	
to reclaim [rɪˈkleɪm]	(Land) zurückgewinnen, rekultivieren	
acre [ˈeɪkə]	Morgen (Flächenmaß)	
wildlife [ˈwaɪldlaɪf]	Tier- und Pflanzenwelt, Natur	
to breed [briːd]	sich vermehren	
ranching [ˈrɑːntʃɪŋ]	Viehwirtschaft	

113
in relation to [ɪn rɪˈleɪʃn tə]	in Bezug auf
built-in [ˌbɪltˈɪn]	eingebaut
carbon footprint [ˌkɑːbən ˈfʊtprɪnt]	CO_2-Fußabdruck
to dissolve [dɪˈzɒlv]	auflösen
to glue [gluː]	kleben
greenhouse gas [ˌgriːnhaʊs ˈgæs]	Treibhausgas
incinerator [ɪnˈsɪnəreɪtə]	Müllverbrennungsanlage
toxic [ˈtɒksɪk]	giftig, toxisch
to conduct sth [kənˈdʌkt]	etw durchführen
to eliminate [ɪˈlɪmɪneɪt]	entfernen, eliminieren
hazardous [ˈhæzədəs]	gefährlich, schädlich
CO_2 equivalent [siː əʊ tuː ɪˈkwɪvələnt]	CO_2-Äquivalent
emission [ɪˈmɪʃn]	Ausstoß, Emission
mercury [ˈmɜːkjəri]	Quecksilber

T
to aim [eɪm]	darauf abzielen, wollen
aim [eɪm]	Ziel
to gather [ˈgæðə]	sammeln, zusammentragen
to persuade [pəˈsweɪd]	überzeugen
substance [ˈsʌbstəns]	Stoff, Substanz
climate [ˈklaɪmət]	Klima
to harm [hɑːm]	schaden, Schaden zufügen
carbon [ˈkɑːbən]	Kohlenstoff
consumer [kənˈsjuːmə]	Verbraucher/in
poisonous [ˈpɔɪzənəs]	giftig
tin [tɪn]	Zinn
chromium [ˈkrəʊmiəm]	Chrom
to disappear [ˌdɪsəˈpɪə]	verschwinden
to end up [ˌend ˈʌp]	(irgendwo) landen
landfill [ˈlændfɪl]	Mülldeponie
to release [rɪˈliːs]	freisetzen
to link [lɪŋk]	in Verbindung bringen
precious metals *pl* [ˌpreʃəs ˈmetlz]	Edelmetalle
to dump [dʌmp]	(Müll) abladen, verfrachten
profitable [ˈprɒfɪtəbl]	einträglich, profitabel
dead [ded]	(Akku:) leer
guide [gaɪd]	Anleitung

record [rɪˈkɔːd]	Bilanz, Ergebnis(se)
to expand on sth [ɪkˈspænd ɒn]	ausführlich über etw sprechen
manufacture [ˌmænjuˈfæktʃə]	Herstellung, Fertigung
to deal with sth [ˈdiːl wɪð]	mit etw fertig werden, etw bewältigen
to extract [ɪkˈstrækt]	(Rohstoffe) gewinnen
contract length [ˈkɒntrækt leŋθ]	Vertragsdauer
to cut down on sth [ˌkʌt ˈdaʊn ɒn]	etw reduzieren
comment [ˈkɒment]	Kommentar
to point out sth [ˌpɔɪnt ˈaʊt]	auf etw hinweisen
to damage [ˈdæmɪdʒ]	schädigen
to illustrate [ˈɪləstreɪt]	veranschaulichen

114
robot [ˈrəʊbɒt]	Roboter
assembly robot [əˈsembli rəʊbɒt]	Montageroboter
widespread [ˈwaɪdspred]	verbreitet
to perform [pəˈfɔːm]	(Tätigkeit) ausführen
arc welding [ˈɑːk weldɪŋ]	Lichtbogenschweißen
assembly system [əˈsembli sɪstəm]	Montageanlage
material handling [məˈtɪəriəl hændlɪŋ]	Materialtransport, Fördertechnik
to collaborate [kəˈlæbəreɪt]	zusammenarbeiten
collaboration [kəˌlæbəˈreɪʃn]	Zusammenarbeit
to take delivery [ˌteɪk dɪˈlɪvəri]	Ware entgegennehmen, eine Lieferung in Empfang nehmen
delivery note [dɪˈlɪvəri nəʊt]	Lieferschein
extent [ɪkˈstent]	Ausdehnung
distance [ˈdɪstəns]	Entfernung, Strecke
heaviness [ˈhevɪnəs]	Gewicht
mass [mæs]	Masse
overhead [ˈəʊvəhed]	Überkopf-, obere/r/s
to assign [əˈsaɪn]	zuweisen, vergeben
to insulate [ˈɪnsjuleɪt]	isolieren
conductor [kənˈdʌktə]	Leiter
to communicate sth [kəˈmjuːnɪkeɪt]	etw übermitteln
payload [ˈpeɪləʊd]	Nutzlast
working envelope [ˈwɜːkɪŋ envələʊp]	Arbeitsraum
reach [riːtʃ]	Reichweite
controller [kənˈtrəʊlə]	Steuerung, Steuereinheit, Controller
protection class [prəˈtekʃn klɑːs]	Schutzklasse

115
serial number [ˈsɪəriəl nʌmbə]	Seriennummer
total price [ˌtəʊtl ˈpraɪs]	Gesamtpreis

	power supply cable ['paʊə səplaɪ keɪbl]	Netzkabel		clog [klɒg]	Verstopfung
	labelling plate ['leɪbəlɪŋ pleɪt]	Beschriftungsplatte		to block [blɒk]	verhindern, blockieren
	contents ['kɒntents]	Inhalt		to heat [hiːt]	erhitzen
				to jam [dʒæm]	blockieren, verstopfen
				wavy ['weɪvi]	wellenförmig

T
gantry crane ['gæntri kreɪn]	Portalkran
type plate ['taɪp pleɪt]	Typenschild
Hold on. [ˌhəʊld 'ɒn]	Moment mal!
handbook ['hændbʊk]	Handbuch
documentation [ˌdɒkjumen'teɪʃn]	Unterlagen, Dokumentation
to be up and running [bi ˌʌp ən 'rʌnɪŋ]	laufen, im Einsatz sein
error ['erə]	Fehler, Irrtum

				pattern ['pætn]	Muster
				vibration [vaɪ'breɪʃn]	Vibration
				wobble ['wɒbl]	Wackeln
				sudden ['sʌdn]	plötzlich
				sharp [ʃɑːp]	scharf
				inertia [ɪ'nɜːʃə]	Trägheit
				visible ['vɪzəbl]	sichtbar
				print [prɪnt]	Ausdruck
				bracket ['brækɪt]	Halterung
				to suffer from ['sʌfə frəm]	unter etw leiden
116	sales department ['seɪlz dɪpɑːtmənt]	Verkauf(sabteilung), Vertrieb	119	fail [feɪl]	Fehldruck
	sales representative ['seɪlz reprɪzentətɪv]	Vertreter/in		prototype ['prəʊtətaɪp]	Prototyp
				at the beginning [ɪn ðə bɪ'gɪnɪŋ]	anfangs
117	stringing ['strɪŋɪŋ]	Fadenzug		satisfactory [ˌsætɪs'fæktəri]	zufriedenstellend
	string [strɪŋ]	Faden			
	feature ['fiːtʃə]	Teil, Bestandteil		to inform [ɪn'fɔːm]	informieren, mitteilen
	layer ['leɪə]	Schicht		inspection [ɪn'spekʃn]	Überprüfung, Kontrolle
	to shift [ʃɪft]	verschieben			

T
customer service [ˌkʌstəmə 'sɜːvɪs]	Kundendienst
to forward ['fɔːwəd]	weiterleiten
terrible ['terəbl]	furchtbar, fürchterlich
desert ['dezət]	Wüste
to harden ['hɑːdn]	aushärten
filament coil ['fɪləmnt kɔɪl]	Filamentspule
to exit sth ['eksɪt]	aus etw treten
to cool [kuːl]	abkühlen
to retain [rɪ'teɪn]	behalten
to solidify [sə'lɪdɪfaɪ]	fest werden
to exceed [ɪk'siːd]	überschreiten

	misaligned [ˌmɪsə'laɪnd]	falsch ausgerichtet			
	splitting ['splɪtɪŋ]	Spaltung			
	filament ['fɪləmnt]	Filament (drahtförmige thermoplastische Kunststoffe)			
	clogged [klɒgd]	verstopft			
	extruder [ɪk'struːdə]	Extruder			
118	reproduction [ˌriːprə'dʌkʃn]	Wiedergabe			
	extrusion [ɪk'struːʃn]	Extrusion			
	to interact [ˌɪntər'ækt]	zusammenspielen			
	to extrude [ɪk'struːd]	herauspressen, herausdrücken, extrudieren			
	printer resin ['prɪntə rezɪn]	geschmolzener Filamentkunststoff		unsatisfactory [ˌʌnˌsætɪs'fæktəri]	unzureichend, unbefriedigend
	settings pl ['setɪŋz]	Voreinstellungen	120	to apologize [ə'pɒlədʒaɪz]	sich entschuldigen
	to distort [dɪ'stɔːtɪd]	verzerren		to react to sth [ri'ækt tə]	auf etw reagieren
	to resolve [rɪ'zɒlv]	lösen		action ['ækʃn]	Maßnahmen
	multiplier ['mʌltɪplaɪə]	Multiplikator		at one's expense [ət wʌnz ɪk'spens]	auf jds Kosten
	to increase [ɪn'kriːs]	erhöhen, vergrößern		X-ray machine ['eks reɪ məʃiːn]	Röntgengerät
	to decrease [dɪ'kriːs]	verkleinern, verringern			
	to ooze [uːz]	tropfen, quellen			
	hairy ['heəri]	haarig			
	to deposit [dɪ'pɒzɪt]	ablagern			
	to be due to sth [bi 'djuː tə]	an etw liegen			

T
dental clinic [ˌdentl 'klɪnɪk]	Zahnklinik
scratched [skrætʃt]	verkratzt
dented ['dentɪd]	verbeult
casing ['keɪsɪŋ]	Gehäuse
to get sth sorted [ˌget 'sɔːtɪd]	etw klären, sich um etw kümmern
business ['bɪznəs]	Angelegenheit, Sache
superior [suː'pɪəriə]	Vorgesetzte/r

	typically ['tɪpɪkli]	normalerweise, üblicherweise			
	retraction [rɪ'trækʃn]	Rücksaugung			
	to enable [ɪ'neɪbl]	einschalten			
	to edit ['edɪt]	bearbeiten, editieren			
	tab [tæb]	Reiter			
	printer head ['prɪntə hed]	Druckkopf			
	course [kɔːs]	Verlauf			
	jam [dʒæm]	Stau		spelling ['spelɪŋ]	Schreibweise

Unit word list

	consignment [kən'saınmənt]	Warensendung	
	to **fulfil an order** [fʊl,fıl ən 'ɔːdə]	einen Auftrag abwickeln, eine Bestellung ausführen	
121	**transcript** ['trænskrıpt]	Mitschrift	
	record ['rekɔːd]	Datensatz	
	I realize that. [aı 'rıəlaız ðæt]	Das ist mir bewusst.	

UNIT 12

122	**(job) application** [,æplı'keıʃn]	Bewerbung
	to **apply for a job** [ə,plaı fər ə 'dʒɒb]	sich um eine Stelle bewerben
	to **qualify** ['kwɒlıfaı]	einen/den Abschluss machen
	job agency ['dʒɒb eıdʒənsi]	Arbeitsagentur, Arbeitsvermittlung
	mechanical engineering technician [mı,kænıkl ,endʒı'nıərıŋ teknıʃn]	Maschinenbautechniker/in
	mechatronics technician [,mekə'trɒnıks teknıʃn]	Mechatroniker/in

T
	listener ['lısnə]	Hörer/in
	computer aided [kəm'pjuːtər eıdıd]	computerunterstützt
	experienced [ık'spıəriənst]	erfahren
	transmitter [træns'mıtə]	Sender
	antenna [æn'tenə]	Antenne
	ideally [aı'diːəli]	idealerweise

123	**soldering** [səʊdərıŋ]	Weichlöten
	job opportunities pl [dʒɒb ,ɒpə'tjuːnətiz]	Arbeitsmöglichkeiten
	career prospects pl [kə'rıə prɒspekts]	berufliche Perspektiven
	job offer ['dʒɒb ɒfə]	Stellenangebot
	to **come across sth** [,kʌm ə'krɒs]	auf etw stoßen
	CV (curriculum vitae) [,siː 'viː, kə,rıkjələm 'viːtaı]	Lebenslauf
	agent ['eıdʒənt]	hier: zuständige/r Mitarbeiter/in
	standardized ['stændədaızd]	genormt
	potential [pə'tenʃl]	möglich, potenziell
	self-assessment [,self ə'sesmənt]	Selbsteinstufung
	mobility [məʊ'bıləti]	Freizügigkeit, Mobilität
	to **acquire** [ə'kwaıə]	erlangen, erwerben
	supplement ['sʌplımənt]	Zusatz, Ergänzung
	holder ['həʊldə]	Inhaber/in
124	**job advert(isement)** ['dʒɒb ædvɜːt/ ədvɜːtısmənt]	Stellenanzeige

	benefits pl ['benıfıts]	Zusatzleistungen, Sozialleistungen
	to **be shortlisted** [bi 'ʃɔːtlıstıd]	in die engere Auswahl kommen
	recruitment agency [rı'kruːtmənt eıdʒənsi]	Personalvermittlung
	metalwork ['metlwɜːk]	Metallbau
	salary ['sæləri]	Gehalt
	negotiable [nı'gəʊʃiəbl]	verhandelbar
	renewable [rı'njuːəbl]	verlängerbar
	to **face sth** [feıs]	mit etw konfrontiert sein
	chronic ['krɒnık]	dauerhaft
	shortage ['ʃɔːtıdʒ]	Mangel
	in high demand [ın ,haı dı'mɑːnd]	sehr gefragt
	commitment [kə'mıtmənt]	Engagement
	willingness ['wılıŋnəs]	Bereitschaft
	ability [ə'bıləti]	Fähigkeit
	drive [draıv]	Tatendrang, Motivation
	starting salary ['stɑːtıŋ sæləri]	Einstiegsgehalt
	opportunity [,ɒpə'tjuːnəti]	Gelegenheit, Möglichkeit
	initial [ı'nıʃl]	erste/r/s
125	**(metal) fabricator** ['fæbrıkeıtə]	Metallbauer/in
	vacancy ['veıkənsi]	offene Stelle
	metalworker ['metlwɜːkə]	Metallarbeiter/in
	fabrication [fæbrı'keıʃn]	Verarbeitung, Herstellung
	handrail ['hændreıl]	Geländer, Handlauf
	railings pl ['reılıŋz]	Gitter, Geländer
	structural work [,strʌktʃərəl 'wɜːk]	Rohbauarbeiten
	site installation ['saıt ınstəleıʃn]	Vor-Ort-Montage
	driving licence ['draıvıŋ laısns]	Führerschein
	to **involve** [ın'vɒlv]	mit sich bringen, beinhalten
	site work ['saıt wɜːk]	Arbeit vor Ort
	annual(ly) ['ænjuəl]	jährlich
	paid holiday [,peıd 'hɒlədeı]	bezahlter Urlaub
	public holiday [,pʌblık 'hɒlədeı]	gesetzlicher Feiertag
	equivalent [ı'kwıvələnt]	gleichwertig

P
	to **establish** [ı'stæblıʃ]	gründen
	mild steel [,maıld 'stiːl]	Baustahl
	to **be dependent on sth** [bi dı'pendənt ɒn]	sich nach etw richten, von etw abhängig sein
	preliminary [prı'lımınəri]	vorläufig, Vor-
	continually [kən'tınjuəli]	ständig
	candidate ['kændıdət]	Bewerber/in
	shift [ʃıft]	Schicht
	to **subsidize** ['sʌbsıdaız]	bezuschussen
	bank holiday BE [,bæŋk 'hɒlədeı]	gesetzlicher Feiertag

	HR department [,eɪtʃ 'ɑː dɪpɑːtmənt]	Personalabteilung	P	to indicate ['ɪndɪkeɪt]	andeuten, darauf hinweisen
	to assume [ə'sjuːm]	davon ausgehen		to keep in mind [,kiːp ɪn 'maɪnd]	daran denken
	occasion [ə'keɪʒn]	Gelegenheit		to stress [stres]	betonen
	to arise [ə'raɪz]	sich ergeben		to progress with sth [prə'gres wɪð]	mit etw vorankommen
126	interviewer ['ɪntəvjuːə]	Person, die ein Vorstellungsgespräch führt		to report to sb [rɪ'pɔːt tə]	jdm unterstehen
	strength [streŋθ]	Stärke		selection process [sɪ'lekʃn prəʊses]	Auswahlverfahren
	weakness ['wiːknəs]	Schwäche	128	mixed up [,mɪkst 'ʌp]	durcheinander
	to irritate ['ɪrɪteɪt]	stören, irritieren		set [set]	vorgegeben, starr, fest
	to flick through ['flɪk θruː]	durchblättern		to grab sb's attention [,græb ə'tenʃn]	jds Aufmerksamkeit fesseln
	pen [pen]	Stift		achievement [ə'tʃiːvmənt]	Leistung
	to disconnect [,dɪskə'nekt]	abschalten		brief [briːf]	kurz, knapp
	landline ['lændlaɪn]	Festnetz(telefon)		academic [,ækə'demɪk]	universitär
	to charge [tʃɑːdʒ]	(Akku) aufladen		socializing ['səʊʃəlaɪzɪŋ]	Ausgehen
	to get disconnected [get ,dɪskə'nektɪd]	(Telefonverbindung:) unterbrochen werden		data protection ['deɪtə prətekʃn]	Datenschutz
	to dress [dres]	sich kleiden		referee [,refə'riː]	Referenz(geber/in)
	bored [bɔːd]	gelangweilt		permission [pə'mɪʃn]	Erlaubnis
	uninterested [ʌn'ɪntrəstɪd]	uninteressiert	129	to seek [siːk]	suchen
	to focus ['fəʊkəs]	sich konzentrieren		school leaving certificate [,skuːl liːvɪŋ sə'tɪfɪkət]	Schulabschluss
	to hang on [,hæŋ 'ɒn]	warten	130	domestic appliance [də,mestɪk ə'plaɪəns]	Haushaltsgerät, Elektrogerät
	to swallow ['swɒləʊ]	schlucken	131	Attn. [ə'tenʃn]	z. Hdn.
	to look the part [,lʊk ðə 'pɑːt]	entsprechend (rollengerecht) aussehen		post [pəʊst]	Stelle
127	clarification [,klærɪfɪ'keɪʃn]	Klarstellung, Klärung		particularly [pə'tɪkjələli]	insbesondere
	expression [ɪk'spreʃn]	Ausdruck		to be keen to do sth [bɪ 'kiːn tə]	jdm liegt sehr daran, etw zu tun
T	in good time [ɪn ,gʊd 'taɪm]	rechtzeitig		on a daily basis [ɒn ə ,deɪli 'beɪsɪs]	jeden Tag, täglich
	to calm down [,kɑːm 'daʊn]	sich beruhigen		fluent ['fluːənt]	(Sprache:) fließend
	impression [ɪm'preʃn]	Eindruck		to benefit sb/sth ['benɪfɪt]	jdm/etw nützen
	Not particularly. [,nɒt pə'tɪkjələli]	Eigentlich nicht.		at short notice [ət ,ʃɔːt 'nəʊtɪs]	kurzfristig
	smart [smɑːt]	(Kleidung:) schick			
	confident(ly) ['kɒnfɪdənt]	selbstbewusst			
	shy [ʃaɪ]	schüchtern			
	habit ['hæbɪt]	Gewohnheit			
	to get into the habit of doing sth [,get ɪntə ðə 'hæbɪt əv]	sich daran gewöhnen, etw zu tun			
	panel ['pænl]	Gremium			
	to relate sth to sth [rɪ'leɪt tə]	etw auf etw beziehen			
	slight(ly) [slaɪt]	geringfügig, etwas			

A–Z word list

Dieses Wörterverzeichnis enthält alle neuen Wörter aus *Metal Matters – 3rd Edition* in alphabetischer Reihenfolge. Nicht angeführt sind Wörter, die zum Grundwortschatz (*Basic word list,* in den Handreichungen für den Unterricht) gehören. Die Zahl nach dem Stichwort bezieht sich auf die Seite, auf der das Wort zum ersten Mal erscheint. Wörter aus den Hörverständnisübungen sind zusätzlich mit einem **T** (Transkript) und Wörter aus den *Partner files* mit einem **P** gekennzeichnet.

A

ability *124* Fähigkeit
abnormal *70* ungewöhnlich, anormal
abrasion dust *37* Abriebstaub
abrasive sand *80* Abrasivsand
to **absorb** *35* absorbieren, aufnehmen
academic *128* universitär
acceleration *103* Beschleunigung
access *86T* Zugang; ~ **to sth** *69T* Zugriff auf etw
to **access sth** *69T* auf etw zugreifen
accessible, freely ~ *97T* frei zugänglich
accessories pl *17* Zubehör
to **accommodate** *31* aufnehmen, unterbringen
according to *7* gemäß, entsprechend, zufolge
account *112* Konto; **key** ~ **management** *11F* Großkundenbetreuung
accuracy *56* Genauigkeit
accurate(ly) *16* genau
acetone *76* Aceton
to **achieve** *59* erreichen
achievement *128* Leistung
acid *15* Säure
to **acquire** *123* erlangen, erwerben
acre *112* Morgen *(Flächenmaß)*
action *120* Maßnahmen
to **activate** *83* aktivieren, betätigen
to **adapt** *96* anpassen
adaptor *70* Adapter
addition *60* Ergänzung, Erweiterung
to **adjust** *56* regeln, einstellen
adjustable *56T* regelbar, einstellbar; ~ **spanner** *27* Rollgabelschlüssel
adjuster, eccentric ~ **for brake** *106* Einsteller Exzenter Bremse
to **administer sth** *77* etw geben, etw erteilen
administration *77* Verwaltung
advanced *24* fortschrittlich, modern
to **advise** *56* beraten
to **affect sb/sth** *112* sich auf jdn/etw auswirken, negative Auswirkungen auf jdn/etw haben
to **age** *37* altern
ageing *37* Alterung
agency, job ~ *122* Arbeitsagentur, Arbeitsvermittlung; **recruitment** ~ *124* Personalvermittlung
agenda *32* Tagesordnung
agent *123* hier: zuständige/r Mitarbeiter/in
aggregate *95* Aggregat
aggressive *87* aggressiv
aid, first ~ *15* Erste Hilfe
to **aim** *113T* darauf abzielen, wollen
aim *113T* Ziel
air, combustion ~ *104* Verbrennungsluft; **forced** ~ *104* Zwangsluft; **hot** ~ **blower** *81* Heißluftgebläse
air conditioner *70* Klimaanlage
air conditioning system *52* Klimasteuerung, Klimaanlage
air-flow rate *85* Luftdurchsatz
airtight *71* luftdicht
alarm, to set off the ~ *76* Alarm auslösen
to **align** *51* ausrichten
Allen head wrench *27* Innensechskantschlüssel, Inbusschlüssel
alloy, fusible ~ *70* Schmelzlegierung
along *9* entlang
alphabetical *47* alphabetisch
alternating *62* wechselnd; ~ **current (AC)** *84* Wechselstrom
alternative *21* Alternative
aluminium BE *34* Aluminium
aluminum AE *34* Aluminium
ambient temperature *70* Umgebungstemperatur
ambulance *77* Rettungswagen
amount *69* Menge, Betrag; **fixed** ~ *112* Pauschalbetrag
to **analyse** *60* analysieren
and so on *10T* und so weiter
angle *27* Winkel; **right** ~ *53* rechter Winkel
to **announce** *32* ankündigen
annual(ly) *125* jährlich
antenna *122T* Antenne
to **apologize** *120* sich entschuldigen
apparent, nominal ~ **power** *62* Nennscheinleistung
to **appear** *32* erscheinen, auftreten, vorkommen
appliance, domestic ~ *130* Haushaltsgerät, Elektrogerät; **electrical** ~ *15* Elektrogerät
application *32* Antrag, Bewerbung; *70* Anwendung
to **apply sth** *35* etw anwenden; *37* (Flüssigkeit usw.) auftragen; ~ **for a job** *122* sich um eine Stelle bewerben
appointment *65* Termin
apprentice *6* Auszubildende/r, Lehrling
apprenticeship *6* Lehre, Ausbildung
appropriate *73* entsprechend, passend, geeignet; **if** ~ *52* gegebenenfalls
approximate(ly) *46* ungefähr, zirka
apron *31* Schlosskasten
arc: ~ **eye** *14* verblitztes Auge; ~ **welding** *114* Lichtbogenschweißen
to **argue against/for sth** *91* sich gegen/für etw aussprechen, gegen/für etw argumentieren
to **arise** *125F* sich ergeben
arrangement *64* (Termin-)Vereinbarung, Vorbereitung
arrow *105* Pfeil
artificial *34* künstlich
aspect *78* Gesichtspunkt, Aspekt
to **assemble** *16* zusammenbauen, montieren
assembly *27* Montage; ~ **instructions** pl *38* Montageanleitung; ~ **line** *27* Fertigungsstraße, Montageband; ~ **point** *76* Sammelplatz; ~ **robot** *114* Montageroboter; ~ **system** *114* Montageanlage; **carriage** ~ *31* Werkzeugschlitten; **ready-**~ **model** *37* Fertigmodell
assessment, self-~ *123* Selbsteinstufung; **fire risk** ~ *79* Brandrisikobewertung, -analyse
to **assign** *114* zuweisen, vergeben
to **assist** *91* assistieren, helfen, unterstützen
assistance *32* Hilfe, Unterstützung
to **assume** *125F* davon ausgehen
assurance, quality ~ *92* Qualitätssicherung
to **attach** *32* (E-Mail:) anhängen
attached, to be ~ **to sth** *14* mit etw verbunden sein; **with a room** ~ *65* mit einem Nebenraum
attachment *69* (E-Mail:) Anhang
to **attend** *18* (Schule) besuchen; ~ **sth** *112* an etw teilnehmen
attendant, swimming pool ~ *56* Bademeister/in

attention *98* Aufmerksamkeit; to
   attract sb's ~ *50* jds Aufmerksamkeit
   wecken; to **grab sb's ~** *128* jds Aufmerksamkeit fesseln; to **pay (special) ~
   to sth** *49T* (besonders) auf etw achten
Attn. *131* z. Hdn.
to **attract sb's attention** *50* jds Aufmerksamkeit wecken
auction *102* Versteigerung, Auktion;
   to **buy sth at ~** *103* etw ersteigern;
   to **sell at ~** *102* versteigern
audience *7* Publikum
automated *80* automatisch
automation *6* Automatisierung,
   Automation; **~ system** *93* Automatisie-
   rungssystem, -anlage
automotive *7T* Automobil-
available *21* lieferbar, verfügbar;
   to **make sth ~** *59* etw zur Verfügung
   stellen
to **avoid** *13* vermeiden
award *86* Auszeichnung, Preis
awareness, cultural ~ *87* Kulturbewusstsein, kulturelle Sensibilität
axis, axes *9T* Achse, Achsen; **four-
   ~** *9T* vierachsig
axle *37* Achse; **displacement ~** *37*
   Verdrängerachse

B

back: ~ to back *41* Rücken an Rücken;
   ~ gear *31* (Räder-)Vorgelege
background *77* Hintergrund
ball bearing *93* Kugellager; **6-point ~
   cage** *97T* sechsfach kugelgelagerter
   Laufwagen
bandsaw *29* Bandsäge
bank holiday BE *125F* gesetzlicher
   Feiertag
bar *40* Barren; **~ chart** *54* Säulendiagramm
barrier, light ~ *84* Lichtschranke
to **base** *96* basieren, fußen
base *29* Basis, Sockel; *36* Grundkörper;
   ~ line *39T* Grundlinie
based in ... *8* mit Sitz in ...; to **be ~
   ...** *13* seinen Sitz in ... haben, in ... sein
basis, on a daily ~ *131* jeden Tag,
   täglich
batch *11* Charge, Los
battery *56T* Batterie, Akku; **~ pack** *70*
   Akku; **rechargeable ~** *56T* wiederaufladbare Batterie, Akku
battery-powered *109* batteriebetrieben
bearing *37* Lager; **ball ~** *93* Kugellager; **friction ~** *37* Gleitlager, Gleitlagerung; **main ~** *52* Hauptlager(ung)
beat per minute *56T* Schlag pro Minute
bed slideways *31* Maschinenbett
beginning, at the ~ *119* anfangs

behalf, on ~ of sb *20* für jdn, in jds
   Namen
bench *77* Werkbank
benchmark *59* Maßstab
to **bend** *35* biegen
bend, sharp ~ *75* Knick, enge Kurve
bending, tight ~ *75* starke Krümmung
to **benefit (from sth)** *18* (von etw) pro-
   fitieren; **~ sb/sth** *131* jdm/etw nützen
benefits pl *124* Zusatzleistungen,
   Sozialleistungen
beside *9T* neben
beyond *48* über, jenseits
biodiversity *112* Artenvielfalt
birth, place of ~ *12* Geburtsort
bit, drill ~ *71* Bohrer, Bohrspitze
blast furnace *104* Hochofen
to **block** *14T* versperren, blockieren;
   118 verhindern
block *40* Klotz, Block
to **blow** *85* blasen
blower, hot air ~ *81* Heißluftgebläse;
   Roots ~ *104* Roots-Gebläse, Drehkolbengebläse
board *6* Aufsichtsrat; **circuit ~** *70*
   Leiterplatte, Platine; **distribution
   ~** *73* Stromverteilung
body *98* (Brief:) Haupttext; *102* (Auto:)
   Karosserie; **pump ~** *104* Pumpengehäuse
bodywork *105* Wagenaufbau, Karosserie
boiler, gas ~ *70* Gaskessel
bolt *27* Schraube (zur Befestigung von
   Muttern); **hex ~** *28* Sechskantschraube; **machine ~** *28* Maschinenschraube
to **book** *64* reservieren, buchen
to **bore** *30* innendrehen
bore *39T* Bohrung
bored *126* gelangweilt
borehole *39T* Bohrloch
to **bow** *87* sich verbeugen
bracket *118* Halterung
to **brainstorm** *14T* Ideen sammeln
brake *47* Bremse; **~ shoes** pl *106*
   Bremsbacken; **eccentric adjuster for
   ~** *106* Einsteller Exzenter Bremse; **~
   spindle** *60* Spindelbremse; **~ horsepower** *103T* Pferdestärken-Einheit in
   UK u. USA;
branch *10* Niederlassung; *19* Ast, Zweig
brass *37* Messing
breakdown *17* Ausfall, Störfall
breathing *14* Atmung
to **breed** *112* sich vermehren
brief *128* kurz, knapp
bright *56T* (Licht:) hell, gleißend
to **bring up sth** *69T* etw zur Sprache
   bringen
brochure *32* Broschüre
buffet breakfast *86T* Frühstücksbüfett

to **build up** *37* sich anreichern, sich
   bilden
builder, machine ~ *17* Maschinen-
   bauer/in
building *7* Bauwesen
built-in *113* eingebaut
bulk: ~ order *109* Großbestellung,
   Großauftrag; **~ production** *58*
   Massenfertigung
to **bump into sth** *15* gegen etw stoßen
burn *77* Verbrennung
business *120T* Angelegenheit, Sache;
   ~ partner *65* Geschäftspartner/in;
   to **do ~ with sb** *33* mit jdm Geschäfte
   machen
button, emergency stop ~ *15* Not-Aus-
   Taster
to **buy sth at auction** *103*
   etw ersteigern
by *56T* (Abmessungen:) mal;
   ~ tomorrow *64* bis morgen

C

cabinet, control ~ *49* Steuerungskasten; **switch ~** *52* Schaltschrank
cable *6* Kabel; **charging ~** *78* Ladekabel; **connecting ~** *97T* Anschlusskabel;
   data ~ *71* Datenkabel, Datenleitung;
   power ~ *71* Stromkabel, Stromleitung;
   power supply ~ *115* Netzkabel;
   ~ trunk *71* Kabelkanal; to **lay
   ~s** *71T* Kabel/Leitungen verlegen
CAD engineer *10* Technische/r Zeich-
   ner/in
cage, 6-point ball bearing ~ *97T*
   sechsfach kugelgelagerter Laufwagen
calibration equipment *108*
   Kalibriergerät(e)
to **call back** *20* zurückrufen
to **calm down** *127T* sich beruhigen
candidate *125F* Bewerber/in
canteen *19* Kantine
capabilities pl *59* Möglichkeiten,
   (Leistungs-)Vermögen
capacitance *24* Kapazität
capacity *84* Leistung; *103* Hubraum;
   tank ~ *102* Tankinhalt
cap nut *28* Überwurfmutter, Hutmutter
carbon *113T* Kohlenstoff; **~ fibre** *34*
   Kohlefaser; **~ footprint** *113* CO_2-
   Fußabdruck
carburettor *103* Vergaser
care *103T* Sorgfalt; to **take ~** *74*
   aufpassen; to **take ~ of sth** *32* sich
   um etw kümmern, etw bearbeiten, etw
   erledigen
career prospects pl *123* berufliche
   Perspektiven
carriage *97T* Schlitten; **~ assembly** *31*
   Werkzeugschlitten

to carry: ~ **sth** *25* etw mit sich führen; ~ **out sth** *68* etw durchführen
cart, tool ~ *60* Werkzeugwagen
case *56* Gehäuse
casing *120T* Gehäuse
casting *31* Gussstück
cast iron *34* Gusseisen
castor *47* Rolle
catalogue *33* Katalog
to catch fire *70* in Brand geraten, Feuer fangen
category *15* Kategorie
to cause sth do to sth *37* dazu führen, dass etw etw tut
ceiling *98* (Zimmer-)Decke
central lubrication *51* Zentralschmierung
centre *30* Reitstockspitze; **live** ~ *31* verfahrbare Führungsspitze; ~ **line** *52* Mittellinie, Achse; ~ **punch** *24* Körner
centrifugal *104* zentrifugal, Zentrifugal-
ceramic paste *37* Keramikpaste
ceremony, prize-giving ~ *86* Preisverleihung
certificate, school leaving ~ *129* Schulabschluss
certified *79* geprüft, zertifiziert
chafing *51* Abscheuerung
chain, power supply ~ *52* Stromversorgungskette
chain-dotted line *39* strichpunktierte Linie
chairman *6* Vorsitzende/r
challenge *16* schwierige Aufgabe, Herausforderung
chamfer *39T* Fase
change, to make ~**s** *11* Änderungen vornehmen
characteristics pl *96* Merkmale, Eigenschaften
to charge *126* (Akku) aufladen
charge, to be in ~ **of sth** *10T* für etw zuständig/verantwortlich sein
charger *70* Ladegerät
charging cable *78* Ladekabel
chart *10* Diagramm, Tabelle; **bar** ~ *54* Säulendiagramm; **organization** ~ *10* Organigramm; **pie** ~ *54* Tortendiagramm
chassis *103* Fahrgestell
to check: ~ **in** *86* sich anmelden, einchecken; ~ **out** *86* sich abmelden, auschecken
chemicals pl *84* Chemikalien
chip: ~ **conveyor** *58T* Späneförderer; ~ **removal** *49T* Späneförderung; ~ **tank** *60* Spänebehälter; **flying** ~**s** *31* herumfliegende Späne
chisel *27* Meißel

chromium *113T* Chrom
chronic *124* dauerhaft
chronological(ly) *77* chronologisch
chuck *29* Spannfutter, Bohrfutter; ~ **jaw** *48* Futterbacke, Klemmbacke; **power** ~ *52* Kraftspannfutter
circle *40* Kreis
circuit board *70* Leiterplatte, Platine
circuit breaker, residual current ~ **(RCCB)** *73* FI-Schutzschalter, Fehlerstromschutzschalter
circular *30* kreisförmig
circumference *39* Umfang
to clamp *31* einspannen
clamp, hold down ~ *29* Niederhalter
clamping: ~ **force** *51* Spannkraft; ~ **surface** *97F* Aufspannfläche
clarification *127* Klarstellung, Klärung
to clarify *100* klären, abklären
clarity *42* Klarheit, Deutlichkeit
to classify *34* klassifizieren
to clean up *112* reinigen, saubermachen, aufräumen
cleaning *37* Reinigung
to clear space *112* Platz schaffen
clearance *52* Spiel; **ground** ~ *102* Bodenabstand
client *20* Kunde/Kundin
climate *113T* Klima
to climb *54* steigen
climb *54* Anstieg
clinic, dental ~ *120T* Zahnklinik; **outpatient** ~ *98* Ambulanz
clog *118* Verstopfung
clogged *117* verstopft
close, complimentary ~ *33* (Brief:) Schlussformel
close-up photo *25* Nahaufnahme
closely, more ~ *78* näher, genauer; ~ **related to** *105* eng verwandt mit
cloth *37* Tuch
clothing, protective ~ *14T* Schutzkleidung
cloud storage *90* Datenspeicherung in der Cloud
clutch *31* Kupplung
CNC milling *8* CNC-Fräsen; ~ **machine** *9T* CNC-Fräse
CO₂ equivalent *113* CO₂-Äquivalent
coefficient *93* Koeffizient
coil, filament ~ *119T* Filamentspule
to collaborate *114* zusammenarbeiten
collaboration *114* Zusammenarbeit
collar *96* Spannhals; **blue** ~ **workers** pl *55* Arbeiter/innen; **white** ~ **workers** pl *55* Angestellte
colleague *10T* Kollege/Kollegin
column *25* (Text:) Spalte; *29* Säule
to combine *18* verknüpfen, kombinieren

combustion: ~ **air** *104* Verbrennungsluft; **internal** ~ **engine** *104* Verbrennungsmotor
to come: ~ **across sth** *123* auf etw stoßen; ~ **off** *95T* sich lösen, abgehen; ~ **up with sth** *80T* sich etw ausdenken, sich etw einfallen lassen
comment *113* Kommentar
commercial *70* gewerblich
to commission *17* in Betrieb nehmen
commissioning *60* Inbetriebnahme
commitment *124* Engagement
common sense *14T* gesunder Menschenverstand
to communicate sth *114* etw übermitteln
communication, means of ~ *68* Kommunikationsmittel
company, multinational ~ *7* internationaler Konzern; **to join a** ~ *19* bei einem Unternehmen anfangen
compatibility *96* Kompatibilität
to compete *79* konkurrieren
competition *79* Konkurrenz
competitor *7* Wettbewerber/in, Konkurrent/in
complaint *112* Beschwerde, Reklamation
complicated *62* kompliziert
complimentary close *33* (Brief:) Schlussformel
component *59* Bauelement
composed, to be ~ **of sth** *29* aus etw bestehen
compound *34* Verbundwerkstoff; *93* Verbindung; ~ **rest** *31* Kreuzschlitten; ~ **slide** *31* Kreuzschlitten
to compress *61* verdichten, komprimieren
compressed air *17* Druckluft
compressive stress *35* Druckbelastung, Druckspannung
computer aided *122T* computerunterstützt
computerized *12* Computer-
concave *39T* konkav
to concern sth *11* etw betreffen
conclusion *35* Schluss; **in** ~ *91* abschließend
condition *16* Zustand; *55* Bedingung
to conduct sth *113* etw durchführen
conductivity, thermal ~ *36* Wärmeleitfähigkeit
conductor *114* Leiter; ~ **cross-section** *62* Leiterquerschnitt
cone *40* Kegel, Konus
conference *54* Tagung, Konferenz
confident(ly) *127T* selbstbewusst
configuration *59* Einstellung, Konfiguration

to **configure** *92* einrichten, konfigurieren
to **confirm** *20* bestätigen
confirmation *98* Bestätigung
to **conform to sth** *70* einer Sache entsprechen
conical *41* konisch, kegelförmig
to **connect (sth to sth)** *9T* (etw mit etw) verbinden, (etw an etw) anschließen
connecting: ~ cable *97T* Anschlusskabel; **~ pipe** *11* Verbindungsrohr, -leitung
connection *49T* Anschluss; **~ terminal** *51* Verbindungsklemme
connector *6* Verbinder, Stecker; **plug ~** *52* Stecker, Steckverbinder
to **consider sth** *69T* etw in Betracht ziehen, über etw nachdenken
consignment *120* Warensendung
to **consist of sth** *96* aus etw bestehen
constraint *52* Auflage
to **construct** *81* bauen, konstruieren
construction *7* Bau
construction *8* Konstruktion(sabteilung); **~ site** *57F* Baustelle
consultancy *79* Beratung
consumer *113T* Verbraucher/in
consumption, fuel ~ *103* Kraftstoffverbrauch; **power ~** *57* Stromverbrauch
contact *73* Kontaktperson
to **contain** *29* enthalten
container *100* Behälter, Box, Container
to **contaminate** *112* verunreinigen, kontaminieren
contamination *112* Verunreinigung, Kontamination
contents *115* Inhalt
context menu *62* Kontextmenü
continually *125F* ständig
to **continue to do sth** *19* mit etw weitermachen
continuous line *39* durchgezogene Linie
continuously *97T* fortwährend, ständig, kontinuierlich
contour *62* Kontur
contract *80T* Vertrag; **~ length** *113* Vertragsdauer
to **contrast** *55* gegenüberstellen, vergleichen
control: ~ cabinet *49* Steuerungskasten; **~ centre** *61* Steuerzentrale; **~ dial** *29* Drehregler; **~ panel** *48* Steuerkonsole; **~ unit** *31* Steuergerät
controlled *9T* gesteuert

controller *114* Steuerung, Steuereinheit, Controller; **pneumatic ~** *95* pneumatischer Regler
conventional *93* herkömmlich, konventionell
convertible *102* Cabriolet
convex *39T* konvex
conveyor *80* Förderband, Förderer, Fördersystem; **chip ~** *58T* Späneförderer
to **cool** *103T* kühlen; *119T* abkühlen
coolant *31* Kühlmittel
cooler *36* Kühlkörper
cooperation *11* Zusammenarbeit
coordinates pl *92* Koordinaten
to **cope with sth** *58T* mit etw zurechtkommen
copper *34* Kupfer
to **copy in sb** *69T* jdn auf CC / in den Verteiler setzen
corridor *9T* Flur, Gang
correctness *42* Richtigkeit
corrosion *52* Korrosion
coupling *84* Kupplung
course *118* Verlauf
to **cover** *7* (Thema) behandeln; *14T* verdecken, abdecken; *79* absichern, erfassen
cover *56T* Hülle, Tasche; **~ profile** *96* Abdeckungsprofil; **safety ~** *15* Sicherheitsabdeckung; **slip-on ~** *56T* Einstecktasche
covering letter *32* Anschreiben, Begleitschreiben
crack *52* Riss
crane, gantry ~ *115T* Portalkran
crankshaft *37* Kurbelwelle
crash *76* Krach, Schlag, Rums; **~ helmet** *35* Sturzhelm
crate *71* Kiste; **packing ~** *98* Packkiste
to **create** *96* (Datei) anlegen
credit, Documentary Letter of C~ *109* Dokumentenakkreditiv
cropland *112* Anbaufläche
cross drive *52* Querantrieb
cross section *30* Querschnitt; **conductor ~** *62* Leiterquerschnitt
cross slide *31* Querschlitten; **~ taper** *52* Keilleiste des Planschlittens
cross slot screw *27* Kreuzschlitzschraube
to **crush** *49* zerquetschen
cube *40* Würfel
cubical *40* würfelförmig
cultural awareness *87* Kulturbewusstsein, kulturelle Sensibilität
current *24* Strom; **~ gain** *24* Stromverstärkung; **alternating ~ (AC)** *84* Wechselstrom; **nominal ~** *62* Nennstrom; **rated ~** *70* Nennstrom; **three phase ~** *49T* Drehstrom;

residual ~ circuit breaker (RCCB) *73* FI-Schutzschalter, Fehlerstromschutzschalter
currently *79* zurzeit, gegenwärtig, momentan
custom-made *92* speziell angefertigt, individuell gefertigt
customer, regular ~ *94* Stammkunde/-kundin; **~ service** *119T* Kundendienst
to **customize** *59* nach Kundenwunsch fertigen; *96* individuell anpassen
customs *73* Zoll; **~ inspector** *73* Zollinspektor/in
to **cut: ~ down** *112* (Baum) fällen; **~ down on sth** *113* etw reduzieren
cutoff, thermal ~ *70* thermische Abschaltung; **thermal ~ fuse** *70* Thermosicherung
cutter, milling ~ *17* Fräser
cutter, multi-toothed ~ *30* mehrzahniges Fräswerkzeug
cutting: ~ mechanic *17* Schneidwerkzeugmechaniker/in; **~ section** *52* Spanquerschnitt; **~ speed** *17* Schnitt-, Schneidegeschwindigkeit; **~ tool** *29* Schneidwerkzeug; **hot ~ system** *96* Heißschneidesystem; **waterjet ~** *8* Wasserstrahlschneiden
CV (curriculum vitae) *123* Lebenslauf
cycle *62* Zyklus; **multi-thread ~** *62* Mehrgewindezyklus
cylinder *37* Zylinder; **servo-brake ~** *106* Servobremszylinder
cylindrical(ly) *41* zylindrisch

D

daily, on a ~ basis *131* jeden Tag, täglich
to **damage** *113* schädigen
damage *52* Schaden; **fire ~** *76* Brandschaden
damaged *14T* beschädigt, defekt
to **darken** *37* nachdunkeln
darkroom *57* Dunkelkammer
data pl *17* Daten, Angaben; **~ cable** *71* Datenkabel, Datenleitung; **~ protection** *128* Datenschutz; **~ sheet** *102* Datenblatt
date of delivery *94* Lieferdatum
day, at the end of the ~ *18* letzten Endes; **the other ~** *58T* neulich
dead *113T* (Akku:) leer
deadly *48* tödlich
deafness *14* Taubheit
to **deal with sth** *43* sich mit etw befassen; *57F* sich um etw kümmern; *77* mit etw umgehen; *113* mit etw fertig werden, etw bewältigen
dealer *7T* Händler/in

A–Z word list

decal *48* Aufkleber
decibel *49T* Dezibel
decrease *54* Abnahme, Sinken
to decrease *54* abnehmen, sinken; *118* verkleinern, verringern
deep *18* tief, vertieft
defect *35* Schaden, Fehler
to define *78* definieren
to deform *35* verformen
deformation *52* Verformung
degree *18* Abschluss; *46* Grad; *69* Maß
delivery: **~ note** *114* Lieferschein; **~ terms** pl *56T* Lieferbedingungen; **date of ~** *94* Lieferdatum; **to take ~** *114* Ware entgegennehmen, eine Lieferung in Empfang nehmen
demand, in high ~ *124* sehr gefragt
dense *36* dicht
density *36* Dichte
dent *24* Vertiefung
dental clinic *120T* Zahnklinik
dented *120T* verbeult
department *8* Abteilung
dependent, to be ~ on sth *125F* sich nach etw richten, von etw abhängig sein
to deposit *118* ablagern
depth *24* Tiefe
desert *119T* Wüste
design *15* Gestaltung, Design
desired *37* gewünscht
desktop machine *95* Tischgerät
to destroy *112* zerströren
destruction *112* Zerstörung
to detect *92* erfassen
detection, temperature ~ *71* Temperaturmessung, -erfassung
to develop *6* entwickeln
deviation *92* Abweichung
device *24* Gerät
to diagnose *24* diagnostizieren, feststellen
dial *29* Anzeige, Regler; **control ~** *29* Drehregler
diameter *11* Durchmesser; **inside ~** *24* Innendurchmesser; **outside ~** *24* Außendurchmesser
to dictate *32* diktieren
die plate *27* Formplatte
digit *21* Ziffer
dimension line *39* Bemaßungslinie
dimensions pl *39* Abmessungen, Dimensionen
dining room *86T* *(Hotel:)* Speisesaal
to dip *105* senken
directions pl *9* Wegbeschreibung; **to give ~** *9* den Weg beschreiben
dirt *14T* Schmutz, Dreck
to disappear *113T* verschwinden
to disappoint *106T* enttäuschen

to disassemble *37* auseinanderbauen, demontieren
disassembly *97T* Zerlegen, Demontage
disc turret, 12-station ~ reception *60* 12-fach-Revolverscheiben-Werkzeugaufnahme
discharge *60* Auswurf
to disconnect *126* abschalten
disconnected, to get ~ *126* *(Telefonverbindung:)* unterbrochen werden
discount *94* Rabatt
to discuss *14* diskutieren, besprechen, (über etw) sprechen
to dismantle *97T* demontieren, zerlegen
to dismount *52* abmontieren
dispatch *8* Versand(abteilung)
to dispatch *33* versenden
to displace *52* verschieben
displacement axle *37* Verdrängerachse
to dissolve *113* auflösen
distance *61* Abstand; *114* Entfernung, Strecke
to distort *118* verzerren
distorting *35* verformend, deformierend
distortion *48* Verzug
to distract *15* ablenken
to distribute *35* verteilen
distribution, power ~ *6* Stromverteilung; **~ board** *73* Stromverteilung
to disturb *112* stören
to divide *42* teilen, unterteilen
division *10* Geschäftsbereich, Division, Sparte; **head of ~** *10* Bereichsleiter/in
DIY kit *95* Bausatz
Documentary Letter of Credit *109* Dokumentenakkreditiv
documentation *115T* Unterlagen, Dokumentation
domestic *70* Haushalts-; **~ appliance** *130* Haushaltsgerät, Elektrogerät
dominant *87* dominant
dose *57* Dosis
dot *32* Punkt
double ended ring spanner *27* Doppelringschlüssel
double open ended spanner *27* Doppelmaulschlüssel
downwards *81* abwärts, nach unten
draft *81* Entwurf
drag knife *96* Schleppmesser
drastic(ally) *55T* drastisch
to draw: **~ in sth** *104* etw einziehen; **~ up** *79* *(Text)* erstellen, *(Liste)* aufstellen
drawer *28* Schublade, Schubfach
to dress *126* sich kleiden
to drill *11* bohren
drill *21* Bohrer; **electric ~** *26* Elektrobohrmaschine; **~ bit** *71* Bohrer, Bohrspitze

drilling *8* Bohren, Bohrabteilung; **~ machine** *9T* Bohrmaschine
to drip off *81* abtropfen
to drive *30* antreiben
drive *49* Antrieb; *124* Tatendrang, Motivation; **cross ~** *52* Querantrieb; **left-hand ~** *105* Linkslenker, Linkslenkung; **linear ~** *92* Linearantrieb; **rear wheel ~** *103* Hinterradantrieb; **tool ~** *60* Werkzeugantrieb; **~ power** *60* Antriebsleistung; **~ unit** *93* Antriebseinheit, -aggregat; **final ~ ratio** *103* Achsübersetzung; **linear ~ profile** *96* Linearachsprofil
driving: **~ licence** *125* Führerschein; **~ pulley** *31* Antriebsscheibe
drop *37* Tropfen; *54* Fall, Sinken
to drop *54* sinken, fallen
droplet *37* Tröpfchen
dual system *18* duales System
due to *15* aufgrund von, wegen; **to be ~ sth** *118* an etw liegen
to dump *113T* *(Müll)* abladen, verfrachten
dump, waste ~ *112* Müllhalde
dust *37* Staub; **abrasion~** *37* Abriebstaub
duty *17* Pflicht, Aufgabe
dynamics *59* Dynamik

E

ear protection *14* Gehörschutz
earth, protective ~ *62* Schutzleiter, Schutzerde
eccentric adjuster for brake *106* Einsteller Exzenter Bremse
ecological *64* ökologisch, Öko-
ecosystem *112* Ökosystem
edge *41* Kante
to edit *118* bearbeiten, editieren
edition *98* *(Zeitschrift etc.:)* Ausgabe
education system *18* Bildungssystem, Schulsystem
effect, overall ~ *15* Gesamteindruck, Gesamtwirkung
efficiency *78* Effizienz
efficient *59* leistungsfähig, effizient
e.g. *34* z.B.
either *42* eines (von mehreren)
to eject *48* auswerfen, herausschleudern
elastic(ally) *35* elastisch
elasticity *36* Elastizität
electric: **~ current** *84* (elektrischer) Strom; **~ drill** *26* Elektrobohrmaschine
electrical appliance *15* Elektrogerät
electrical engineer *12T* Elektroingenieur/in, Elektrotechniker/in; *17* Elektriker/in

electrician *17* Elektriker/in
electrocution *49* (Tötung durch) Stromschlag
electronics, industrial ~ *6* Industrieelektronik
to eliminate *113* entfernen, eliminieren
emergency *14T* Notfall; **~ cut out switch** *14T* Not-Aus-Schalter; **~ exit** *15* Notausgang; **~ services** pl *77* Einsatzkräfte, Rettungsdienste; **~ stop button** *15* Not-Aus-Taster
emission *113* Ausstoß, Emission
to employ sb *6* jdn beschäftigen
employee *7* Angestellte/r, Beschäftigte/r
to enable *118* einschalten
to enclose *98* (Brief:) beifügen
enclosure *98* (Brief:) Anlage
end switch *85* Endschalter
to end up *113T* (irgendwo) landen
endstop *85* Endanschlag
energy engineer *68* Energieingenieur/in, Energietechniker/in
to engage *105* einschalten
engaged *20* (Telefon:) besetzt
engine *36* Motor; **~ layout** *103* Motoranordnung; **8 inline ~** *105* Achtzylinder-Reihenmotor; **frontmounted ~** *103* Frontmotor; **internal combustion ~** *104* Verbrennungsmotor; **Stirling ~** *36* Stirlingmotor; **supercharged ~** *103* Kompressormotor
engineer's hammer *27* Schlosserhammer
engineering *16* Technik, Ingenieurwissenschaft, Maschinenbau
to engrave *95T* (ein)gravieren
engraving, laser ~ *93* Lasergravur; **~ needle** *96* Graviernadel
to enquire about sth *56* sich nach etw erkundigen
enquiry *32* Anfrage
to ensure *59* garantieren, sicherstellen
to entangle *49* (sich/etw) verfangen
to enter sth *18* etw (Ausbildung usw.) beginnen, mit etw anfangen; *26* etw betreten; *62* etw (Daten) eingeben
entrance *9* Eingang
entry, no ~ *15* Einfahrt verboten
entry-level user *59* Einsteiger/in
envelope, working ~ *114* Arbeitsraum
environmental standard *70* Umweltnorm
equipment *7T* Geräte, Ausstattung
equipped with sth *30* mit etw ausgestattet
equivalent *20* Entsprechung, Übersetzung; *125* gleichwertig; CO_2 **~** *113* CO_2-Äquivalent
error *115T* Fehler, Irrtum

to establish *101* etablieren, schaffen, aufbauen; *125F* gründen
to estimate *61* schätzen
event *32* Veranstaltung
everyday *78* Alltags-
exactly faced *53* genau bearbeitet
exam, to pass an ~ *19* eine Prüfung bestehen
to exceed *119T* überschreiten
except for *21* außer
excerpt *11* Auszug
excess *37* überschüssig
excessive *53* übermäßig
exclusive *62* exklusiv
Excuse me. *13* Verzeihung. Entschuldigung.
exhaust manifold *106* Auspuffkrümmer
to exist *105* existieren
exit, emergency ~ *15* Notausgang; **fire ~** *15* Notausgang
to exit sth *119T* aus etw treten
to expand *36* sich ausdehnen; **~ on sth** *113* ausführlich über etw sprechen
expansion, thermal ~ *36* Wärmeausdehnung
expense, at one's ~ *120* auf jds Kosten
experience, job ~ *18* Berufserfahrung; **work ~** *26* Praktikum
experienced *122T* erfahren
expert staff *18* Fachpersonal
to express sth *109* etw zum Ausdruck bringen
expression *127* Ausdruck
to extend *108* erweitern
extension *21* Durchwahl
extent *114* Ausdehnung
external tooth lock washer *28* außengezahnte Zahnscheibe
to extinguish *77* löschen
extinguisher, fire ~ *15* Feuerlöscher
extra *49T* Sonderzubehör, Zusatzausstattung, Extra
to extract *113* (Rohstoffe) gewinnen
to extrude *118* herauspressen, herausdrücken, extrudieren
extruder *117* Extruder
extrusion *118* Extrusion
eye: ~ contact *85* Blickkontakt; **~ protection** *14* Augenschutz, Schutzbrille; **arc ~** *14* verblitztes Auge

F

to fabricate *30* fertigen, herstellen
fabrication *125* Verarbeitung, Herstellung
fabricator *125* Metallbauer/in
face *53* Fläche; **~-to-face** *69T* persönlich
to face: ~ sth *124* mit etw konfrontiert sein; **exactly ~ed** *53* genau bearbeitet

facilities pl *86T* Einrichtungen
fact, in ~ *13* tatsächlich, eigentlich
factory *6* Fabrik, Werk; **~ floor** *9* Fertigungsbereich, Werkshalle; **~ manager** *20* Betriebsleiter/in, Werksleiter/in
fail *119* Fehldruck
fair *32* Messe; **trade ~** *34* (Branchen-, Handels-)Messe
faithfully, Yours ~ *33* ... und verbleiben mit freundlichen Grüßen
fall *54* Absturz
to fall *54* abstürzen; **~ off** *15* herunterfallen
family business *6* Familienunternehmen
fan *52* Ventilator; **ventilation ~** *70* Ventilator
far, as ~ as *11* soweit
farming area *112* Landwirtschaftsfläche(n)
to fasten sth to sth *31* etw an etw befestigen
fastener *27* Verbindungselement; **snap ~** *100* Schnappverschluss
to feature *91* (Merkmal) aufweisen
feature *30* Teil, Sonderanfertigung; *39T* (technisches) Merkmal; *57* Funktion; *117* Bestandteil
to feed *31* vorschieben; *104* zuführen
feed *84* Einzug; **manual ~** *30* manueller Vorschub; **power ~** *30* automatischer Vorschub; *52* Stromzuführung; **~ rate** *17* Vorschubgeschwindigkeit; *97T* Vorschub; **~ reverse gear** *31* Vorschub rückwärts
feedback *43* Rückmeldung(en)
feeding system *83* Einzug
ferrous metals pl *34* Eisenmetalle
fibre, carbon ~ *34* Kohlefaser; **glass ~** *34* Glasfaser
field *79* Bereich, Gebiet
figures pl *55* Zahlen, Ziffern
filament *117* Filament; **~ coil** *119T* Filamentspule
file, flat ~ *27* Flachfeile; **personnel ~** *12* Personalakte; **work ~** *96* Arbeitsdatei
to fill *14T* (Regal) befüllen
film *40* Folie
to filter *80T* filtern
filter: ~ insert *52* Filtereinsatz; **~ press** *64* Filterpresse
final drive ratio *103* Achsübersetzung
finance *6* Finanz, Finanzen
financial year *55* Geschäftsjahr
fingerprint *37* Fingerabdruck
finish, surface ~ *30* Oberfläche(nbeschaffenheit)
finished *9T* fertig; **~ product** *9T* Fertigware, Fertigprodukt

A–Z word list

finishing date *73* Fertigstellungstermin
fire: ~ brigade *77* Feuerwehr;
  ~ damage *76* Brandschaden; **~ exit** *15* Notausgang; **~ extinguisher** *15* Feuerlöscher; **~ protection** *79* Brandschutz; **~ risk assessment** *79* Brandrisikobewertung, -analyse;
  ~ safety *79* Brandschutz; **risk of ~** *49* Brandgefahr; **to catch ~** *70* in Brand geraten, Feuer fangen;
  to put out a ~ *76* einen Brand löschen
firm *8* Firma
first aid *15* Erste Hilfe
first-aider *76* Sanitäter/in
first of all *10* zunächst, zuallererst
to fit *11* passen; **~ sth with sth** *47* etw mit etw ausstatten; **~ out sth** *105* etw ausstatten
fit, tight ~ *52* enger Sitz
fitted with *100* ausgestattet mit
fitter *10* Monteur/in; **Mechanical F~** *16* Maschinenmonteur/in
fitting *10* Montage; **~ piece** *75* Anschlussstück
to fix *71T* befestigen; *75* *(Problem:)* lösen
fixed amount *112* Pauschalbetrag
flammable, highly ~ *15* leicht entzündlich
flame *76* Flamme
flange *11* Flansch
flash *76* Stichflamme
flat *30* eben; **~ file** *27* Flachfeile; **~ washer** *28* Unterlegscheibe
to flatten out *54* sich stabilisieren, sich einpendeln (bei)
flexibility *59* Flexibilität
flexible *35* biegsam
to flick through *126* durchblättern
floor: ~ plan *9* Grundriss, Lageplan;
  ~ tray *83* Bodenwanne; **factory ~** *9* Fertigungsbereich, Werkshalle; **ground ~** *86T* Erdgeschoss
flooring *71* Fußboden
fluctation *54* Schwankung(en), ständige Veränderung
to fluctuate *54* schwanken, sich ständig verändern
fluent *131* *(Sprache:)* fließend
fluid *104* Flüssigkeit
flyer *32* Faltblatt
flying chips *31* herumfliegende Späne
flywheel *11* Schwungrad
to focus *126* sich konzentrieren
to fold *85* klappen
to follow: as ~s *37* folgendermaßen, wie folgt
footprint, carbon ~ *113* CO$_2$-Fußabdruck
to force *85* zwingen, *hier:* drücken

force *35* Kraft; **~ of gravity** *85* Schwerkraft; **clamping ~** *51* Spannkraft; **quill ~** *52* Pinolenanstellkraft
forced air *104* Zwangsluft
foreman/-woman *10* Vorarbeiter/in, Meister/in
forklift truck *71* Gabelstapler
to form *24* formen, bilden
formal *13* formell, förmlich
formation *112* Bildung
to forward *119T* weiterleiten
to found *6* gründen
foundation *6* Grundlage
four-axis *9T* vierachsig
to fracture *35* brechen, zerbrechen
frame *105* Gestell; **tube ~** *105* Rohrgestell
freely accessible *97T* frei zugänglich
freight *60* Fracht, Beförderung
frequency *62* Frequenz
frequently *30* oft, häufig
friction *93* Reibung; **~ bearing** *37* Gleitlager, Gleitlagerung
front-mounted engine *103* Frontmotor
fuel *102* Kraftstoff; **~ consumption** *103* Kraftstoffverbrauch; **~ tap** *106* Benzinhahn
to fulfil an order *120* einen Auftrag abwickeln, eine Bestellung ausführen
function *17* Funktion
furnace, blast ~ *104* Hochofen
fusage, NH-~ *73* NH-Sicherungen
fuse *62* Sicherung; **slow-blow ~** *62* träge Sicherung; **thermal (cutoff) ~** *70* Thermosicherung; **~ box** *73* Sicherungskasten
fusible alloy *70* Schmelzlegierung

G

to gain *18* erwerben
gain, current ~ *24* Stromverstärkung
gallery walk *15* Galerierundgang
gallon *102* Gallone *(UK = 4,45l; US = 3,78l)*
gantry *95T* Portal; **~ crane** *115T* Portalkran
gas *17* Gas; **greenhouse ~** *113* Treibhausgas; **~ boiler** *70* Gaskessel
gate *86T* Tor, Einfahrt
to gather *52* sich sammeln; *113T* sammeln, zusammentragen
gear *31* Zahnrad; *103T* Gang; **back ~** *31* (Räder-)Vorgelege; **feed reverse ~** *31* Vorschub rückwärts; **reverse ~** *103T* Rückwärtsgang; **top ~** *103* höchster Gang; **valve ~** *103* Ventile; **~ ratio** *103* Übersetzung; **~ train** *30* Getriebe;
~s pl *31* Gangschaltung

gearbox *103* Schaltgetriebe; **4 speed manual ~** *103T* Viergang-Handschaltgetriebe
gearing *93* Verzahnung
gears pl *31* Gangschaltung
general practitioner (GP) *57F* Allgemeinarzt/-ärztin, Hausarzt/-ärztin
generation *18* Generation; *62* Erzeugung; **power ~** *6* Stromerzeugung
generator shaft *106* Lichtmaschinenwelle
to get: ~ at sth *69T* auf etw hinauswollen; **~ ready** *87* sich bereit machen, sich fertig machen; **~ started** *9T* loslegen, anfangen
gib *53* Bolzen
glance, at a ~ *55T* auf einen Blick
glass fibre *34* Glasfaser
global player *6* international agierendes Unternehmen
gloves pl *15* Handschuhe
glue *71* Klebstoff
to glue *113* kleben
to go: ~ down *54* sinken; **~ off** *77* *(Alarm:)* losgehen; **~ on** *11* währen, dauern; **~ on with sth** *9T* mit etw weitermachen; **~ up** *54* steigen
goggles pl**, safety ~** *15* Schutzbrille
goods pl *9T* Ware(n); **household ~** *35* Haushaltsartikel
government *112* Regierung
to grab *85* greifen; **~ sb's attention** *128* jds Aufmerksamkeit fesseln
gramme BE *56T* Gramm
graph *54* Diagramm, Grafik; **line ~** *54* Liniendiagramm
graphic image *69T* Grafik, Schaubild
graphical *62* grafisch
grasp, at a single ~ *60* mit einem Griff
gravity, force of ~ *85* Schwerkraft
grazing *112* Weideland
to grease *48* einfetten, schmieren
greenhouse gas *113* Treibhausgas
grid *7* Raster
to grind *104* schleifen
grinder, off-hand ~ *29* Handschleifmaschine
grinding *8* Schleifen, Schleiferei; **~ machine** *9T* Schleifmaschine
gripper *85* Greifer
groove *39T* Nut
gross *57* brutto
ground: ~ clearance *102* Bodenabstand; **~ floor** *86T* Erdgeschoss
groundwater *112* Grundwasser
to guarantee *98* garantieren
guarantee period *101* Garantiezeit
guard *14T* Schutzvorrichtung
guidance *93* Führung

to **guide** *24* leiten, führen
guide *113T* Anleitung
guideline *15* Richtlinie
guideway *52* Führungsschiene
guiding rail *93* Führungsschiene

H

habit *127T* Gewohnheit; to **get into the ~ of doing sth** *127T* sich daran gewöhnen, etw zu tun
habitat *112* (natürlicher) Lebensraum
hacksaw *26* Bügelsäge; **power ~** *29* Maschinenbügelsäge
hairy *118* haarig
hammer *14T* Hammer; **engineer's ~** *27* Schlosserhammer; **soft faced ~** *27* Schonhammer
handbook *115T* Handbuch
handfile *26* Handfeile
handle *100* Griff
to **handle sth** *71T* etw behandeln
handling, material ~ *114* Materialtransport, Fördertechnik
hand-out *35* Arbeitsblatt, Informationsblatt, Merkblatt
handrail *125* Geländer, Handlauf
hands-on *18* praktisch
hand tool *25* Handwerkzeug
handwheel *41F* Handrad
to **hang** *73* hängen; **~ on** *126* warten
to **harden** *24* härten; *119T* aushärten
hard hat *14T* Schutzhelm
hardly ever *27* kaum, fast nie
hard-wearing *35* strapazierfähig, verschleißfest
to **harm** *113T* schaden, Schaden zufügen
hazard *14* Gefahr
hazardous *113* gefährlich, schädlich
head *9T* Leiter/in, Chef/in; **~ of division** *10* Bereichsleiter/in
headline *6* Überschrift
head office *6* Zentrale, Sitz
headquarters pl *74* Zentrale, Hauptsitz
headstock *31* Spindelkasten
health *14* Gesundheit; **~ and safety** *14* Arbeitssicherheit, Sicherheit am Arbeitsplatz
heat *80T* Hitze
to **heat** *118* erhitzen
heating *16* Heizung
heaviness *114* Gewicht
heavy metals pl *34* Schwermetalle
height *31* Höhe
helmet, crash ~ *35* Sturzhelm
hemisphere *40* Halbkugel
hemispherical *40* halbkugelförmig
hermetic sealing *70* hermetische Abdichtung

hex: ~ bolt *28* Sechskantschraube; **~ nut** *28* Sechskantmutter
hexagon screw *27* Sechskantschraube
HGV (heavy goods vehicle) *92* Lkw
highly flammable *15* leicht entzündlich
high-pressure nozzle *84* Hochdruckdüse
high voltage *15* Hochspannung
hillside *112* Hang
to **hold** *29* halten; **~ up** *13* aufhalten; **~ the line** *20* (Telefon:) am Apparat bleiben; **H~ on.** *115T* Moment mal!
hold down clamp *29* Niederhalter
holder *123* Inhaber/in; **tool ~** *31* Werkzeughalter
holiday, bank ~ BE *125F* gesetzlicher Feiertag; **paid ~** *125* bezahlter Urlaub; **public ~** *125* gesetzlicher Feiertag
hood *49T* Schutzhaube; *105* Motorhaube; **protective ~** *31* Schutzhaube
horizontal *54* waagrecht, horizontal
horsepower *105* PS; **brake ~** *103T* Pferdestärken-Einheit in UK u. USA
hose *51* Schlauch; **pneumatic ~** *71* Druckluftschlauch, Pneumatikschlauch; **tight ~** *75* gespannter Schlauch
hot: ~ air blower *81* Heißluftgebläse; **~ cutting system** *96* Heißschneidesystem
to **house** *31* beherbergen
household goods pl *35* Haushaltsartikel
housing *31* Gehäuse
HR department *125F* Personalabteilung
Human Resources (HR) *12* Personalabteilung
humidity *51* Feuchtigkeit
hydraulic *11* hydraulisch, Hydraulik-; **~ power unit** *95* Hydraulikaggregat; **~ pressure** *48* Hydraulikdruck
hyphen *32* Bindestrich

I

ideally *122T* idealerweise
to **identify** *26* identifizieren, bestimmen
if I were you *57* an deiner/eurer/Ihrer Stelle
illness *13* Krankheit
to **illustrate** *113* veranschaulichen
image, graphic ~ *69T* Grafik, Schaubild
immediately *48* sofort, unverzüglich
impact *112* Auswirkung(en), Folge(n)
impeller *104* Flügelrad, Impeller
imperfect *53* mangelhaft
impression *127T* Eindruck
impressive *56T* beeindruckend, eindrucksvoll
improperly *48* nicht richtig
improvement *43* Verbesserung
inch *102* Zoll
incident *76* Vorfall

incinerator *113* Müllverbrennungsanlage
to **include** *11* einbeziehen, aufnehmen; **~ sth in sth** *104* etw in etw einbauen
including *6* einschließlich
incorrect *53* fehlerhaft
increase *54* Zunahme, Anstieg
to **increase** *54* zunehmen, ansteigen; *118* erhöhen, vergrößern
increased *62* gesteigert
indentation *35* Eindruck, Einkerbung
independent *95T* unabhängig
index card *42* Karteikarte
to **indicate** *127F* andeuten, darauf hinweisen
indication *32* Hinweis, Anzeichen
individual(ly) *56T* einzeln
inductance *24* Induktivität
industrial *17* industriell, Industrie-; **~ electronics** *6* Industrieelektronik; **~ mechanic** *17* Industriemechaniker/in
inertia *118* Trägheit
to **inform** *119* informieren, mitteilen
initial *124* erste/r/s
initials pl, **reference ~** *98* (Brief:) Zeichen
injury *49* Verletzung(en)
inline, 8 ~ engine *105* Achtzylinder-Reihenmotor
input screen *62* Eingabemaske
insert, filter ~ *52* Filtereinsatz; **nylon ~ lock nut** *28* Sicherungsmutter mit Nylon-Einsatz
inside *37* Innenseite, das Innere; **~ address** *98* Innenadresse; **~ diameter** *24* Innendurchmesser
to **insist on sth** *79* auf etw bestehen
inspection *119* Überprüfung, Kontrolle; **visual ~** *52* Sichtprüfung; **~ mirror** *24* Kontrollspiegel
to **install** *17* installieren
installation, site ~ *125* Vor-Ort-Montage; **~ instruction** *96* Montageanleitung
instruction *15* Anweisung; *60* Einweisung; **installation ~** *96* Montageanleitung
instructions pl, **maintenance ~** *51* Wartungsanleitung; **safety ~** *46* Sicherheitshinweise
to **insulate** *114* isolieren
intake *104* Zufuhr, Ansaugung; **~ manifold** *104* Ansaugkrümmer
to **integrate** *70* integrieren, einbauen
integrated *60* integriert
integration *90* Einbindung, Integrierung
intended *37* vorgesehen, beabsichtigt
to **interact** *118* zusammenspielen

interface *62* Schnittstelle, (Bedien-)Oberfläche; **parallel ~** *95* Parallel-Schnittstelle
interior *83* Innen-; *105* Innenausstattung
intermediate *96* Zwischen-
internal *68* intern; **~ combustion engine** *104* Verbrennungsmotor; **~ tooth lock washer** *28* innengezahnte Zahnscheibe
to **interrupt** *70* unterbrechen
to **interview sb** *32* mit jdm ein Vorstellungsgespräch führen
interviewer *126* Person, die ein Vorstellungsgespräch führt
introductions pl *12* Bekanntmachen, Vorstellen
to **invent** *78* erfinden
investment *60* Investition
to **invite sth** *42* zu etw auffordern
to **involve** *125* mit sich bringen, beinhalten
involved (in sth) *77* (an etw) beteiligt
iron *34* Eisen; *70* Bügeleisen; **cast ~** *34* Gusseisen; **soldering ~** *24* Lötkolben
irregular *30* uneben
to **irritate** *126* stören, irritieren
issue *112* Frage, Problem
item *33* Artikel; *80* Gegenstand; *90* Punkt
itinerary *65* Reiseplan

J
jam *118* Stau
to **jam** *118* blockieren, verstopfen
jaw, chuck ~ *48* Futterbacke, Klemmbacke
jewellery *15* Schmuck
jigsaw *26* Stichsäge
job: ~ advert(isement) *124* Stellenanzeige; **~ agency** *122* Arbeitsagentur, Arbeitsvermittlung; **~ application** *122* Bewerbung; **~ description** *12* Stellenbeschreibung; **~ experience** *18* Berufserfahrung; **~ offer** *123* Stellenangebot; **~ opportunities** pl *123* Arbeitsmöglichkeiten; **~ title** *16* Berufsbezeichnung; **to do one's ~** *50* jds Aufgabe erfüllen
to **join a company** *19* bei einem Unternehmen anfangen
journey *13* Fahrt, Anreise

K
keen, to be ~ to do sth *131* jdm liegt sehr daran, etw zu tun
to **keep: ~ on sb** *18* jdn behalten; **~ up sth** *10T* etw aufrecht erhalten

kerb *103* Bordstein; **~ weight** *102* Leergewicht
key: ~ account management *11F* Großkundenbetreuung; **~ word** *85* Schlagwort, Stichwort
king pin *106* Achsschenkelbolzen
kit *38* Bausatz
knife, drag ~ *96* Schleppmesser
knock *84* Stoß, Schlag
to **knock over sth** *77* etw umstoßen

L
L-shaped *41* L-förmig
to **label** *39* bezeichnen, etikettieren
label *11* Etikett, Siegel
labelling plate *95* Typenschild; *115* Beschriftungsplatte
labour *79* Arbeit
ladder *15* Leiter
lag, time ~ *84* Zeitverzögerung
landfill *113T* Mülldeponie
landline *126* Festnetz(telefon)
lap *56T* Bahn (im Schwimmbecken)
laser: ~ beam printer *70* Laserdrucker: **~ engraving** *93* Lasergravur
last but not least *10T* zu guter Letzt
latest *57* neueste/r/s
lathe *20* Drehbank; **~ operator** *31* Dreher/in
to **lay cables** *71T* Kabel/Leitungen verlegen
layer *117* Schicht
layout *8* Raumaufteilung, Plan; **engine ~** *103* Motoranordnung
lead *34* Blei
to **lead (to sth)** *9T* (zu etw) führen
leakage *51* Leck, undichte Stelle; *112* Austreten, Versickern
least, last but not ~ *10T* zu guter Letzt
leather *105* Leder
to **leave a message** *20* eine Nachricht hinterlassen
leeway *53* Abdrift
left-hand drive *105* Linkslenker, Linkslenkung
legislation *80* Gesetze, Gesetzgebung
length *31* Länge; **contract ~** *113* Vertragsdauer; **turning ~** *60* Drehlänge
Letter of Credit, Documentary ~ *109* Dokumentenakkreditiv
level *52* Stand, Pegel; **sound ~** *49* Lärmpegel, Geräuschpegel
to **level off** *54* sich stabilisieren, sich einpendeln (bei)
lever *31* Hebel
licence, driving ~ *125* Führerschein
to **lift** *74* heben, anheben
lift: ~ cabin *11* Aufzugskabine; **~ shaft** *11* Aufzugsschacht

lifting: ~ equipment *93* Hebegeräte, Hebezeuge; **~ system** *11* Hubsystem
to **light** *76* sich entzünden
light *101F* Scheinwerfer; **~ barrier** *84* Lichtschranke; **naked ~s** pl *15* offene Flammen; **surgery ~** *98* Operationslampe, -leuchte
light metals pl *34* Leichtmetalle
light-weight *35* leicht
to **limit** *84* begrenzen, beschränken
limit, power ~ *96* Leistungsobergrenze
line, base ~ *39T* Grundlinie; **centre ~** *52* Mittellinie, Achse; **chain-dotted ~** *39* strichpunktierte Linie; **continuous ~** *39* durchgezogene Linie; **dimension ~** *39* Bemaßungslinie; **~ graph** *54* Liniendiagramm; **~ manager** *10* direkte/r Vorgesetzte/r; **voltage** *49* Netzspannung; **~ drive** *92* Linearantrieb; **~ track profile** *96* Linearachsprofil; **~ unit** *85* Lineareinheit; **to hold the ~** *20* (Telefon:) am Apparat bleiben
to **link** *113T* in Verbindung bringen
link, motion ~ *36* Kulisse, Kulissenführung
liquid *17* Flüssigkeit
to **list** *10T* (in einer Liste) aufführen
listener *122T* Hörer/in
live centre *31* verfahrbare Führungsspitze
load, permissible ~ *94* zulässige Last; **tool ~** *62* Antriebslast der Werkzeuge; **no-~ running** *49* Leerlaufbetrieb
lobe *104* Nocken
to **lock** *49* abschließen, verschließen
lock, transport ~s pl *60* Transportsicherungen
locker *9T* Schließfach, Spind; **~ rooms** pl *8* Umkleideräume
long-time *19* langfristig
longitudinal *103* längs
to **look the part** *126* entsprechend (rollengerecht) aussehen
look, to have a ~ around *9T* sich umsehen
loose *24* locker
lorry BE *17* Lkw
loss *112* Verlust
Ltd *33* GmbH
lube system *52* Schmierung
lubricant *37* Schmiermittel
to **lubricate** *37* schmieren
lubrication, central ~ *51* Zentralschmierung

M

to **machine** *30* (maschinell) bearbeiten
machine, desktop ~ *95* Tischgerät;
  ~ bolt *28* Maschinenschraube;
  ~ builder *17* Maschinenbauer/in;
  ~ operator *59* Maschinenbediener/in, Maschinenführer/in; **~ tool** *29* Werkzeugmaschine
machinery *14T* Maschinen
madam *33* Dame
main: ~ bearing *52* Hauptlager(ung);
  ~ switch *49* Hauptschalter
mainly *16* hauptsächlich
to **maintain** *79* warten, instand halten
maintenance *15* Wartung, Instandhaltung; **~ instructions** pl *51* Wartungsanleitung; **M~ Technician** *16* Wartungstechniker/in; **regular ~ routines** pl *51* regelmäßige Wartung(sarbeiten)
to **make up sth** *21F* sich etw ausdenken
malleable *35* formbar
manifold, exhaust ~ *106* Auspuffkrümmer; **intake ~** *104* Ansaugkrümmer
manner *43* Art (und Weise)
manual *46* Handbuch; **operating ~** *49T* Betriebsanleitung; **user ~** *37* Benutzerhandbuch, Betriebsanleitung
manual feed *30* manueller Vorschub
manually *80* von Hand
manufacture *113* Herstellung, Fertigung
to **manufacture** *6* fertigen, herstellen
manufacturing: ~ company *79* Fertigungsbetrieb, Produktionsunternehmen; **small series ~** *59* Kleinserienfertigung
to **mark** *24* kennzeichnen, markieren;
  ~ out *27* anreißen, anzeichnen
marketplace *59* Markt, Marktplatz
mass *114* Masse; **~ production** *17* Massenproduktion
mat *80* Matte
material *9T* Werkstoff, Material;
  ~ handling *114* Materialtransport, Fördertechnik
mathematical operation *46* Rechenoperation
maximum speed *103* Höchstgeschwindigkeit
means: ~ of communication *68* Kommunikationsmittel; **~ of transport** *60* Transportmittel
to **measure** *24* messen
measurement *46* Maß, Maßangabe, Messung; **~ run** *92* Messfahrt
measures pl *68* Maßnahmen
measuring: ~ equipment *92* Messgerät(e); **~ room** *8* Messraum;
  ~ station *92* Messplatz, Messstation;
  ~ tool *24* Messwerkzeug

mechanic, cutting tool ~ *17* Schneidwerkzeugmechaniker/in; **industrial ~** *17* Industriemechaniker/in; **precision ~** *17* Feinwerkmechaniker/in
mechanical *35* mechanisch; **M~ Design Engineer** *16* Konstruktionsmechaniker/in; **~ engineering** *6* Maschinenbau; **~ engineering technician** *122* Maschinenbautechniker/in; **M~ Fitter** *16* Maschinenmonteur/in
mechanics *18* Mechanik
mechatronic systems engineer *17* Mechatroniker/in
mechatronics *18* Mechatronik;
  ~ technician *122* Mechatroniker/in
medical *7T* medizinisch;
  ~ equipment *56* medizinische Geräte, Medizintechnik
medium-sized *7* mittelgroß, mittelständisch
to **meet** *92* (Anforderungen usw.) erfüllen
to **melt** *70* schmelzen, zum Schmelzen bringen
memo *70* Notiz, Kurzmitteilung, Aktenvermerk
to **mention** *11* erwähnen, nennen
mercury *113* Quecksilber
meshing *104* ineinandergreifend
message, to leave a ~ *20* eine Nachricht hinterlassen; **to take a ~** *20* etw ausrichten
messiness *14T* Unordnung, Unsauberkeit
metal, ferrous ~s pl *34* Eisenmetalle; **heavy ~s** pl *34* Schwermetalle; **light ~s** pl *34* Leichtmetalle; **non-~s** pl *34* Nichtmetalle, Steine und Erden;
  non-ferrous ~s pl *34* Buntmetalle;
  precious ~s pl *113T* Edelmetalle;
  sheet ~ *28* Blech; **~ fabricator** *125* Metallbauer/in
metalwork *124* Metallbau
metalworker *125* Metallarbeiter/in
method *68* Art (und Weise), Weg; **~ of payment** *107* Zahlungsweise
micrometre *11* Mikrometer
microphone *101F* Mikrofon
mild steel *125F* Baustahl
miller *106T* Fräser/in
millimetre *16* Millimeter
milling: ~ cutter *17* Fräser;
  ~ machine *29* Fräsmaschine
mind, to have sth in ~ *57* an etw denken, sich etw vorstellen; **to keep in ~** *127F* daran denken
to **mind, Never ~.** *90T* Macht nichts.
mind map *19* Mindmap

mine *104* Bergwerk, Grube, Mine;
  ~ shaft *104* Schacht, Stollen
mining *112* Bergbau, Abbau, Förderung
minor *14T* klein(er/e/s), geringfügig
mirror, inspection ~ *24* Kontrollspiegel
misaligned *117* falsch augerichtet
to **mix** *80T* mischen
mixed up *128* durcheinander
mixture *81* Mischung, Gemisch
mobile *20* Handy, Mobiltelefon
mobility *123* Freizügigkeit, Mobilität
model-maker *95T* Modellbauer/in
modification *62* Änderung, Modifikation
to **modify** *49T* verändern, modifizieren
moisture *37* Feuchtigkeit
monitoring *62* Überwachung, Kontrolle
more closely *78* näher, genauer
motion *93* Bewegung; **~ link** *36* Kulisse, Kulissenführung
motor *29* Motor
mould *17* Gussform
to **mount** *17* montieren
mounting *9T* Montage
moveable *49T* beweglich
moving parts pl *49* bewegliche Teile
multi-thread cycle *62* Mehrgewindezyklus
multi-toothed cutter *30* mehrzahniges Fräswerkzeug
multimeter *24* Multimeter
multinational *7* internationaler Konzern
multiplier *118* Multiplikator

N

naked lights pl *15* offene Flammen
natural *34* natürlich
nearby *71T* in der Nähe
needle, engraving ~ *96* Graviernadel
negotiable *124* verhandelbar
net *57* netto
Never mind. *90T* Macht nichts.
next door *76* nebenan
NH-fusage *73* NH-Sicherungen
noise *19* Lärm
no-load running *49* Leerlaufbetrieb
nominal: ~ apparent power *62* Nennscheinleistung; **~ current** *62* Nennstrom; **~ pressure** *84* Nenndruck
non-ferrous metals pl *34* Buntmetalle
non-metals pl *34* Nichtmetalle, Steine und Erden
noon *64* Mittag
notice *76* Warnhinweis, Hinweisschild; **at short ~** *131* kurzfristig
nozzle *84* Düse; **high-pressure ~** *84* Hochdruckdüse
numerous *59* zahlreich

nut *27* Mutter; **cap ~** *28* Überwurfmutter, Hutmutter; **hex ~** *28* Sechskantmutter; **nylon insert lock ~** *28* Sicherungsmutter mit Nylon-Einsatz; **square ~** *28* Vierkantmutter; **wheel ~** *106* Radmutter; **worm-and-~ steering** *103* Zahnstangenlenkung
nylon insert lock nut *28* Sicherungsmutter mit Nylon-Einsatz

O

occasion *125F* Gelegenheit
to **occur** *52* auftreten, vorkommen
odd *105* merkwürdig, seltsam
offer, job ~ *123* Stellenangebot
off-hand grinder *29* Handschleifmaschine
office, head ~ *6* Zentrale, Sitz
to **oil** *38* ölen
to **ooze** *118* tropfen, quellen
to **open: ~ out** *9T* sich öffnen, sich verbreitern; **~ up new opportunities** *59* neue Möglichkeiten/Chancen eröffnen
to **operate** *24* funktionieren, arbeiten; **~ sth** *56T* etw bedienen, etw betreiben
operating: ~ manual *49T* Betriebsanleitung; **~ temperature** *70* Betriebstemperatur; **~ theatre** *98* Operationssaal; **~ voltage** *62* Betriebsspannung
operation *31* Betrieb; **mathematical ~** *46* Rechenoperation
operational, directly ~ *96* direkt einsatzbereit
operator *59* Maschinenbediener/in, Maschinenführer/in; **lathe ~** *31* Dreher/in; **machine ~** *59* Maschinenbediener/in, Maschinenführer/in
opportunity *124* Gelegenheit, Möglichkeit; **job ~ies** pl *123* Arbeitsmöglichkeiten; to **open up new ~ies** *59* neue Möglichkeiten/Chancen eröffnen
to **opt for sth** *96* sich für etw entscheiden
optimum *85* optimal
option *58T* Möglichkeit, Alternative, Option
oral *75* mündlich
order, bulk ~ *109* Großbestellung, Großauftrag; **order, reverse ~** *47* umgekehrte Reihenfolge; **trial ~** *98* Probebestellung; **~ code** *94* Bestellcode, Bestellschlüssel; **~ sheet** *106T* Bestellschein; to **fulfil an ~** *120* einen Auftrag abwickeln, eine Bestellung ausführen; **in good running ~** *103T* in gutem Zustand, in Schuss
organization chart *10* Organigramm
outer ring *11* Außenring

outpatient clinic *98* Ambulanz
output *79* Produktion; **power ~** *103* Leistung
outside diameter *24* Außendurchmesser
outstanding *59* herausragend, außergewöhnlich
overall *14T* Schutzanzug; **~ effect** *15* Gesamteindruck, Gesamtwirkung; **~ score** *43* Gesamtpunktzahl; **~ size** *97F* Gesamtmaße
to **overhaul** *74* überholen, wieder instandsetzen
overhead *114* Überkopf-, obere/r/s; **~ valve** *103T* obenliegendes Ventil
to **overheat** *70* sich überhitzen, zu heiß werden
overhung *52* auskragend, hervorstehend
to **overload** *84* überlasten
overtime: ~ work *19* Überstunden; to **~ work** *19* Überstunden machen
overview *34* Übersicht
own, on one's ~ *7* alleine
oxidation *37* Oxidation
oxygen *104* Sauerstoff

P

to **pack** *98* verpacken
package *60* Paket, Sendung
to **package** *56T* verpacken
packaging *56* Verpackung; **~ crate** *98* Packkiste
padlock *100* Vorhängeschloss
paid holiday *125* bezahlter Urlaub
paint spraying *14* Spritzlackieren
to **palletize** *80T* palettieren
palletizer *80* Palettierer
palm, sweaty ~s pl *37* verschwitzte Handflächen
panel *127T* Gremium; **control ~** *48* Steuerkonsole; **~ beating** *14* Spenglerarbeiten
parallel interface *95* Parallel-Schnittstelle
parameter *62* Parameter
part *16* Bauteil; to **look the ~** *126* entsprechend (rollengerecht) aussehen
partially *37* teilweise
participant *60* Teilnehmer/in
particular *19* speziell
particularly *131* insbesondere; **Not ~.** *127T* Eigentlich nicht.
partner *6* Gesellschafter/in
party, third ~ *112* Dritte/r
to **pass an exam** *19* eine Prüfung bestehen
passenger car *17* Pkw
past sth *9* an etw vorbei, hinter etw
paste, ceramic ~ *37* Keramikpaste
to **patent** *104* patentieren

patina *37* Patina
pattern *118* Muster
pay *13* Bezahlung, Gehalt
to **pay (special) attention to sth** *49T* (besonders) auf etw achten
payload *114* Nutzlast
payment *98* Zahlung; **method of ~** *107* Zahlungsweise; **terms** pl **of ~** *98* Zahlungsbedingungen
peak *54* Spitzenwert
to **peak** *54* einen Spitzenwert erreichen
pellet, thermal ~ *70* thermisch geschütztes Gehäuse
pen *126* Stift
to **perform** *114* (Tätigkeit) ausführen; **~ sth** *57* (Theater usw.:) etw aufführen, etw spielen
performance *59* Leistung
period, guarantee ~ *101* Garantiezeit
permanent *14* dauerhaft; *18* unbefristet
permissible load *94* zulässige Last
permission *128* Erlaubnis
personnel *12* Personal
personnel file *12* Personalakte
to **persuade** *113T* überzeugen
petrol BE *103* Benzin; **~-non return valve** *106* Benzin-Rückhalteventil
phase *62* Phase
Phillips screw *27* Kreuzschlitzschraube
photocopier *70* Kopiergerät
physical *36* physikalisch
pie chart *54* Tortendiagramm
pile *14T* Stapel
to **pin** *15* (mit einer Nadel) befestigen, anheften; **~ sth to sth** *87* etw an etw befestigen
pin, king ~ *106* Achsschenkelbolzen
pipe *17* Rohr, Röhre; **connecting ~** *11* Verbindungsrohr, -leitung
pipeline *17* (Rohr-)Leitung
piping *52* Rohrleitungen; *75* Leitung, Schlauch
piston *11* Kolben; **working ~** *37* Arbeitskolben
to **place an order** *56T* einen Auftrag erteilen, eine Bestellung aufgeben
place of birth *12* Geburtsort
plant *80T* Werk, Betrieb; **power ~** *17* Kraftwerk; **production ~** *17* Produktionsanlage, Fertigungsbetrieb
plastic(ally) *35* plastisch
plastics *17* Kunststoff
plate *39T* Platte; **die ~** *27* Formplatte; **type ~** *115T* Typenschild
platform trolley *47* Plattformwagen, Transportwagen
play-free *97T* spielfrei

pliers pl *17* Zange; **side cutting** ~ *27* Seitenschneider; **waterpump** ~ *27* Wasserpumpenzange
plug connector *52* Stecker, Steckverbinder
to **plug in** *15* einstecken
plunger pump *84* Kolbenpumpe, Plungerpumpe
pneumatic *61* pneumatisch; ~ **controller** *95* pneumatischer Regler; ~ **hose** *71* Druckluftschlauch, Pneumatikschlauch
to **point out sth** *113* auf etw hinweisen
poisonous *113T* giftig
polish *37* Politur
to **polish** *37* polieren
polite(ly) *33* höflich
politics *13* Politik
to **pollute** *80T* verschmutzen
pollution *112* Verschmutzung
to **pop over** *106T* vorbeikommen
poppet valve *106* Tellerventil
population *112* Bevölkerung
portable *56* tragbar, mobil
to **position** *81* platzieren
post *131* Stelle
poster *14* Plakat
to **postpone** *65* (nach hinten) verschieben
potential *123* möglich, potenziell
powder *38* Pulver
to **power** *103* antreiben; ~ **up** *48* einschalten, hochfahren
power, drive ~ *60* Antriebsleistung; **nominal apparent** ~ *62* Nennscheinleistung; ~ **cable** *71* Stromkabel, Stromleitung; ~ **chuck** *52* Kraftspannfutter; ~ **consumption** *57* Stromverbrauch; ~ **distribution** *6* Stromverteilung; ~ **feed** *30* automatischer Vorschub; *52* Stromzuführung; ~ **generation** *6* Stromerzeugung; ~ **hacksaw** *29* Maschinenbügelsäge; ~ **limit** *96* Leistungsobergrenze; ~ **output** *103* Leistung; ~ **plant** *17* Kraftwerk; ~ **rating** *105* Nennleistung; ~ **supply** *52* Stromversorgung; ~ **supply cable** *115* Netzkabel; ~ **supply chain** *52* Stromversorgungskette; ~ **tool** *28* Elektrowerkzeug; ~ **transmission thread** *62* Bewegungsgewinde; **hydraulic** ~ **unit** *95* Hydraulikaggregat
powerful *87* mächtig
Pozidriv screw *27* Pozidriv-Kreuzschlitzschraube
practitioner, general ~ **(GP)** *57F* Allgemeinarzt/-ärztin, Hausarzt/-ärztin
precautions pl, **safety** ~ *48* Sicherheitsvorkehrungen, Sicherheitsmaßnahmen

precious metals pl *113T* Edelmetalle
precise *17* präzis, genau
precision *16* Präzision, Genauigkeit; ~ **mechanic** *17* Feinwerkmechaniker/in
predefined *62* vordefiniert
preliminary *125F* vorläufig, Vor-
to **pre-load** *94* vorspannen
prepared *7* bereit, vorbereitet; to **be** ~ **to do sth** *85* bereit sein, etw zu tun
pre-planning *16* Vorausplanung
presentation *18* Vortrag, Präsentation
to **press** *48* drücken
press, filter ~ *64* Filterpresse
pressure *84* Druck; **hydraulic** ~ *48* Hydraulikdruck; **nominal** ~ *84* Nenndruck; **high-**~ **nozzle** *84* Hochdruckdüse
pretty *9T* ziemlich
to **prevent** *17* verhindern
prewar *105* Vorkriegs-
price: ~ **per unit** *106* Stückpreis, Einzelpreis; **total** ~ *115* Gesamtpreis; ~ **list** *98* Preisliste
print *118* Ausdruck
printer, laser beam ~ *70* Laserdrucker; ~ **head** *118* Druckkopf; ~ **resin** *118* geschmolzener Filamentkunststoff
prize-giving ceremony *86* Preisverleihung
probe *92* Sonde
process *10T* Ablauf, Prozess, Verfahren; **production** ~ *17* Fertigungsablauf, Produktionsprozess; **selection** ~ *127F* Auswahlverfahren
to **process** *96* verarbeiten
producer *6* Hersteller, Produzent
product, finished ~ *9T* Fertigware, Fertigprodukt
production *7* Produktion, Fertigung, Herstellung; **mass** ~ *17* Massenproduktion; **serial** ~ *58* Serienfertigung, Serienproduktion; ~ **plant** *17* Produktionsanlage, Fertigungsbetrieb; ~ **process** *17* Fertigungsablauf, Produktionsprozess; ~ **system** *17* Fertigungssystem, Produktionssystem
productivity *59* Produktivität
profile *6* Porträt, Beschreibung, Profil
profiled *96* profiliert
profitable *113T* einträglich, profitabel
to **program** *17* programmieren
programming *62* Programmieren
to **progress with sth** *127F* mit etw vorankommen
to **project** *53* ausladen, vorstehen
Project Manager *16* Projektleiter/in
projection *53* Ausladung
prolonged *37* (lang) anhaltend

prompt *84* Stichwort; ~ **card** *42* Moderationskarte
proof *79* Nachweis(e), Beleg(e)
property *35* Eigenschaft
prospective customer *101* potenzielle/r Kunde/Kundin
prospects pl, **career** ~ *123* berufliche Perspektiven
to **protect** *98* schützen
protection *14* Schutz; **data** ~ *128* Datenschutz; **ear** ~ *14* Gehörschutz; **eye** ~ *14* Augenschutz, Schutzbrille; **fire** ~ *79* Brandschutz; ~ **class** *114* Schutzklasse
protective: ~ **clothing** *14T* Schutzkleidung; ~ **earth** *62* Schutzleiter, Schutzerde; ~ **hood** *31* Schutzhaube
prototype *119* Prototyp
to **protrude** *48* vorstehen, herausragen
public holiday *125* gesetzlicher Feiertag
pulley, driving ~ *31* Antriebsscheibe; **V-belt** ~ *106* Keilriemenscheibe
pulse and blood pressure monitor *56* Puls- und Blutdruckmessgerät
to **pump** *61* pumpen
pump *27* Pumpe; **plunger** ~ *84* Kolbenpumpe, Plungerpumpe; ~ **body** *104* Pumpengehäuse
punch, centre ~ *24* Körner
purchasing *6* Einkauf
purpose *11* Zweck, Absicht
push-button *83* Drucktaster, Taster
to **put:** ~ **sb through** *20* (Telefon:) jdn durchstellen; ~ **out a fire** *76* einen Brand löschen

Q

qualification *18* Abschluss, Qualifikation
qualified *18* Fach-, mit Abschluss, qualifiziert
to **qualify** *122* einen/den Abschluss machen
quality: ~ **assurance** *92* Qualitätssicherung; ~ **control** *10* Qualitätskontrolle; ~ **management** *79* Qualitätsmanagement, Qualitätssicherung
quantity *69* Menge
quarter *55* Quartal
quarterly *55* vierteljährlich, Quartals-
quill *52* Pinole; ~ **force** *52* Pinolenanstellkraft
quotation *94* Preisangebot, Kostenvoranschlag
quoted *103* angegeben

R

racing car *105* Rennwagen
rack *31* Zahnstange
radiation *57* Strahlung
radius, radii *39T* Radius, Radien

rail *93* Schiene; **guiding ~** *93* Führungsschiene
railings pl *125* Gitter, Geländer
ranching *112* Viehwirtschaft
range *70* Bereich, Umfang; *103* Reihe, Produktlinie; **a broad ~ of** *70* eine große Auswahl von
to rank *15* einstufen, (in einer Rangliste) bewerten
ratchet *26* Ratschenschlüssel
rated current *70* Nennstrom
rating, power ~ *105* Nennleistung
ratio *102* Verhältnis; **final drive ~** *103* Achsübersetzung; **gear ~** *103* Übersetzung
re *109* bezüglich, betreffs
reach *114* Reichweite
to reach (over) *77* greifen
to react to sth *120* auf etw reagieren
to read out sth *46* etw vorlesen
to readjust *52* nachjustieren
ready, to get ~ *87* sich bereit machen, sich fertig machen
ready-assembly model *37* Fertigmodell
ready built *96* fertig montiert
to re-align *52* neu ausrichten, nachjustieren
to realize: ~ sth *77* etw (be)merken; **I ~ that.** *121* Das ist mir bewusst.
to ream *30* reiben
rear wheel *103* Hinterrad; **~ drive** *103* Hinterradantrieb
to reassemble *37* wieder zusammenbauen
to rebuild *37* neu aufbauen; *107* erneuern, umbauen
reception *8* Empfang, Rezeption; *60* Aufnahme; **12-station disc turret ~** *60* 12-fach-Revolverscheiben-Werkzeugaufnahme
receptionist *86* Empfangsmitarbeiter/in
rechargeable battery *56T* wiederaufladbare Batterie, Akku
to reclaim *112* (Land) zurückgewinnen, rekultivieren
to recognize *15* erkennen; *18* anerkennen
recommendation *91* Empfehlung
record *77* Aufzeichnung(en); *113* Bilanz, Ergebnis(se); *121* Datensatz
recording *90* Aufzeichnung, Aufnahme
to recover *55T* sich erholen
recruitment *18* Einstellung, Anwerbung (von Personal); **~ agency** *124* Personalvermittlung
rectangle *40* Rechteck
rectangular solid *40* Quader
rectilinear solid *47* geradkantiger Körper

to reduce *11* senken, reduzieren, verringern
to refer to sth *35* auf etw verweisen, sich auf etw beziehen
referee *128* Referenz(geber/in)
reference *98* Referenz; **with ~ to** *101* mit Bezug auf, bezüglich; **~ initials** pl *98* (Brief:) Zeichen
refinery *17* Raffinerie
to refresh *8* auffrischen
refreshment *13* Erfrischung
refrigeration *17* Kühlung, Kühl-
regard, R~s *33* Mit freundlichen Grüßen; **Best ~s** *33* Mit freundlichen Grüßen
to regrease *37* nachfetten
regular: ~ customer *94* Stammkunde/-kundin; **~ maintenance routines** pl *51* regelmäßige Wartung(sarbeiten)
to regulate *78* regeln
regulations pl *70* Vorschriften; **warranty ~** *49* Garantiebedingungen
to reject *57* ablehnen, zurückweisen
to relate sth to sth *127T* etw auf etw beziehen
related: ~ to sth *14* bezüglich etw; **closely ~ to** *105* eng verwandt mit
relating to *16* bezüglich, betreffend
relation, in ~ to *113* in Bezug auf
to release *113T* freisetzen
relevant *49T* relevant, wichtig, entsprechend
reliability *70* Zuverlässigkeit
reliable *96* zuverlässig
to relocate sth *70* etw verlegen, etw verlagern
relocation *70* Verlegung, Verlagerung
to relubricate *37* nachschmieren
removal, chip ~ *49T* Späneförderung
to remove *15* entfernen, abheben; *30* abtragen; *50* (Kleidung usw.) ausziehen
to renew *52* erneuern
renewable *124* verlängerbar
repetitive *92* (sich) wiederholend
replacement *104* Ersatz
to re-play *90* erneut abspielen
reply *33* Antwort
to reply *33* antworten
to report to sb *76* sich bei jdm melden; *127F* jdm unterstehen
report update *72* aktueller Bericht
to represent *20* darstellen, vertreten
representative *59* Vertreter/in; **sales ~** *116* Vertreter/in; **union ~** *54* Gewerkschaftsvertreter/in
to reproduce *96* kopieren, reproduzieren
reproduction *118* Wiedergabe
reputation *10T* Ruf

request (for sth) *32* Bitte (um etw); **on ~** *60* auf Anfrage
to request: ~ sth *94* um etw bitten; **as ~ed** *109* wie gewünscht
required *52* erforderlich
requirement *58* Anforderung, Voraussetzung
research *6* Forschung; *91* Recherche
to research sth *79* etw recherchieren, sich über etw informieren
reservation *86T* Reservierung
to reserve *65* reservieren
residual current circuit breaker (RCCB) *73* FI-Schutzschalter, Fehlerstromschutzschalter
resilient *35* federelastisch
resin *70* Harz; **printer ~** *118* geschmolzener Filamentkunststoff; **~-seal** *70* Gießharzverguss; **~-sealed** *70* mit Gießharz vergossen; **~-sealer** *72* Versiegelungsanlage; **~-sealing unit** *71* Versiegelungsanlage
to resist *35* einer Sache widerstehen
resistance *24* Widerstand
to resolve *118* lösen
to respect *87* respektieren, achten
response *13* Antwort, Reaktion; **in ~ to** *35* als Reaktion auf
responsibility *16* Aufgabe, Zuständigkeit, Verantwortlichkeit
rest, compound ~ *31* Kreuzschlitten; **steady ~** *52* Lünette
to restart *48* neu starten
to restore *102* restaurieren; *112* wiederherstellen, wieder in den ursprünglichen Zustand versetzen
to result in sth *14* etw zur Folge haben
to retain *119T* behalten
retraction *118* Rücksaugung
to reuse *80T* wiederverwenden
to reverse *112* umkehren, rückgängig machen
reverse: ~ gear *103T* Rückwärtsgang; **~ order** *47* umgekehrte Reihenfolge; **feed ~ gear** *31* Vorschub rückwärts
revolution *103T* Umdrehung
rid, to get ~ of sth *58T* etw loswerden
right angle *53* rechter Winkel
rigid(ly) *31* starr, fest
rigidity *93* Steifigkeit
rise *54* Anstieg
to rise *54* ansteigen
risk: ~ of explosion *49* Explosionsgefahr; **~ of fire** *49* Brandgefahr; **fire ~ assessment** *79* Brandrisikobewertung, -analyse
robot *114* Roboter
rock *112* Fels, Stein
rod *24* Stab

role *6* Rolle
rolled *41* gewalzt, Walz-
roller *81* Rolle, Walze
Roots blower *104* Roots-Gebläse, Drehkolbengebläse
rotary vane *104* Drehkolben
to rotate *30* rotieren, sich drehen
rotation *31* Rotation, Drehung
rough *9* grob; *35* rau
roughness, surface ~ *92* Oberflächenrauigkeit
round *9T* Runde
rpm *103* U/min
rubber *47* Gummi
rubbish *14T* Abfall, Müll
rugged *31* robust, stabil
rule *14T* Vorschrift, Regel; **as a ~** *37* in der Regel
ruler *24* Lineal
to run *6* (Unternehmen usw.) führen
run, measurement ~ *92* Messfahrt; **trial** ~ *37* Probelauf
running, no-load ~ *49* Leerlaufbetrieb; **in good ~ order** *103T* in gutem Zustand, in Schuss; **up and** ~ *71T* betriebsbereit; **to be up and** ~ *115T* laufen, im Einsatz sein
to rupture *35* reißen, zerreißen
to rust *38* rosten

S

saddle *41F* Sattel
safe, to keep sb ~ *14T* jdn schützen
safety *14* Sicherheit; **health and** ~ *14* Arbeitssicherheit, Sicherheit am Arbeitsplatz; ~ **cover** *15* Sicherheitsabdeckung; ~ **goggles** pl *15* Schutzbrille; ~ **instructions** pl *46* Sicherheitshinweise; ~ **officer** *73* Sicherheitsbeauftragte/r; ~ **precautions** pl *48* Sicherheitsvorkehrungen, Sicherheitsmaßnahmen; ~ **shoes** pl *14T* Sicherheitsschuhe; ~ **sign** *15* Sicherheitsschild, Hinweisschild
salary *124* Gehalt; **starting** ~ *124* Einstiegsgehalt
sales *6* Verkauf, Vertrieb; *55* Umsatz, Umsätze, Verkaufszahlen; ~ **department** *116* Verkauf(sabteilung), Vertrieb; ~ **representative** *116* Vertreter/in
salesperson *57* Verkäufer/in
salutation *33* (Brief:) Anrede
sand, abrasive ~ *80* Abrasivsand
satisfactory *119* zufriedenstellend
satisfied *79* zufrieden
scaffold *46* Gerüst
scale *24* Skala

to schedule *90T* planen, (Termin) ansetzen
scheme *18* Programm, Plan; *109* Schema
school leaving certificate *129* Schulabschluss
scientist *6* Wissenschaftler/in
score, overall ~ *43* Gesamtpunktzahl
scraper, three corner ~ *27* Schabeisen mit dreieckiger Ziehklinge
scratched *120T* verkratzt
scratching *35* Verkratzen
screen *10T* Leinwand, Bildschirm; *14T* Schutzschirm; **input** ~ *62* Eingabemaske
to screw *96* schrauben
screw *11* Schraube (zur Befestigung von Teilen mit Innengewinde); **cross slot** ~ *27* Kreuzschlitzschraube; **hexagon** ~ *27* Sechskantschraube; **Phillips** ~ *27* Kreuzschlitzschraube; **Pozidriv** ~ *27* Pozidriv-Kreuzschlitzschraube; **Security T** ~ *27* Torx-TR-Schraube; **sheet metal** ~ *28* Blechschraube; **slotted** ~ *27* Schlitzschraube; **thread cutting machine** ~ *28* gewindeschneidende Maschinenschraube; **Torx** ~ *27* Torxschraube
screwdriver *17* Schraubendreher, Schraubenzieher
seal *49T* Siegel
sealing, hermetic ~ *70* hermetische Abdichtung; ~ **point** *52* Dichtstelle
seat, Is this ~ taken? *87* Ist hier besetzt?
seater, 4 ~ *102* Viersitzer
section *9T* Bereich; *49T* Abschnitt; **cutting** ~ *52* Spanquerschnitt
sector *7* Bereich, Branche, Sektor
secure *86T* sicher, bewacht
securely *48* fest, sicher
Security T screw *27* Torx-TR-Schraube
sedan *105* Limousine
to seek *129* suchen
to select *69T* auswählen
selection *17* Auswahl; ~ **process** *127F* Auswahlverfahren
self-assembled *37* selbst zusammengebaut
self-assessment *123* Selbsteinstufung
to sell at auction *102* versteigern
semicircle *39T* Halbkreis
sense, to make ~ *58T* vernünftig sein, sinnvoll sein, einleuchten
sensitive, to be ~ to sth *70* empfindlich auf etw reagieren
separate *9T* getrennt
to separate *82* trennen

serial: ~ **number** *115* Seriennummer; ~ **production** *58* Serienfertigung, Serienproduktion
series *59* Serie, Baureihe
to serve *31* dienen; *86T* servieren
to service *27* warten, überprüfen
service *7* Dienst, Dienstleistung; ~ **check** *20* Wartung, (routinemäßige) Überprüfung, Inspektion
servicing *17* Wartung, (routinemäßige) Überprüfung
servo-brake cylinder *106* Servobremszylinder
session *90* Sitzung
to set *48* einstellen; ~ **up** *51* aufbauen, einrichten; *64* (Treffen usw.) vereinbaren; ~ **off the alarm** *76* Alarm auslösen; ~ **up standards** *79* Normen aufstellen
set *27* Satz; *128* vorgegeben, starr, fest
set-up *62* Aufspannung
settings pl *118* Voreinstellungen
to settle *37* sich ablagern, sich festsetzen
severe(ly) *48* stark, schwer
shaft *11* Welle; **generator** ~ *106* Lichtmaschinenwelle; **lift** ~ *11* Aufzugsschacht; **mine** ~ *104* Schacht, Stollen; **water-pump** ~ *106* Wasserpumpenwelle
to shake hands with sb *87* jdm die Hand geben
shape *35* Form
shaped *24* geformt; **L-**~ *41* L-förmig
to share sth *9T* sich etw teilen
sharp *118* scharf; ~ **bend** *75* Knick, enge Kurve
sheet *40* Blech; **data** ~ *102* Datenblatt; **order** ~ *106T* Bestellschein; ~ **metal** *28* Blech; ~ **metal screw** *28* Blechschraube
shelf, shelves *14T* Regal, Regale
shelving *14T* Regale
shift *125F* Schicht
to shift *117* verschieben
shock *35* Stoß, Stöße; **to be in** ~ *77* unter Schock stehen
shortage *124* Mangel
shortlisted, to be ~ *124* in die engere Auswahl kommen
shouting *76* Geschrei
to shut down sth *15* etw ausschalten
shy *127T* schüchtern
side cutting pliers pl *27* Seitenschneider
signature *98* Unterschrift
signpost *42* Hinweise zur Orientierung der Zuhörer in einer Präsentation
silvery-grey *35* silbrig-grau

A–Z word list

sincerely, Yours ~ *33* Mit freundlichen Grüßen
single workpiece *59* Einzelteil
sinkhole *112* Erdfall, Doline
sir *33* Herr
site: construction ~ *57F* Baustelle; **~ installation** *125* Vor-Ort-Montage; **~ work** *125* Arbeit vor Ort; **on ~** *74* vor Ort
size *7* Größe; **overall ~** *97F* Gesamtmaße
sketch *9* Skizze
to sketch *81* skizzieren
skilled worker *10* Facharbeiter/in
to skim *70* *(Text)* überfliegen
to slide *31* gleiten
slide *53* Schlitten; *69T* *(Präsentation:)* Folie; **compound ~** *31* Kreuzschlitten; **cross ~** *31* Querschlitten; **cross ~ taper** *52* Keilleiste des Planschlittens
slideways, bed ~ *31* Maschinenbett
sliding surface *37* Gleitfläche
slight(ly) *127T* geringfügig, etwas
slip-on cover *56T* Einstecktasche
size, overall ~ *97F* Gesamtmaße
slotted screw *27* Schlitzschraube
to slow down sth *38* etw (ab)bremsen
slow-blow fuse *62* träge Sicherung
small series manufacturing *59* Kleinserienfertigung
smart *127T* *(Kleidung:)* schick
to smear *52* beschmieren
to smoke *15* rauchen
smooth(ly) *17* reibungslos; *30* glatt, ruhig
snap fastener *100* Schnappverschluss
socializing *128* Ausgehen
socket wrench *27* Steckschlüssel
soft faced hammer *27* Schonhammer
soil erosion *112* Bodenerosion
soldering *123* Weichlöten; **~ iron** *24* Lötkolben
solid *40* (dreidimensionaler) Körper; **rectangular ~** *40* Quader; **rectilinear ~** *47* geradkantiger Körper
to solidify *119T* fest werden
solution *7* Lösung
to solve *52* lösen
to sort out sth *39T* etw klären
sorted, to get sth ~ *120T* etw klären, sich um etw kümmern
sound level *49* Lärmpegel, Geräuschpegel
source *37* Quelle
spanner, adjustable ~ *27* Rollgabelschlüssel; **double ended ring ~** *27* Doppelringschlüssel; **double open ended ~** *27* Doppelmaulschlüssel
spare part *102* Ersatzteil

speaker *101F* Lautsprecher
Speaking. *21* *(Telefon:)* Am Apparat.
special tool *17* Spezialwerkzeug
specialist *17* Fachmann/-frau, Spezialist/in; **~ supplier** *102* Fachhändler/in
specific *39* speziell, bestimmt, konkret; **~ torque** *103* spezifisches Drehmoment
specifically *72* ausdrücklich; *96* eigens, speziell
specifications pl *39* technische Daten, Spezifikationen
speed, maximum ~ *103* Höchstgeschwindigkeit; **cutting ~** *17* Schnitt-, Schneidegeschwindigkeit; **4-~ manual gearbox** *103T* Viergang-Handschaltgetriebe
spelling *42* Rechtschreibung; *120* Schreibweise
sphere *40* Kugel
to spill *9T* *(Wasser)* verschütten, verspritzen; *77* *(Flüssigkeit:)* laufen, auslaufen
spindle *29* Spindel; **~ brake** *60* Spindelbremse
split lock washer *28* Federring, Federscheibe
splitting *117* Spaltung
spraying, paint ~ *14* Spritzlackieren
to spread *76* sich ausbreiten
square nut *28* Vierkantmutter
stability *96* Stabilität
to stack *100* stapeln
stackable *100* stapelbar
stacking system *85* Stapeleinheit
staff, expert ~ *18* Fachpersonal; **trained ~** *49T* Fachpersonal
stainless steel *96* Edelstahl
stairs pl *9T* Treppe
stand *32* (Messe-)Stand; *36* Ständer
standard, environmental ~ *70* Umweltnorm; **to set up ~s** *79* Normen aufstellen
standardization *79* Normung
standardized *123* genormt
standstill *37* Stillstand
started, to get ~ *9T* loslegen, anfangen
starting: ~ point *9* Ausgangspunkt; **~ salary** *124* Einstiegsgehalt
to state *32* angeben, erklären, sagen
statement *76* Aussage, Schilderung
stationary *92* ortsfest, stationär
status *73* Stand, Zustand, Status
steady rest *52* Lünette
steel *17* Stahl; **mild ~** *125F* Baustahl; **stainless ~** *96* Edelstahl
steering *103* Lenkung; **worm-and-nut ~** *103* Zahnstangenlenkung
stepper motor *95* Schrittmotor

to stick *48* kleben; **~ with sth** *58T* bei etw bleiben, sich an etw halten
Stirling engine *36* Stirlingmotor
stock, in ~ *33* auf Lager, verfügbar
to stomp *76* trampeln, treten
stone *34* Stein
storage *69T* (Daten-)Speicherung; *100* Aufbewahrung, Lagerung; **cloud ~** *90* Datenspeicherung in der Cloud
straight *75* gerade; **~ ahead** *9* geradeaus
strength *126* Stärke
stress *34* Betonung; *35* Belastung; **compressive ~** *35* Druckbelastung, Druckspannung
to stress *127F* betonen
strict *80* streng
string *117* Faden
stringing *117* Fadenzug
strip *40* Leiste, Streifen
stroke *103* Hub
structural work *125* Rohbauarbeiten
structure *6* Aufbau, Struktur
to structure *7* aufbauen, strukturieren
study *112* Untersuchung, Studie
stuff *14T* Sachen, Zeug
subject, to be ~ to sth *37* einer Sache unterliegen
subject line *32* Betreffzeile
subsidiary *8* Niederlassung
to subsidize *125F* bezuschussen
substance *113T* Stoff, Substanz
to suck in *85* ansaugen
sudden *118* plötzlich
to suffer from *118* unter etw leiden
sufficient *60* ausreichend, genügend
to suit sth *70* (passend) für etw
suitable *13* geeignet, passend
to sum up *91* zusammenfassen
sunlight *56T* Sonnenlicht
supercharged engine *103* Kompressormotor
supercharger *103T* Kompressor, Turbolader; **twin-screw ~** *104* Doppelschnecken-Turbolader
superior *120T* Vorgesetzte/r
to supervise *10T* überwachen, beaufsichtigen
supervised *19* unter Aufsicht
supervisor *8* Ausbildungsleiter/in, Abteilungsleiter/in, Vorgesetzte/r
supplement *123* Zusatz, Ergänzung
supplier *11* Zulieferer, Lieferant/in; **specialist ~** *102* Fachhändler/in
supply, power ~ *52* Stromversorgung; **power ~ chain** *52* Stromversorgungskette; **water ~** *16* Wasserversorgung
to supply *56T* zur Verfügung stellen, liefern

to **support** *29* tragen, halten, stützen; *43* (Argumentation) untermauern
support *31* Träger, Halter; *90* Unterstützung
to **suppose** *106T* vermuten, glauben
surface *30* Oberfläche, Fläche; **clamping ~** *97F* Aufspannfläche; **sliding ~** *37* Gleitfläche; **~ finish** *30* Oberfläche(nbeschaffenheit); **~ roughness** *92* Oberflächenrauigkeit; **~ water** *112* Oberflächenwasser
surgery light *98* Operationslampe, -leuchte
surrounding area *112* Umgebung
surroundings pl *112* Umgebung
survey *68* Umfrage
suspension *105* Aufhängung
to **swallow** *126* schlucken
sweaty palms pl *37* verschwitzte Handflächen
swimming pool: ~ attendant *56* Bademeister/in; **~ complex** *56T* Bäderlandschaft, Schwimmbadanlage
switch *14T* Schalter; **end ~** *85* Endschalter; **main ~** *49* Hauptschalter; **emergency cut out ~** *14T* Not-Aus-Schalter; **~ cabinet** *52* Schaltschrank
to **switch on/off** *14T* ein-/ausschalten
switching device *49* Schaltgerät
to **swivel** *29* schwenken
swivelling head *30* Schwenkkopf
syllable *34* Silbe
symmetrical *41* symmetrisch
to **synchronize** *69T* abgleichen, synchronisieren
system-guided *96* systemgeführt

T

tab *118* Reiter
table *54* Tabelle
tail *105* Heck
tailstock *30* Reitstock
to **take: ~ on sb** *18* jdn einstellen; **~ over sth** *79* etw übernehmen; **~ sth apart** *49T* etw auseinandernehmen; **~ turns** *9* sich abwechseln; **~ up time** *69T* Zeit beanspruchen; **Is this seat taken?** *87* Ist hier besetzt?
talk *14* Vortrag
to **talk sb through sth** *39T* etw mit jdm durchgehen
tank *52* Tank; **~ capacity** *102* Tankinhalt
tap, fuel ~ *106* Benzinhahn
taper *30* Kegel; **cross slide ~** *52* Keilleiste des Planschlittens
target group *7* Zielgruppe
to **tarnish** *37* anlaufen
technical drawing *16* technische Zeichnung

teething problems pl *53* Kinderkrankheiten, Anlaufschwierigkeiten
telecommunication *6* Fernmeldetechnik, Telekommunikation
temperature, ambient ~ *70* Umgebungstemperatur; **operating ~** *70* Betriebstemperatur; **~ detection** *71* Temperaturmessung, -erfassung
template *16* Vorlage, Schablone
temporary *14* vorübergehend
tension *52* Spannung
term *46* Begriff
terminal, connection ~ *51* Verbindungsklemme
terms pl **of payment** *98* Zahlungsbedingungen
terrible *119T* furchtbar, fürchterlich
test technician *10* Prüftechniker/in
theatre, operating ~ *98* Operationssaal
thermal: ~ conductivity *36* Wärmeleitfähigkeit; **~ cutoff** *70* thermische Abschaltung; **~ expansion** *36* Wärmeausdehnung; **~ (cutoff) fuse** *70* Thermosicherung; **~ pellet** *70* thermisch geschütztes Gehäuse
thermoplastic pl *96* Thermoplaste
thickness *24* Stärke, Dicke
third party *112* Dritte/r
thoroughly *37* gründlich
to **thread** *30* Gewinde schneiden
thread *28* Gewinde; **multi-~ cycle** *62* Mehrgewindezyklus; **power transmission ~** *62* Bewegungsgewinde; **~ cutting machine screw** *28* gewindeschneidende Maschinenschraube
three corner scraper *27* Schabeisen mit dreieckiger Ziehklinge
three phase current *49T* Drehstrom
throttle *105* Drosselklappe, Gaspedal
tight *52* eng, fest, knapp; **~ bending** *75* starke Krümmung; **~ fit** *52* enger Sitz; **~ hose** *75* gespannter Schlauch
to **tighten** *11* (Schraube) festziehen
till *9* bis
time, in good ~ *127T* rechtzeitig; **on ~** *71T* rechtzeitig, pünktlich; to **take up ~** *69T* Zeit beanspruchen; **waste of ~** *69T* Zeitverschwendung; **~ lag** *84* Zeitverzögerung
timetable *64* Programm, Fahrplan, Flugplan
tin *113T* Zinn
tip *24* Spitze
titanium *34* Titan
title, job ~ *16* Berufsbezeichnung
tolerance *11* Toleranz; **out of ~** *11* außerhalb der Toleranz
tool *9T* Werkzeug; **cutting ~** *29* Schneidwerkzeug; **machine ~** *29*

Werkzeugmaschine; **measuring ~** *24* Messwerkzeug; **power ~** *28* Elektrowerkzeug; **special ~** *17* Spezialwerkzeug; **turning ~** *17* Drehwerkzeug; **~ cart** *60* Werkzeugwagen; **~ drive** *60* Werkzeugantrieb; **~ holder** *31* Werkzeughalter; **~ load** *62* Antriebslast der Werkzeuge; **~ maker** *17* Werkzeugmacher/in; **~ trolley** *26* Werkzeugwagen
toolbox *25* Werkzeugkasten
to **top up** *52* nachfüllen
top-heavy *14T* kopflastig
torque *103* Drehmoment; **specific ~** *103* spezifisches Drehmoment
Torx screw *27* Torxschraube
total price *115* Gesamtpreis
touch, to get in ~ with sb *64* sich mit jdm in Verbindung setzen; to **keep in ~** *74* in Verbindung bleiben, Kontakt halten
tough *35* zäh
tour *9* Rundgang
toxic *113* giftig, toxisch
track *102* Spurweite
trade *18* Gewerbe, Branche; **~ fair** *34* (Branchen-, Handels-)Messe; **~ magazine** *98* Fachzeitschrift
to **train** *17* ausbilden, eine Ausbildung machen; **~ sb** *83* jdn schulen
train, gear ~ *30* Getriebe
trained staff *49T* Fachpersonal
trainee *6* Auszubildende/r, Praktikant/in
trainer *14* Ausbilder/in, Dozent/in
training *7T* Ausbildung; **vocational ~** *6* Berufsausbildung, **~ company** *8* Ausbildungsbetrieb; **~ course** *14* Lehrgang, Schulung; **~ package** *60* Schulungspaket
transcript *121* Mitschrift
transformer *70* Transformator
transistor *24* Transistor
transmission, power ~ thread *62* Bewegungsgewinde
to **transmit** *84* übertragen
transmitter *122T* Sender
to **transport** *80* befördern, transportieren
transport, means of ~ *60* Transportmittel; **~ locks** pl *60* Transportsicherungen
transportation *71T* Beförderung, Transport
to **trap** *49* einklemmen
tray, floor ~ *83* Bodenwanne
tread *102* Spurweite
to **treat** *103T* behandeln
trial *90* Test, Probe; **~ order** *98* Probebestellung; **~ run** *37* Probelauf

triangle *40* Dreieck
to **trickle** *77* rinnen, (in einem Rinnsal) laufen
trolley *46* Wagen; **platform ~** *47* Plattformwagen, Transportwagen; **tool ~** *26* Werkzeugwagen
troubleshooting *52* Fehlersuche
truck, forklift ~ *71* Gabelstapler
trunk, cable ~ *71* Kabelkanal
tube *40* Rohr; **~ frame** *105* Rohrgestell
turn, in ~ *29* wiederum, seiner-/ihrerseits; to **be one's ~** *43* an der Reihe sein; to **take ~s** *9* sich abwechseln
to **turn** *17* sich drehen; *29* drehen
turner *10* Dreher/in
turning *8* Drehen, Dreherei; **~ length** *60* Drehlänge; **~ machine** *9T* Drehmaschine; **~ tool** *17* Drehwerkzeug
twin-screw supercharger *104* Doppelschnecken-Turbolader
type plate *115T* Typenschild
typically *118* normalerweise, üblicherweise

U

ultimate *105* vollendet, ultimativ
ultrasonic *9T* Ultraschall-; **~ ultrasonic sensor** *83* Ultraschallsensor
unavailable, to **be ~** *20* (Telefon:) nicht zu sprechen sein
unbeatable *59* unschlagbar
underneath *73* unter, unterhalb
underscore *32* Unterstrich
understanding *11* Verständnis
uninterested *126* uninteressiert
union *54* Gewerkschaft; **~ representative** *54* Gewerkschaftsvertreter/in
unit *54* Einheit; **control ~** *31* Steuergerät; **drive ~** *93* Antriebseinheit, -aggregat; **linear ~** *85* Lineareinheit; **price per ~** *106* Stückpreis, Einzelpreis
universal *60* universell, Universal-
unknown *33* unbekannt
unless, not ~ *37* nicht bevor; nur (dann) wenn
unlimited *96* unbegrenzt
to **unpack** *71T* auspacken
to **unplug** *48* ausstecken, vom Stromnetz trennen
unsatisfactory *119* unzureichend, unbefriedigend
unsteady *52* wackelig
unsupported, to **be ~** *53* keine Unterstützung haben
up and running *71T* betriebsbereit; to **be ~** *115T* laufen, im Einsatz sein
update (on sth) *32* aktuelle Informationen (zu etw); **report ~** *72* aktueller Bericht

upwards *81* aufwärts, nach oben
urban environment *112* städtischer Raum
urgent *104* eilig, dringend
usage *84* Verwendung
user *59* Anwender/in; **~ manual** *37* Benutzerhandbuch, Betriebsanleitung

V

V-belt *51* Keilriemen; **~ pulley** *106* Keilriemenscheibe
vacancy *125* offene Stelle
valve *84* Ventil; **overhead ~** *103T* obenliegendes Ventil; **petrol-non return ~** *106* Benzin-Rückhalteventil; **poppet ~** *106* Tellerventil; **~ gear** *103* Ventile
vane *103T* Schaufel, Läufer; **rotary ~** *104* Drehkolben
VAT (value added tax) *104* MwSt (Mehrwertsteuer)
vehicle *17* Fahrzeug
to **ventilate** *104* belüften
ventilation *14T* Belüftung; **~ fan** *70* Ventilator
ventilator *14T* Abzug, Ventilator
venue *32* Veranstaltungsort
vernier callipers pl *24* Messschieber
versatile *92* vielseitig verwendbar
version *70* Ausführung, Modell
vertical *54* senkrecht, vertikal
vessel *17* Gefäß, Behälter
vibration *118* Vibration; **~-critical** *62* schwingungskritisch; **~-cushioned** *85* schwingungsgedämpft; **~ testing** *24* Schwingprüfung, Vibrationsprüfung
vice *27* Schraubstock
video conferencing *90* Videokonferenz
view *13* Aussicht
vintage car *102* Oldtimer
virtually *96* praktisch
visible *118* sichtbar
visual inspection *52* Sichtprüfung
visuals pl *50* visuelle Hilfsmittel
vocational: ~ college *18* Berufsschule; **~ training** *6* Berufsausbildung
voicemail *20* Mailbox
void *37* unwirksam, ungültig
voltage *24* Spannung; **high ~** *15* Hochspannung; **line ~** *49* Netzspannung; **operating ~** *62* Betriebsspannung
volume *55T* Volumen

W

to **wander** *24* wandern
warehouse *100* Lagerhalle, Lager
to **wait,** to **keep sb ~ing** *13* jdn warten lassen

warning *49* Hinweis, Warnhinweis
warranty *37* Garantie; **~ regulations** pl *49* Garantiebedingungen
to **wash: ~ down sth** *80T* etw abwaschen; **~ off sth** *80* etw abwaschen
washer *27* Unterlegscheibe; **flat ~** *28* Unterlegscheibe; **external tooth lock ~** *28* außengezahnte Zahnscheibe; **internal tooth lock ~** *28* innengezahnte Zahnscheibe; **split lock ~** *28* Federring, Federscheibe
washing: ~ machine *80T* Waschmaschine; **~ system** *80* Waschanlage
to **waste** *84* verschwenden, vergeuden
waste: ~ of time *69T* Zeitverschwendung; **~ dump** *112* Müllhalde; **~ water** *64* Abwasser
water supply *16* Wasserversorgung
water-pump shaft *106* Wasserpumpenwelle
waterjet *8* Wasserstrahl; **~ cutting** *8* Wasserstrahlschneiden
waterproof *56T* wasserdicht
waterpump pliers pl *27* Wasserpumpenzange
wavy *118* wellenförmig
way, by the ~ *9T* übrigens, à propos
weakness *126* Schwäche
wear *17* Abnutzung, Verschleiß
to **weigh** *56T* wiegen
weight *11* Gewicht; **kerb ~** *102* Leergewicht
to **weld** *14* schweißen
welder *76* Schweißer/in
welding *14* Schweißen; **arc ~** *114* Lichtbogenschweißen
well known *7* bekannt
wheel, rear ~ *103* Hinterrad; **rear ~ drive** *103* Hinterradantrieb; **~ nut** *106* Radmutter
wheelbase *102* Radstand
wheelchair *86T* Rollstuhl
widespread *114* verbreitet
wilderness *112* Wildnis
wildlife *112* Tier- und Pflanzenwelt, Natur
willingness *124* Bereitschaft
window shield *52* Schutzscheibe
wiper *52* Abstreifer
wire *40* Draht
to **wire** *49T* verkabeln, anschließen
wiring *52* Verkabelung
wish, Best ~es *33* Mit freundlichen Grüßen
to **withstand sth** *35* etw aushalten, einer Sache widerstehen
wobble *118* Wackeln
wooden *98* Holz-
work: ~ experience *26* Praktikum; **~ file** *96* Arbeitsdatei

to **work overtime** *19* Überstunden machen
workbench *9T* Werkbank
worker, skilled ~ *10* Facharbeiter/in; **blue collar ~s** pl *55* Arbeiter/innen; **white collar ~s** pl *55* Angestellte
working: ~ envelope *114* Arbeitsraum; **~ hours** pl *19* Arbeitszeiten; **~ piston** *37* Arbeitskolben; **~ space** *52* Arbeitsbereich; *97F* Arbeitsraum
workpiece *17* Werkstück; **single ~** *59* Einzelteil

workplace *8* Arbeitsplatz
works *7* Fabrik, Werk
workshop *14* Werkstatt; **~ manager** *18* Werkstattleiter/in
worm-and-nut steering *103* Zahnstangenlenkung
to **worry** *9T* Bedenken haben, sich Sorgen machen
wrench *14T* Schraubenschlüssel; **Allen head ~** *27* Innensechskantschlüssel, Inbusschlüssel; **socket ~** *27* Steckschlüssel

to **write up sth** *19* etw *(Text)* ausarbeiten
writing, in ~ *69T* schriftlich

X
X-ray *57* Röntgen; **~ machine** *120* Röntgengerät

Z
zinc *34* Zink

Basic technical vocabulary (German–English)

Berufe – jobs

Ausbilder/in	training supervisor
Auszubildende/r	apprentice
Dreher/in	turner
Elektriker/in	electrician, electrical engineer
Facharbeiter/in	skilled worker
Feinwerkmechaniker/in	precision mechanic
Konstruktionsmechaniker/in	construction mechanic
Machinenbauer/in	machine builder
Mechatroniker/in	mechatronic systems engineer
Meister/in	foreman/-woman
Schneidwerkzeug-mechaniker/in/in	cutting tool mechanic
Techniker/in	state-certified engineer
Technische/r Zeichner/in	CAD engineer
Teilezurichter/in	metal dresser
Werkstattleiter/in	workshop manager
Werkzeugmacher/in	toolmaker

Handwerkzeuge – hand tools

Bandsäge	bandsaw
Bügelsäge	hacksaw
Elektrobohrmaschine	electric drill
Feile	file
Flachrundzange	snipe-nose pliers
Gewindebohrer	tap
Hammer	hammer
Innensechskanntschlüssel	hex key
Körner	centre punch
Maulschlüssel	open-ended spanner
Meißel	chisel
Schlagdorn	pin punch
Schraubendreher	screwdriver
Spitzsenker	countersink
Stichsäge	jigsaw
Wasserpumpenzange	waterpump pliers
Zapfensenker	counterbore

Werkzeugmaschinen – machine tools

Bohrmaschine	drilling machine
Fräsmaschine	milling machine
Hubsäge	power hacksaw
Schleifmaschine	grinding machine
Drehmaschine	lathe
Winkelschleifer	angle grinder

Messintrumente – measuring instruments

Gewinde-Grenzlehrdorn	thread plug gauge
Grenzlehrdorn	plug gauge
Grenzrachenlehre	snap gauge
Lineal	rule
Messgerät	gauge
Messschieber	vernier callipers
Tiefenmessgerät	depth gauge

Verbindungselemente – fixing devices

einfache flache Unterlegscheibe	plain flat washer
Federscheibe	spring washer
Flügelmutter	wing nut
Flügelschraube	wing screw
Halbrundkopfniete	panhead rivet
Halbrundkopfschraube mit Querschlitz	slotted panhead bolt
Innensechskant-geschwindestift	Allen set screw
Innensechskantschraube	hexagon socket cap bolt
Nagel	nail
Rundkopfniete	round head rivet
Rundkopfschraube	round head screw
Sechskantschraube	hexagon head bolt
Senkkopfniete	countersunk rivet
Senkkopfschraube mit Querschlitz	slotted countersunk bolt
Zahnscheibe	shakeproof washer
Zylinderkopfschraube	slotted cheesehead bolt

Tätigkeiten – actions

(ab)schleifen	to grind
(an)fasen	to chamfer
befestigen	to fasten, fix
biegen	to bend
bohren	to bore, drill
drehen	to turn
ersetzen	to replace
formen	to shape
fräsen	to mill
hartlöten	to braze
lösen	to loosen
montieren	to assemble
nachfüllen	to refill
ölen	to oil
polieren	to finish
rändeln	to knurl
reparieren	to repair
schmieren	to grease
schweißen	to weld
weichlöten	to solder

Talking about numbers

Cardinal numbers

0	oh/nought/null (*AE*) zero
1	one
2	two
3	three
4	four
5	five
6	six
7	seven
8	eight
9	nine
10	ten
11	eleven
12	twelve
13	thirteen
14	fourteen
15	fifteen
16	sixteen
17	seventeen
18	eighteen
19	nineteen
20	twenty
21	twenty-one
22	twenty-two
23	twenty-three
24	twenty-four
30	thirty
40	forty
50	fifty
60	sixty
70	seventy
80	eighty
90	ninety
100	one hundred

Ordinal numbers

1st	first
2nd	second
3rd	third
4th	fourth
5th	fifth
6th	sixth
7th	seventh
8th	eighth
9th	ninth
10th	tenth
11th	eleventh
12th	twelfth
13th	thirteenth
14th	fourteenth
15th	fifteenth
16th	sixteenth
17th	seventeenth
18th	eighteenth
19th	nineteenth
20th	twentieth
21st	twenty-first
22nd	twenty-second
23rd	twenty-third
24th	twenty-fourth
30th	thirtieth
40th	fortieth
50th	fiftieth
60th	sixtieth
70th	seventieth
80th	eightieth
90th	ninetieth
100th	one hundredth

In English you say:
101 — one hundred **and** one
235 — two hundred **and** thirty-five
1,563,765 — one million, five hundred **and** sixty-three thousand, seven hundred **and** sixty-five
1 563 765
You use commas or spaces (and not a point) after the thousands (or millions) in large numbers.

Decimals

In English, you write decimals with a point, not a comma.

0.25	oh/nought point two five (*BE*) zero point two five (*AE*)
3.76	three point seven six
55.37	fifty-five point three seven
1.585	one point five eight five

Fractions

¼	a/one quarter
⅓	a/one third
½	a/one half
⅔	two-thirds
¾	three-quarters
⁵⁄₁₆	five sixteenths
1½	one and a half

1 m^2	one **square** metre
1 m^3	one **cubic** metre
5^2	five **squared**
10^4	ten **to the power** of four

Symbols

+	plus/and
−	minus
±	plus or minus
×	multiplied by/times by (6 mm × 2 mm)
÷	divided by
=	is equal to/equals
≠	isn't equal to/doesn't equal
≈	is approximately equal to
<	is less than
>	is greater/more than
μ	micro- (one millionth)
%	per cent (*auch*: percent)
°	degree

Conversion tables

Area

English to metric	1 square inch (in^2)	= 6.452 square centimetres
	1 square foot (ft^2)	= 0.0929 square metres
	1 acre (ac)	= 4,047 square metres
	1 square mile (m^2)	= 2.59 square kilometres
Metric to English	1 square centimetre	= 0.155 square inches
	1 square metre	= 10.764 square feet
	1 square kilometre	= 0.3861 square miles
English to English	1 square foot	= 144 square inches
	1 acre	= 43,560 square feet
	1 square mile	= 640 acres

Distance

English to metric	1 inch (in)	= 2.54 centimetres
	1 foot (ft)	= 30.48 centimetres
	1 yard (yd)	= 0.9144 metres
	1 mile (mi)	= 1.609 kilometres
Metric to English	1 centimetre	= 0.3937 inches (3/8 inch)
	1 metre	= 39.37 inches (3 feet, 3 3/8 inches)
	1 kilometre	= 0.62137 miles
English to English	1 foot	= 12 inches
	1 yard	= 3 feet
	1 mile	= 5,280 feet

Energy/Force

English to metric	1 horsepower (hp)	= 0.746 kilowatts
	1 ounce-force	= 0.278 newtons
	1 pound-force (lbf)	= 4.448 newtons
	1 foot pounds (ft-lb)	= 1.355 newtons-metres/joules
	1 inch pounds	= 0.112 newtons-metres
	1 pounds per foot	= 14.59 newtons-metres
	1 British thermal unit (BTU)	= 1055 joules
Metric to English	1 kilowatt	= 1.341 horsepower
	1 newton	= 3.597 ounce-force
	1 newton	= 0.224 pound-force
	1 newtons-metres / 1 joule	= 0.738 foot pounds
	1 kilojoule	= 0.948 British thermal units

Mass/Weight

English to metric	1 ounce (oz)	= 28.35 grams
	1 pound (lb)	= 0.453 kilograms
	1 UK ton ('long ton')	= 1,016 kilograms
	1 US ton ('short ton')	= 907 kilograms
Metric to English	1 gram	= 0.035 ounces
	1 kilogram	= 2 pounds, 3.3 ounces
English to English	1 pound	= 16 ounces
	1 UK ton ('long ton')	= 2,240 pounds
	1 US ton ('short ton')	= 2,000 pounds
Metric to metric	1 metric tonne (t)	= 1,000 kilograms

Temperature

Fahrenheit (F) to Celsius: subtract 32, then multiply by 5, then divide by 9
Celsius to Fahrenheit: multiply by 9, then divide by 5, then add 32

Volume

English to metric	1 fluid UK ounce (fl oz)	= 28.41 millilitres
	1 UK pint (pt)	= 0.568 litres
	1 UK quart (qt)	= 1.137 litres
	1 UK gallon (gal)	= 4.546 litres
	1 fluid US ounce	= 29.57 millilitres
	1 US pint	= 0.473 litres
	1 US quart	= 0.946 litres
	1 US gallon	= 3.785 litres
	1 cubic inch (in^3)	= 16 cubic centimetres
	1 cubic foot (ft^3)	= 0.03 cubic metres
Metric to English	1 litre	= 0.568 UK pints
	1 litre	= 0.473 US pints
English to English	1 pint	= 16 fluid ounces
	1 quart	= 2 pints
	1 gallon	= 4 quarts

Abbreviations

A	amp(ere)	dB	decibel	LAN	local area network
V	volt	FM	frequency modulation	WLAN	wireless local area network
W	watt	UHF	ultra-high frequency	LED	light-emitting diode
AC	alternating current	Hz	hertz		
DC	direct current	MHz	megahertz	rpm	revolutions per minute
F	farad	GHz	gigahertz		
kWh	kilowatt hour				
R	resistance				
RCD	residual current device				

Irregular verbs

be – was/were – been	sein	let – let – let	lassen
become – became – become	werden	lose – lost – lost	verlieren
begin – began – begun	anfangen, beginnen	make – made – made	machen
break – broke – broken	brechen	mean – meant – meant	meinen, bedeuten
bring – brought – brought	bringen	meet – met – met	treffen
build – built – built	bauen	pay – paid – paid	bezahlen
burn – burnt/burned – burnt/burned	(ver)brennen	put – put – put	setzen, stellen, legen
buy – bought – bought	kaufen	read – read – read	lesen
catch – caught – caught	fangen	ride – rode – ridden	reiten, fahren
choose – chose – chosen	wählen	ring – rang – rung	klingeln, anrufen
come – came – come	kommen	rise – rose – risen	(an)steigen
cost – cost – cost	kosten	run – ran – run	laufen, rennen
cut – cut – cut	schneiden	say – said – said	sagen
do – did – done	tun, machen, erledigen	see – saw – seen	sehen
draw – drew – drawn	zeichnen	sell – sold – sold	verkaufen
dream – dreamt – dreamt	träumen	send – sent – sent	senden, schicken
drink – drank – drunk	trinken	shake – shook – shaken	schütteln
drive – drove – driven	fahren	set – set – set	setzen, stellen
eat – ate – eaten	essen	show – showed – shown	zeigen
fall – fell – fallen	fallen	shut – shut – shut	schließen
feed – fed – fed	füttern, ernähren	sing – sang – sung	singen
feel – felt – felt	(sich) fühlen, empfinden	sit – sat – sat	sitzen
fight – fought – fought	kämpfen	sleep – slept – slept	schlafen
find – found – found	finden	smell – smelt/smelled – smelt/smelled	riechen
fit – fit/fitted – fit/fitted	passen		
fly – flew – flown	fliegen	speak – spoke – spoken	sprechen
forget – forgot – forgotten	vergessen	spell – spelt/spelled – spelt/spelled	buchstabieren
get – got – got (AE gotten)	bekommen, erhalten	spend – spent – spent	ausgeben, verbringen
give – gave – given	geben	stand – stood – stood	stehen
go – went – gone	gehen, fahren	steal – stole – stolen	stehlen
grow – grew – grown	wachsen	swim – swam – swum	schwimmen
hang – hung – hung	hängen	take – took – taken	nehmen
have – had – had	haben	teach – taught – taught	unterrichten, beibringen
hear – heard – heard	hören	tear – tore – torn	(zer)reißen
hide – hid – hidden	(sich) verstecken	tell – told – told	sagen, erzählen
hit – hit – hit	schlagen, aufprallen auf	think – thought – thought	denken
hold – held – held	halten, festhalten	throw – threw – thrown	werfen
keep – kept – kept	behalten	understand – understood – understood	verstehen
know – knew – known	kennen, wissen		
lay – laid – laid	legen	wake – woke – woken	wecken
lead – led – led	führen, leiten	wear – wore – worn	tragen (Kleidung)
learn – learnt/learned – learnt/learned	lernen	win – won – won	gewinnen
		write – wrote – written	schreiben
leave – left – left	abfahren, verlassen, weggehen		

Acknowledgements

S. 7: Shutterstock / OPOLJA; **S. 8/1:** Shutterstock / Vladimir Nenezic; **S. 8/2:** Fotolia / Kzenon; **S. 8/3:** Fotolia /Erwin Wodicka; **S. 8/4:** Fotolia / Cynthia Lawing Salvia; **S. 8/5:** Fotolia / industrieblick; **S. 8/6:** Fotolia / Cybrain; **S. 8/7:** Fotolia / Monkey Business; **S. 8/8:** Fotolia / Andrey Armyagov; **S. 8/9:** Shutterstock / Chuck Rausin; **S. 8/10:** Fotolia / srki66; **S. 8/11:** Shutterstock / Andrey Eremin; **S. 10:** Shutterstock / teh_z1b; **S. 12/1:** Shutterstock / Djomas; **S. 12/2:** Fotolia / Vadym Zaitsev; **S. 12/3:** Shutterstock / Monkey Business Images; **S. 12/4:** Shutterstock / Firma V; **S. 12/5:** Shutterstock / UncleOles; **S. 12/6:** Fotolia / ajr_images; **S. 14:** Shutterstock / ESB Professional; **S. 16/1:** Fotolia / pololia; **S. 16/2:** Shutterstock / Syda Productions; **S. 16/3:** Fotolia / industrieblick; **S. 16/4:** Shutterstock / bikeriderlondon; **S. 16/5:** Fotolia / WavebreakmediaMicro; **S. 16/6:** Shutterstock / Kzenon; **S. 18:** Fotolia / industrieblick; **S. 22:** Fotolia / ahavelaar; **S. 24/1:** Fotolia / bruno135_406; **S. 24/2:** Shutterstock / Minerva Studio; **S. 24/3:** Shutterstock / kurhan; **S. 25/1:** Fotolia / J.M.; **S. 25/2:** Fotolia / naruedom; **S. 25/3:** Fotolia / krasyuk; **S. 25/4:** Fotolia / photobalance; **S. 25/5:** Fotolia / PhotographyByMK; **S. 25/6:** Fotolia / Shahril KHMD; **S. 26/1:** Fotolia / naruedom; **S. 26/2:** Fotolia / Popova Olga; **S. 26/3:** Fotolia / Kevin Mayer; **S. 26/4:** Fotolia / grgroup; **S. 26/5:** Fotolia / stoleg; **S. 26/6:** Fotolia / fotos-v; **S. 26/7:** Georg Aigner, Landshut; **S. 27:** Fotolia / Fobosvobos; **S. 28/1:** Fotolia / sergey7; **S. 28/2:** Shutterstock / goodluz; **S. 28/3:** Shutterstock / goodluz; **S. 29/1:** Fotolia / Kadmy; **S. 29/2:** Fotolia / tm-photo; **S. 29/3:** Fotolia / Kzenon; **S. 29/4:** Fotolia / Fotolia RAW; **S. 29/5:** Georg Aigner, Landshut; **S. 29/6:** Fotolia / isaac74; **S. 29/7:** Fotolia / Andrey Armyagov; **S. 30:** Shutterstock / Vereshchagin Dmitry; **S. 34/1:** Shutterstock / Thanakorn Hongphan; **S. 34/2:** Shutterstock / Scanrail1; **S. 34/3:** Shutterstock / gualtiero boffi; **S. 36:** Georg Aigner, Landshut; **S. 37:** Fotolia / the_lightwriter; **S. 40/1-5:** Georg Aigner, Landshut; **S. 41/1:** ODI; **S. 41/2:** Jan Richter, Freiberg; **S. 42:** Shutterstock / ESB Professional; **S. 45:** Shutterstock / John_Silver; **S. 48:** Fotolia / mbongo; **S. 51/1-8:** Georg Aigner, Landshut; **S. 53:** Shutterstock / Monkey Business Images; **S. 56:** Shutterstock / FabrikaSimf; **S. 57:** Fotolia / sudok1; **S. 58:** DMG MORI Europe Holding AG, München; **S. 59:** DMG MORI Europe Holding AG, München; **S. 62:** Siemens AG; **S. 64:** Shutterstock / Rawpixel.com; **S. 67:** Shutterstock / mariva2017; **S. 68/1:** Shutterstock / ESB Professional; **S. 68/2:** Shutterstock / mimagephotography; **S. 68/3:** Shutterstock / racorn; **S. 71:** Shutterstock / Mila Supinskaya Glashchenko; **S. 74/1:** Shutterstock / emel82; **S. 74/2:** Shutterstock / michaeljung; **S. 74/3:** Shutterstock / Baloncici; **S. 74/4:** Fotolia / piotr_roae; **S. 74/5:** Shutterstock / Baloncici; **S. 74/6:** Shutterstock / Aleksandar Tasevski; **S. 74/7:** Shutterstock / safakcakir; **S. 74/8:** Shutterstock / garmoncheg; **S. 77:** Shutterstock / ChiccoDodiFC; **S. 78/1:** Fotolia / alice_photo; **S. 78/2:** Fotolia / Björn Wylezich; **S. 78/3:** Fotolia / ake1150; **S. 78/4:** Fotolia / Avantgarde; **S. 79/1:** Shutterstock / Oleg Golovnev; **S. 79/2:** Shutterstock / AJR_photo; **S. 80/1:** Hilmer Metallbau, Atting; **S. 80/2:** Hilmer Metallbau, Atting; **S. 80/3:** Shutterstock / Andrey Burmakin; **S. 82/1:** Klaus Hilmer, Carina Rauscher, Andreas Nachtwey; **S. 82/2:** Shutterstock / abimages; **S. 82/3:** Fotolia / Alexander; **S. 82/4:** Shutterstock / Africa Studio; **S. 83/2:** Klaus Hilmer, Carina Rauscher, Andreas Nachtwey; **S. 84/1-4:** Klaus Hilmer, Carina Rauscher, Andreas Nachtwey; **S. 85/1-2:** Klaus Hilmer, Carina Rauscher, Andreas Nachtwey; **S. 86/1:** Shutterstock / leungchopan; **S. 86/2:** Shutterstock / Lisa F. Young; **S. 86/3:** Shutterstock / Rehan Qureshi; **S. 86/4:** Shutterstock / SnowWhiteimages; **S. 92:** Fotolia / Phuchit; **S. 95:** Georg Aigner, Landshut; **S. 96:** Stepcraft GmbH & Co. KG, Menden; **S. 100:** Shutterstock / TaraPatta; **S. 105:** mauritius images / Alamy / nawson; **S. 106/1-6:** Georg Aigner, Landshut; **S. 106/7:** Fotolia / aleksandrn; **S. 106/8:** Shutterstock / Apinunt Sukhapinda; **S. 106/9-12:** Georg Aigner, Landshut; **S. 112:** Shutterstock / Jason Benz Bennee; **S. 114/1:** Fotolia / zapp2photo; **S. 114/2:** Fotolia / xiaoliangge; **S. 117:** Simplify3D; **S. 119:** Jan Richter, Freiberg; **S. 120:** Shutterstock / Daniel M Ernst; **S. 122/1:** Shutterstock / Monkey Business Images; **S. 122/2:** Shutterstock / racorn; **S. 122/3:** Shutterstock / SpeedKingz; **S. 127:** Shutterstock / Michal Kowalski; **S. 132:** Shutterstock / baranq; **S. 136/1-4:** Jan Richter, Freiberg; **S. 140:** Jan Richter, Freiberg; **S. 147:** Autopstenhoj

Wir danken folgenden Firmen für ihre freundliche Unterstützung:

Stepcraft GmbH & Co. KG (https://www.stepcraft-systems.com/en/cnc-3d-systems/stepcraft-2-420)

Halfords Group PLC (http://www.halfords.com/motoring/car-accessories/car-security)

Simplify3D (https://www.simplify3d.com/support/print-quality-troubleshooting)